This Strange Loneliness

This
Strange
Loneliness

Heaney's Wordsworth

PETER MACKAY

McGill-Queen's University Press
Montreal & Kingston • London • Chicago

© McGill-Queen's University Press 2021

ISBN 978-0-2280-0571-1 (cloth)
ISBN 978-0-2280-0572-8 (paper)
ISBN 978-0-2280-0751-7 (ePDF)
ISBN 978-0-2280-0752-4 (ePUB)

Legal deposit first quarter 2021
Bibliothèque nationale du Québec

Printed in Canada on acid-free paper that is 100% ancient forest free
(100% post-consumer recycled), processed chlorine free

Library and Archives Canada Cataloguing in Publication

Title: This strange loneliness : Heaney's Wordsworth / Peter Mackay.
Names: Mackay, Peter, 1979– author.
Description: Includes bibliographical references and index.
Identifiers: Canadiana (print) 2020037673X | Canadiana (ebook) 20200376802
 | ISBN 9780228005728 (softcover) | ISBN 9780228005711 (hardcover)
 | ISBN 9780228007517 (PDF) | ISBN 9780228007524 (ePUB)
Subjects: LCSH: Heaney, Seamus, 1939-2013—Criticism and interpretation.
 | LCSH: Wordsworth, William, 1770-1850—Influence.
Classification: LCC PR6058.E2 Z75 2021 | DDC 821/.914—dc23

This book was typeset in 10.5/13 Sabon.

Contents

Acknowledgments   vii

Introduction   3

1   Advancements of Learning   29

2   Fosterage and Poetic Influence   66

3   Places and Displacements: Haunted Ground   109

4   The Necessity of an Idea of Transcendence   150

5   "Total Play and Truth in Earnest": Heaney's Late Style   199

Notes   247

Works Cited   301

Index   329

Acknowledgments

This book originated in a PhD I completed some years ago at Trinity College Dublin under the supervision of Terence Brown; without his reassurance and guidance (and financial support from the college) I would not have been able to finish the degree. During my time at Trinity I was also lucky to have wide-ranging discussions with and receive advice from Eve Patten, Gerry Dawe, Elmer Kennedy-Andrews, Ronan Kelly, Brendan Kennelly, Stephen Matterson, Eoin McCarthy, Bernice Murphy, Jenny McDonnell, Brendan O'Connell, Will Megarry, Heinrich Hall, Liam Prut, John Guerin, Joe Guerin, Rodrigue Alcazar, Neven Brady Leddy, Thomas Davreaux, Laura Jarque, Zuzana Kollárovitsová, Jo Day, and Lærke Recht.

The book subsequently evolved (sometimes following a deeply subterranean course) as I held posts as a research fellow on the Arts and Humanities Research Council-funded Irish and Scottish Poetry Project based at Queen's University; an adjunct lecturer at Trinity College Dublin, University College Dublin, and Edinburgh University; and then as a lecturer in literature at the University of St Andrews. I am grateful to many people I encountered throughout this period for discussions about Heaney, Wordsworth, and many other aspects of contemporary and Romantic poetry which have influenced this book in one way or another: Fran Brearton, Edna Longley, Ciaran Carson, Michael Longley, Cairns Craig, Alan Gillis, David Wheatley, Máire Ní Annrachaín, Fiona Stafford, Peter McDonald, Guinn Batten, Michael Brown, Leontia Flynn, Sinéad Morrissey, Eoghan Walls, Alex Wylie, Rob Dunbar, Iain S. MacPherson, Wilson McLeod, Christopher Whyte, Robert Crawford, Andy Murphy, Gill Plain,

viii   Acknowledgments

Nick Roe, Sam Haddow, Anindya Raychaudhuri, Katie Garner, Jane Stabler, Dom Hale, Henry Hart, Adam Potkay, and Ron Schuchard.

Michael Parker and the American Philosophical Society kindly helped in my search for articles and lectures, and I have been shown great forebearance by the staff of various libraries including Trinity College Dublin, the National Library of Ireland, the National Library of Scotland, Queen's University Belfast, and, especially, Kathy Shoemaker in the Stuart A. Rose Library of Emory University. I am also grateful to the College of William and Mary for the invitation to be a visiting scholar there, and to the University of St Andrews for a research grant to visit Emory University, which was crucial to this book. I thank Seamus Heaney's estate and Faber and Faber for permission to quote from his published works and from archival material in Emory University's Manuscripts, Archives, Rare Books Library, in the National Library of Ireland, and in the library of Queen's University, Belfast. The following are reprinted by permission of Farrar, Straus and Giroux: "At Toombridge" and excerpt/s from "Late in the Day" from *Electric Light* by Seamus Heaney. Copyright © 2001 by Seamus Heaney. Excerpts from "Lightenings, Squarings and Weighing In" from *Opened Ground: Selected Poems, 1966–1996* by Seamus Heaney. Copyright © 1998 by Seamus Heaney. Excerpts from "In Time" from *Selected Poems 1988–2013* by Seamus Heaney. Copyright © 2014 by the Estate of Seamus Heaney. Excerpts from "The Loaning" and "The Sand Pit" from *Station Island* by Seamus Heaney. Copyright © 1984 by Seamus Heaney. All other quotations are covered by the principle of Fair Use in academic publications.

Mark Abley at McGill-Queen's University Press has been a wonderfully helpful and encouraging editor; I am heavily indebted to him, and to Kate Merriman, Kathleen Fraser, and Filomena Falocco at the press, for their work on the book. The reviewers for the press provided much excellent advice on how to improve the text; similarly, Patrick Crotty generously read through a near-finished manuscript and helped bring out any virtues that it has – slán leat, a chara. I have also received invaluable emotional and financial support from my family (Joan, Derek, and John Angus), and an immeasurable amount of patience, help, and intellectual stimulus from Miriam Gamble, who endured more conversations about the twists and turns of the process than anyone should ever have to bear.

I am, finally, grateful to Seamus Heaney for having helped me with various notes and queries, and for his generous hospitality; this book is dedicated to his memory.

This Strange Loneliness

Introduction

In *Stepping Stones*, Seamus Heaney attests the "staying power" of poetry, even of nursery rhymes he had learned before he went to school. Asked about the effect those poems had on him, he responds: "I'm not sure. The main thing is that they stay with you for a lifetime. Poems learned early on, poems with a truly imaginative quality, end up being sounding lines out to the world and into yourself."[1] Characteristically for Heaney, poetry's effects work in two directions: as a means of understanding or probing the world on the one hand and the self on the other; in both, poetry is a means of imaginative exploration. Also characteristically, Heaney's thinking about poetry is framed through, and depends upon, a pun – those "sounding lines" which tie the basic poetic structure to a maritime (or fishing) metaphor. "Sounding lines" appear repeatedly (though erratically) throughout Heaney's career, from the Blackstaff anthology / magazine *Soundings '72* he edited, through his description of John Montague's poems as "sounding lines, rods to plumb the depth of a shared and diminished culture," to a public conversation about translation between Heaney and Robert Hass published under the title *Sounding Lines* in 2000.[2] The metaphor also aligns Heaney with a particular way of thinking about poetry, in which the art form is a probing of unknown and uncanny depths (of the psyche, of geography, or of history), a way of thinking associated particularly, in anglophone poetry, with William Wordsworth's "spots of time."[3]

The "spots of time" are the generative structure of Wordsworth's *Prelude*, nodes of memory which "retain / A vivifying virtue" and offer a "beneficent influence" by which "our minds / Are nourished and invisibly repaired."[4] One of these "spots" describes the first

4   This Strange Loneliness

week of Wordsworth's residence in Hawkshead, after the death of his mother. He spends half an hour on the banks of Esthwaite Lake observing a pile of garments on the far shore, with the "breathless stillness" of the water disturbed only by leaping fish; the next day, "went there a company, and in their boat / Sounded with grappling-irons and with long poles" and caught a dead man who "bolt upright / Rose with his ghastly face."[5] The death of his mother feeds into the presentiment of the discovery of this second corpse; "the breathless stillness" of one kind of death is disturbed by the possibility of a violent, ghastly return of the dead. Placed against Heaney's "sounding lines," what the grappling-irons trawling Esthwaite discover offers a tempering warning to any naive understanding about what might arise from exploration of the "depths of a shared and diminished culture": these too might offer up something "ghastly" and yet insistent, something dead which presents itself "bolt upright," some "terror even."[6]

This book plumbs the poetic relationship between Seamus Heaney and William Wordsworth, and especially the ways in which Heaney reconfigures what "Wordsworth" means to him at different points in his poetic career. Although there are significant differences of tenor, aesthetic, and humour between the Derry Nobel Laureate and the Lakeland Laureate, the work of Wordsworth was one of the foremost among Heaney's lifelong touchstones, gaining in significance over the years, helping the Northern Irish poet create his own personal "inscape" or "instress." Wordsworth was not the only lifelong influence (the words "inscape" and "instress" are those of Gerald Manley Hopkins, another poet whose influence can be traced from Heaney's earliest writings); however, he was, as Neil Corcoran comments, "probably the most deeply informing presence" in Heaney's work (not least for his contributions to the idea of poetic influence as a "deeply informing presence").[7] Late in his life Heaney continued to attest to Wordsworth's importance as one of the poetic voices that had stayed with him longest. Speaking in *Stepping Stones* about his time in "the master's room" of Anahorish primary school, Heaney recalls: "The poem that I remember best from that time is Wordsworth's 'Fidelity': 'A barking sound the Shepherd hears, / A cry as of a dog or fox ... ' It's about a dog that stays for weeks in this lonely dale in the mountains, keeping watch by the body of its master after he has fallen to his death off a cliff. What got to me was the description of the fells and the tarn and the sinister

Introduction 5

atmosphere."[8] At St Columb's College, Derry, Wordsworth (along with Keats) became "a definite long-term influence on me. The grip I got on poems like 'Michael' and 'Resolution and Independence,' the deep familiarity with the Preface to *Lyrical Ballads*, stood to me for the rest of my life."[9] "Stood to me": while talking about poetry Heaney has a persuasive and determined eloquence about the "good" that poetry can do, its benign influence, its role as "corroboration," "fortification," or "redress." This is true even, or especially, when the first impulse or delight of reading a poem comes, as in "Fidelity," from an unsettling source, whether it be the "sublime" loyalty of the dog or the uncanny fidelity of the poem's descriptive power: it is a poem in which an echo – that central poetic metaphor – is created by "Crags [that] repeat the Raven's croak / In symphony austere."[10]

"Symphony," the "sounding together" of different voices ("austere" or otherwise), is one possible model for poetic influence (and different ways in which we might understand "influence" will be a recurring theme through this book). Both Heaney and Wordsworth tend towards a generally (but not solely) benign understanding of poetic influence, in which it is imagined as the result of corroborative echoes, conjoined voices or harmonies, or confluent streams, rather than an agonistic struggle. Musical and, given Wordsworth's predilections, fluvial metaphors are more appropriate than those of debt and conflict. As Heaney suggests, "any account of Wordsworth's music must sooner or later come to the river"; "One could not grow up in the Lake District," as John Beer notes, "without being aware of water flowing and pouring on all sides – often from seemingly inexhaustible sources."[11] Poetic musicality, and poetic influence, can both be figured by the merging of different murmurs, the intermingling of manifold rivers, streams, and rivulets.

If this is an "inexhaustible" process, it is also one that might at times be invisible, submerged, or subterranean: an underground stream that only occasionally rises to the surface. Heaney and Wordsworth, tellingly, use this image in quite different ways. Wordsworth pictures the imagination as a "stream" that we can trace from its birth in "darkness" in a "blind cavern," and that comes "to light / And open day" only then to disappear and reappear as it is "bewildered and engulfed" before rising "once more / With strength, reflecting in its solemn breast / The works of man and face of human life."[12] These fluvial meanderings trace a course for Wordsworth from the natural, through "human life," to the divine, binding the three: from

6 This Strange Loneliness

the river's "progress" he draws "The feeling of life endless, the great thought / By which we live, infinity and God." Heaney does not, however, assent to such a religious culmination. When he uses a similar image in "The Sandpit" in *Station Island* (1984), the transcendental is carefully (and literally) concretized, but in a way that nevertheless argues for the value of persistence and endurance, for the aggregation of meaning, and for the possibility of self-discovery and the re-discovery of childhood wonder. Heaney describes a builder, working on a new housing estate:

> His touch, his daydream of the tanks,
> his point of vantage on the scaffolding
> over chimneys and close hills at noontime,
> the constant sound of hidden river water
> the new estate rose up through –
> with one chop of the trowel he sent it all
> into the brick for ever. [13]

The "sound of hidden river water" is not silenced or lost in the brick. Rather, it "has not stopped travelling in / in the van of all that followed," and it persists through the completion of the estate, and the lives lived on it, until it culminates in the adult poet remembering (or re-imagining) his childhood self: "And my own hands, the size of a grandchild's, / go in there, cold and wet, and my big gaze / at the sandpit opening by the minute." There is a shared sense of wonder (that grandchild's "big gaze") at the persistence and limitlessness of life, and a Wordsworthian tracing of how childhood events resonate through to adulthood (of how the "Child is Father of the Man").[14] Rather than being imagined on a transcendental plane, however, in Heaney's poem that "life endless" is carried by mundanely concretized "works of man": bricks. Heaney's world is ultimately earthy, soily, and physical, rather than infinite and ethereal. Nevertheless, these poets share an intimation "of life endless" or, as the sandpit suggests, of memory opening itself to itself, in an eternal process of self-discovery. Heaney's poetry, in other words, taps into the same hidden rivers as Wordsworth's, but is able to use them to create "new estates" that are not beholden to the poet of the Derwent, and were not always (at least in Heaney's earliest work) that respectful towards him.

Introduction

PUKING ROMANTIC VERSE
AND PROSPECTS OF THE MIND

In "There's Rosemary," an early – and for him very rare – short story, Heaney satirizes romantic visions of the west of Ireland. The story, published in 1961 in *Gorgon*, the Queen's University student magazine, describes a trip taken by a newlywed couple to Galway. Their honeymoon is shadowed by an earlier holiday the man had taken there, and an earlier relationship, sparked when he meets a girl, "Grainne," standing alone at the deck-rail of a ferry. She is staring down at "the swollen corpse of a mangy grey dog floating along the harbour-wall, its disgusting rotund belly glistening in the cold morning sun. The oil-scummed water was hitting the wall with an opaque slap."[15] This inauspicious encounter leads to them sharing "their inferiority complexes and basic shyness and bad poetry," and then, implicitly, more. This is not, however, how he remembers it to his wife: instead he recalls a day trip with "the footballers ... to the Aran Islands and tour[ing] all round Connemara in jaunting cars. I wrote reams of puking Romantic verse when I came to recollect it in tranquillity."[16] The twist at the end of the story is that the man discovers from his wife, who is unaware of the particular significance, that Grainne subsequently went to the Isle of Man for an abortion. There is a dismissal of epiphany in the story: it centres around multiple absences (the dog, the aborted fetus), and the lie now festering at the heart of the married couple's relationship. At stake is what and how we remember or misremember. The title reworks lines spoken by Ophelia ("There's *Rosemary*, that's for remembrance; pray, love, remember"), but the Wordsworthian model of poetic remembrance, of "emotion recollected in tranquillity," is not favoured: it results only in "puking Romantic verse."[17]

This story is, unsurprisingly, not representative of Heaney's future career. It comes in the same issue of *Gorgon* as a "superfluous and unsolicited editorial" in which Heaney labelled himself with apparent sincerity an "ex-poet" (with his undergraduate doubts and uncertainties he could not predict the twelve volumes of poetry, the translations, the books of essays and interviews, the honorary doctorates, the university professorships, the T.S. Eliot and Forward and Nobel prizes).[18] Nor is it representative of his future poetic allegiances: it lightly dismisses a poetic relationship that would continue throughout his career, evolving, enduring, and informing Heaney's thinking about poetry and poetics all his life.

8   This Strange Loneliness

When he was first collecting occasional essays, lectures, reviews, and broadcasts for publication in *Preoccupations* (1980), he gave Wordsworth almost the first word (almost, since the epigraph to the book comes from Yeats, and the foreword mentions Auden and Kavanagh). The book opens with a 1978 BBC Radio 4 broadcast (retitled "Omphalos") in which Heaney describes the importance of his "first place," the Derry countryside he grew up in, and the different languages that named that countryside. "In the names of its fields and townlands," Heaney recounts, "in their mixture of Scots and Irish and English etymologies, this side of the country was redolent of the histories of its owners. Broagh, The Long Rigs, Bell's Hill; Brian's Field, the Round Meadow, the Demesne; each name was a kind of love made to each acre. And saying the names like this distances the places, turns them into what Wordsworth once called a prospect of the mind. They lie deep, like some script indelibly written into the nervous system."[19] Conversely, Wordsworth is given (again almost) the last word in *Stepping Stones* (2008), the book-length interview between Dennis O'Driscoll and Heaney that takes the place of an autobiography. O'Driscoll's final questions are repeated from Heaney's poem "Keeping Going" – "Is this all? As it was / In the beginning, is now and shall be?" – and Heaney answers that "If those questions had to be translated into Latin they'd begin with the word 'Nonne,' which indicates that the answer they expect is 'yes.' Fundamentally they're saying what William Wordsworth said long ago: that it is on this earth 'we find our happiness, or not at all.' Which is one reason for keeping going."[20] Repeated recourse to the same poet is as revealing of Heaney as of Wordsworth: as Heaney himself notes, "when poets turn to the great masters of the past, they turn to an image of their own creation, one which is likely to be a reflection of their own imaginative needs, their own artistic inclinations and procedures."[21] Certainly, in "There's Rosemary," "Omphalos," and *Stepping Stones*, Heaney discovers, depending on his artistic and personal needs, preoccupations, and concerns, different reflections of himself.

"Omphalos," for example, carefully balances multiple histories and competing relationships to place. Naming here is not an act of claiming or of possession; nor is it only a form of "love-making" with all the problems this raises. (Patricia Coughlan rightly criticizes Heaney's reliance, here and elsewhere, on a "land-woman metaphoric equation" and his tendency to see "self-formation as a

Introduction

struggle ... however metaphorically or virtually, as *against* the feminine"; this includes a form of sexual struggle.)[22] Naming is here, instead, an act of both internalization and estrangement: a writing deep into the nervous system that is also a "distancing," the interplay of competing political birthrights or cultural traditions. The title "Omphalos" (the Greek for the navel) itself suggests multiple influences. Heaney famously relates it to the sound of a pump in the farmyard of his childhood home, merging classical inheritances with rural and domestic verisimilitude, but it also has literary (and literary critical) connotations.[23] It is haunted by Joyce's *Ulysses* – where Buck Mulligan associates the Martello Tower with the phrases "To ourselves ... the new paganism ... omphalos" and then imagines "a national fertilising farm to be named *Omphalos*, with an obelisk hewn and erected after the fashion of Egypt."[24] However, it is also (less obviously) underpinned by critical study of Wordsworth's work. In 1964, Geoffrey Hartman diagnosed Wordsworth's "omphalos or spot syndrome" as the "attraction to specific place" that underlies Wordsworth's "spots of time"; for Hartman, as he later expanded, these omphaloi are "specific locations that could restore poetic strength and lead to a future as strong as the past," through the preservation of memories and historical traces.[25]

Heaney does not present his own "omphalos" here as a Joycean paganist site of fertilization, but as a Hartmanian location of continuity between the future and the past.[26] Heaney's allusion is to Book II of the *Prelude*, where Wordsworth is remembering childhood excursions at dawn, sitting "upon some jutting eminence ... when the vale / Lay quiet in an utter solitude": "Oft in those moments such a holy calm / Did overspread my soul that I forgot / That I had bodily eyes, and what I saw / Appeared like something in myself, a dream, / A prospect in my mind."[27] Heaney misquotes the poem: for him it is "a prospect *of* the mind" rather than a "prospect *in* the mind" as it appears in both the 1805 and 1850 versions of Wordsworth's poem.[28] The misquotation suggests subtle differences in emphasis between his project and Wordsworth's. The prospect *in* Wordsworth's mind is a result of "holy calm" in which the external world ("what I saw") is internalized and turned into a mental landscape, through the interaction of natural and mental processes – "winter snows," "summer shade," "my dreams," and "my waking thoughts" – and the mediation of the "spirit of religious love in which / I walked with nature."[29] This "love" bound him to the natural world so that he was under a "like dominion" to the birds, breezes, and fountains; any creative impulse from within the poet was, in comparison, "An auxiliar light" to this dominion.[30]

The emphasis has shifted in Heaney's passage. This process of deep, indelible inscription is now strangely also, through the "saying" of the names, an act of "distancing." Both poets are interested in how this process might be a means of "transport," of dislocation as well as location, but for Heaney it hints at some level of defamiliarization as well as of deep identification: it is a doubled relationship.[31] Two decades later, Heaney repeats this misquotation in a discussion of Edwin Muir's "October in Hellbrunn"; here he is explicit that the Wordsworthian idea of "prospect" involves the "mirroring of outer and inner things."[32] Heaney compares Muir's poetry to "the simplicity of Wordsworth's ballad poems of that season [when Dorothy and William had 'withdrawn to the South of England in the 1790s'], in which the greening of vegetation and the startle of birdsong are analogies for the shoots of self-healing he was experiencing." In Muir's poem, a "park scene has become what Wordsworth called 'a prospect of the mind': the images dwell in two places at one time"; for both poets, "poetry was a necessary part of an effort at self-restoration and self-integration, an aspect of the attempt to align powers of the self with powers of the cosmos."[33]

This doubled dwelling and belief in the possibility of "self-integration" might seem overly optimistic: there is no sense that dwelling "in two places at one time" might lead precisely away from "integration" towards a more complex sense of self; and there appears to be an underpinning faith in a turn to the self that transcends, or simply ignores, political or historical circumstances. What, though, if the "inner and outer things" do not mirror each other? Perhaps as a result of such doubts, the possibility of psychic displacement (as well as renewal) underlies the allusion in *Stepping Stones*. Although a metaphysical response might be expected to the questions "Is this all? As it was / In the beginning, is now and shall be?" Heaney's allusion to Wordsworth stymies any such expectation. He quotes from the stanza that contains the famous exclamation "Bliss was it in that dawn to be alive, / But to be young was very heaven!" and the context is Wordsworth's hope for the political and social change that might follow the French Revolution (rather than the earlier hope for "self-restoration and self-integration").[34] Wordsworth describes the joy of being involved in a project of world creation, of thinking

Introduction

with "fervour upon management / Of nations, what it is and ought to be," and with the possibility of this being enacted not, crucially, "in Utopia – subterraneous fields, / Or some secreted island, heaven knows where! / But in the very world which is the world / Of all of us, the place in which in the end / We find our happiness, or not at all."[35] Wordsworth's "bliss" and "fervour" were temporary and provisional, and would be undone by Britain declaring war on France, and his being separated from Annette Vallon and their daughter, Caroline. (Heaney was well aware of this subtext: in 1969, after he had won the Somerset Maugham Award, the Heaneys travelled to France, "Making stops and digressions all over the place – to Blois, for example, where Wordsworth had met Annette Vallon.")[36]

Heaney retains the (non-quietist) political and ethical dimensions of Wordsworth's poem. Happiness is to be found only "in this world" and this gives a reason stoically to persist, to endure, to "keep going." In effect this is a restatement of a liberal humanist sense of the continuity of social, political, and ethical projects across historical distance, based in part on Wordsworth's own writing, as in Book X of *The Prelude*, where he claims that "There is / One great society alone on earth, / The noble living and the noble dead. / Thy consolation shall be there."[37] M.H. Abrams's gloss of this passage uses it as an example of an ideology common to Wordsworth and other Romantic writers, "whose mission was to assure the continuance of civilization by reinterpreting to their drastically altered condition the enduring humane values, making whatever changes were required in the theological systems by which these values had earlier been sanctioned. Chief among these values were life, love, liberty, hope, and joy."[38] This is the mission Heaney identifies with at the end of *Stepping Stones*: the endurance of "humane values" and the belief in a sense of "great society" (those "great masters of the past"). He alludes to it, however, through a passage that bespeaks dashed revolutionary idealism. There is the desire for some continued ideal of "civilization," but this is coloured by a "late-humanist" awareness that this ideal is diminished by belatedness, by an embattled sense of inherent human possibility and goodness, or by the loss of revolutionary ardour and religious succour. Late Heaney, unlike late Wordsworth, does not renounce such youthful ideals; despite the knowledge that such idealism needs to be tempered, he reasserts it as a reason for "keeping going."

The central concern of this book is the willed and perhaps surprising persistence of Wordsworth (and a Wordsworth-influenced

12 This Strange Loneliness

humanism) in Heaney's poetic landscape: how Wordsworth remained a presence from Heaney's earliest writings to his last, in the face of various poetic, critical, cultural, and political pressures, and personal and aesthetic divergences. In a 1981 essay, Darcy O'Brien expressed surprise at Heaney's saying, in 1973, that he had been "getting a lot out of Wordsworth lately." "I failed to see," O'Brien comments, "what possible connection there could be between the two poets. Personality defied the alliance: Wordsworth tediously earnest, slow, relentlessly profuse; Heaney spare, quick, sharp, clear, in his own phrase, as the bleb of an icicle. The two minds appeared to have as much in common as vinegar and treacle ... As for poetic form, Heaney had more in common with the Japanese than with the English Romantics."[39] This is an unfair caricature of Wordsworth, but the terms of difference O'Brien lights upon are nevertheless notable: a matter of personality and poetic form, the lack of "any common ground of experience."[40] O'Brien's article also outlines many of the things that the poets *do* share, but predicts the likely end of that commonality: "My guess is that he will leave behind Wordsworthian reflections and Wordsworthian nature for a time, charting new territory, perhaps returning some day to Wordsworthian matter and manner, perhaps not."[41] Strangely, perhaps, there never was such a clear "leaving behind" of Wordsworth at any point in Heaney's career. Although he did repeatedly find "other beacons," in O'Brien's words, he never recanted entirely from certain Wordsworthian poses (and it is perhaps in a wry nod to his late friend's comments that in a 2007 article Heaney used Wordsworth as a critical framework through which to discuss Japanese poetry).[42] Indeed, the importance of "durability," and the belief that "for poetry to matter, the amount of it you know isn't as important as the meaning any small bit of it can gather up over a lifetime," is another lesson Heaney learned from his ongoing and changing relationship with Wordsworth. As he notes in a 2002 interview, "Wordsworth I just gradually grew up to. He has always been a mountain on the horizon. Wordsworth helps you to think about poetry as a way of taking the measure of yourself and the world, and yourself-in-the-world."[43]

READING HEANEY READING WORDSWORTH

Examining how Heaney used Wordsworth "to think about poetry as a way of taking the measure of yourself and the world" allows us to retrace some of the fault-lines in contemporary poetry: the ongo-

Introduction 13

ing viability of the "Romantic," humanist lyric subject, and the vexed relationship between the aesthetic and the historical, and between "poetry" and "politics." Wordsworth is one of the most commonly recurring focuses, touchstones, and even problems of Heaney's criticism, and Heaney turns to him repeatedly to explore his own evolving justification for poetry, and also – as in Heaney's remarkably careful delineation of his childhood reading – to weave his "deep familiarity" with Wordsworth into the story of his own education and development as a poet.[44] Because of these repeated returns, Wordsworth features in Heaney's lectures and essays with a frequency and complexity that far exceeds the attention he paid to early influences such as Hopkins or Hughes, or later ones such as Robert Lowell. The only poet to compare, the only one who seems to be a similar problem that repeatedly needs to be addressed, is Yeats.

Neil Corcoran, discussing "Heaney's writings on Yeats," imagines that they "would almost make a book [like Louis MacNeice's 1941 *The Poetry of W.B. Yeats*]," which would be "relatively slim, but intellectually substantial."[45] A book of "Heaney on Wordsworth" would be as intellectually weighty, and somewhat fatter, comprising essays, lectures, interviews and reviews, as well as various manuscript fragments. Providing a full outline of the contents of this putative book would try the patience of all but the most specialist reader; what follows is thus simply a brief sketch. There are numerous essays, lectures, and broadcasts in which Wordsworth is discussed in depth as the main focus, or one of the main focuses, of attention. These include Heaney's 1974 BBC broadcast, *William Wordsworth Lived Here: Seamus Heaney at Dove Cottage*; the lectures "Feeling into Words" (1974), "The Makings of a Music: Reflections on Wordsworth and Yeats" (1978), and *Place and Displacement: Recent Poetry of Northern Ireland* (1984); Heaney's introduction to his 1988 *Essential Wordsworth*; and the 2006 lecture "Apt Admonishment: Wordsworth as an Example?" These could be accompanied by the following: extracts from various essays and interviews in which Wordsworth is used as a critical comparator or touchstone, of which the most important for my purposes is "The Indefatigable Hoof-Taps: Sylvia Plath" (1988); the numerous articles, essays, and lectures in which Wordsworth appears as an element of what Heaney refers to as his "keyboard of references"; and Heaney's comments and asides about Wordsworth in television and radio broadcasts. Finally, there are, of course, Heaney's poems. Many of these, as the following pages show, explicitly or implicitly respond to, echo, or critique Wordsworth's work, starting with uncollected poems written before the publication of *Death of a Naturalist* (1966) and ending with "Had I not Been Awake"" and "A Kite for Aibhín," from *Human Chain* (2010). (Some of these echoes ring louder than others. Michael O'Neill, discussing "Personal Helicon," from *Death of a Naturalist*, cautions that it would be "absurd to find Wordsworth everywhere in such passages": this book risks absurdity, at times, as it attempts to tease out how the relationship between the poets develops in even the most unlikely places.[46])

Across these articles, lectures, and poems, however, Heaney turns to only a relatively small number of poems by Wordsworth: there is little fidelity, for example, to "Fidelity." He limits himself almost entirely to passages from *The Prelude*, "There Was a Boy," "Resolution and Independence," "The Thorn," "Michael," "The Ruined Cottage," "A Slumber Did My Spirit Seal," "The Solitary Reaper," and "Ode: Intimations of Immortality." Later Wordsworth is apparently of little interest: Heaney includes only four poems written after 1807 in his *Essential Wordsworth*, although two of these – "Loud Is the Vale!" and the "Extempore Effusion Upon the Death of James Hogg" – are also mentioned enthusiastically in passing in his late criticism.[47] Heaney's taste in Wordsworth's work was, in general, largely determined by his early reading: as Hugh Haughton has commented, aside from "the Two-Part *Prelude*," which was first published in 1979, and which Heaney includes entire in his *Essential Wordsworth*, the Wordsworth he turns to in his own poetry and criticism is largely "the figure he read at school at St Columb's College, Derry, and at Queen's, Belfast, and again on returning to Ireland after Berkeley in the early 1970s."[48]

This is not to say, however, that how Heaney reads these poems does not change: indeed, the evolution of these readings is one of their main sources of interest. "Wordsworth," as Patricia Horton notes, "is a shape-changer in Heaney's prose, prone to metamorphosis depending on Heaney's priorities, agenda and anxieties. He is a 'rooted' Wordsworth in 'The Makings of a Music,' a 'displaced' Wordsworth in *Place and Displacement*, and finally a 'whole' Wordsworth in *The Essential Wordsworth*."[49] (Heaney's shift towards the "marvellous" with the attendant possible resurrection of the "idea of the poet as a transcendent genius" is also, as Horton notes, to some extent Wordsworthian.[50]) Horton's analysis is astute

Introduction 15

and accurate, but not quite the whole story: Wordsworth appears in Heaney's poetics in different ways at other times, depending on those shifting "priorities, agenda and anxieties." Long before "The Makings of a Music," Heaney had been interested in Wordsworth as an "educational" poet and thinker (he had considered writing an MA thesis on the subject); from this Heaney developed an interest in Wordsworth as providing an insight into childhood understanding, development, and repression, which reappears in Heaney's criticism in the 1990s and 2000s. The poets also shared an interest in poetic "influence" and how this can be related in complicated ways to ideas of "fosterage." Moreover, two turns occur after Horton's discussion of the poets was published: a rethinking of poetic and cultural relationships in Britain and Ireland through a "four nations" or "Britannic" approach, which necessarily impinges on Heaney's relationship with Wordsworth; and the late emphasis on endurance or keeping going, Heaney's own celebration of "resolution and independence." The following chapters thus sketch out a picture of Heaney's Wordsworth that add "educational," "epiphanic," "influential," "post-secular," "enduring," and "excessive" dimensions to the "rooted," "displaced," and "whole" figures Horton describes.

Horton's work is part of a healthy body of criticism on Heaney's relationship with Wordsworth that includes numerous reviews, essays, and general studies stretching from Christopher Ricks's 1966 *New Statesman* review of *Death of a Naturalist* onwards: any book on Heaney and Wordsworth has dues to pay, not least to cover its author's belatedness. Among the most useful critical sources, alongside Horton's work, are an excellent unpublished PhD thesis by Michael Kinsella, and perceptive readings of particular poems and facets of their relationship by Nicholas Roe, Edna Longley, Edward Larrissy, and Darcy O'Brien. There are, however, three studies that have been particularly influential on this current book, by Hugh Haughton, Guinn Batten, and Fiona Stafford, and which will appear at various points.[51] Haughton's nuanced essay "Power and Hiding Places: Wordsworth and Seamus Heaney" (2006) is the most comprehensive previous treatment of the poets and is especially useful for identifying how "influence" is crucial to both poets and for its discussion of the extent to which Heaney is "an avowed heir to the Wordsworthian defense of poetry" (in the face of waxing and waning critical attitudes to Romanticism).[52] Batten's "Heaney's Wordsworth and the Poetics of Displacement" is a persuasive application of feminist and psychoanalytic theories to Heaney's various readings of the Romantic poet, and in particular their use of "sound/mother/place" as a combined, complicated, and "displacing" force.[53] Her discussion of how Heaney is "doubled by place" and "situates the experience of embodiment *as* displacement within Ireland's particular history of dispossession" is particularly compelling, as is her identification of Heaney's use and abandonment of the Romantic trope of the "self-inwoven simile" as a means of "mutually implicating poet and place."[54] Stafford's *Local Attachments: The Province of Poetry* (2010) also deals at length with Heaney's readings of Wordsworth and their versions of "place." Stafford fruitfully locates her discussion alongside readings of other important Romantic figures (Keats, Scott, and Burns) to argue for the way that Heaney's careful negotiations of the poetic traditions of these islands, and their different versions of the "local," is salutary; but this must, as later chapters discuss, come with heavy caveats. Indeed, whether one chooses to focus on Heaney as a "local" rather than an international poet, say (or as a "Irish" poet, or a "post-Romantic" poet), depends on the limits and limitations of the critical approach one is taking.

BAD DEBTS?

As the substantial body of criticism on both poets suggests, the relationship between Heaney and Wordsworth can be approached through various critical lenses, each of which brings its own complications, tensions, and anxieties. Since this book focuses primarily on Heaney and how he reads, misreads, and rewrites Wordsworth (rather than on Wordsworth himself), the most pertinent critical contexts are discussions of the legacy of Romanticism, the nature of poetic influence, and the extensive criticism of Heaney's oeuvre (and contemporary Irish poetry more generally). Running through each of these tends to be a wider question of whether poetry should be treated as a phenomenon unto itself – as an art form first and foremost with its own rules, value judgments, and responsibilities – or whether it should be read historically, as a series of socially, politically, and psychologically rooted and motivated gestures, responses, and evasions (and these questions are complicated by Heaney's own repeated exploration of them). Given this last, one of the underpinnings of this book is a belief that what authors say they are doing, and do not say they are doing, is still useful for interpreting the texts they produce: writers have always been revealing, if unreliable, critics and self-critics, and different "texts" they produce can clearly influence, inform, and rework each other. Such self-reflexive texts can, of course, be approached with the same critical distances, freedoms, and responsibilities as poems, novels, or short stories; and to ignore the contiguity between texts that respond intertextually to Wordsworth in the manner of Heaney's "Feeling into Words" and his *Stations* would be perverse and provide at best a limited reading.

That Heaney's and Wordsworth's poems can fruitfully be read through the lenses of postcolonialism, deconstruction, and feminism is unquestioned, and it is necessary to bear in mind that Heaney (like any informed contemporary writer) was aware of these critical tendencies and approaches. His own writing will often provide a series of clues, evasions, and dead-ends to such critical strategies (although the critical direction Heaney provides is perhaps less playfully misleading than that, say, of Paul Muldoon). Given the theoretical and philosophical discussions of literature over the course of his lifetime, that Heaney would persist with a broadly liberal-humanist attitude to the relationship between writers is even more worthy of scrutiny. This book thus attends more to how Heaney frames his own readings of and relationship with Wordsworth than how that relationship can be explored in the light of deconstruction or postmodernism (say) or the various twists, turns, and controversies in the arguments for and against postcolonial or "revisionist" readings of Irish literature (or indeed the convergences and divergences in how theoretical practice has evolved in Irish studies – and Heaney studies in particular – and studies of Romanticism).[55] It does, however, take the weight of these broader critical questions as they exert pressure at important points in Heaney's career; thus, it is worth briefly unpicking some of the most important threads.

How we understand the term "Romantic poetry" has changed markedly since Heaney started writing about Wordsworth. "Romanticism" or "Romantic poetry" are themselves contested, and largely indefinable, terms: there is rightly a critical preference at least for a plural "Romanticisms," with its sense of multiple, and at times incompatible, threads, and a recognition that whatever "Romanticism" may or may not be (or have been), it manifested itself differently depending on national, historical, racial, and gender contexts. From the 1970s onwards, different waves of theoretical analysis – including those with deconstructionist, new-historicist, postcolonial, or environmental bents – have seen aesthetic or humanist or transcendental approaches to reading literature criticized and undermined; as a result, the idea of (Romantic) poetry as a reified area of knowledge, set aside from political contingency, has been repeatedly attacked (despite a counterinsurgency that would seek out possible religious, quasi-religious, or "post-secular" roles for poetry). The extent to which such critical debates impinged on Heaney's own writing about Romanticism is, however, debatable. It is broadly true that Heaney has not, as Haughton claims, "noticeably engaged with the post-Freudian or deconstructionist Wordsworth of Bloom, De Man, and Hartman, or with the politically fraught Wordsworth of the newer historicists, such as Jerome McGann, Alan Liu, and Nicholas Roe."[56] This does not mean, however, that the changing landscape of Romantic criticism has not influenced his reading of Wordsworth in more subterranean ways (indeed the same is true of deconstruction and other theoretically driven approaches to literature, which for all Heaney's wariness can be heard echoed by various ideas, tropes, or manoeuvres in his work).[57] That is, the evolving discussions of Romanticism overlap in certain ways with both Heaney's own poetry and prose, and how it has been criticized.

Romantic poetry, especially that of Wordsworth, often stands accused of political negligence, of "displac[ing] and idealiz[ing]" (this is Jonathan Bate's criticism of Jerome McGann's "Romantic Ideology") as it "privileges imagination at the expense of history ... [and] covers up social conditions as it quests for transcendence"; or, indeed, it is accused of "hid[ing] history in order, finally, to reflect the self," as Alan Liu suggests of the Wordsworthian georgic.[58] Often, as Edna Longley argues while discussing Yeats's poetry, the "Romantic quest for transcendence – Muldoon's quinquereme – is repeatedly dashed against the rocks of history."[59] Heaney has been criticized, even by critics generally well-disposed to him, for similar historical "bad faith." Horton, for example, argues that Heaney ultimately "uses Wordsworth to privilege the idea of the poet as a transcendent genius, and while he does give some sense of the politics of the period, this is ultimately only to uphold the view that such a world is antithetical and hostile to the psychic equilibrium of the poet."[60] Critics less favourably inclined towards Heaney's poetics have made more damaging accusations: David Lloyd, for one, attacks Heaney's belief in the poet as a guarantor of bourgeois continuity, seeing rather a figure who poses a false questioning of the

Introduction 19

self in a "rhetoric of compensation" that "uncritically replays the Romantic schema of a return to origins which restores continuity through fuller self-possession."[61]

Reading Heaney as a last bastion (witting or unwitting) of Romantic transcendence is, however, to oversimplify the matter. Much of Heaney's criticism is deliberate and "critical" in its replaying of the Romantic schema Lloyd outlines, and queries whether such "self-possession" is possible given the demands on (Northern) Irish poets during the Troubles to respond to the political and social circumstances in which they found themselves. The political contexts have added particular weight and urgency to (Romantic) arguments about "transcendence" or historical burial, with the risks of either taking an overly transcendental line (becoming a "botaniser among the hedgerows," as Michael Longley suggests) or saturating your work "with 'Ireland'" (in Edna Longley's phrase) only too apparent.[62] Questions of how poetry can "answer its circumstances" rather than seek to transcend them, and whether a "rhetoric of compensation" can ever compensate, are crucial. For most sympathetic critics it is Heaney's attempt to address and balance historical circumstance and poetic demands that is most salutary about his work. As Patrick Crotty puts it, "much of the authority of Heaney's poetry derives from his successful quest for avenues of aesthetic approach to ethical and political concerns"; these concerns must be faced, but without them overwhelming the distinct aesthetic requirements of poetry.[63]

Part of Heaney's treading of the line between the historical and the transcendent actually comes in a careful distancing from elements of Romanticism: Heaney's mistrust of "puking Romantic verse recollected in tranquillity" does not fade entirely. In "The Fully Exposed Poem," for example, Heaney's review of *Sagittal Section* and *Interferon, or On the Theatre*, translations of the work of Miroslav Holub, he bemoans how "In spite of a period of castigation about the necessity for 'intelligence' and 'irony,' poetry in English has not moved all that far from the shelter of the Romantic tradition. Even our self-mocking dandies pirouette to a narcotic music. The dream's the thing, not the diagnosis. Inwardness, yearnings and merging of the self towards nature, cadences that drink at spots of time – in general the hopes of poets and readers still realize themselves within contexts like these. We still expect the poetic imagination to be sympathetic rather than analytic. 'Intellect' still seems to summon its rhyme from Wordsworth's pejorative 'dissect.'"[64] The point of the review is to advocate a distinctly non-Romantic, scientific, and intellectual approach to poetry; since this is so fundamentally different from Heaney's own poetics, it can be read in part as ironic self-commentary (and elsewhere he will argue precisely for the importance of "dreams" and "trances" to poetry). Nevertheless, the review does show that Heaney felt the need at times to distance himself from the "Romantic" (or a particular caricature of it), even when flagging up elements that chime with his own work (such as the location of the self in nature or the celebration of the narcotic over the intellectual).

The "Romantic tradition" is nevertheless here presented as being, to some extent, inescapable: even self-mocking dandies cannot separate themselves from it. One might consider that Paul de Man's claim that we still "think" Romantically is pertinent, that "with romanticism we are not separated from the past by that layer of forgetfulness and that temporal opacity that could awaken in us the illusion of detachment."[65] This is not borne out, however, by the rest of Heaney's criticism, in which there is always a sense of historical detachment (even if this sense is illusory). Although he wrote critically on Clare, Burns, Shelley, and Keats as well as Wordsworth as part of an ongoing conversation with a Leavisite "great tradition" of previous writers across many periods, countries, and languages, these figures are always compared to poets from other epochs and historical contexts in a way that takes due account of each poet's historical distinctiveness. Thus, Heaney's reading of Wordsworth is complicated by the intervening examples of Yeats, Joyce, Eliot, MacDiarmid, Hughes, Kavanagh, Lowell, Mandelstam, Milosz, Plath, Bishop, Muldoon, and others. In each instance their historical rootedness – their timeliness rather than their timelessness – is as important as their communication or co-ordinance across generations or centuries. "The Romantic symbol with its offer of totalization and timelessness" may have "exerted a profound attraction," but it was not the only attraction.[66]

Attention to the historical and cultural context of his precursors helps Heaney avoid the bland levelling of an F.R. Leavis- or Harold Bloom-informed canon-building, in ways that chime – perhaps unexpectedly – with the techniques and motivations of postcolonial criticism. Access to the canon is not equally shared or enjoyed; the act of alluding to Romantic writers, say, has the potential, as postcolonial criticism would remind us, of being both a private act of

Introduction

identification and a public disavowal that reshapes the power dynamics of the language used; these acts might sit uneasily together.[67] For Heaney such questions of linguistic and cultural possession and dispossession are most often introduced through Joyce's *Portrait of the Artist as a Young Man*, in which (in a quotation Heaney repeatedly uses) Stephen Dedalus exclaims, "How different are the words *home, Christ, ale, master*, on his lips and on mine! I cannot speak or write these words without unrest of spirit. His language, so familiar and so foreign, will always be for me an acquired speech."[68]

Such attention to "foreign familiarity" has only recently been consistently present in studies of Romantic legacies. George Bornstein, writing in the 1970s, could comment (albeit with caveats that this is a "romantic" opinion) that "the representativeness of Wordsworth's or Keats' minds make them in fact more accessible than Yeats' quirky Celts."[69] Yeats, that is, is not *as* representative as the "original romantics" and the way he fastened his "visions to a national landscape" (which is not that of England) was at best "quirky." Irish "patriotism," as against the English version is, as Patrick Kavanagh wryly notes, "a different kettle of potatoes altogether."[70] Recent discussions of Romantic legacies do, however, take into account the fact that the flavour of the words "history" or "transcendence" or "Romanticism" itself depends on who is uttering them, and that Irish responses to "English" Romanticism are complex, and may include an unsettling, postcolonial, Bhabhian "mimcry" or (as Fiona Stafford suggests) a "lingering Yeatsian 'love.'"[71] Michael O'Neill's *The All-Sustaining Air*, for example, shows how critics can be attentive to the "historical differences and cultural dissonance" involved in the relationship between Northern Irish poets and Romanticism, and especially their simultaneous "looking back to and backing off from the Romantics."[72] O'Neill argues that the Romantic legacy entails a "bifocal" approach for contemporary poets, "a post-Romantic doubleness of vision, one marked by a generous scepticism, by an inclusive irony" whose ability "to enact and criticize longing and desire is part of its fascinating doubleness," and which can then create an aesthetic "which implies that art is at once autonomous and shaped by historical circumstance, which licenses transcendental questing while valuing the meanest flower that blows."[73] And O'Neill acknowledges that this raises particular problems for Northern Irish poets, who in turn raise particular questions about the "Romantic": he comments that "double-takes are at work in

22 This Strange Loneliness

Northern Irish poets such as Seamus Heaney and Derek Mahon" in which "Post-Romanticism sees its own face in the mirror held up by Romanticism; but it persuades us, too, that Romanticism's features were always ready to grow into the expressions worn by the post-Romantic."[74]

The national dimension is unavoidable and should be used to undermine any singular notion of the Romantic: within "Romanticism" itself there is a need to recognize distinct Irish strains. As Julia Wright argues, Irish Romanticism possessed a particular tenor which tended to query and undermine imperial tendencies within English Romanticism by paying a different form of attention to the land: Irish Romanticism did not "bury" history into a continuous, pastoralized English landscape, or subsume "the binary opposition of country and city within the larger imaginative structure of universal, peaceful empire."[75] The land was too troubled and troubling to allow this: debates about land ownership and usage and the process of mapping the landscape were explicitly involved in questions of colonialism, power imbalances, and cultural conflict. "Romantic" evasions or elisions of history have a different dimension in Irish literature, in other words, because the relationship between geography and history (and land ownership) is framed differently. The "quaking sod" of a "national consciousness" (in Daniel Corkery's tendentious phrase) might be a place where history is not just "buried" but – as the troubling metaphor of the bog bodies suggests – preserved, with poetry then becoming, in Heaney's words from "Feeling into Words," "a dig, a dig for finds that end up being plants."[76] (This may seem tangential to Heaney, who rarely discusses Irish Romantic writers. However, David Lloyd criticized Heaney's identity politics precisely on the grounds of a "nationalist" emphasis on the land, on the belief that "through its rootedness in the primary soil of Ireland, the mind of Ireland will regain its distinctive savour.")[77]

The imagery O'Neill uses above chimes with Heaney's own: the need to take a "bifocal" approach is central to Heaney's attitude not just to Romanticism but to the relationship between poetry and politics, and also the political situation in Ireland. Doubleness, the fact of being "Janus-faced," is one of Heaney's repeated preoccupations, and in a discussion of Louis MacNeice in *The Redress of Poetry*, he mentions how "MacNeice's bifocal vision ... is, as they say, 'part of the solution.'"[78] The bifocals Heaney describes are of a distinctly political, rather than Romantic, hue. Thus, while it is true,

Introduction
23

as O'Neill argues, that "In the uses made by contemporary Northern Irish poets of the Romantic inheritance, Romanticism's own splits and divisions are multiplied and refracted," it is important that different types of doubleness, or "bifocal vision," exist outside, or long predate, Romantic poetry; and they also include a complicating view of "English" literature.[79] Heaney was, of course, wary of being subsumed neatly into an "English" or "British" literature. In *An Open Letter* (1983), for example, he responds to his inclusion in *The Penguin Book of Contemporary British Poetry*, edited by Blake Morrison and Andrew Motion, with the assertion that his "passport's green"; earlier, in "Feeling into Words" he had complained: "I speak and write in English, but do not altogether share the preoccupations and perspectives of an Englishman. I teach English literature, I publish in London, but the English tradition is not ultimately home. I live off another hump as well."[80] Elsewhere he expresses this in more anxious terms. In *Among Schoolchildren* (1984) he describes how "The official British culture, if you like, was at odds with the anthropological culture," to the extent that the experience of that education could be interpreted in diametrically opposed ways. "Was I two persons or one?," he asks. "Was I extending myself or breaking myself apart? Was I being led out or led away? Was I failing to live up to the aspiring literary intellectual effort when I was at home, was I betraying the culture of the parish when I was at the university?"[81]

These questions perhaps mark a limit for Heaney's identification with Wordsworth, the moment when it is wrong to argue for Heaney being "Wordsworth Redivivus" (a tendency Edna Longley noted particularly "among English critics"), without acknowledging that he is, in his own terms, also "Sweeney Redivivus."[82] This awareness of cultural distance, otherness, and fragmentation is crucial to Heaney's own negotiations with Wordsworth: there is a necessary level of nuance in how he deals with the English poet. Heaney himself was certainly aware, and distrustful, of the tendency to identify the two poets. In the "Glanmore Sonnets" (discussed in chapter 3) Heaney has his wife reject any association between Dorothy and William's life and "the strange loneliness" Heaney had brought his family to in Wicklow: "She interrupts: / 'You're not going to compare us two?'"[83] Such acts of dis-identification were, perhaps, more necessary in later years when Heaney appeared to have been granted the mantle of Wordsworth's poetic "heir" to the extent that he had the honour of opening the Jerwood Centre at Dove Cottage in

24   This Strange Loneliness

Grasmere in 2005. Speaking on the *Today* program on BBC Radio 4, Heaney was fulsome in his praise: "as a student, Wordsworth's poetry meant a lot to me, in fact it's when I was starting out to write and the concentration on memory and on 'ordinary incidents' as he said 'with a certain light of the imagination thrown over them' and the other thing about Wordsworth, he said a marvelous thing in a letter once, he said that he wrote in order to show that men who don't wear fine clothes can also have deep feelings, so there is much to be commended about that particular genius, I think."[84] (A suggestive slip: Heaney remembers the "light of the imagination" rather than the "colouring of the imagination," as it is in the Preface to *Lyrical Ballads*).

Similarly, when interviewed the following day on *Front Row*, again on BBC Radio 4, Heaney demurred (in part through humility) about any comparison between the two. "Well," he said, "I don't think myself and Wordsworth have much in common, apart from my own gratitude for his poetry of memory and his sense of spots of time having a fructifying influence, as he said. I mean, Wordsworth is the greatest English poet after we look past Yeats, I think, and I would be loath to make too much identification between myself and him."[85] In these radio interviews, while there is affection, there is also distancing, the careful emphasis on them not having "much in common" (even if that "not much" still encompasses the "poetry of memory" and the "spots of time": not an insignificant legacy). However, despite the strategic placement of Yeats between himself and Wordsworth, Heaney's feeling of gratitude towards Wordsworth, and of the fructifying influence his poetry might have, are perhaps more central to Heaney's own defence of poetry than these comments might suggest.

Heaney's interest in Wordsworth is ultimately rooted in his need to defend poetry – in questions of what the value of poetry is, and what its role might be in the world. His criticism worries over matters of cultural identity, legacy, and poetic tradition, circling and returning to ultimately irresoluble questions and oppositions: the question, for example, of "How with this rage shall beauty hold a plea / Whose action is no stronger than a flower?" or (repeated in his preface to *Preoccupations* and the foreword to *Finders Keepers*) "How should a poet properly live and write? What is his relationship to be to his own voice, his own place, his literary heritage and his contemporary world?"[86] This repeated questioning suggests, as O'Donoghue

Introduction 25

argues, that Heaney's "abiding concerns have remained unchanged"; but it also gives the impression that the process of repeated questioning is perhaps more important than the hope of any answer.[87] As this book shows, Wordsworth's work is central to Heaney's never-ending process of questioning the value of poetry, from the use of lines from Book XI of the *Prelude* in the 1974 lecture "Feeling into Words" as the basis for "a view of poetry which I think is implicit in the few poems I have written that give me any right to speak," through the blunt asking of the question, "What is my apology for poetry?" in a Glanmore home that is uncannily mapped onto the Wordsworths' in Grasmere, to a late interest in Wordsworth's encounter with a leech-gatherer in "Resolution and Independence."[88] Wordsworth's narrator in this poem asks, "How is it that you live, and what is it that you do?" and this question could, when asked on an ethical rather than literal plane, easily stand alongside Heaney's other acts of self-questioning as epigraph to his prose.[89]

Fundamentally, Heaney's answers come through a critical and careful restatement of a liberal humanist defence of literature, given added impetus by the violence in Northern Ireland. As he suggests, during the Troubles the "hoary old chestnuts about the relationship of literature to life lost their hoar and were all of a sudden new again."[90] This willingness to re-ask questions and to explore those "hoary old chestnuts" (without a set or expected answer) is particularly prevalent and important in Heaney's later years. In *Stepping Stones*, for example, discussing the way in which Czesław Miłosz stuck throughout his life to the "Christian humanist wager," Heaney credits him with "visionary obstinacy rather than arrested development": such humanism is not retrograde, but an acknowledgment of the importance of "vision," even when it is fading or historically circumscribed. The comparison he uses (while admitting this is "pushing the case") is Wordsworth. "You could argue," Heaney comments, "that there's something analogous to Miłosz's deployment of the full orchestra after Auschwitz in Wordsworth's response to the loss of visionary gleam in his great 'Ode': it was only when the gleam had fled that Wordsworth opened all the gorgeous stops. There's nothing else in his work as deliberately orchestral and linguistically plenary as the Immortality Ode."[91] If Heaney is himself subscribing to humanism here, it is best viewed as a "late" or "belated" (or, for John Dennison, "post-Christian") humanism, conscious and even defensive about humanist claims of the value of literature.[92] The horrors of Auschwitz are not to be ignored, in other words, but neither do they negate the power – and beauty – of music or poetry.

There is a nuanced, and doubled, approach to humanism and religious belief here, as there had been in "Saw Music," the third section of "Out of This World" in *District and Circle* (2006), which he wrote in memory of Miłosz. In this poem Heaney refuses to repeat the catechistic renunciation of the world, preferring to celebrate the "untranscendent music of the saw" that his friend "might have heard in Vilnius or Warsaw."[93] "Untranscendent" does not appear in the *Oxford English Dictionary* and, although it is not strictly Heaney's invention, it is a clear example of how his poetry criticism relies upon (even in rejection) a Catholic terminology and worldview. Heaney himself repeatedly stressed the way in which Catholic thinking helped form his thinking. In *Stepping Stones*, for example, Heaney notes how his childhood was structured around Catholic ritual and mystery, and how he was "oversupplied" with religion in his youth: "I lived with, and to some extent lived by, divine mysteries: the sacrifice of the Mass, the transubstantiation of bread and wine into the body and blood of Christ, the forgiveness of sin, the resurrection of the body and the life of the world to come, the whole disposition of the cosmos from celestial to infernal, the whole supernatural population, the taxonomy of virtues and vices." He adds that "like many Catholics, lapsed or not – I am of the Stephen Dedalus frame of mind: if you desert this system, you're deserting the best there is, and there's no point in exchanging one great coherence for some other ad hoc arrangement."[94] However, as Gail McConnell notes, the negative "untranscendent," along with other negations such as "unbaptized" and "unroofed," expresses Heaney's "hesitant" relationship towards Catholic ritual (the participation in the Eucharist), acknowledging the symbolic power of its transformations, but redirecting this to assert "faith in language and in poetry's capacity to transform the elements and alter reality."[95] For McConnell, Heaney throughout his career draws "on Catholic forms of signification in order to re-imagine and re-image historical violence" and his approach to poetry as a whole is described in terms of a re-working of "Catholic iconography and sacramentalism" (in which poetry is a "vocation" or "covenant").[96] Catholicism provides Heaney with a vocabulary to describe the workings of the poetic mind, the relationship between the poet,

Introduction   27

poetry, and the world: however, this language is used throughout in a secular or skeptical (and certainly unorthodox) fashion.

As such, the celebration of the "untranscendent" is the end point of Heaney's apologetic poetic journey and his response to Wordsworth. Late Heaney is a poet who "credits marvels" but not one who believes in them; he accepts the "necessity of an idea of transcendence," but does so with a post-Christian conviction that god is absent, that the "definite / Presence" has "withdrawn."[97] All that is left, then, is "visionary obstinacy," or the in-spite-of-it-all gorgeousness of Wordsworth's "Immortality Ode." In the raging against the dying of the light, and the fading of the gleam, the knowledge "that it is on this earth 'we find our happiness, or not at all'" becomes in itself (obstinate) sustenance enough: as long as everything on this earth lies "bedded in a quickening soil."[98]

THIS BOOK

Drawing extensively on uncollected prose and poetry and archive material and on Heaney's repeated discussions of Wordsworth, the following chapters allow for a comprehensive understanding of Heaney's complex and multi-faceted response to Wordsworth. Although I engage with the work of previous critics, the central questions that this book poses have not been addressed in previous discussions of their relationship. These include the following: what did Heaney gain from Wordsworth's educational theories? How and why does he adopt and adapt the Wordsworthian epiphanic model? What are the political complications of their relationship, and are the cultural politics of their relationship best seen in light of ongoing dialogues between (Northern) Ireland and England, or a more broadly defined archipelagic approach? What does their relationship reveal about poetic influence (or poetic "fosterage")? And, finally, why is Wordsworth's influence so durable for Heaney, and to what extent does a belief in "durability" become self-sustaining?

Behind these questions lie various beliefs: that Heaney's response to Wordsworth is inextricably bound up with his broader defence of poetry; that this defence is as likely to be found in his poems as in his criticism; that it is as likely to be influenced by poems as by more formal, discursive *ars poeticas*; and that his defence of poetry is always, necessarily, contingent, and recognizes poetry is dependent on and responsive to historical and political circumstance.[99] Focusing

28 This Strange Loneliness

as it does on his relationship with Wordsworth, this book does not offer a comprehensive reading of Heaney's poetry and poetics, but instead gives an alternative way of reading Heaney's oeuvre, which will often foreground relatively unexplored parts of Heaney's oeuvre (uncollected poems and reviews, manuscripts, radio and television broadcasts) to give as full a picture of their relationship as possible. This way of reading is attentive – using a fluvial image shared by both poets – to the way poetic influence can be like an underground river, at times on the surface, at times hidden. The "river" of influence can, in the words of Heaney's poem "The Sandpit," be sent with "one chop of the trowel ... into the brick for ever," and so be made material for the future continuities and restorations of poetry.[100]

A personal note: the first time I met Seamus Heaney was at a reading at Trinity College Dublin, when my PhD supervisor Terence Brown introduced me – slightly mischievously – as a graduate student from the Outer Hebrides of Scotland, a native Gaelic speaker, and someone working on the influence of William Wordsworth on Seamus Heaney. "Ah," said Heaney, a (defensive) twinkle in his eye, "'Will no one tell me what she sings?' and all that." This line, from Wordsworth's "The Solitary Reaper," I took to be half-recognition and half-warning. "Who are you to say what I sing?" on the one hand, but, on the other, a shared sense of distance from the English poetic mainstream, a recognition that there are different songs, and different ways of understanding songs. One of the recurring themes of this book is the way in which nationality, and the cultural, social, and political pressures and tensions that exist between Northern Ireland, the Republic of Ireland, and Britain, necessarily impinge upon and muddy Heaney's poetic and critical relationship with Wordsworth; another is the considered, open, and complicated way in which Heaney fords these muddied waters. That I come at the Irish and English poetic traditions from a different angle, from a different island in this cultural archipelago, and from within a poetic tradition (the Scottish one) that Heaney often used as a third, complicating factor in the oppositions of "Ireland" and "England" is – I hope – an opening rather than a disqualification. I do not aim, in the role of disgruntled Highlander, to answer the unanswerably rhetorical question, "Will no one tell me what she sings?" or to fall into the two categories of people Heaney tried to keep his distance from ("shits and sycophants").[101] Rather, I try to listen into and sound out the distinct voices and tones in their "symphony austere," and to trace the underground rivers that flow between them.

I

Advancements of Learning

AMPLER PROSPECTS

In *Stepping Stones*, Heaney describes how, while a teacher at St Thomas's Secondary Intermediate School in Ballymurphy, he took a fourth-year class to see the birthplace of Louis MacNeice. MacNeice's poem "Carrickfergus" had featured in the anthology they were using, *Rhyme and Reason*. Heaney suggests that this trip may have been in some way a "confirmation" for the pupils, while also encouraging their teacher to view both art and education as "two-way processes." "What's on offer is one thing," he proposes, and "what's picked up is another. The temperament and disposition of the ones on the receiving end are decisive, and so are the quality and suitability of the thing being offered. I think, for example, that the Louis MacNeice poem – plus the visit to Carrick – must have meant something to a number of them. They'd have got some kind of confirmation from finding a familiar name and place brought to book like that, some new grip on what they knew, some new freedom within it. I believe education can offer ampler prospects and a change of perspective or a reason for aspiration."[1] There are etymological games being played here, alongside the punning on "brought to book." "Ample" is derived from the Latin *amplus* (large, capacious, abundant), but is related to *ampla*, "grip" or "handle." "Ampler prospects" enable not only a broader, more abundant perspective, but also a groundedness, the "new grip" the pupils got on "what they knew," expanding their horizons while also rooting them in the world around them. Education, in this imagining, creates a doubled relationship between the individual and the rest of the

30   This Strange Loneliness

world that serves – to borrow one of Heaney's favourite terms – to "fortify" you.[2] It has the Christian overtones of a "confirmation," an initiation into maturity or an (adult) community that was previously closed to you but is nevertheless "familiar."

This mode of thinking about education stretches back to an early stage of Heaney's career. In 1968, while he was working as a teacher-trainer at St Joseph's College of Education, Heaney began to sketch out "a Workbook for Students of Poetry" entitled *The Gentle Flame*. In his notebooks of the period there is a handwritten draft of an introduction, and then of a first chapter, "Handling Experience," which proposes an extended agricultural metaphor for how the act of reading – and writing poetry – should be approached: "Farmers used to describe the process of harvesting certain crops as 'handling' – handling hay, handling peat, and the term could be appropriately extended to the harvesting of literature ... Literature is one way of handling experience."[3] The introduction, meanwhile, relies on the imagery of echo-sounding: "The justification of many of the extracts ~~here~~ is meant to fulfil the function of an echo-sounder on the herring trawler: to suggest roughly the depth, motion and direction that shoals of thought running under the surface of the mind before the poem was caught."[4] The attention paid to both physical texture and subterranean currents of thought is typical of Heaney's attitude to poetry at this point: poems are to be considered "a human activity and birth, distant, even indeterminate in its conception and as matter-of-fact and mysterious as any other human birth."[5]

Often in Heaney's early work, this understanding of the "matter-of-fact" and the "mysterious" as a basis for education is intertwined with an appreciation of Wordsworth's poetry. This includes the lecturely banal, such as Heaney's 1977 notebook, in which he has noted down, on the back of a draft of "The Harvest Bow," a possible essay question: "'Wordsworth's visionary moments are convincing because of their origins in the matter-of-fact.' Discuss."[6] But it also encompasses a range of ideas, metaphors, and puns – earlier versions of the "ampler prospects," new "grip," and "familiarity" in *Stepping Stones* – which gesture, at least in part, back to Wordsworth's thinking. That Heaney's discussions of "education," in the broadest sense, might be sanctioned or underpinned by Wordsworth's work is suggested by one of the cul-de-sacs of Heaney's career. After graduating from Queen's University, Heaney considered returning to Queen's to pursue a postgraduate degree, with a "thesis on Wordsworth's

Advancements of Learning   31

educational ideas in mind."[7] Although this thesis was never written, Wordsworth's influence casts a long shadow over Heaney's career as a teacher, educator, and writer of poems "about" education. In particular, Wordsworth's explorations of poetic "epiphanies" cast this shadow: the epiphany becomes for Heaney a model of how an "ampler prospect" might be revealed, either in poetry or in education.

KICKING AGAINST THE CLASSROOM

It is easy to forget that Heaney was for most of his life a professional educator, and that his careers as poet and teacher cannot entirely be separated. After St Thomas's (his only position in a school), he taught at St Joseph's College of Education, was a lecturer at Queen's University Belfast, head of the English Department at Carysfort College, Dublin, and then professor at Harvard and Oxford universities, with various other visiting teaching, lecturing, or residency roles. Outside the classroom and lecture hall, he published numerous lectures, articles, and reviews arguing for greater attention to poetry as an educational tool, for the benefits of creative writing in the classroom, and – in some of his earliest reviews – for a progressive approach to teaching.

These early reviews engage with passionate debates about the need for educational reform. In "Evangelists," for example, published in the *New Statesman* in July 1965, Heaney reviewed John Holt's influential *How Children Fail* (1964), which would go on to sell over a million copies worldwide, alongside *Experiments in Education at Sevenoaks* (1965), a description of another attempt at educational reform; in "Kicking Against the Code," published in November of that year, he reviewed *English versus Examinations*, edited by Brian Jackson (1965), and R.F. Mackenzie's *Escape from the Classroom* (1965).[8] In both reviews, Heaney comes across as a conscientious educator keen to help reshape the profession and improve methods of teaching for the benefit of pupils. In his analysis of *English versus Examination*, Heaney approves of how the journal had opposed the "artificial division between 'language' and 'literature' and the tyranny of textbooks," and especially the emphasis on examinations: "Examinations, which are testing devices – hence mechanical and inflexible in their methods – have so affected the idea of English in schools that mechanical competence and information have replaced sensibility and the development of imagination as teaching ideals."[9]

32   This Strange Loneliness

Heaney is clearly in favour of a learner-centred education, with an emphasis on experience and "delight," and the rejection of mechanistic systems.[10] He hails *Experiments in Education in Sevenoaks* for its focus on "creativity" and approach to teaching art (in a way that suggests that Heaney was weighing the merits of "craft" and "technique" long before his famous 1974 lecture "Feeling into Words"): "After various experiences of, and delight in, these media [paint, collage, and print], he proceeds to use the media expressively, gradually realising the necessity of craftsmanship and technique."[11] Similarly, in his draft notes for a lecture from 1966 (which also argues against examinations), Heaney suggests that in "composition" two elements are involved: "*inspiration* and craftsmanship or technique."[12] These terms will be refined over coming decades; but it is clear that his thinking about education – this lecture was aimed at schoolteachers – was tightly bound up with his ideas about his own artistic practice and poetic practice more generally.

Certainly, in "Kicking Against the Code" Heaney is not solely an educational idealist. He offers Holt a mild rebuke for his depiction, in the later chapters of *How Children Fail*, of a "utopian classroom, buzzing with curiosity and experiment, where the teacher would be superfluous," but which "lacks the close attention to the realities of school life which distinguishes the earlier chapters."[13] Where Heaney was resistant to Holt's "utopian classroom," he approves of Mackenzie's escape from it, and especially the way that this is grounded in Mackenzie's own practical experience. Mackenzie was the headmaster of Braehead Secondary School in Buckhaven, Fife, and his book outlines his ultimately unsuccessful attempts (in the face of local authority resistance) to secure a hunting lodge in the Highlands where the school could bring pupils for extended periods of time outdoors in a natural environment. An English teacher by training, Mackenzie hoped to transform the educational system to encourage individual exploration of the world, and to nurture curiosity. He draws on Coleridge as a touchstone ("Coleridge said that is was one of the functions of poetry to let people see things freshly and with a sense of wonder. He could have said the same of education") and attempts to instill a culturally and historically informed sense of place in his pupils, by taking them far from the classroom.[14] Mackenzie's prose comes close to what would now be marketed as literary non-fiction, with a tendency towards thick description and careful observation: "There were different shades of red in the spring, the reds of alder, birch and elm. They [his pupils] picked up a skull and identified it as a badger's and knew that a small leg bone lying in peat was the bone of a hare and not a pheasant."[15] His overarching aim is to inculcate deep knowledge of a place, rather than the accumulation of dislocated "facts": he aims for "not just knowledge of bits of the past, Sparta and Plato and the Aztecs, but an awareness of continuity, of a fourth dimension, time, so that you can see the Braes of Lochaber as they have altered in time. Into this understood framework, little random pieces of the jigsaw fit, filling out and amplifying the picture of life on earth, so that they get the hang of things."[16]

This feeling of personal "amplification" resonates with Heaney's comments in *Stepping Stones* discussed in the introduction; Mackenzie's heightened sense of place and understanding of historical continuity can also be traced in the idea of the antediluvian "world-schooled ear" Heaney will try to access in "Gifts of Rain" in *Wintering Out* in 1972.[17] This influence is not, however, likely direct, but a shared interest in a "Romantic" educational tradition which insists on a relationship between the internal life of the pupils and the external stimulus of the natural world. Heaney comments (with ironic distance), "Mr Mackenzie is something of a visionary and something of a satirist ... He would turn each pupil into an Émile and compare the result with the standard product. But such an experiment was denied him. And what the hell is everyone so smug about, he would like to know. His anger is generated by a comparison of what might have been achieved and what he has been forced to accept. His reform schemes were based on his long experience and experimental class outings on the Scottish hills and moors. There is nothing of the fussy-do-gooder in his make-up. Rousseau or Wordsworth might have written like this in the situation."[18]

This, as with Heaney's other reviews, lauds an alternative to what was then the dominant mode of teaching, an education in which delight, enrichment, "natural" accomplishment, sensibility, and imagination replace mechanical competence, academic forcing, and examination. These concerns were not separate from Heaney's thinking about poetry. In a 1965 review of Edward Lucie-Smith's *Confessions and Histories*, for example, he comments that "In every individual there exists a conflict between a dream of self-realization and the demands of society or circumstances."[19] The poetry review shares the focus on "self-realization": notably,

34   This Strange Loneliness

though, Heaney argues that "self-realization" comes not through books but through personal experience – the textbook is a force of "tyranny." (Much later, in a 1997 interview with John Quinn, "My Education," Heaney would again stress the importance of "practical" or empirical experience, with a telling distinction: "Our townhouse was a farmhouse – not a book house – going about its farm business, but there was an education of a kind in that too. It was very, very close to the primal issues of a life and death."[20]) The education he celebrates in these reviews is one which would side with the farm (or the natural world) over the book: an "education," as he noted, which might parallel the ideas espoused by "Rousseau or Wordsworth."

EVERY GREAT POET IS A TEACHER

Why, though, might Wordsworth "have written like this"? While not attempting to second-guess the thesis Heaney never wrote, it is still necessary to trace out some of the features of Wordsworth's approach to education that will eventually influence Heaney. As with much to do with Heaney's response to Wordsworth, this subject actually takes into account a small part of Wordsworth's oeuvre. There are various ways in which Wordsworth was interested in "education" which do not feature directly in Heaney's version of the poet: they are, however, important for the way they inform Wordsworth's thinking more broadly. One is the association of education with religion, which extends from Wordsworth's earliest surviving poem, the juvenile "Lines on the Bicentenary of Hawkshead School," which outlined the role of religion in the development of "education" in Britain – "science with joy saw Superstition fly / Before the lustre of Religion's eye" – to his "Speech at the Laying of the Foundation Stone of the New School in the Village of Bowness" in 1836, which took as its theme the "education of a sincere Christian ... an education not for time but for eternity."[21] It may seem slightly odd that Wordsworth's persistent reliance on religion does *not* feature to any considerable extent in Heaney's response to him, given his own interest in how the mysterious and the matter-of-fact intertwine; however, as "Superstition" commonly stood in for Catholicism in the eighteenth- and nineteenth-century context (with "enthusiasm" a parallel shorthand for Protestantism), it is perhaps no surprise Heaney is not drawn to such sectarian triumphalism.[22]

Similarly, Heaney does not engage with Wordsworth's interest, from at least 1808 onwards, in a national system of education that could take into account the local or environmental contexts of pupils in different parts of the country (the problems with national education systems were quite different by the time Heaney was teaching). Writing to Francis Wrangham in June 1808, Wordsworth complained that "any plan of national education in a country like ours is most difficult to apply to practice ... Heaven and Hell are scarcely more different from each other than Sheffield and Manchester, etc. differ from the plains and Vallies of Surrey, Essex, Cumberland, or Westmorland" (one assumes that Sheffield and Manchester are here associated with "hell").[23] Wordsworth's answer, slightly confusingly, is a trickle-down model: he encourages Wrangham to begin "Education at the top of society; let the head go in the right course and the tail will follow."[24]

Following this interest in a national system for education came his support for Andrew Bell's "Madras System." This was a system devised in India and then transported back to the United Kingdom: Bell was originally concerned with the education of the "half-cast" "orphan and distressed male children of the European military," and in particular the need to combat "the very first maxims which the mothers of these children instil into their infant minds[;]... an infallible mode of forming a degenerate race."[25] He subsequently developed this into a monotorial or "emulation" system in which the schoolmaster taught the most advanced pupils, who then taught those below them, and so on, with the "tail" clearly following the "head" (thus allowing for both "the inward improvement of the individual" and a top-down model for disseminating it across the country).[26] Shortly after writing to Wrangham in June 1808, Wordsworth discovered Bell's *Experiment in Education Made at the Asylum of Madras*: in a subsequent letter he describes it as "a most interesting work" which "entitles him to the fervent gratitude of all good men"; although he suggests that it does not make any "material change" to his views, he does "strenuously recommend [it] wherever it can be adopted."[27] One of the merits of the system was, as Wordsworth notes, that its "efficiency" is "chiefly shewn in the treatment of slow Boys. – One Boy advances *more rapidly* than another, but *all* are made to advance according to their talents"; it also had the advantage of avoiding corporal punishment.[28] Bell visited the Wordsworths in 1811 and then 1812 ("Dr Bell," Wordsworth commented, "changes his mind, I fear,

36 This Strange Loneliness

often, and has something of a plaguey manner, but he is a most excellent Creature"), and they got on so well that Wordsworth undertook "a disagreeable employment for Dr Bell; viz to select and compose with Mr Johnson's assistance 20 pages of monosyllabic lessons for Children."[29] Within three years, he was effusive, writing to Thomas Poole that "Next to the art of Printing it [the Madras System] is the noblest invention for the improvement of the human species."[30]

This comment comes alongside a gloss on a passage from *The Excursion* (1815) in which Wordsworth pictures an ideal balance between a formal, utilitarian education based on the Madras System, and a laissez-faire approach to education rooted in freedom, activity, idleness, and pleasure:

> A few short hours of each returning day
> The thriving prisoners of their village-school:
> And thence let loose, to seek their pleasant homes
> Or range the grassy lawn in vacancy;
> To breathe and be happy, run and shout,
> Idle – but no delay, no harm, no loss.[31]

That the children are "thriving prisoners" is predicated on the fact that they are incarcerated in school only for those "few short hours." This picture of education is part of a desire for national cohesion and development based on a hope that "this imperial Realm ... shall admit / An obligation, on her part, to "teach" / Them who are born to serve her and obey," and in particular to "inform the mind with moral and religious truth / Both understood and practiced."[32] (As we shall see in chapter 4, similar concerns with a cohesive education – serving to mend the rifts of the Troubles – are to the fore in Heaney's later thinking about education: they do not, however, have Wordsworth's imperial emphasis on obligation, serving, and obeying.)

Wordsworth's enthusiasm for Bell's system would ultimately cool, for a combination of reasons. These may have included Wordsworth's changing personal relationship with Bell, his political opposition to many of Bell's supporters, and the failure of his own children to succeed within the system; however, it also suggests his ultimate disapproval of emulation, which, as Alison Hickey notes, treats pupils as "part of a machine" rather than as individuals who need to be "drawn out."[33] Certainly, by 1828 Wordsworth was criticizing, in a letter to Hugh James Rose, Dr Bell's "sour-looking teachers in petticoats" and comparing their "mechanism" unfavourably with "Shenstone's school-mistress, by her winter fire and in her summer garden seat"; by this point, "Emulation" was seen as "cousin-german to Envy."[34] (The Wordsworths and Bell did, however, remain friends until Bell's death in 1832, even if Bell's decision to endow a school in St Andrews in Fife using £120,000 gathered from "England and the English Church" remained a sore point: "it is half of it likely to be wasted among Scotch lawyers."[35])

Wordsworth's support for the Madras System can be seen as a temporary though persistent addition to what would be the mainstay of his educational theories: the thinking of Jean-Jacques Rousseau. These can also be traced through *The Excursion*; and they are the only element of Wordsworth's various experiments with education that will directly feed into Heaney's own ideas. Rousseau – especially in his Émile, ou De *l'éducation* (1762) – had been a huge influence on Wordsworth through the 1790s, before the Lake Poet recanted his revolutionary politics. In Émile, Rousseau argues that the natural landscape can provide a moral education.[36] A male child (Émile's education is quite different from that of his wife-to-be, Sophie) should be guided through a controlled natural environment in which he makes his own discoveries. The point is to circumvent, as far as possible, the social and cultural strictures that serve, in Rousseau's view, to stunt or tarnish humankind's original God-given goodness: "Tout est bien, fortant des mains de l'Auteur des choses: tout dégénere entre les mains de l'homme" [God makes all things good: all things degenerate in the hands of man].[37] As Lucy Newlyn notes, William and Dorothy raised their foster-child, Basil Montagu Jr, in accordance with the suggestions of Émile: Basil had, in Dorothy's words, "no other companions, than the flowers, the grass, the cattle, the sheep."[38]

Wordsworth's poetry, as well as his domestic life, was informed by Rousseau's philosophy. The beneficial effect of (psychological and physical) immersion in the natural world is a defining theme of both *The Prelude* and the *Lyrical Ballads*. The complicated (partial) rejection of book learning in Book V of the 1805 *Prelude*, as Mary Jacobus argues, "subsumes literature under the heading of Nature," in a way that would accord with Rousseau's ideas.[39] In the *Lyrical Ballads* the benefits of such subsuming are repeatedly made clear. "Lines Written in Early Spring," for example, modulates the terms of the first sentence of *Émile* into a repeated lamentation of "what man has made of man": this is in the context of a celebration of

38 This Strange Loneliness

pantheistic infusion, and a worrying about any "creed" that would doubt the ability of the natural world to feel "pleasure."[40] "Lines Written at a Small Distance from My House," meanwhile, versifies the relationship between William, Dorothy, and Basil, and celebrates "natural" education over book learning. On "the first mild day of March," the poem begins, there is "blessing in the air," associated with "Love, now a universal birth." Yielding to this "power" (and "to the bare trees, and mountains bare") for one moment may give more "Than fifty years of reason": and so both "Edward" (Basil) and the poet's "sister" are encouraged to put on their "woodland dress, / And bring no book; for this one day / We'll give to idleness."[41] "Expostulation and Reply" and "The Tables Turned" also stage the clash between natural and bookish or "intellectual" learning to support the idea that you should "Let Nature be your teacher."[42] "Expostulation and Reply" lauds the "wise passiveness" through which we can "feed" our minds, since there are "powers, / which of themselves our minds impress" (in preference to "books ... that light bequeath'd / To beings else forlorn and blind!").[43] "Tables Turned" continues the theme: books are a "dull and endless strife"; there is more "life" in the song of the linnet or the throstle; "science and art" are but "barren leaves"; and "Our meddling intellect / Misshapes the beauteous forms of things; / – We murder to dissect."[44] Pointedly, the approach here is based on questions of morality as well as knowledge: "One impulse from a vernal wood / May teach you more of man; / Of moral evil and of good, / Than all the sages can."[45]

There are contradictions underpinning Wordsworth's dismissal of book learning: there is both overstatement and a deliberately anti-philosophical application of philosophy that might stem from Wordsworth's turn against French revolutionary intellectualism. Rather than being a blank slate on which the natural world could leave its impress, the human mind (and the memory in particular) is an active force: a child's experience is, in the words of "Tintern Abbey," at least "half-created" by the child. "Wise passiveness" is a pose to be adopted, but one which is – paradoxically – active. But there is also a more fundamental contradiction: this book of poems tells the reader to reject book learning. One point of the poems is surely the revelation of this contradiction; the reader is then cast in the role of Schiller's "sentimental" poet, in search of lost nature, rather than the "naive" poet, who, without any form of bookish intervention, *is* nature (with the poignancy of loss and distance

Advancements of Learning

then felt alongside the desire for natural inspiration).[46] Despite its apparent self-abasement, Wordsworth's poetry then takes on the educational role of nature for all his readers, who by virtue of being part of the reading public have suffered a book-derived separation from the natural world: *this* book is the consolation for the rift that books have caused.

How such a natural or poetic education (and redemption) might work is another matter. Wordsworth gives numerous examples in his poetry of the late 1790s and early 1800s, especially the *Lyrical Ballads* and the early versions of *The Prelude* (poems that appear commonly in Heaney's criticism). The boat-stealing and skating passages in *The Prelude*, "There Was a Boy," and "Nutting" all, for example, figure moments of revelation which combine a Rousseau-esque idea of the natural world as a moral teacher with an associationist understanding of how that "education" might occur (good and evil are to be learned through an "associationist" impulse, in a manner derived from David Hartley's theories, which Wordsworth and Dorothy had encountered through Coleridge, and which viewed memory primarily as a creative function).[47] In each of these poems, a young boy, alone in a natural landscape, is made hypersensitive to his surroundings by the power of his imagination; while he is "stilled" and "listening into" the landscape, a religio-mystical force within it works upon him, entering his mind, stimulating and encouraging his imagination or his moral sensibility, and providing a form of mental landscaping. In the language of "Tintern Abbey," they are experiences which are "half-created" and half-perceived: the important elements are, on the one hand, the "stillness" of the communion and a necessary "wise passiveness" on the part of the poet-figure and, on the other, the combined workings of the imagination and some external force, be that force "ye beings of the hills," or "Nature," or the "Wisdom and Spirit of the Universe."[48]

These poems are among what Heaney describes in his 1974 lecture "Feeling into Words" as "the high moments of Wordsworth's poetry," moments which "occur when the verse has carried us forward and onward to a point where line by line we do not proceed but hang in a kind of suspended motion, sustained by the beat of the verse as a hanging bird is sustained by the beat of its wing, but, like the bird, holding actively to one point of vantage, experiencing a prolonged moment of equilibrium during which we feel ourselves to be conductors of the palpable energies of earth and sky."[49] In the boat-stealing incident, for example, Wordsworth uses the ambiguities of the word "still" – the poet's boat leaves "behind her still on either side / Small circles glittering idly in the moon"; the cliff "still, / For so it seemed, with purpose of its own / And measured motion, like a living thing / Strode after me" – to create a sense of "arrested motion" (in Susan Wolfson's words) or dynamic stability, a moment in which stasis and motion are combined.[50] This heightened state of tension is created by a combination of the landscape and the boy's imagination: a state in which, for weeks afterwards, "huge and mighty forms that do not live / Like living men, moved slowly through the mind / By day, and were a trouble to my dreams."[51] It is not only that something "uncanny and terrifying occurs," as Heaney comments in a manuscript lecture on *The Prelude*, but that this sense of fear and uncanniness persists.[52] In "There Was a Boy," meanwhile, the stasis, the arrested motion, is created by the enjambed "hung / Listening," in which there irrupts an epiphany of sorts: "the voice / Of mountain torrents" is carried "far into his heart"; "the visible scene" enters "unawares into his mind / With all its solemn imagery."[53]

The heightened landscape of "Nutting" is slightly different: it has a susurrant supernatural dimension, as the grove is filled with "the murmur and the murmuring sound" of "fairy water-breaks" that "murmur on / for ever" and the poet wonders if it "was a bower beneath whose leaves / The violets of five seasons re-appear / And fade, unseen by any human eye."[54] But the rebuke that the boy receives from the landscape after he desecrates the grove – in an act with sexual undertones – once more comes through heightened awareness of the "silent trees and the intruding sky." This rebuke, and the lesson the boy learns, is the most clearly moral of these experiences: addressing a "dearest Maiden" at the end of the poem, the poet can rather portentously tell her to "move along these shades / In gentleness of heart with gentle hand / Touch, – for there is a spirit in these woods."[55]

These poems are all examples of what was being discussed, when Heaney was a young lecturer at Queen's University Belfast, as the "Greater Romantic Lyric" (and would later be labelled by Harold Bloom as the "Wordsworthian crisis poem").[56] M.H. Abrams coined the label "Greater Romantic Lyric" for a poetic structure in which there is a "repeated out-in-out process, in which mind confronts nature and their interplay constitutes the poem."[57] For Abrams, there is a similar pattern in Wordsworth's "Tintern Abbey," "Ode:

Intimations of Immortality," and ("with a change in initial reference from scene to painting") in "Elegiac Stanzas Suggested by a Picture of Peele Castle, in a Storm" (as well as in Coleridge's "The Eolian Harp," "Frost at Midnight," "Fears in Solitude," and "Dejection: An Ode" and in Shelley's "Stanzas Written in Dejection" and "Ode to the West Wind"). These poems all "present a determinate speaker in a particularized, and usually a localized, outdoor setting" who "begins with a description of the landscape; an aspect or change of aspect in the landscape evokes a varied but integral process of memory, thought, anticipation, and feeling which remains closely intervolved with the outer scene. In the course of this meditation the lyric speaker achieves an insight, faces up to a tragic loss, comes to a moral decision, or resolves an emotional problem."[58] Various interpretations and modifications have been proposed for this overall pattern: George Bornstein, for example, substitutes "'vision' for 'meditation'" to suggest a poetic structure of "description-vision-evaluation" (Bornstein, like Abrams, allows for a work of art to be the object of the "description").[59] When read as models of "education," however, these poems offer a visionary learning process in which there is not only intellectual or psychic development but also a sense of lingering loss. When one returns to one's self or one's being-in-the-world, there is a necessary feeling of difference and estrangement, or having moved on in time, and having been diminished as well as nurtured by the process. The "return" of the Romantic vision is always, necessarily, helical rather than circular: the visionary gleam is always fled, the self is always displaced.[60]

Education might prove a crisis or diminishment in Wordsworth's thinking in other ways as well. In a letter to Sir George Beaumont in February 1808, Wordsworth makes what would on the surface appear to be his grandest and most definitive claim about poetry and education: "Every great Poet is a Teacher: I wish either to be considered as a Teacher, or as nothing."[61] Here, however, Wordsworth is responding to scathing reviews of his *Poems in Two Volumes*, published the previous year, which had described his work variously as "flimsy, puerile thoughts, expressed in such feeble halting verse we have seldom seen," "a very paragon of silliness and affectation," "calculated to excite disgust and anger in a lover of poetry," and "namby-pamby."[62] Wordsworth strongly disagreed with these criticisms – "my Poems must be more nearly looked at before they can give rise to any remarks of much value, even from the strongest

42   This Strange Loneliness

minds" – but in the face of them he is keen to proclaim the poems'
intellectual strength and improving purpose.[63] Yoking poetry to education threatens, however, to deny poetry any independent status, to
turn it into a form of philosophy or social agent: there is no role for
the "poet" aside from that of the teacher. If he is "to be considered
as a Teacher, or as nothing," then there is a serious risk that he (with
his "flimsy thoughts") might be considered "nothing."

"THE PLAY WAY": THE POET AS TEACHER

Of Wordsworth's various approaches to education, two are particularly resonant for Heaney. One is the ambiguous relationship
between poetry and teaching: the sense that poetry might be nothing
but teaching, or that poetry might risk being subsumed by it. And
the second is Wordsworth's model of "natural" education, the structure of "description-vision-evaluation," and the sense of loss, as well
as growth, this involved. Where Wordsworth tended to approach
education from a theoretical perspective, however (there were few
chalk smudges on his sleeves), Heaney always treated education as a
practical problem, based on his own teaching experience. "The Play
Way," for example, uses Heaney's time in the classroom to explore
various Wordsworthian ideas about education: that it involves a give-
and-take between the individual mind and the external world (the
process of half-creating, half-perceiving); the psychological inter-
change with and nourishment possible from the natural world (or
a work of art); and the belief that beneficial education often comes
through an "idleness" that allows you to appreciate the "beauteous
forms of things" (at least, if idleness is equated to "playing").[64]

"The Play Way" (first published in 1964) presents a lesson in
which, as the poem's "lesson notes" suggest, "*Teacher will play /
Beethoven's Concerto Number Five / And class will express themselves freely / In writing.*"[65] There is, perhaps, too much credence
given to this possible "freedom," both in terms of the boys' ability to
achieve it and the ease with which art brings its possible liberations.
The music works

> its private spell behind eyes
> That stare wide. They have forgotten me
> For once. The pens are busy, the tongues mime
> Their blundering embrace of the free

Advancements of Learning

Word. A silence charged with sweetness
Breaks short on lost faces where I see
New looks. Then notes stretch taut as snares. They trip
To fall into themselves unknowingly.[66]

Art is here a stimulus for fundamental, personal transformation. Through exposure to art (either Beethoven's concerto or the poem describing the experience), even that which appears most solid or most established can be seen anew. The first image of the poem – "sunlight pillars through glass" – uses what would become a typical Heaneyesque transformation, in which a concrete noun ("pillar") becomes a fluid, operative, and (here) illuminating verb.[67] Haecceity, or "thisness," becomes – through the magic of art – an otherness, an airy possibility. There are hints of the paternalistic (the "lost faces," the miming tongues) and a concerted belief in the "authority" of art ("each authoritative note" of the music); however, this is balanced by a faith in self-discovery, and the representation of a heightening and a transformation that is fundamentally private and internal. Art might provide a trap (the "snare," the "trip"), but it is one in which your "true" self will be caught, as you are "drawn out" of yourself and so, paradoxically, carried deeper into yourself.[68]

The poem echoes, and reveals various intellectual debts to, T.S. Eliot and Matthew Arnold. Beethoven's music mixes "memory and desire with chalk dust" in a bathetic, downplaying allusion to the first lines of *The Waste Land*, "April is the cruelest month, breeding / Lilacs out of the dead land, mixing / Memory and desire."[69] The "silence charged with sweetness," meanwhile, suggests the title of the first chapter of Matthew Arnold's *Culture and Anarchy* (1869), "Sweetness and Light." Education in this approach entails illuminating the quotidian and, conversely, "thickening" potentiality through the influence of art, whether it be the Beethoven that is being played or indeed the Eliot that is alluded to. Slightly oddly, there is a similar process in another poem in *Death of a Naturalist*, "Churning Day," in which churned butter is described as "coagulated sunlight": the classroom, like the butter-churn, becomes a location of golden transformation, of "light" combined with material substance.[70] Less lacteally, a much later poem, the uncollected villanelle "The Singing Classes," repeats the image of sunlight illuminating dust and "stasis" from "The Play Way," and the possibility of imaginative and artistic transformation: "Roll-books. Ink-wells. Motes in sunlight. Stasis. /

44 This Strange Loneliness

Andersen and Grimm. The Golden Fleece. / And tuning forks. The struck note quails and passes."[71]

Although "The Play Way" does not have the same emphasis on the transience of the experience, it does suggest that the learning experience repeats the Wordsworthian (and more broadly "Romantic") idea of self-discovery through estrangement. In "The Play Way," self-knowledge comes from an inward and unconscious "fall": the boys "trip / To fall into themselves unknowingly." This might reflect what Leon Gottfried identifies as Arnold and Wordsworth's "powerful conviction ... that the true direction for reform lay in the inward improvement of the individual," or the broader Romantic metaphorical tendency "to move inside and downward instead of outside and upward, hence the creative world is deep within, and so is heaven or the place and presence of God" (this is Northrop Frye writing, like Gottfried, in 1963, the year before "The Play Way" was published).[72] Heaney's subsequent writing would certainly repeatedly encourage such inward questing. A script for *Explorations*, a BBC Northern Ireland schools radio program, broadcast in May 1968, begins, "You can explore inwards as well as outwards, obviously. Your head is a world that contains oceans, continents, the lonely constellations. It can make room for constellations to come, galaxies that have not yet been named."[73] And through the 1970s and 1980s the "master-tropes" of Heaney's work are, as Jahan Ramazani notes, "the excavation and exhumation of the dead" and "Dantean and Virgilian voyages to the nether world."[74]

"The Play Way" is not, however, just a negotiation with artistic precursors and the Romantic metaphor of the fall (or, indeed, a foreshadowing of Heaney's own poetic directions to come); it is also an engagement with contemporary pedagogical debates. Some of the tensions present in "The Play Way" are made explicit in "Educating the Epsilons," a contemporaneous review Heaney wrote of David Holbrook's 1964 *English for the Rejected*.[75] Holbrook attempts – Heaney approvingly notes – to use art to educate the children of the "backward streams," and proposes that schools be "geared towards the less academic child" to create "a more humane, civilized, atmosphere," a process in which what would now be called creative writing has a central role.[76] Heaney is not entirely complimentary to Holbrook (or his privileged position as a Cambridge Fellow), but does acknowledge his basic point that "not by intelligence alone is a man educated." "Everyone," Heaney writes, "is possessed of an urge to create, everyone is to some extent an artist. And just as Shakespeare came to terms with certain doubts and fears when he wrote *King Lear* and Milton eased and ordered his pain in *Samson Agonistes*, so, Mr Holbrook implies, every child who is not actually mentally handicapped can attain some degree of self-knowledge through written expression of unconscious conflict and some degree of self-respect through this achievement."[77] With its emphasis on "unconscious impulses and desires," and the possibility of the pupils writing out their "unconscious conflict," Holbrook's approach is fundamentally Freudian. As Heaney wryly notes, "it is not surprising that apart from 'love' and 'imagination' which are the keynotes of the book, the two words in the index with the most references are 'phantasy' and 'sex.'"[78] Heaney himself – in a way that is telling for the markedly un-Freudian tenor of "The Play Way" – demurs: "I wonder if children really can resolve sexual struggles by imaginative writing."[79]

Where Heaney does agree with Holbrook, however, is on his emphasis on a "poetic function," defined as "the capacity to explore and perceive, to come to terms with, speak of and deal with experience *by the experience of the whole mind and all kinds of apprehensions, not only intellectual ones.*"[80] Heaney supports the idea that "good writing comes from personal experience treasured and selected by the imagination, and that a textbook approach to the teaching of accurate expression is doomed with duller children"; this is a repetition, for a classroom setting, of Wordsworth's claim in his Preface to *Lyrical Ballads* that poetry takes its origin from "emotion recollected in tranquillity," and is a process in which "incidents and situations from common life" have a "certain colouring of imagination" thrown over them.[81] (In an early editorial in the Queen's student magazine *Gorgon*, Heaney had already argued, in an echo of the Preface, that "the first poems spring from a nascent feeling for language – language as sounds, as a vehicle for emotional expression" and that "poems can grow from a single emotion approached through different words.")[82]

Against such demands for poetry (or education) "The Play Way" is an interesting failure. In creative writing workshop-speak, it tells rather than shows. As readers, we do not have access to the transformative experiences of the students listening to Beethoven; instead, we are, along with the teacher, spectators, left looking at "new looks," without having any sense of what they portend. The poem presents education – or epiphany – as spectator-sport: the claim the students

46   This Strange Lonchness

"trip / to fall into themselves unknowingly" then seems both presumptive and somewhat patronizing. It is as if we were stood on the banks of Ullswater, watching the young Wordsworth in his stolen boat, without having access to his new-found perception of the "huge and mighty forms that do not live / Like living men," but presuming to know that this is what he is experiencing; this is precisely the issue raised in Wordsworth's "Solitary Reaper" when he asks of the Highland girl singing, "Will no one tell me what she sings?"[83]

This problem of perspective is perhaps why poems about teaching, as opposed to poems about learning, are relatively rare in Heaney's oeuvre, and, when they appear, do not in any simple way celebrate the role of the teacher.[84] The uncollected "Writer and Teacher," published in the *Irish Times* in 1965, makes it clear that these two identities exist in conflict. The poem describes "A humble master of two trades" but gives a clearer sense of his "mastery" of teaching. The children are taught to evade "The market place and the headline," to "use [their] eyes," to "tell small truths instead of lies / In big words that sound fine," to "breed tenderness in bone- / Heads" and to "look / With love at movement in the street / To celebrate each joy they meet."[85] As a writer, though, the subject of the poem is less "successful": "His work says little that is new," says "one slick review"; and the final line – "But the pupils are his masterpiece" – is (from the pen of an ambitious writer) tonally ambiguous. For all its celebration of a "master of two trades," the poem also suggests a terror of entrapment. Its full, looping rhymes (it consists of three sextillas, rhymed aabccb), and its final rhyming of "masterpiece" and "The lessons cease" produce an air of claustrophobia, completeness, and finality: the master who "keeps to his room" is contained within the full-stopped, enclosed stanza. Like the teacher of "The Play Way," he "celebrate[s] each joy [the boys] meet"; and like that teacher he is removed from the individual liberation and self-discovery experienced; as the pupils are freed, the teacher is entrapped.

Any sense of entrapment is not, however, just thematic: Heaney's memories of his time as a teacher were, at best, conflicted. "Writer and Teacher" reads, at least in part, as a sketch of the short-story writer Michael McLaverty, Heaney's headmaster and mentor at St Thomas's Intermediate School, where (although McLaverty's own writing days were behind him) he was one of the main redeeming features of what was otherwise a depressing experience.[86] Following his graduation from Queen's in 1961, Heaney had (like many of his generation, the first beneficiaries of the 1947 Northern Irish Education Act) taken up a career in teaching, after rejecting a scholarship to undertake further research at Oxford University.[87] St Thomas's came as a culture shock. In *Finders Keepers* he remembers finding himself standing "in front of a class of deprived and disaffected adolescent boys, many of whom would end up a decade later as active members of the provisional IRA"; in *Stepping Stones*, Heaney recalls being "unhappy," "inexperience[d] in the classroom," and also "lack[ing] full commitment," with a "lingering feeling that [he] was now a bit off course" in a "non-literary" environment of colleagues who were often "oafs and gobshites."[88] Part of the problem was the difficulty of "liberating" himself in the classroom. In a 1997 interview "My Education" he explains that he found teaching "agonizing ... It takes a long time to learn the mixture of freedom within yourself and attention to the student in front of you that makes for good teaching."[89] Liberation, as he had written ten years earlier, came only on weekends: "Saturday morning is a good time of the week for a young teacher, a breathing space between the lift-off of Friday evening and the *adagios* of Sunday. Liberation walks with you if you have got out on the town by eleven o'clock, especially if it is the mid-sixties and you are out on Botanic Avenue, the *Boule-Miche* of the north, sniffing the chic of ground coffee from Bells' new upmarket grocery shop or gazing at new titles in Mr Gardner's ever-expanding book emporium, the hub of the action."[90]

ADVANCEMENTS OF LEARNING

Any "liberation" of the teacher was, in other words, hard-won and fleeting; in the 1960s, though, Heaney's interest was more in the liberation – and "advancement" – of the learner. Before it was published as *Death of a Naturalist*, Heaney's first collection of poetry had the working title "Advancements of Learning" (Heaney sent a manuscript of that name to Dolmen Press for consideration in late 1964). Rand Brandes notes that this working title, with its allusion to Francis Bacon, is "almost too literary and self-conscious for the elemental ambience of the book as it later became."[91] There are various ways, however, in which Bacon's book offers a useful context for Heaney's keen-eyed descriptions of the natural world. It is not just that, as Henry Hart argues, Bacon debunks "supernatural forms of knowledge and advocate[s] an empirical approach to learning,"

48   This Strange Loneliness

which is certainly true, but that even "empirical" knowledge is, for Bacon, a matter of illumination and revelation.[92] "The knowledge of man," Bacon claims, "is as the waters, some descending from above, and some springing from beneath: the one informed by the light of nature, the other inspired by divine revelation."[93] This balancing between intense experience and description of the phenomenological world, and the revelation of a "truth" behind it, is central to "The Play Way" (and the whole of *Death of a Naturalist*): it is, of course, also the basis of the epiphanic structure Heaney would have found in Wordsworth's work.

It is by now a critical commonplace to identify Wordsworth's influence among the many running through *Death of a Naturalist*. In an early review in *The New Statesman*, Christopher Ricks established the central terms when he equated the farm machines and mulch in Heaney's poetry with "beauty" and the poet's experience of a multitude of frogs supplanting quaint frogspawn with "fear" to invoke Wordsworth's claim of having been fostered alike by beauty and by fear; this line of argument was extended by Elmer Kennedy-Andrews onto a mystical or spiritual plane with his suggestion that the "fear" in both poets is "enlarging and provocative of growth," rather than "restrictive and paralysing," possibly in an "effort to affirm a 'visionary power.'"[94] Fiona Stafford notes the eerie way in which Heaney's use of "fructified" in "Personal Helicon" appears to echo Wordsworth's description of the spots of time in the 1805 manuscript version of *The Prelude*: a text whose existence Heaney would not have been aware of in the 1960s.[95]

More attention can be paid, however, to the specifically educational mechanics of *Death of a Naturalist*, and in particular "Blackberry-Picking," "Advancements of Learning," "The Barn," and the title poem. These are, in Neil Corcoran's phrase, "written in the margin" of Wordsworth's poetry, inasmuch as they all express in similar ways the young poet's wide-eyed, childish wonder at finding himself in the world, and describe how that wonder develops, through a fearful experience, into some level of greater understanding or linguistic control.[96] In each, as in the poems by Wordsworth discussed above, a young poet-figure finds himself alone, separated from human society in a heightened landscape in which there is a tension between action and inaction, or stillness and movement. In the midst of this tension the young poet experiences an epiphany in which his imagination is extended and he is "educated," which means that he can return to

Advancements of Learning

social / communal "reality" with a greater sense of his own linguistic powers, emotional complexity, or sexual maturity. The isolation is, as Jonathan Allison notes, important: in the Romantic tradition within which Heaney is working, poetry is "a quest for supernatural vision" and the price one "must pay for such revelation is solitude."[97]

"Death of a Naturalist" presents Heaney's pattern of solitary revelation most fully. A young poet-figure ducks through hedges to the frog-filled flax-dam, which – although it lies "in the heart / Of the townland" – is cut off from human society by the hedges that surround it.[98] It is a place in which life and decay exist side by side: there are "dragon-flies, spotted butterflies," but there is also rotting flax, "weighted down by huge sods," and bubbles that "gargled delicately," exploding into and beyond maturity. The flax-dam is also balanced precariously between movement and stasis, created by the bluebottles that "Wove a strong gauze of sound around the smell" of the flax-dam: this is a gauze which exists both as stable single entity and as a mass of individual insects. In this heightened landscape fear leads to knowledge: the narrator (irrationally) fears that the adult frogs will take revenge on him for collecting frogspawn, and this leads to the realization that "if I dipped my hand the spawn would clutch it."[99] The "education" here is an increase in sexual awareness (with concomitant guilt), and also in linguistic competence: how, as Heaney would later put it in a letter, one learns to "linguify" experience.[100] The guilt, sexual knowledge, and linguistic ability intertwine, as the childish vocabulary and understanding of sexuality at the beginning of the poem ("the mammy frog / Laid hundreds of little eggs and this was / Frogspawn") develops into a physical and violent onomatopoeia ("cocked," "hopped," "plop"; "pulsed," "blunt," "clutch") and disgusted similes and metaphors: "gross-bellied frogs," "cocked like sods," "loose necks pulsed like snails," "poised like mud grenades."[101]

Linguistic development here contributes to knowledge, but also seems to provide more elaborate means for you to frame your guilt and to expose yourself to censure. In "The Barn" and "An Advancement of Learning," however, the development of linguistic ability becomes a bulwark against, and corrective to, the (sublime) fear the poet experiences. These poems form a pair, offering a problem and its resolution. The eponymous barn is transmogrified by the young boy's imagination, in which the relationship between presence and absence, between reality and metaphor, becomes confused.

The poem describes how "The dark gulfed like a roof-space," but the power of simile fails: the dark, after all, actually *is* a roof-space, and what opens up is a "gulf" in the ability of metaphor to understand and explain experience. This creates a space in which nightmarish fears of violence emerge, in which "farmyard implements, harness, plough-socks" become an "armoury" and in which the young narrator is overwhelmed by his own fantasies: he "lay face-down to shun the fear above. / The two-lugged sacks moved in like great blind rats."[102] As Andrews argues, this plays out in miniature "the liquefaction of set limits occasioned by fear" which was "for Wordsworth, what engendered his sense of the mysterious unity of Being."[103]

Heaney does not, however, embrace this "fear" here or see it leading to a greater "unity" with the outside world. But where "The Barn" presents all-consuming, paralyzing fear, "An Advancement of Learning" (once more following the pattern of the Greater Romantic Lyric) shows how that fear can be faced down. The narrator takes the embankment path until he is "well away from the road now."[104] Time metaphorically stops: the poet finds himself face to face with a rat that "clockworked aimlessly a while" before standing staring at the poet. Instead of burying his face in the ground, however, the young boy stares back "With deliberate, thrilled care" at it, taking it all in: "The tapered tail that followed him, / The raindrop eye, the old snout." Crucially, as the boy masters the art of metaphorical description, his fear dissipates: it never entirely vanishes, however, even when transmuted into poetry. "Fear," as Heaney later suggests in an interview, "is the emotion that the muse thrives on. That's always there"; fully to overcome your "fear" would mean the end of inspiration, of development, or of education.[105] As the end of "Storm on the Island" exclaims, "strange, it is a huge nothing that we fear," leaving the doubled possibility that there is "nothing" to fear, but also that we do fear "nothingness," and in that fearing our imagination is stimulated.[106]

In an important way, that is, an enabling – though complicated – "nothingness" underlies these poems (Catriona Clutterbuck astutely comments that "nothingness" in Heaney's early work not only "enables the ideal of creative freedom" but also "interrogates that ideal").[107] The poems do not reveal a "true" empirical understanding of the world but bring the awareness that our understanding of the world cannot exist outside language; as Elmer Kennedy-Andrews argues, these poems suggest that "meaning, far from preceding language, is an effect produced by language."[108] The end of "Personal Helicon" (and so of the collection) suggests that is possible to "see oneself" through "rhyme," through setting "the darkness echoing."[109] This self-knowledge comes through the use of language itself, rather than the revelation of a spiritual or religious force active in the universe. Thus, in his revisions to "An Advancement of Learning," Heaney changes the poem from being the discussion of a theological problem (the poet probes why he is afraid of rats that are "perfect" and unfallen and so "theologically preferable") to a linguistic problem: how to describe the rat, and so control it though language.[110]

Kennedy-Andrews suggests that, "Like Wordsworth who spoke of 'The Bible of the Universe' as a store of 'types and analogies of the infinite,' Heaney found in nature a system of symbols and a machinery of realization."[111] There is a marked difference, however, between Wordsworth's "store of types and analogies" and Heaney's "system of symbols," as a result of the presence and absence of the "infinite" as source and guarantor of their systems. *Death of a Naturalist* does suggest the discovery of a linguistic "machinery of realization" (and a subsequent ability to know oneself), but because of Heaney's removal of the religio-mystical elements of the narrative of the fall, his epiphanies do not, in Hart's words, "reveal God as in the showing forth of Christ to the Magi in the orthodox epiphany" (but nor do they, like Joyce's epiphanies, unveil "the *quidditas* of objects and events").[112] Heaney's poems do not go beyond their "machinery of realization," language itself, in search of the "infinite": they discover only the connections and separations that language causes between the mind and the world. "Fosterage," a poem in *North* dedicated to Michael McLaverty, opens with a quotation from Wallace Stevens's 1945 "Description without Place": "Description is Revelation." Already in *Death of a Naturalist* there is the suggestion that *all* that could be revealed is the act of description itself; acts of revelatory description do, though, bring their own succour.[113]

EPIPHANY AND AMPLIFICATION

I have been brandishing the word "epiphany" somewhat recklessly. This is perhaps permissible since by the time Heaney himself started writing, the "poetry of epiphany" was already something of a cliché: as Geoffrey Hartman noted in his 1964 *Wordsworth's Poetry, 1787–1814*, "accidental epiphanies" had already become "almost a modern staple."[114] The epiphany as Heaney would have encountered it was in part the great Romantic and Victorian moment of revelation, revelation of divine presence, of human insignificance, of mystery: "Wordsworth's spots of time ... Coleridge's 'flashes,' Shelley's 'best and happiest moments,' Keats's 'fine isolated verisimilitude,' Browning's 'infinite moment,' Arnold's 'gleaming' moments, and Tennyson's 'little things ... that strike on a sharper sense.'"[115] These were, however, tempered by and approached through Joyce's reformulation of the epiphany into the revelation not just of divine presence (as Aquinas thought), but of haecceity, a moment in which an object's *quidditas* (its essence) is revealed through a moment of radiance or *claritas*: "*Claritas* is *quidditas* ... Its soul, its whatness, leaps to us from the vestment of its appearance. The soul of the commonest object ... seems to us radiant. The object achieves its epiphany."[116] The epiphany is thus a moment of distancing, as well as of illumination, in which not only something's essence but also its essential otherness is revealed. In Northrop Frye's words, the Joycean epiphany is "an actual event, brought into contact with the creative imagination, but untouched by it, so that it preserves the sense of something contained by the imagination and yet actual in its own terms."[117] These epiphanies are not, however, fully illuminating: they gesture towards the ghostly possibility of an immanent divine presence (a sublime) that will never fully be understood. "Whither is fled the visionary gleam?," Wordsworth asks in "Ode: Intimations of Immortality": after the moment of epiphany, the visionary gleam necessarily flees; there is always a sense of diminishment, a "fall." This is a diminishment, however, that paradoxically redeems itself: it is a "fortunate fall" in Daniel Tobin's words, or one that enables "openness," in which the "sublime" is made productive rather than overpowering.[118]

In Heaney's poetry, as "The Play Way" suggests, the experience of epiphany is often connected to such a "fortunate fall," a fall that is not debilitating but that occurs *into* knowledge or self-discovery. Certainly, "falling" is a multifaceted metaphor in Heaney's work. Often, as Henry Hart argues, Heaney imagines himself as another Adam, falling from a "pastoral, childhood Eden," into "painful recognitions of enervating labor, decay, starvation, sexual turmoil, and fears of natural and political catastrophe"; at other times, though, the poet can also be seen to fall with Satan and – in the process of this fall – gain a doubled perspective or "two consciousnesses."[119]

Thus, in "Waterfalls," from *Death of a Naturalist*, the poet's eye "rides over and downwards, falls with / Hurtling tons that slabber and spill / Falls, yet records the tumult thus standing still."[120] "Waterfalls" might respond to one of Heaney's Queens' lecturers, Lawrence Lerner, whose "Phoenix as Waterfall," published in the 1957 *Domestic Interiors and Other Poems*, features the Gerard Manley Hopkins-heavy lines "so did I fall, a fell glory; in the passes / My people bustled and tumbled at my call. / Now I can trudge and paddle through other grasses; / I fell dying; I dribble after my fall."[121] Lerner's "dribbling" becomes the "slabber[ing] and spill[ing]" of Heaney's waterfall; more importantly, though, rather than the (post-coital?) debilitation of Lerner's poem, there is an air of detachment in Heaney's "record[ing]" that can control and calm the "tumult."

This is part of a broader downward tendency in Heaney's work towards "control" or knowledge. Until *Station Island* (1984) at least, the "path" of poetry is itself most commonly viewed as a downwards journey: it entails a trek or dig into the unconscious, the bog, the underworld, or the past, with the hope of retrieving from those depths whatever one can make use of to fortify oneself, or to sharpen and heighten one's perceptions. Heaney is a poet often interested in the Gothic – such as the irruptions of a violent past from the bogs of Ireland and Denmark in the bog poems of *Wintering Out* and *North* – but this is usually to learn from and to put to use horrifying elements from the past: he actively digs into the past, or lowers his sounding-lines into it, with the aim of summoning ghosts (though whether these ghosts can then be controlled is another matter).[122] In a similar way, part of the interest in "falling" is a search for knowledge that can be derived from the experience; another part, though, is the desire for something that will cushion the blow – and poetic form might offer such a cushion.

Discussing Robert Lowell's work, Heaney suggests that "no matter how much the poem insisted on breakdown or the evacuation of meaning from experience, its fall toward a valueless limbo was broken by the perfectly stretched safety net of poetic form itself."[123] Poetic form stands in here for an absent religious or moral certainty: it provides "value" where otherwise there would be none. If Romanticism is, in T.E. Hulme's terms, a form of "spilt religion," Heaney's rewriting of the fall is a process of learning *how* to spill religion, how to "mess up, falsify and blur the clear outlines of human

54 This Strange Loneliness

experience": his focus on bogs, slime, and turf (and, as he says in a 1973 interview, of taking "the English lyric and make it eat stuff that it has never eaten before") is then a Derry equivalent of Hulme's "pouring a pot of treacle over the dinner table."[124] There are debates about the extent to which the religion being spilt in *Death of a Naturalist* is distinctively Catholic: about whether, as Nicholas Roe argues, Heaney resists the "redemptive adequacy" of the spot of time due to its relationship (through *The Prelude*) to "the spiritual journal and autobiography of puritan tradition," or whether it is going too far to read these poems in terms of "confessional theology."[125] What is being rejected is perhaps less important, however, than what is being chosen to replace it. In his adaptation of theology, as Gail McConnell argues, Heaney is far from discovering the "presence of Christ"; instead the presence he discovers "is what [W.K.] Wimsatt calls the 'fullness of actually presented meaning' in the well-made poem."[126] More important than any residual theological aspect of the epiphany is its elevating (or formal) poetic role, the way it makes a poem mean more than its constituent parts. When he looks back at his student poems in "Feeling into Words," their lack of "epiphany" (in his experience of writing them) is a major failing. "At the university," he recalls, "I kept the whole thing at arm's length, read poetry for the noise and wrote about half a dozen pieces for the literary magazine. But nothing happened inside me. No experience. No epiphany. All craft – and not much of that – and no technique."[127]

"Epiphany" would later be replaced in Heaney's criticism by other terms, the language that Heaney had earlier used for education. In "Two Voices," Heaney's 1980 review of the Australian poet A.D. Hope's book of essays *New Cratylus*, for example, the acts of writing and reading are both understood as moments of revelation, quickening, or amplification: "A surprise and a gratitude ensue in the writer and reader as that original nervous energy translates itself into phrases and rhythms. A personality reveals itself, the current quickens, the volume of the language amplifies."[128] This blurring of educational and poetic moments is perhaps unsurprising: one of the "two voices" he identifies in Hope's book is "the habitual tone of the educator, expository, working from first principles, spiced with quotation and anecdote" (he is not so explicit about what the other voice is).[129] There is almost a circular argument here: poems operate as epiphanies, which reveal the validity, "thisness," and worth of poetry to both poet and reader; in doing so, they provide the

Advancements of Learning 55

possibility of continuous growth and development. In the 1980s, Heaney will express this in terms of Jungian psychic growth; in the 1960s and early 1970s, however, he does not make the mechanism for this development explicit. Instead, by repeating and modulating the poetic structure of epiphany as a model for education, what Heaney has gained is that the doubled nature of the epiphany (both process and object of illumination) can help explain how you can develop a linguistic "grip" on the world: through developing the means of describing the world in richer and stranger detail the world itself is transformed, is amplified.

VIOLENCE AND REPOSE

Such a model, however, depends on a confidence in the beneficent nature of the world that is being "amplified," or on the extent to which language itself might be salvific, or redeem pain, suffering, death, war, nothingness, or any other unpalatable truth that might be revealed through the moment of epiphany, even if there is no immanent divine presence. The persistence of Heaney's preoccupation with the epiphany might suggest that it is, in itself, a source of anxiety and doubt as much as of creative inspiration. I would compare Heaney's interest in the epiphany to Paul Muldoon's obsessive returns to the sonnet; for Alan Gillis, Muldoon's reconfigurations, tinkerings with, and explosions of the form suggest that "there is a great big hole at the heart of Muldoon's sonnets ... over and around which the sonnets proceed" and "which is variously associated in his work with pain, betrayal, bereavement, death, and disempowerment."[130] The epiphanic structure raises the question of what there is beyond our reality and, in the absence of divine revelation or "Real Presence," a similar "great vacuity" or "pervasive emptiness" (in Gillis's words) can be seen to lurk at the heart of Heaney's epiphanies. This is the "nothingness" that might be feared in "Storm on the Island," or indeed "The heart of a vanished world" (to borrow the title of Heaney's 2001 article on David Thomson), or "an inner emptiness," a phrase Heaney adopts from Eugenio Montale in his 1996 lecture "Keeping Time."

There is another, perhaps more pressing, concern as well: the extent to which epiphanies could encompass the irruption of violence (historical, political, sectarian) that Heaney could not help but address in his poetry, without offering too easy a resolution or meaning. Such

56   This Strange Loneliness

doubts pervade "Violence and Repose," Heaney's complex review (published in *Hibernia* in 1973) of *Gradual Wars*, the first poetry collection by his school-friend Seamus Deane. In its opening gambit, Heaney offers a nuanced but pared-back version of the "epiphany." "The poems here which give immediate pleasure," he claims, "are a number of lyrics that speak in a natural tentative voice of moments of hiatus. They are epiphanies; image and rhythm are restrained and unornamented, their effects are pure."[131] "Epiphanies," in this run of adjectives, are related to hiatus, restraint, lack of ornamentation, purity, naturalness, and tentativeness. They are also, as the review goes on, a performance "on the tightropes of miniature, imagist forms, in the pause of held breath." Were Deane content to limit himself to this, "he could achieve an art of nuance and definition at least as delicate as anything in Robert Creeley"; however, "this wise passiveness, this silence, is the silence between the stretched coils of a spring. It is not indolent, emotionally or intellectually, for there is an ironist in this poet who is guardian to the imagist."[132] There is a compaction here – on the "repose" side of this ambivalent review – of Romantic and Modernist poetic theory, of Wordsworthian "wise passiveness" and Imagistic miniaturism trans-Atlantically sponsored by Creeley. But this is not the point or ultimate effect of Deane's collection. As Heaney argues, "the repose of the finished thing is the antithesis of what the book is generally concerned with. The tone is typically nervous, highly-strung, on the edge of violence or catastrophe, in the face or the aftermath of some climax: hinging and unhinging, shuddering, detonating, steepening, throbbing, welling, hurtling, such verbs signal 'a radical unease,' and the related nouns appear like semaphores all through the book: doom, throes, precipice, salvoes, spasm."[133] There is a conflict, that is, between Heaney's reposeful adjectives and Deane's "radically uneasy" verbs and nouns, between "pain at the crunch of history" and "aspiration towards the eloquent artefact"; this is a necessary conflict in light of "the large poetic challenge we all face, how to combine the bitterness and tragedy of our present history with the exigencies of a modern poetic technique." For Heaney, at its best, Deane's "art is tough and delicate"; however, when it does not work, his technique isn't always "adequate" and "One has often the sense of energy and argument over-shooting the landing ground of the form, a sense of verbal overkill that disturbs the essentially incantatory quality of his rhythms. Too many words spoil the poem." [134]

Deane does not, perhaps, always give "silence" the due Heaney feels he should. In a BBC NI program broadcast in 1973, Heaney praises some of "the most attractive poems" in *Gradual Wars* as being "about moments of rare inner realization, moments of silence and composure when the confusion of the world disappears."[135] For John Dennison, Heaney here presents "the emerging notion of poetry as a reconciling space, now a separate order in which the traumatic imprint of history is somehow brought in ameliorative relationship with lyric expression."[136] Poetry then becomes a matter of an "adequate technique" that can combine "history" and the "eloquent artefact," or indeed "history" and "modern poetic technique," a complicated self-consumption which Dennison calls a "doubled duality."[137] This may be, as Dennison argues, a "formalist sidestep" (although he is perhaps too quick to condemn Heaney for tending "towards the simplicity of dualism, rather than the difficulty of establishing an adequate art within the wreck of 'history'").[138] However, I would suggest that this is more of a crisis for Heaney's poetic method than Dennison acknowledges, and that there is no "formalist sidestep" that Heaney can take. It is not just a case of developing an "adequate technique"; rather, Heaney feels the need to reshape his own models of poetic thinking, models that have, more or less, held firm through *Death of a Naturalist, Door into the Dark* (1969), and *Wintering Out* (1972), but which have foundered in his most explicitly "Wordsworthian" – and least successful – endeavour to date, the series of prose poems published as *Stations*.

STATIONS AND THE SPOTS OF TIME

As Heaney outlines in his introduction to *Stations* (1975), he had begun these prose poems while he was in Berkeley, California in 1970 as experiments along Wordsworthian lines: they "had been attempts to touch what Wordsworth called 'spots of time,' moments at the very edge of consciousness, which had lain for years in the unconscious as active lodes or nodes."[139] However, he had laid them to one side, blocked on the one hand "by the appearance of Geoffrey Hill's *Mercian Hymns*: what I had regarded as stolen marches in a form new to me had been headed off by a work of complete authority," and on the other by the worsening political situation he encountered on his return to Belfast: "a month after the introduction of internment my introspection was not confident enough to pur-

58 This Strange Loneliness

sue its direction. The sirens in the air, perhaps quite rightly, jammed those tentative if insistent signals."[140]

Competitive anxiety with Hill was one thing, the felt need for more direct political engagement quite another; and this called into question the validity of such absorbed introspection. Only after recording a TV documentary in Grasmere, *William Wordsworth Lived Here*, and after he had removed himself to "the "hedge-school" of Glanmore, did Heaney return to and complete the poems, in May and June 1974. In drafts the response to Wordsworth's poetry was explicit: Heaney used the working title "Seed-Time" and had as one of the epigraphs a passage from *The Prelude* (which he would later use in the "Singing School" section of *North*): "Fair seed-time had my soul, and I grew up / Foster'd alike by beauty and by fear; / Much favour'd in my birthplace, and no less / In that beloved Vale to which, erelong / I was transplanted."[141] Heaney's approach is quite different from Wordsworth's: as he acknowledges, "Glanmore is not Grasmere."[142] The phrase "spots of time" suggests the thickened interrelationship of place and time, a chronotopic space in which the repeated layerings of the past are revealed. Unlike some new historicist critics, I do not read these passages as moments in which historical and political concerns are elided in favour of a personal retrospection or introspection; instead, I agree with Saree Makdisi that they allow Wordsworth to resist a singular version of "modernity" or of the present – they unsettle the present moment through the irruption of an uncontrollable (and haunting) past.[143] In Wordsworth's work these episodes broadly consider – like his epiphanies – the manner in which childhood experiences of the transcendental or divine in the natural landscape can restore and nourish our minds in later years. They are moments in which the child's imagination is extended by the natural world, moments,

> Which with distinct preeminence retain
> A vivifying virtue, whence, depressed
> By false opinion and contentious thought,
> Or aught of heavier or more deadly weight
> In trivial occupations and the round
> Of ordinary intercourse, our minds
> Are nourished and invisibly repaired[.][144]

The child's imagination also works, however, on the natural world: in the 1805 *Prelude* these are experiences when "We have had deep-

Advancements of Learning

est feeling that the mind / Is lord and master, and that outward sense / Is but the obedient servant of her will."[145] The mind becomes "master" of the senses and of engagement with the external world; the nourishment is then self-willed, and not a matter of passive engagement. However, this "mastery" of the mind is balanced against a sense of being penetrated: what the spots of mind bring is "A virtue, by which pleasure is enhanced, / That penetrates, enables us to mount / When high, more high, and lifts us up when fallen."[146]

What is being penetrated here is unclear: it could be internal or external mysteries, or it could be the mind penetrating into the senses and, by exploring their workings, "lifting" us above "trivial occupations and the round / Of ordinary intercourse."[147] But then the ambiguity is precisely the point: Wordsworth isn't so much justifying the ways of God to men as using an idea of God to defer explaining the ways of men. The inexpressible and ineffable are central to the spots of time. In the first spot (in which Wordsworth gets lost, aged four, on the moors near Penrith) the poet is faced with the sight of a wind-blown girl carrying a pitcher on her head. The poet tells us that he "should need / Colours and words that are unknown to man / To paint the visionary dreariness" which attended the scene: he would need a superhuman language to describe it.[148] Similarly, in the second spot of time there is an inexplicable, mysterious, divine presence that causes the experience to resonate throughout the poet's life. Wordsworth remembers how, after waiting in vain for his father (who dies shortly afterwards) on a storm-blown hillside, "With trite reflections on morality, / Yet with the deepest passion, I bowed low / To God who thus corrected my desires."[149] God is the corrective to the poet's misguided desires; God provides the moral or meaning of the spot of time (opaque though it is to us as readers); and God may cause the experience to resonate throughout the narrator's later life. The poet believes that he relives the experience; yet, what causes him to, he does not know: he does "not doubt / That in this later time ... When I am in the woods, unknown to me / The workings of my spirit thence are brought."[150] The spots of time take on a sanctity, a mysterious, permanent, eternal nature: in the 1799 *Prelude* (which Heaney would not have known at this point) they are "images to which in following years / Far other feelings were attached – with forms / That yet exist with independent life, / And, like their archetypes, know no decay."[151]

When it comes to the spots of time in Heaney's *Stations*, however, the archetypes and the workings of the spirit are not divine, but

60   This Strange Loneliness

sectarian. The poems are (as with Wordsworth's) a form of personal pilgrimage back to childhood memories and locations. A "psychic *turas*," as Heaney describes them, they are "stations that I have often made unthinkingly in my head": this journey involves an uncanny sense of repetition, the combination of novelty and deep familiarity, "the excitement of coming for the first time to a place I had always known completely."[152] This is not just the recovery of deep-lying mental resources, but also the carving out of cultural territory. When some of the poems were published in the *Irish Times* in July 1975 under the title "Autobiographical Borings," it was with the suggestion that they were "narrow shafts let down into one stratum of a northern consciousness, bits to drill the compacted years of G.A.A. sports days and ceilidhe bands, that embattled culture of feiseanna and Gaeltacht scholarships, family rosaries and *Faith of Our Fathers*" (and as such, the *Irish Times* presented them under the journalistic label "Northern Ireland: A Special Report").[153] This is a place, in other words, already mapped and marked by historical and sectarian tensions. As Heaney notes, when he returned to the poems in Glanmore, helped by that sense of "remove," "the sectarian dimension of the pre-reflective experience presented itself as something to be uttered also," with more force than had previously been the case in his poems, the repeated brooding violence of *Death of a Naturalist* notwithstanding.[154]

In such circumstances, the validity of Wordsworthian "introspection" is necessarily questioned: linguistic and religious experience cannot be reified to an ahistorical plane or "exist with independent life." If the poems acknowledge a form of "transplantation," in Wordsworth's botanical metaphor, they also reveal the operations of incision, violent grafting, and usurpation (as well as "fostering"). And religion in *Stations* is always and necessarily sectarian and partisan, at times a form of identity politics, at times a series of empty postures and antagonisms. When Heaney tells in "Cloistered," for example, of his days as an "ascetic" boy at St Columb's College, he dismisses the impetus behind the rituals of Catholicism as being merely "exhilarated self-regard."[155] "Faith" is a matter of exclusion, "the faith of our fathers" and any expression of Catholic belonging is necessarily a matter of resisting Protestant oppression: "We lived there too. / We stared into the pennanted branches and held the tableau. / In spite of dungeon, fire and sword. Implacable."[156]

Language in the prose poems is also necessarily already historically tainted. It is a matter of "codes" and catechisms, phrases that

Advancements of Learning

"atrophy" and get "camouflaged by parasites and creeping greenery," or of "big concepts" that you have to move between "like a double agent." In a draft "Station" poem (which was never published), this is a matter of "Finding a Voice," of balancing "good pronunciation" against "guttural fidelities," with the concern that the former might hide "bigotry" and "abdications" while the latter might be "too pious."[157] Generally, in *Stations* the manner of telling of the tale is at least as important as the tale itself: tongues are "kindly" or "bad" or "gifted"; voices are "far-off, searching for something," "strange," "back-biting," "big"; words are "heraldry" or "combination" locks or are "passwords" to be "carefully enunciated." Language, in other words, leads to a feeling of displacement, of not belonging. In "England's Difficulty" Heaney notes that "The word 'enemy' had the toothed efficiency of a mowing machine" but that – listening to Lord Haw Haw's wartime broadcasts – he lodged "with 'the enemies of Ulster,' the scullions outside the walls" (sectarian tension is tinged here by the wartime context of his earliest memories).[158] There is also a gauging of sectarian insult – rather than precise detail – obvious from the drafts of the poems. In "Kernes," as it appears in "Autobiographical Borings," Dixon, the representative Loyalist schoolboy, declaims, "I could beat every bastardin' fenian in the school!" and "And fuck the pope, every time!"; by *Stations* it is "I could beat every fucking papish in the school!" and "No surrender! Up King Billy every time!"[159] Given the atmosphere, each insult is as likely – and as interchangeable – as the other.

Despite the understanding of how sectarianism underpins speech, these poems also (necessarily as prose poems) revel in language as a rich, almost over-determined, medium. Thus in the first station, "Cauled," the poem oscillates between images of being born and being caught – "Green air *trawled* over his arms and legs ... Little tendrils *unsprung*, new veins lit in the shifting leaves, a *caul of shadows* stretched and *netted* around his head again."[160] The language and imagery in the poems is exact, indeed over-exact, and showy; as Anne Stevenson notes, the poems "cut us out by their very artistry."[161] Heaney's imagery owes more to his later adult mystification of this experience than to the experience itself. The child surely could not himself have considered this experience to be, in any way, a birth, and Heaney can only work his way back to the original childhood event (when he is lost in a field) through other peoples' telling of the tale: "They thought he was lost. For years they talked about it until he found himself at the root of their kindly tongues, sitting like a big fieldmouse in the middle of the rig."[162]

At other points, Heaney is too controlling of what the "spots of time" might mean, too generously offering keys to their interpretation; thus, they are occasionally overwrought. "Overcooked as well as raw" is Haughton's assessment, while Marie Heaney thought (as Heaney recalls in interview) "that they aren't realized or thrown free, that they are like private family memories, pious."[163] The balance between the private and public is not successfully managed. The end of "Sinking the Shaft," for example, about the pump that is the source of the sound "Omphalos," is too explicit about the totemic quality of childhood memories: "snouted, helmeted, the plunger like an active gizzard, the handle dressed to a clean swoop, set on a pediment inscribed by the points of their trowels, I suppose we thought it never could be toppled."[164] In "The Sabbath-Breakers," meanwhile, Heaney looks for an indigenous metaphor for the oppression the Catholic minority face (the context is vandalism of a Gaelic Football pitch): "Call it a pattern. We called it a tournament ... Call it a pattern. We can hardly call it a pogrom."[165] Demurring from the historical connotations of "pogrom," Heaney settles on the defiant – in the context – notion of a "pattern," a "vernacular religious and secular assembly on the day designated for commemorating the patron saint of an area."[166] In "Inquisition," meanwhile, the relationship between language and threatened violence in "the Gents" (an earlier name for the poem) is perhaps made too apparent: "What combination should have slipped open to that proffered 'brother'? One barred the door, the other caught my hand in a grip alive with some pincer alphabet."[167] The pincer grip of Heaney-the-remembering-adult is anxiously felt, offering a (restrictive) code or combination through which to understand his memories.

This overt steering is less of a problem when the memories engage clearly with a literary precursor than when they are presented as more "purely" autobiographical: Heaney always excelled at finding literary models through which to explore his own experience. Two of the *Stations*, "The Discharged Soldier" and "July," engage with Wordsworth's poetry, beyond the overarching adoption of the spot of time as a model. Both open ambiguous distances between Heaney and Wordsworth's work, while also freeing Heaney, to some extent, from the requirements of autobiographical verisimilitude. "The Discharged Soldier" (which had previously been called "An Ulster Twilight") alludes to an episode in Book IV of *The Prelude*. Here,

Advancements of Learning

63

Wordsworth encounters a soldier by the roadside, and walks him to a nearby cottage where he procures aid for him. The soldier is not, however, entirely present: in the 1805 version he cuts a "ghastly figure"; by the 1850 version he is a "ghostly figure"; and when he tells the poet "of what he had endured / From hardship, battle, or the pestilence," there was "in all he said ... a strange half-absence, and a tone / Of weakness and indifference, as of one / Remembering the importance of his theme / But feeling it no longer."[168] Through the allusion, Heaney is drawing a parallel between the Napoleonic Wars and the First World War, or rather the difficulty of talking about experiences in those wars. Danny, his "shell-shocked" discharged soldier, tells "yarns" of "Flanders," a name that "sounded heavy as an old tarpaulin being dragged off a wet load" and "once or twice a month his artesian and desolate wailing lifted over the fields": in an allusion to *Treasure Island* (Heaney has acknowledged his childhood love of Stevenson) he is "My shell-shocked Pew, stamping the parish with his built-up hoof, proffering the black spot of his mouth."[169] Danny's uncontrollable "artesian" wailing may have more in common with the compulsive need of Coleridge's Ancient Mariner to tell his story; certainly for the young Heaney the main feeling he inspires is fear, "I dreaded the twilit road" (a possible echo of "Like one that on a lonesome road / doth walk in fear and dread"?). The disapproval of Danny – the quoted "Oh there's a badness there for sure" – is ultimately sanctioned, rather than challenged, by the allusion to *Treasure Island* (the "ghostly" still retains the "ghastly").

In "July," meanwhile, the hammering of the drums of an Orange band is balanced against various allusions to Romantic poetry in a series of assertions and negations. "The drumming started in the cool of the evening," it begins, "as if the dome of air were lightly hailed on. But no. The drumming murmured from beneath that drum."[170] The "dome of air" invokes Coleridge's "Kubla Khan" (with the poet's claim that "with music loud and long, / I would build that dome in air"), but more directly Shelley's "The Cloud":

> the winds and sunbeams with their convex gleams
> Build up the blue dome of air,
> I silently laugh at my own cenotaph,
> And out of the caverns of rain,
> Like a child from the womb, like a ghost from the tomb,
> I arise and unbuild it again.[171]

64   This Strange Loneliness

Shelley's laughing defiance in the face of death is immediately negated,
however, by the inversion of "hailed *on*. But *no*": "No Surrender," in
effect, to such life-giving resistance. Indeed, one is tempted to anach-
ronistically read Heaney's poem as an echo of "Ulster Says No":
the very landscape combines to defeat any Wordsworthian inspired
natural energy and persistence after death. Heaney alludes to Wordsworth's "A Slumber Did My Spirit Seal," but instead of Lucy's
spirit which "Roll'd round in earth's diurnal course / With rocks
and stones and trees!," in "July" the hills serve to repeat the echoes
of the drums: "The hills were a bellied sound-box resonating, a low
dyke against diurnal roar, a tidal wave that stayed, that still might
open."[172] Pulsing beneath the landscape is the "diurnal roar" of the
Lambeg drum: the hills themselves become an anvil on which "tuns
and ingots were being beaten thin." The poem ends with a rejection of the inspiring Romantic wind – that "corresponding breeze"
or "West Wind" – through a pun on the shared etymological root
of "winnow" and "wind": "And so my ear was winnowed annu-
ally." Rather than being inspired by a natural force, the poet's ear
was informed, pared down, and reduced by the land-filling sound of
the drums. What price now the nourishing and repairing power of
Wordsworth's spots of time? The *Stations* tend rather to show the
effects of "false opinion and contentious thought": in the face of
a particular kind of instruction or resonation, the poems offer not
"repair" but resistance.

The music of Beethoven in "The Play Way" seems to find its nega-
tion in the Lambeg drum of "July." The promise of "amplification"
that is found in epiphanies of education is shown not necessarily to
be beneficial or desirable: the natural landscape does not necessarily
provide nourishment or repair but might be "a bellied sound-box
resonating" that might amplify and open a wave of sectarian hatred
and violence. Tripping to fall into yourself "unknowingly" might be
the discovery of one's own propensity to violence: the "grip" that
you get on things might easily be a drumstick or worse. The question
is one of agency, of whether we can outstrip the circumstances of
our education: as Heaney asks of a figure in the uncollected poem
"Woodcut" (1971), "Is he a loom or a spool / For his speech? Is he
force-fed / Or finding these words?"[173]

What "July" suggests, then, is a rejection of the Romantic project,
and of the liberal humanist project (the "humanist wager"): a rejection of the belief that art, like the natural landscape, can educate

Advancements of Learning

you through an act of (self-)revelation in which you gain your ability to describe the world around you in more detail. Such acts of revelation no longer guarantee a kind of higher moral, religious, or social knowledge. This rejection is, however, not complete. Among the manuscripts for *Stations* is the draft poem "Oral English" (the reworking of "Finding a Voice") in which Heaney imagines transcending the sectarianism and class assumptions of his upbringing, the way his voice might be conditioned by violence, or rural origins, or (Northern) Irishness:

> But, can I make a trampoline of a tongue set like a tripwire?
> ~~Well, dammit! If it hasn't taken to rhetorical questioning, getting uppity in its old age.~~[174]

The "trampoline" is an echo of the end of Paul Muldoon's "Dancers at the Moy" (published in 1973) in which the corpses of horses – destined for war, and slaughtered at the onset of unexpected peace – are buried under foundations of houses, and "Give their earthen floors / The ease of trampolines."[175] Not for the last time would Muldoon (whom Heaney had taught at Queen's and supported in his career) offer Heaney an alternative to his own tendency towards piety or excessive seriousness. The conversation staged here is between a dangerous, historically informed playfulness – as in Muldoon's poem – and a (racially charged) self-critical voice that would urge you to know your own place, to not get "uppity." The fact that this second voice is struck out means at least a temporary victory for imaginative playfulness, for the trampoline over the tripwire (this victory would not become permanent until *The Spirit Level*, and the decision to "walk on air against your better judgement").[176] But it also perhaps suggests how the Romantic models he had been exploring – the epiphany, the spot of time, the idea of the poem as a moment of "education" – do not have to be jettisoned. Rather, there is a need to combine a lightness of touch with an understanding of political and historical difficulty; a sense that his reworking of Romanticism – and of Wordsworth in particular – needs to be grounded in the historical formations, and disruptions, of place; and a confirmation that although poetic "influence" may be primarily a matter of complex cultural and political interactions, rather than an innocent, natural, flow, it could still – in spite of this – be a matter of "play."

2

Fosterage and Poetic Influence

WORKING THE COMPOST

That compost of childhood experience, that rich packed stratum of half-remembered and half-forgotten feeling is certainly the basis of the poetic imagination, but poetic work is carried out under the influence of other powers as well, pre-eminently under the influence of all the great poets who have already written.[1]

In an unpublished lecture on "The Prelude," Heaney offers horticultural and traditional images for the relationships between poets or poems. "Poetic work" is a matter of good composting, of transmuting the influence of the poets of the great tradition, and poetic influence is, here, complex and layered: like the poetic imagination, it might be as much a matter of half-forgetting as it is of half-remembering. The idea of "influence" is itself also "composted," built up through various "conditioning metaphors, dead or alive," to borrow Eleanor Cook's words, which shape how we talk about the relationships between poems or poets, and how these ebb, flow, and under- or overwhelm.[2] Such metaphors might include the fluvial images in my introduction or the educational, horticultural, or devotional images in the previous chapter: "underground streams," "transplantations," "patterns," "apprenticeships," "nourishment." Other metaphors, meanwhile, appeal to the biological, musical, erotic, or criminal. Indeed, almost any area of human experience can be adopted to talk about the relationships between poets. They can be seen (and this list is alphabetical, but by no means comprehensive) as a matter of adaption, adoption, aftering, altering, amplification, anxiety, appropriation, atrophy, authority, belatedness, borrowing, brotherhood, burden, colonization, commodification, community, competition, completion, debt, echo, emulation, enclosure, encounter, encroachment, filiation, fleecing, flirting, geniality, gift-giving, gratitude, harmony, hybridity, hybridization, inheritance, intertextuality, intimidation, invasion, legacy, "magical transference and visionary reanimation," mimicry, mining, misprision, pick-pocketing, resonance, sisterhood, "strenuous tussle," theft, transformation, translation, trespass, trysting, undermining, and versioning; one might also feel that one owes a "monstrous debt" or agree with Osip Mandelstam's noisy suggestion that "a citation is a cicada."[3] Poetic "influence," in other words, is shorthand for a very diverse range of interactions, engagements, defences, and suppressions, reflecting a complex range of possible positions on both sides: influence is never a simple (and rarely entirely innocent) process, and is often a matter of play, companionship, and fellow-travelling rather than – or as well as – intergenerational "debt."

In the 1970s, the question of how poetic influence works, and how poets relate to each other, came to be one of Heaney's main critical preoccupations (in a way that builds on his discussions of developing poetic "technique" in the previous decade). Just as his broader poetics of this period focused on the need to find "befitting emblems of adversity," his explorations of influence sought appropriate emblems (or metaphors) for influence, especially those that could be used to stress how "influence" can be seen as a beneficent force. The (largely implicit) target here is Harold Bloom's formulation of poetry as necessarily being "anxious" or agonistic. It is a critical commonplace to emphasize Heaney's anti-Bloomian positivist approach to influence, to trace not an "anxiety" of influence but "an acceptance of, a revelling in, or even at times a disgust with, the poet's inherited resources," in which "the desire to establish difference and originality is productive not only of anxiety but also of acknowledgement and admiration."[4] The phrase the "anxiety of influence" itself is repeatedly revised in criticism of Heaney's work (so often that one might suspect some critical anxiety at play), as a "perplexed 'anxiety of trust,'" as the "buoyancy of influence" (echoing Heaney himself), or the "anxiety of authorship."[5]

In this chapter, I explore different approaches to influence, and anxiety, and discuss various metaphors for poetic influence that Heaney uses in his prose, and ways in which influence is seen as

68   This Strange Loneliness

beneficent or troubling; first, however, I need to draw a broad distinction. In Heaney's poems up until *Station Island* there is often the sense of places and texts being "haunted" by previous texts, of predecessors being unruly, and possibly dangerous, ghosts (this I explore in the next chapter). In his prose, however, there is little "anxiety," in the non-technical, emotional sense. Previous poets are encouraging forces rather than blocking presences: they could help form an inscape, they could be relied upon to generously *do* or *be* in your service. Rather than antagonistic conflict, the poetic tradition could offer "hope" as well as "challenge"; "pastness" is, as Heaney comments on Neruda, "to a greater or lesser degree enabling."[6]

This is perhaps no surprise. Heaney came to poetic maturity in a time when poetic influence was less "anxious" about itself, a time, for example, when Leon Gottfried could quote Eliot to the effect that Arnold's writing on Wordsworth was "not so much a criticism of Wordsworth as a testimonial of what Wordsworth had done for *him*."[7] And indeed, Heaney's approach to influence is informed at least in part by Wordsworth's view of influence, whether natural or poetic, as generally (but not entirely) beneficent. Unlike Keats, for whom Milton was a famously oppressive precursor ("life to him would be death to me"), Wordsworth could construct his own autobiographical epic *The Prelude*, as W.J. Harvey had taught Heaney at Queen's, out of the wreck of Milton's Eden.[8] As Heaney himself argues, referring to Book III of *The Prelude*, for Wordsworth "the influence of the spirit of the place [Cambridge University], and the sense that he was treading ground that had been trodden by his great predecessors, spoke to him and acted as a kind of steadying and admonitory presence. Chaucer, Spenser, Milton haunted him gently and regularly."[9] As Heaney's comments suggest, this gentle "haunting" involved a sense of inferiority alongside a jovial companionship. Wordsworth remembers how he "could not print / Ground where the grass had yielded to the steps / Of generations of illustrious men, / Unmoved"; he could, however, laugh with Chaucer "Beside the pleasant Mills of Trompington."[10]

There are, I suggest, three ways in particular through which Heaney develops an understanding of a "steadying and admonitory" influence that stimulates the poetic imagination: the models of poetic "touchstones" and "traditions"; a willed form of imaginative identification; and the idea that influence might be understood through a form of "fosterage." Each of these shapes and determines

Fosterage and Poetic Influence 69

his relationship with Wordsworth, and the last (fosterage) has origins in Wordsworth's poetry as well as in the customs and laws of Gaelic Ireland: this joint origin will accrue cultural and political significance the more insistently Heaney returns to it (especially as he does so in the face of criticism of "fictive" reclamations of the past). In general, each can be seen as a way of achieving a form of poetic authority – what Heaney describes as "the authority to do your own work – *auctoritas*, yourself as the *auctor* of the work" – and doing so without feeling that authority to be a crushing burden.[11]

TRADITIONS, TALENTS, AND TOUCHSTONES

Much of Heaney's consideration of poetic history relies, implicitly and explicitly, on the idea of a poetic "tradition" traced out by T.S. Eliot. In "Learning from Eliot," the Eliot Centenary lecture he delivered at Harvard in 1988, Heaney remembers owning a copy of Eliot's prose while he was a student at Queen's, "in a little purple-colored Penguin book ... reminiscent of a confessor's stole" and reading and rereading "Tradition and the Individual Talent": "most important of all ... was a definition of a faculty which he called 'the auditory imagination'" (which Eliot had formulated in an essay on Matthew Arnold).[12] The idea Eliot develops in "Tradition and the Individual Talent" of a "historical sense" which "involves a perception, not only of the pastness of the past, but of its presence" is crucial to all of Heaney's prose: it underpins an ability to make historical comparisons and to trace distinct patterns of influence and kinship, particularly when balanced alongside another idea derived from Matthew Arnold, that of the poetic touchstone.[13] For Arnold, in "The Study of Poetry" (1880), "touchstones" were "lines and expressions of the great masters" which can be used to detect "the presence or absence of high poetic quality, and also the degree of this quality, in all other poetry which we may place beside them."[14] As Heaney notes in his lecture "The Sense of Place" (1977), these touchstones were "high points of imaginative experience, 'those recollections which are our standards and our beacons.' Arnold's touchstones were literary, drawn from the whole field of European poetry."[15] Where Arnold's touchstones were "lines and expressions," however, Heaney frequently used the (undefined) "achievement" or complete oeuvre of a poet (especially Wordsworth, Yeats, Osip Mandelstam, or Czesław Miłosz) as a measure against which to judge poets whose reputations are less canonically secure. This perpetuates the idea of a canon based on biography as much as on artistic work. As Neil Corcoran argues, Heaney employs a "vocabulary of recognition, or rhetoric of tribute" which "compounds a moral and aesthetic judgement: it implies that the poet's life as well as his work (or the quality of the life, with its gestures and alignments, as it can be read out of his work) is in some sense accountable, available to scrutiny, proposed as pattern and imitation."[16] (Choices of poetic touchstones will of course also often be "self-legitimizing" and serve to celebrate and laud poets whose aesthetics or artistic practices are similar to one's own; this is certainly true for Heaney.[17])

"Traditions and an Individual Talent," an essay from 1972, can then be seen as a way of developing Eliot's ideas of poetic tradition while also weighing Wordsworth and Hugh MacDiarmid, the Scottish poet and instigator of the Scottish Renaissance, against each other, and in the process helping to create a critical environment sympathetic to Heaney's own poetics. Throughout runs the silent recognition of the older meaning of "talent" as a measure of weight, a token of value. The central impetus is the recognition of value and of importance, as the essay compares Wordsworth's and MacDiarmid's careers and developing oeuvres. "Both," Heaney suggests, "discovered early a way of affiliating an individual talent to a submerged tradition; both professed a diction that was deliberately at variance with prevalent modes; both wrote classic lyric poetry in a short period of intense creativity and followed this by turning their lyric discoveries towards more ambitious goals, producing long meditative poems that wove their personal poetic and public worlds into a single major artistic form."[18] This can be seen as self-reflexive artistic credo as much as critical analysis, with its emphasis on "submerged traditions" (Heaney had published the first of his bog poems in *Wintering Out* in 1972) and lyric intensity; there is perhaps even a prophetic look ahead to Heaney's own turn towards a "long meditative" poem in "Station Island" (1984).

It is also an act of personal thanks as much as of celebration of MacDiarmid's importance and achievement. MacDiarmid – along with poets such as Norman MacCaig and Sorley MacLean, and the critic Alasdair Macrae – had shown Heaney great hospitality in Scotland. This is not just, then, as Eugene O'Brien has suggested, a slightly dry attempt to "pluralize Eliot's sense of tradition" but an example of Heaney using his position, as he would throughout his career, to advocate on behalf writers (and friends) who he felt were due wider recognition.[19] Heaney clearly assumes that his readers (the readership of the fortnightly Irish periodical *Hibernia* in 1972) will accept Wordsworth's status as a canonical poet; equally – and probably rightly – he appears to assume that they will not be so convinced of MacDiarmid's. Where Wordsworth needs no introduction, MacDiarmid does, and Wordsworth *is* that introduction. Bridges are being built, poetic communities forged, perhaps at the cost of nuance: Heaney both underplays the differences between the ways in which their diction "was deliberately at variance with prevalent modes" and overstates, for mild comedic purposes, how much MacDiarmid would have objected to being compared "with an Englishman."[20]

What is at stake in this essay is the idea of – and ability to be part of – a poetic "tradition" of the kind Eliot had outlined; certainly, Eliot's words pervade the essay. Heaney promotes an "auditory imagination" that trusts, in Heaney's words, in "a poetry that communicates before it is understood" or, in Eliot's, in a "feeling for syllable and rhythm" that penetrates "far below the conscious levels of thought and feeling."[21] And Heaney rewrites Eliot's "Little Gidding" (with its emphasis on "purify[ing] the dialect of the tribe") to argue that MacDiarmid "set out not so much to purify as to restore the language of the tribe, with a passion that was as philological as it was poetic."[22] This distinction is important, as it, to some extent, avoids the nationalistic (as well as tribal) elements of Eliot's thinking. Such strains were present in the focus on national histories in "Tradition in the Individual Talent" in his depiction of a historical sense which compelled one to write "with a feeling that the whole of the literature of Europe from Homer and within that the whole of the literature of his own country has a simultaneous existence and composes a simultaneous order."[23] This is clearly an issue if one does not sit easily within the literature of one "country," but straddles different national borders, or has different "rights" on the English language.

Joyce, as is often the case in Heaney's prose of the 1970s, is relied upon to exemplify this linguistic "restoration," to offer a (quasi-postcolonial) response to any sense of English superiority, and to give a model for how self-consciousness about linguistic disenfranchisement – "an uncertainty about language" – could be overcome. "Joyce," Heaney argues, "made a myth and a mode out of this self-consciousness, but he did so by taking on the English language

72 This Strange Loneliness

itself and wrestling its genius with his bare hands, making it lie down where all its ladders start, in the rag-and-bone shop of Indo-European origins and relationships."[24] Joyce offers a way of approaching literary tradition beyond the national boundaries Eliot had emphasized – "the literature of his own country" – and which would have separated rather than connected Wordsworth and (the avowedly Scottish nationalist) MacDiarmid. Instead, there is a turn to the "universal" and a "modern poetry" stripped of the political connotations of Eliot's essay. "In *A Drunk Man Looks at the Thistle*," Heaney writes, "MacDiarmid retrieves for modern poetry the image of the poet offered by the Preface to the *Lyrical Ballads*: a man endued with a lively sensibility, unusual enthusiasm and tenderness, a great knowledge of human nature, a comprehensive soul, a man rejoicing in the spirit of life that is in him and delighted to contemplate similar volitions and passions as manifested in the goings-on of the universe."[25] "Tradition and an Individual Talent," in other words, espouses transhistorical humanism – a sense that the "goings-on of the universe" can be encountered in the same way no matter the historical or political context – sponsored by Wordsworth's Preface on the one hand and Eliot on the other.

If this transhistorical humanism updates the Romantic defence of poetry it does so, as Haughton argues, after a process of cross-fertilization with "modernist poetics," including the work of Eliot, Frost, Lowell, and Mandelstam (as well as MacDiarmid and Joyce).[26] This serves to complicate Heaney's relationship with Romanticism, and indeed, any stable engagement with previous poets. Eliot's tradition not only offers flexibility with its ever-evolving relationship between the present and the past, but also unsettles the past, rendering it uncannily unpredictable and subject to endless future change. The past that is created in the present is then always shifting, and not always in desirable ways. Should we actually aim, like Joyce, to return to where all "ladders start, in the rag-and-bone shop of Indo-European origins and relationships": and can we be sure this would bring cultural or (following the Yeatsian echo of the "rag-and-bone shop of the heart") personal renewal? Or would the experience be somehow more vicarious, more mundane? This last question arises because there is a nineteenth-century fustiness or finicky antiquarianism that inevitably comes with the idea of poetic touchstones. For all of the intellectual heft of Arnold's and Eliot's thinking, both could be seen, with their emphasis on imaginative

Fosterage and Poetic Influence 73

identification across historic periods, as akin to a form of cultural, historic tourism in which another historical period, distant culture, or individual life, is glimpsed and imaginatively inhabited, however briefly. However attractive this may be, it also raises questions about the nature of that tourism, and especially whether it involves a presumptive simplification and commodification of earlier lives. The problems with such imaginative identification – along with the pleasures it entails – are explored in one of Heaney's most extended discussions of Wordsworth, his TV documentary for the BBC, *William Wordsworth Lived Here* (1974).

WILLIAM WORDSWORTH LIVED HERE

William Wordsworth Lived Here is part travel film, part critical appraisal, part love letter: it also has something of the air of the property program *Through the Keyhole,* asking who would live in a house like this (and how might that house shape them). Created for a series commissioned by Antonia Fraser, the program was filmed at Dove Cottage in May 1974 and broadcast in November that year. The point of the series was to have one poet imagine themselves in the place of another and, as ever, Heaney is aware of the requirements of his audience.[27] This is not the medium or forum for the kind of poetic touchstone-ing and arguing of "Tradition and an Individual Talent"; instead, it is, to some extent, a process of de-poeticizing. In his script, Heaney comments that, "Before I came to Grasmere I had no firm visual impressions of the Wordsworth country because one of the striking things about Wordsworth is the way his imagination transformed the external scene into a country of the mind. The landscape became a mindscape."[28] The film, with its necessary insistence on the visual and the material, reverses this journey. The trip to Grasmere makes Heaney aware of the actuality of the Lakes, not just the country of Wordsworth's imagining: he notes his "slight and delightful surprise" that there was a country outside Wordsworth's mind that is so "palpable and compact, so 'monumental' and 'serene.'"[29]

Hugh Haughton, merging the terms from one of Heaney's essays on Dante, describes this film as "a virtuoso exercise in envious identification."[30] Heaney's childhood in Derry and the Heaneys' recent relocation to Glanmore offer a clear basis for such identification; it is less a case of envy, however, than of surprise and affection. Heaney focuses on the Wordsworths' distinctly rural domestic experience:

74

This Strange Loneliness

he notes how they lived on "porridge and potatoes," washed down "with their own home-made beer"; how they fished, and picked mushrooms and herbs; and had deliveries of "peat" (although in her notebook Dorothy only recorded their coal, rather than peat, deliveries).[31] The focus is not solely on William, but tries to reimagine him as a "husband or a father" (and, in an earlier draft, as a teenager) and to picture Dorothy (who gives many of the details of their life there) moving "upstairs like a usurped queen" in October 1802.[32] It is the Wordsworths as gardeners and planters that are of interest to Heaney, with their vegetable patch for broccoli, peas, radishes, and runner beans, their apple trees and wild flowers, and William sinking "his own well": William is in this imagining a "founding father."[33] Alongside this, however, the Wordsworths are considered as inhabitants of a wider, transient community: habitual walkers who would meet "figures who would, sooner or later, find their way into the poetry – vagabonds, discharged soldiers, tinker children, an old leech gatherer."[34] Strangely, Heaney treats these "figures" as elements of the natural landscape, suggesting that Wordsworth's "resolution, his independence as a poet had to do with this capacity to be flooded by the durable, sustaining influences of rock, stream, hill, wind and cloud": vagabonds and leech gatherers merge with the "sustaining influences" of the natural world.[35]

This shift from the human, social, and political to the natural – as the same act of "flooding" – is perhaps the result of Heaney's overarching aim in the program to give a sense of Wordsworth's poetry as emerging from the contemplation of "those natural forms around which his feelings grew pure and steady."[36] Dove Cottage is itself a conduit for natural energies and natural nourishment, "socketed into the hillside, like an elemental power point, an emblem of the poet's instinctive decision to make this new and nourishing connection with his origins"; Grasmere as a whole provides a "hub of the landscape of his youth," a "confluence of energies from the whole circumference of his mind and feelings."[37] In particular, the cottage provides a connection to the subterranean force of underground streams. Heaney notes the "cellar-like atmosphere" in the downstairs rooms of the cottage, which seems "completely appropriate for a man whose inspiration was stored in the cellars of his consciousness, a man who traced the birth of his poetic vocation to the noise of river water murmuring in his infant ear"; meanwhile, "with almost metaphoric force, a branch of the neighbouring stream runs underneath the flagstone" of the larder, reminding Heaney of "Wordsworth's sense of hidden, flowing water as the element which had tutored his poetic voice."[38]

How this tutoring element – this confluence of energies – works, though, is another matter. Heaney offers various models for Wordsworth's relationship to the natural world: not just as a "founding father" but also as someone (combining Keats and Yeats) creating their own "matter of fact Wordsworthian version of a 'magic casement,' opening onto the fairyland of the hillside." Wordsworth's hut, meanwhile, is "an 'Indian shed' as he called it, a moss lined bower," but for Heaney this is not native American, but also Celtic and Christian: "As I say there's something monastic in the whole set-up. Wordsworth sitting composing here like a Celtic monk in his cell in the woods."[39] This combination of natural nourishment, domestic security, and hermetic seclusion ultimately offers Wordsworth an "assuaging influence." Heaney feels the effect of Dove Cottage's "tranquil restoration," a restoration which is fructive and suggests the "incubating mind": the cottage encourages Wordsworth's "Romantic vision of man," in which (in terms taken from the Preface) "the heart of man, and human life" is "founded upon … those 'beautiful and permanent forms of nature.'"[40]

One perhaps should not place too much weight on the details of the program. It is in part an act of cultural tourism and the script is dependent on the exigencies of production and the need to tell a story primarily through the visual means at one's disposal (the cottage, gardens, and surrounding landscape). However, it is clear from the draft materials held at Emory University that the overall thrust of the script had been mapped out in advance. In effect it replays the trajectory of *The Prelude*, suggesting how the influence of the natural world can offer a psychic and emotional "restoration" and lead to "love of man" and a mature "philosophic mind." The broadcast finishes on lines from *The Prelude*:

> The hiding places of my power
> Seem open; I approach, and then they close.
> I see by glimpses now; when age comes on,
> May scarcely see at all; and I would give,
> While yet we may, as far as words can give,
> A substance and a life to what I feel:
> I would enshrine the spirit of the past
> For future restoration.[41]

76   This Strange Loneliness

This does not really offer a convincing conclusion to the (Heideggerian) version of natural dwelling that Heaney had espoused throughout the rest of the broadcast. In the broadcast version he never comments, unlike *The Prelude* itself, on what needed "restoration" and why; and the emphasis on what is "seen by glimpses" only is necessarily complicated by a visual medium. However, this program is serving Heaney's own needs as a writer and reader as well as delivering an authoritative version of the Wordsworth's life in Grasmere. At its most interesting it reveals Heaney (in a televisual version of Eliot's notion of the historical sense) trying to imagine Wordsworth's continued presence, and the conditions that he would find most conducive to composition: "For although it is now a museum it seems to exude a strange residual life – secluded, integrated with the ground, battened down for action, almost hutch like."[42] And, as Heaney makes clear later in 1974, in one of his first major public lectures on poetry, the lines quoted from *The Prelude* play a crucial role in his own understanding of his poetic technique, a technique clearly displaying a Wordsworthian residue.

"FEELING INTO WORDS" AND POETIC AUTHORITY

"Feeling into Words" was delivered in London to the Royal Society for Literature on 17 October 1974. As ever, the audience is important, and the lecture was pitched with assumptions about shared knowledge, and with specific aims, strategies, flatteries, and sleights-of-hand in mind (there is no such thing as a pure, decontextualized discussion of poetry, even though this is how much criticism is often read). Where Heaney had used Wordsworth in "Traditions and an Individual Talent" to make claims about MacDiarmid's significance to an Irish magazine readership audience, here – faced with the Royal Society – he appeals to Wordsworth as a foil for presenting his own poetic practice and aims; in doing so he claims a nuanced and complicated form of allegiance to Wordsworth.

Glossing the lines from *The Prelude* with which he ended *Wordsworth Lived Here* (and which open "Feeling into Words") Heaney curiously identifies his "right to speak" with his reading of Wordsworth. "Implicit in these few lines," he argues, "is a view of poetry which I think is implicit in the few poems I have written that give me any right to speak: poetry as divination, poetry as revelation of the self to the self, as restoration of the culture to itself; poems

Fosterage and Poetic Influence

as elements of continuity, with the aura and authenticity of archaeological finds, where the buried shard has an importance that is not diminished by the importance of the buried city; poetry as a dig, a dig for finds that end up being plants."[43] There is, once more, an Eliotic appeal to tradition here, as much as a gloss of Wordsworth's poem, particularly with the transmutation of "the spirit of the past" into an "element of continuity"; however, the engagement with tradition is both passive and active. Heaney is not simply ceding *auctoritas* to Wordsworth in order "to ventriloquise controversial sentiments through the latter and absolve himself from all consequences," as Shane Alcobia-Murphy argues.[44] Instead, he is also making apparent – and calling into question – that act of ventriloquism. Heaney presents a version of poetry that is both the revelation of something that pre-exists the poet's attention and interest, and also the discovery that this revelation is a form of creation or, at least, "half-creation" (it is notable that a piece of juvenilia quoted in this lecture features the poet's instruction to himself "You should attempt concrete expression, / Half-guessing, half expression").[45] Poetry is, after all, "a dig for finds that end up being *plants*": the double-meaning of "plants," with its invocation not just of growth but also the abuse of power – the planting of evidence – suggests that the identification between Heaney and Wordsworth is less transparent than it might at first appear.

Heaney is ceding authority not primarily to Wordsworth's lines but to what he is reading into them. It is Heaney's acts of reading and misreading that present "poetry as divination," "as revelation of the self to the self" (and so on). These all come through Heaney's own interpretative dig for what is "implicit," which is itself an archeological exploration of the (English) literary tradition to uncover his own place in it. Or rather traditions: one of the recurring motifs of the lecture is the plurality and complexity of types of identification, and ways of locating yourself in the world. Such complexity is imagined through "the exotic listing on the wireless dial: Stuttgart, Leipzig, Oslo, Hilversum," in the jostling lists of the shipping forecast ("Dogger, Rockall, Malin, Shetland, Faroes, Finisterre"), and in the litany of the Blessed Virgin ("Tower of Gold, Ark of the Covenant, Gate of Heaven, Morning Star, Health of the Sick, Refuge of Sinners, Comforter of the Afflicted").[46] Each presents a different, and potentially competing, way of structuring the world, ways that are not politically innocent. In another image from the lecture,

Heaney suggests that "one of the purposes of a literary education as I experienced it was to turn the student's ear into a poetic bugging device": poetic apprenticeship – learning how to negotiate different ways of representing the world – then becomes a matter of spying and skulking, as well as the more standard idea of developing one's poetic "voice" through attention to different influences.[47]

Thus, phrases from Keats, Tennyson, and Wordsworth could be "touchstones of sorts, where the language could give you a kind of aural goose-flesh"; but this appeal to English touchstones is then complicated by a perceived "congruence" between memory, bog, and "for want of a better word, our national consciousness." The question becomes one of how you understand the "intimate connection" between poetic voice and "the poet's natural voice" (with a stress on what a "natural" voice might be), and then with the "national."[48] Finding a "voice" is seen as a process of imitation: "your first steps as a writer will be to imitate, consciously or unconsciously, those sounds that flowed in, that in-fluence."[49] But it is a process that is also implicitly aware of Joycean difference and differentiation. Heaney traces his own growth from the apprentice who signed his poems "*Incertus*, uncertain, a shy soul fretting and all that": this nod to Stephen Dedalus in the tundish scene of Joyce's *Portrait of an Artist* – "My soul frets in the shadow of his language" – suggests the precise form of cultural and linguistic authority (or disqualification) that is at stake while accommodating oneself to a literary tradition (or of that tradition to your purposes).[50] The point of this imitation is to develop a poetic voice which carries with it a level of "authority" (what Heaney will identify in the later lecture "Sounding Auden" as "the rights and weight which accrue to a voice not only because of a sustained history of truth-telling but by virtue also of its tonality").[51]

Unavoidably, there is a political dimension to such questions of truth-telling and authority. In the context of the violence in Northern Ireland, "the problems of poetry," Heaney argues, "moved from being simply a matter of achieving the satisfactory verbal icon to being a search for images and symbols adequate to our predicament"; this search leads to the conclusion that "The question, as ever, is 'How with this rage shall beauty hold a plea?' And my answer is, by offering 'befitting emblems of adversity.'"[52] This answer comes from Yeats's "Meditations in Time of Civil War," but the extraordinary thing about the lecture as a whole – given that it builds up to

Fosterage and Poetic Influence

a discussion of a poetry that could "encompass the perspectives of a humane reason and at the same time to grant the religious intensity of the violence its deplorable authenticity and complexity" in the context of "the tail-end of a struggle in a province between territorial piety and imperial power" – is that each stage of Heaney's argument is underpinned by a discussion of or identification with Wordsworth. This is despite the fact that Wordsworth's "religious intensity" and imperial associations would apparently align him more easily with the "new male cult whose founding fathers were Cromwell, William of Orange and Edward Carson" than the "indigenous territorial numen, a tutelar of the whole island, call her Mother Ireland, Kathleen Ni Houlihan, the poor old woman, the Shan van Vocht."[53]

The identification with Wordsworth is not, however, straightforward, but involves Heaney misreading the older poet and redirecting his energies. So much is clear from Heaney's quotation from *The Prelude* – "The hiding places of my power / Seem open" – and his gloss on it – "Implicit in these few lines ..." Wordsworth's concern in the passage, at least in the 1805 version, is fundamentally with the individual, with the restoration of *himself*: first-person pronouns resound through the passage.[54] Above all Wordsworth is describing how he could rediscover his own childhood (with the implicit understanding that everyone else can do so too). The "hiding places of *my* power" are his childhood years; and the whole passage recapitulates how "The days gone by / Come back upon *me* from the dawn almost / Of life."[55] In Heaney's reading, the focus on the individual moves to the public and the collective. Personal memories become social memories; autobiographical digs become archeological digs; the "revelation of the self to the self" becomes the "restoration of the culture to itself"; the buried shard, no matter how important in itself, is viewed in context of the buried city. Cultural difference necessarily intrudes. This is not just then a case of "cultural osmosis," as Cavanagh argues, in which Heaney and Wordsworth appear "almost as contemporaries, are independent transmitters of a view of poetry" whereby poetry is affirmed "as an ongoing and essentially changeless cultural phenomenon."[56] Rather, as Haughton suggests, their "hiding-places" – and what they might be hiding from or for – are quite different: "Wordsworth's 'hiding-places' are personal, locked into early experiences 'disowned by memory.' Heaney's, by contrast, are communal and cultural, and their archaism is historical as much as psychological."[57] Because of the communal turn in

Heaney's argument, the stress on power and its hiding places brings us into complicated areas. Politically, this social turn could suggest exclusivity and atavism: can there only be one "native culture" for instance? To what extent is the opposition Heaney makes between a "territorial numen" and a usurping or impinging "new male cult" itself a "plant" rather than a "find"?[58] What is the equivalence of the "self" and the "culture"? And what, then, is Wordsworth doing in the middle of all this?

On one level, what Heaney attempts in the lecture is to redeem a form of commonality that would include Wordsworth, rather than excluding him on (cultural) nationalist grounds. And he does so by appealing to a form of mysterious or "mystical kinship" that takes its cues from *The Prelude* itself. The focus on the individualistic in the lines "The hiding places of my power / Seem open ... " can be seen, when taken in context, more as a worrying at how this private "power" and inspiration relates to the rest of humanity. The individual power is representative of a universal "mystery of man," addressed in the lines immediately preceding:

> Oh! mystery of man, from what a depth
> Proceed thy honours. I am lost, but see
> In simple childhood something of the base
> On which thy greatness stands – but this I feel,
> That from thyself it comes, that thou must give,
> Else never canst receive.[59]

As so often in *The Prelude*, the distance between the subject, verb, and object verges on the sublime, and it is extremely difficult to gloss this passage in the third person and retain any of its "power." Man's "greatness" here lies in the mysterious depth of childhood that – as in the "Immortality Ode" – will always be beyond adult recollection. It is at once internal and external, something given and something received, and, above all, it is mysterious: not a matter for rational thought, but for emotional "feeling" and lostness. What every individual shares, their ultimate commonality, is this sense of mystery and loss: and as it is rooted in an abstracted and universal "simple childhood" it will outweigh any questions of race, colour, creed, or nationality.

This sense of a universal mystery is what Wordsworth represents for Heaney in "Feeling into Words," with a particular recognition of the limitations of language when it comes to giving

Fosterage and Poetic Influence   81

"substance," "life," and "spirit" to emotions or the past.[60] As such, he is the embodiment – in Heaney's coining – of "technique." Where "craft" is "what you can learn from other verse" (it is "the skill of making"), technique "involves not only a poet's way with words, his management of metre, rhythm and verbal texture; it involves also a definition of his stance towards life, a definition of his own reality ... Technique entails the watermarking of your essential patterns of perception, voice and thought into the touch and texture of your lines."[61] Heaney had been working towards this distinction for almost a decade, at least since his 1965 review "Evangelists" (with its separation of "craftsmanship and technique") and his draft lecture "On Composition," which distinguished between "*inspiration* and craftsmanship or technique."[62] And it is a distinction that, once more, owes a heavy debt to Eliot. Eliot had made similar claims about "technique" in his review "Professional, Or" (published under the pseudonym "Apteryx" in the *Egoist* in 1918) where he argues that technique is not "what may be learned from a manual of prosody. This is making technique easy ... Technique is more volatile; it can only be learned, the more difficult part of it, by absorption."[63] More important still, though, was C.K. Stead's analysis of Eliot's "Three Voices of Poetry," which shows Eliot engaged in a search for "the voice of the poet's 'soul' – that part of his being which is unknowable, even to himself"; a soul that "expresses itself, not in 'thought,' but by a recreation of diverse experiences into 'feeling' – which in turn becomes ... the essential texture of the poem."[64]

What had begun as a quest for the "spirit of the past" in its "hiding places" in *The Prelude* is now a related search for "essential patterns," a watermark, "what lies hidden" in the pre-verbal state, a poet's "stance towards life" (which will later mutate into the idea of poetry "as a way of taking the measure of yourself and the world, and yourself-in-the-world"), or – as Heaney argues in his editorial to *Soundings* 2 in 1974 – a poet's "authenticity."[65] This search for "essential patterns" might in effect, then, be similar to Keats's, in Walter Jackson Bate's description of him. For Bate, Keats "kept reverting to the larger aims of the great poets of the past – scorning to manicure their details, and seeking instead to recapture their spirit"; this focus on "spirit" or watermarks means Keats [and Heaney] could avoid the paralysis of endeavour and confidence that beset "Matthew Arnold and so many that followed Arnold" in the use of touchstones.[66] (It is quite different from the "use of memory"

82   This Strange Loneliness

that Heaney was fond of in "Little Gidding," which causes "faces and places" that were loved, but have now vanished, "To become renewed, transfigured, in another pattern": there is an "essential pattern" to trace, rather than a transfigured pattern to be created.[67])

The quest for a numinous, hidden essence is related, for Heaney, to the water diviner's "gift for being in touch with what is there, hidden and real, a gift for mediating between the latent resource and the community that wants it current and released."[68] While Heaney reads his own poem "The Diviner" as a poetic representation of technique, for an example of technique in action (and the ability to discover an "objective correlative" for pre-verbal feeling) he turns to Wordsworth's composition of "The Thorn," from *Lyrical Ballads*.[69] "The Thorn," according to Heaney, is a "nicely documented example of feeling getting into words," a "rapid and strange foray where Wordsworth discovered a way of turning the 'lump in the throat' into a 'thought.'"[70] Heaney claims that in the poem Wordsworth donned "the mask of the tale-teller, legitimately credulous, entering and enacting a convention," and through this act "discovered a set of images, cadences and sounds that amplified his original visionary excitement into 'a redundant energy / Vexing its own creation.'"[71] It is Wordsworth's poetic method that is authoritative here: "The Thorn" becomes a model for how poetry can develop both in a natural manner and from a natural source. Heaney describes how Wordsworth endured a storm in the Quantock Hills and asked himself, "Cannot I by some invention do as much to make this thorn permanently an impressive object, as the storm has made it to my eyes at this moment?"[72] The storm is a natural equivalent for poetry – it is "nature's technique for granting the thorn-tree its epiphany" – and Wordsworth's own technical triumph is "to discover a means of allowing his slightly abnormal, slightly numinous vision of the thorn to 'deal out its being.'"[73] Poetry's role is one of mediation, finding a way of making palpable the poet's imaginative response to natural stimuli, of transmuting the "influence" of the natural world: "The storm, in other words, was nature's technique for granting the thorn-tree its epiphany, awakening in Wordsworth that engendering, heightened state which he describes at the beginning of *The Prelude* – again in relation to the inspiring influence of wind."[74]

Heaney's introduction of the distinction between craft and technique operates on an aesthetic plane rather than a social or political one; and there is something forced about the communal aspect introduced through the example of the diviner (diviners are not, after all,

Fosterage and Poetic Influence

necessarily agents of or within a community). At the end of the lecture Heaney withdraws, to some extent, from the emphasis on the communal he had introduced in his reading of *The Prelude*: "I began by suggesting that my point of view involved poetry as divination, as a restoration of the culture to itself. In Ireland in this century it has involved for Yeats and many others an attempt to define and interpret the present by bringing it into significant relationship with the past, and I believe that effort in our present circumstances has to be urgently renewed. But here we stray from the realm of technique into the realm of tradition; to forge a poem is one thing, to forge the uncreated conscience of the race, as Stephen Dedalus put it, is quite another and places daunting pressures and responsibilities on anyone who would risk the name of poet."[75] This is, on one level, an act of disinfection, an attempt to keep the realms of "technique" and "tradition" separate (although the appeals to continuity and community may already mean this attempt is too late). But the desire to retain separate (and equally valid) ways of understanding poetry – as either aesthetically transcendent or politically involved – is itself suggestive of what Heaney has learned from his own reading of Wordsworth during the course of the lecture.

There is a shift, as "Feeling into Words" progresses, in how Heaney uses Wordsworth: from Wordsworth's work providing a model for communal cultural restoration or revivification to Wordsworth's poetic practice being an exemplar for poetic technique, for putting "feeling into words," or mediating the symbols of the natural world; he becomes an example of a poet casting himself into and against nature to produce poetry. Rather than supplying "befitting emblems for adversity," "The Thorn" actually offers a clue towards Wordsworth's implicit, essential, watermarked "voice," an (exemplary) spirit that cannot easily be applied to (political) matters of "tradition," or to the forging of the unconscious of a race. It is as if Wordsworth's example baulks at any attempts to co-opt it to political ends. As Guinn Batten argues, Heaney ultimately opts not to follow the self fully into the "hiding-places" of its power but rather opts to "leave the graves of the self unopened, their secrets intact, lest the 'inquest' of naming them 'have the effect of confining them to what is named.'"[76] Certainly, the ambiguity of Wordsworth's "technical" legacy – and Heaney's reading of it – will persist: in a 2000 interview with Mike Murphy, Heaney notes that "Wordsworth said in his Preface to the *Lyrical Ballads* (I'm still very fond of him), 'In poetry

84   This Strange Loneliness

we see the workings of the spirit reflected in the workings of the universe.' You feel the inner part of yourself, your inner lining, being brought into some kind of co-ordination with what's out there.'"[77] The relationship between the "watermark" and the world remains (perhaps usefully) vague: it might not matter that we never know precisely *what* kind of co-ordination there is between the workings of the spirit and the workings of universe.

FOSTERED ALIKE?

Guinn Batten's essay is in part a thoughtful response to criticism, by Patricia Coughlan in particular, of Heaney's representations of "place" as female (as Mother Ireland, the Sean Vhan Vocht, or as Undine), and in particular that there is an "internal and logical inconsistency in Heaney's effort to be both maternal place and, as poetic son, the oedipal usurper (or reclaimant of place) – both source and subject."[78] Batten's solution is to rephrase the question to focus on how a male poet might identify with (as well as desire) the maternal body: how the poet might, in effect, become both the preserving, nourishing bog and that which is kept there, or "born" from there.[79] This is not a question of self-propagation, but rather an understanding of how familial (and oedipal) relationships might work in ways that outstrip the Freudian: the male poet might identify with a maternal figure; not every "father" has to be fought with and killed. This fluidity (and acknowledgment) of familial relations is particularly relevant to Heaney's thinking about poetry in the 1970s because in this period he repeatedly uses – without theorizing it – a model for poetic influence that is based on a willed familial metaphor: fosterage.

"Singing School," the final section of *North* (1975), has two epigraphs: the first is the by now familiar passage from Book I of the 1805 *Prelude*: "Fair seed-time had my soul, and I grew up / Fostered alike by beauty and by fear, / Much favoured in my birthplace, and no less / In that beloved vale to which erelong / I was transplanted."[80] Elmer Kennedy-Andrews reads this epigraph as showing how Heaney accepts from Wordsworth's poem both the "usefulness and relevance of the English tradition" and "an affirmation of the nurture received from rural, childhood experience."[81] Any sense of nurture or affirmation is, however, immediately challenged by the second epigraph, drawn from Yeats's *Autobiographies*: "He [the

Fosterage and Poetic Influence 85

stable-boy] had a book of Orange rhymes, and the days when we read them together in the hay-loft gave me the pleasure of rhyme for the first time. Later on I can remember being told, when there was a rumour of a Fenian rising, that rifles were being handed out to the Orangemen; and presently, when I began to dream of my future life, I thought I might like to die fighting the Fenians."[82] In a way that is common in Heaney's poetics of the 1970s, binary oppositions accumulate and complicate: beauty and fear, Orange and Fenian, Wordsworth and Yeats. The relationship between these different poles, however, remains necessarily opaque; it is not based on the straightforward opposition of terms, but on the possibility of opposites implicating each other, being subsumed into each other, transcended. As Eamonn Hughes has pointed out, Wordsworth and Yeats are not simply opposed "because Wordsworth was a part of Yeats's cultural 'langue' and both are a part of Heaney's cultural 'langue,'" and in "the autobiographical works from which the oppositions come, the impulse is for both elements to be comprehended."[83] Multiplicity is one of the points here; a multiplicity into which one is educated or "fostered" through the influence of previous literature (that "pleasure of rhyme").

Heaney is clearly identifying Yeats and Wordsworth as two possible poetic "fathers": this might seem to be one of those instances in which Heaney, as Haughton astutely argues, "forged a poetic image of himself out of Wordsworth," and in so doing set up "a Wordsworthian template for reading Heaney."[84] This process of "forging" an image out of a previous poet is a kind of reverse and willed "fosterage," in which poetic influence is acknowledged: the poetic son claims the poetic father. Heaney later repeats this process with Mandelstam, Dante, Lowell, and Miłosz (the latter two in a particularly complicated manner, since he also knew them personally). Fosterage, unlike filiation, is not single or singular, but can be multiple and complex; you can be fostered – or foster yourself to – many different parents, in many different ways, rewriting or reshaping them to suit your present needs, and (in Michael Parker's words) "to pay tribute, to claim kin, but not equality."[85] The relationship the "Singing School" epigraphs suggest between the present moment and previous poetry is, however, far from straightforward. "Singing School" places more pressure on the tension that Heaney had explored in "Feeling into Words" between an abstracted idealized form of poetic influence (a natural "fosterage") and poetic

86   This Strange Loneliness

relationships informed by *realpolitik*: the promise of an idyllic, supportive, non-agonistic relationship between poets is repeatedly undermined. (One question that arises is whether fosterage in the "pleasure of rhyme" actually impels you – like the young Yeats – towards a dream of patriotic violence: it is pertinent, of course, that Heaney is himself entirely antipathetic to the Orange dream of "dying fighting the Fenians.")

In "The Ministry of Fear," the first poem in "Singing School," there is a tentative self-awareness of the poet's relationship to poetic tradition: it presents a form of commonplace-book, a cut-out-and-keep collage reflection on Heaney's time at St Columb's. (This is not without its anxieties: in a draft of one of the "Glanmore Sonnets," "Sensings, Mountings from the Hiding Places," which Heaney wrote at the same time as the poems in *North*, he suggests, dismissively, that he might be no more than "An eleven-plus aesthete / Making the daring leap from quote to quote."[86]) Among the many (daring) allusions that make up the poem, there are at least two to Wordsworth. The title merges an echo of Coleridge's "secret ministry" of frost (from "Frost at Midnight") with Wordsworth's opposition between beauty and fear; by rejecting fear's counterpart (beauty) in the title, however, Heaney suggests a poetic landscape charged with fear, a poetic equivalent of the police state in Graham Greene's novel *The Ministry of Fear* (1943). Heaney then truncates another allusion to Wordsworth's work to enforce this sense of an oppressive environment. When the young Heaney throws the biscuits left to "sweeten his exile" over a fence, the narrator suggests that "It was an act / Of stealth," in a revision of the boat-stealing incident of *The Prelude*, with its "an act of stealth / And troubled pleasure."[87] Gone is the "troubled pleasure," though the "stealth" remains. Stretching the interpretation to breaking point, we might say that alluding to Wordsworth's poetry also has lost its "pleasure" for Heaney: stealth is required and acknowledging the influence of the English does not come without risk. But it is also an "act": Heaney changes the line break to shift the emphasis from an act of *stealth* to an *act* of stealth. The young Heaney's rebellion and the poet Heaney's allusion to Wordsworth are acts – (daring) actions, but also perhaps artificial poses. They are the postured rebellion of one who feels oppressed and trapped, first by his boarding school and second by the world of English literature. This more general sense of oppression is made explicit at the end of the poem: "Ulster was British, but with no right

Fosterage and Poetic Influence 87

on / The English lyric: all around us, though / We hadn't named it, the ministry of fear."[88] Heaney and Wordsworth cannot be "fostered alike," in other words; such a parallel is precluded by their different relationships to the English literary tradition.

I have been presenting fosterage here primarily as a metaphor for a form of poetic relationship or influence (a process of maturation similar to that of Keats's Grecian Urn, the "Foster-child of Silence and slow Time").[89] There is more to it than this, however. David Lloyd has attacked Heaney's tendency to view poetry as an act of "grounding" in which the identity of the writer is assured "in assuring the quasi-procreative relationship between land and culture," and associates this with a retrograde nineteenth-century Irish cultural nationalism, as made manifest in the newspaper *the Nation*: "The slogan of the *Nation* succinctly expresses the ramifications of the nationalist project: 'To foster public opinion and make it racy of the soil.' The act of fostering, by which a people 'separated from their forefathers' are to be given back an alternative yet equally arbitrary and fictive paternity is re-naturalized through the metaphor of grounding: through its rootedness in the primary soil of Ireland, the mind of Ireland will regain its distinctive savour."[90] With his emphasis on archeological metaphors as a means of probing identity, or his repeated invocations of Daniel Corkery's idea of Irish consciousness as a "quaking sod," Heaney is susceptible to such criticisms: he was, however, entirely conscious of this, and repeatedly attempted to avoid being trapped by his own Antaean emphasis on "groundedness." Indeed, what is of interest in Heaney's use of the idea of fosterage is that he does not attempt (at least solely) to reclaim a lost form or savour of Irishness. Rather, he uses "fosterage" as a model for combining different inheritances and different spheres of his own life – poetic, political, and familial – without simplifying how difficult this act of combination will be.

An aside: fosterage is not only literary metaphor for Heaney or Wordsworth – for both it was part of their own lives or family experience. In *The Prelude* Wordsworth is describing both a period of actual fosterage, when he was boarding at Hawkshead Grammar School (his mother had died in 1778, the year before Wordsworth went to Hawkshead, and his father died in 1783 while he was at the school), and a metaphorical fosterage by the natural landscape "in that belovèd vale to which erelong / I was transplanted."[91] It was also a feature of Heaney's own life. He remembers it as one facet

88   This Strange Loneliness

of "the tail-end of a steadier way of life that had persisted right through from medieval times"; indeed, his own father was fostered out along with his siblings among aunts and uncles after the early death of Heaney's grandparents.[92] When Heaney, then, repeatedly imagines his own time as a boarder at St Columb's as a period of fosterage – as in "Alphabets" in *The Haw Lantern* (1987) where Heaney suggests "he was fostered next in a stricter school / Named for a patron saint of the oak wood" – then he is in part doing so in contradistinction to his own father's experience.[93]

In both poets' work, however, "fosterage" *is* more commonly used as a metaphor: in Wordsworth to represent his relationship with the natural landscape, and in Heaney his relationship with literary figures (or advocates of literature). Like Wordsworth, though, setting out on the project of *The Prelude*, Heaney often uses this metaphor at a moment of critical self-definition or shift in poetic direction. This is certainly the case in "Singing School," which as a whole takes stock of the first phase of Heaney's poetic career. The fifth poem in the sequence, "Fosterage," is dedicated to Michael McLaverty and describes how McLaverty "fostered me and sent me out, with words / Imposing on my tongue like obols," advising him to "Go your own way. Do your own work."[94] Foster-fathers, it appears, can also foster one another. Similar advice is reiterated by the spectral figure of James Joyce a decade later in "Station Island," when Heaney seeks another redirection for his career: "What you must do must be done on your own // so get back in harness. The main thing is to write / for the joy of it."[95] Moreover, the last major shift in Heaney's career comes with *Seeing Things* (1991), and is signalled in a poem called "Fosterling."[96] This provides one of the sustaining images for Heaney's late poetry, the idea of "credit[ing] marvels": "fostering," in other words, as well as having clear maturational importance – and importance as a metaphor for growth and development – also has a "marvellous," liberating dimension.

What Joyce calls the "mystical kinship of fosterage, fosterchild and fosterbrother" also has, however, a distinctly Irish significance.[97] Fosterage was a legal practice in medieval Ireland, with both educational and political dimensions. The Brehon law texts of the seventh to ninth centuries describe how "children were commonly sent away to be reared by foster-parents," who would be responsible for "maintaining and training the children in accordance with their parents' rank."[98] Both boys and girls were fostered in what was usually a "cliental" (rather than a patronal) relationship: that is, children would be fostered by parents of a lower social rank. The foster-parents would gain favour with the noble parents (and their child) and the nobles would strengthen the ties of loyalty and obligation that bound the foster-parents to them.[99] The practice also had an international – and possibly anticolonial – element. Fosterage linked Gaelic Ireland to Gaelic Scotland, creating and firming political military alliances (in ways that could undermine, rather than bolster, the status quo). Peter Parkes notes that the "*Annals of Loch Cé* in 1290" record that Domhnall Óg O'Donnell was fostered by "Clann Suibhne of the Hebrides": Domhnall Óg later returned to Ireland with an army of "galloglas" mercenaries from Scotland.[100] As Parkes observes, however, Domhnall Óg's return was deplored by the Christian community in Ireland for political, religious, and eugenic reasons, as possibly leading to a "hybrid, re-paganized Norse-Gaelic population assimilated by fosterage."[101] Concern about cultural "mixing" was also expressed by the English crown (in the Statutes of Kilkenny in 1367) because of the "moral degeneration of fostered Anglo-Irish settlers, and their resultant disloyalty to the English crown": fosterage, alongside alliances through marriage and concubinage, was listed as a treasonable offence.[102] The practice was not, therefore, politically neutral or straightforward; it had a subversive potential as well as a conservative one, depending on your perspective on the purity, genuineness, or authenticity of lines of filiation.[103]

Of interest here is the way in which fosterage offers a model for potentially subversive relationships, and in particular how these might transcend national boundaries. Kate Trumpener's insightful discussion of fosterage and wet-nursing in Irish and Scottish nineteenth-century novels suggests that the nurse is seen as "the bearer of cultural inheritance, able to rouse her grown-up charges from their disaffection with national life into a more committed engagement with its past and present"; crucially, however, the nurse has by this time been "banished" and is "transfigured into a mythic personage, bathed in nostalgia and longing."[104] Something similar is happening in Heaney's poetry: it is not the loss of a personage that is felt, but of a way of thinking, and this becomes mythologized as a means of gaining a fuller access to the past, a greater sense of "right" on the lyric tradition, and an imagined alternative point of origin (an "omphalos" to which Heaney repeatedly returns). A modernized version of fosterage would allow the Irish poet to pick and choose from within the English tradition and still maintain their independence from this tradition: it would allow the creation of political or poetic bonds between families, traditions, and cultures that would otherwise appear at odds. The advice of McLaverty/Joyce can then be seen as the injunction to create your own ancestors, to determine your own (multifaceted) lineage, but to not to be tied or bound by this while you "do your own work."

Such a self-created origin or ancestry is, however, necessarily fictive, and is elsewhere acknowledged not as a beginning but as an end, a "Terminus." This is the title of a poem in *The Haw Lantern* (1987) in which the poet claims that he "grew up in between" and describes how "Baronies, parishes met where I was born. / When I stood on the central stepping stone // I was the last earl on horseback in midstream / Still parleying, in earshot of his peers."[105] As Heaney describes in the 1998 lecture "Something to Write Home About," this poem imagines the meeting of two foster brothers, Hugh O'Neill and the Earl of Essex, who found themselves on opposite sides during the Nine Years' War, and arrange a temporary truce:

> for each of them, this meeting by the river was a mysterious turn, a hiatus, a frozen frame in the violent action, a moment when those on either bank could see what was happening but could not hear what was being said. Both men were alone and exposed to the consequences of their actions; O'Neill was already regarded as a traitor and Essex, by agreeing to a truce with him at this moment, was going to be seen as a betrayer by the Queen and in fact before the end of the year would be executed for treason. O'Neill's ultimate defeat lay ahead also, in a couple of years' time. But for the moment, the balance trembled and held, the water ran and the sky moved silently above them.[106]

The truce arranged between O'Neill and Essex is a temporary one, a balance that "trembled and held" only "for the moment"; this, like the epiphanic moments discussed in the previous chapter, is, in effect, a "spot of time," an ahistorical timeless hiatus that carries its shocking force into the present, in some way "exposing" the present.

Its out-of-time sense of impasse also reveals, however, how "spots of time" might, in themselves, bespeak blockage and stasis rather than fluid in-betweenness. The political weight of this subtext threatens to upset the in-between "balance" of the poem. Heaney relates this image of the foster brothers to the historical context in which he was writing, "the mid-1980s when the political situation in Northern Ireland was totally locked and blocked; ... the post-hunger-strike world, when the IRA's campaign showed no sign of abating and the Thatcher government was prepared to live with what was termed an acceptable level of violence."[107] Both, the comparison suggests, were times when "There was no room for two truths," when friendship or fosterage could come to seem a form of treason, or personal and national allegiances be irreconcilable.[108] This political significance, however, is not apparent from the poem itself; the poem requires the gloss to reveal the political subtext. Shane Alcobia-Murphy criticizes Heaney for his vagueness, for failing to convey the poem's theme that "the inheritance of a divided world is a disabling one, that it traps its inhabitants and corners them in determined positions, saps their will to act freely and creatively."[109] However, this is to take Heaney-the-critic at his word too narrowly: the poem suggests the creative possibility, rather than the entrapment, that might come from an inheritance or imagination that can reach across political division.

"Fosterage" can instead be an antidote to a narrow sense of identity or "origin": rather than the search for a singular father or mother figure, it might allow for a circular process of renewal and self-creation (without the "groundedness" Lloyd had feared). So much would Heaney, at this point in his career, have learned from the work of Paul Muldoon. In Muldoon's "Immram" in *Why Brownlee Left* (1980), the metaphor of fosterage is balanced against an essentialist search for "pedigree" or origins (or, in Harold's Bloom's terms, the desire "to re-beget one's own self, to become one's own Great Original").[110] Rewriting the Irish folktale the Immram Mael Duin, Muldoon also – in a typically playfully serious manner – queries Heaney's obsession with father-figures. He uses "Foster's pool hall" and "Foster's pool room" as the beginning and end locations of "Immram"; where the quest for the "father" bathetically turns up a dead end, a desiccated Howard Hughes figure who "forgives" and "forgets," and the return to "Foster's pool room" offers a circling return that can also be a new beginning.[111] Any quest for pedigree – or self-created pedigree – could, as the poem suggests, lend itself to a narrowly essentialist or exclusivist politics or identity politics, the doubting of "some new strain in my pedigree."[112]

But this had been latent in Heaney's poetry from the beginning, in the fear of that which "festers" – a dark parallel to fosterage – and the wariness of what new life might come from that festering. In a 1966 *New Statesman* article, Heaney describes how in Northern Ireland "Life goes on, yet people are reluctant to dismiss the possibility of an explosion. A kind of doublethink operates: something is rotten, but maybe if we wait it will fester to death."[113] This gives political substance to "Death of a Naturalist," which starts with the image of the flax-dam which "festered in the heart / Of the townland" and ends on the fear of violence.[114] "Festering" is not, however, purely destructive. In the 1960s and early 1970s it suggests the "fouled nest incubating somewhere" that appears in "Summer Home" in *Wintering Out* and reappears in "The Smell," one of the draft poems of "Winter Seeds" (which would become *Stations*): here the solution is "To realize suddenly, / Whip the mat off // That was larval, creeping – / And scald, scald, scald."[115] But from the mid-1970s onwards, "festering" might be generative: there is the hope in "Sibyl" in *Field Work* that "the fouled magma incubate // Bright nymphs" (one thinks of Heaney describing Wordsworth's "incubating mind" in *William Wordsworth Lived Here*).[116] Festering can lead to fostering, that is, like the "vowel of earth / dreaming its root / in flowers and snow" in "Kinship" in *North*, which becomes "a windfall composing / the floor it rots into": it might be an act of productive and successful self-regeneration, rather than an annulling self-inwoven process; a spiral, rather than self-consuming circle.[117]

What is apparent from "Terminus" and "Something to Write Home About" more broadly is the way in which a different set of allegiances, derived from an understanding of literary "fosterage," serves to undermine and complicate a bluntly essentialist approach to identity. This develops from an understanding of poetic influence – outlined in "Feeling into Words" – which views it as organic, natural, sublimated, and "engendering," and in which "in-fluence" is described as "those sounds that flow" into you and enable you to develop your own poetic voice. It is exemplified by the storm in "The Thorn" which becomes "nature's technique for granting the thorn-tree its epiphany, awakening in Wordsworth that engendering, heightened state which he describes at the beginning of *The Prelude*," and which is related to the "inspired influence of wind," that "corresponding, mild, creative breeze."[118] This doubled understanding of influence – that it parallels natural processes and so is

Fosterage and Poetic Influence

"engendering," and that in its heightened state it might present a vision of an apolitical or supra-political realm – is outlined in two lectures from the late 1970s, "The Sense of Place" and "The Makings of a Music."

HUMANIZING INFLUENCE AND THE MAKINGS OF A MUSIC

In the 1977 lecture "The Sense of Place," first delivered at the Ulster Museum, Heaney compares the attitude to the landscape presented by the poet Patrick Kavanagh and the geologist Robert Lloyd Praeger. He uses as a touchstone the Wordsworthian notion of the "primary laws of our nature, the laws of feeling" to argue that "Wordsworth was perhaps the first man to articulate the nurture that becomes available to the feelings through dwelling in one dear perpetual place. In his narrative poem 'Michael,' he talks at one point about the way the Westmorland mountains were so much more than a picturesque backdrop for his shepherd's existence, how they were rather companionable and influential in the strict sense of the word 'influential' – things flowed in from them to Michael's psychic life. This Lake District was not inanimate stone but active nature humanized and humanizing."[119] Heaney then quotes lines from "Michael" that he makes into a model for the (passive) admittance of active "influence," in which "the surface of the earth can be accepted into and be a steadying influence upon the quiet depths of the mind."[120] The poem describes how the "green valleys," streams, rocks, fields, "common air," and hills "impressed" many incidents on Michael's mind, which "like a book, preserved the memory / Of the dumb animals, whom he had saved"; in this process the fields and hills "had laid / Strong hold on his affections, were to him / A pleasurable feeling of blind love, / The pleasure which there is in life itself."[121] Heaney was writing some years before green criticism reclaimed Wordsworth as a poet of Heideggerian rootedness and "belonging"; although he may appear to pre-empt such a reading of Wordsworth, he is also drawing upon millennia of thinking about poetry to describe Wordsworth's ideas about *natural* influence.

Longinus's *On the Sublime* (first century CE) had influenced eighteenth-century writers through the way in which it described, in Jonathan Bate's words, how "sublimity may be achieved by imitating and emulating great writers of the past": the image of Plato diverting "to himself countless rills from the Homeric spring" then became a model for other imitating writers, as did the sense that "inspiration need not be incompatible with imitation; the spirit which possesses the poet may be that of his predecessors."[122] As Heaney recognizes, one of Wordsworth's achievements was to literalize this metaphorical tendency, to remember that "influence," with its metaphoric rills, streams, and fountains, could also come (in a process underwritten by Hartleyan Associationism) from actual rills, streams, and fountains.[123] This happens, however, in Heaney's passage (and Wordsworth's) in such a way that the literary and the natural are held in tremulous balance; it is a two-sided process in which nature is "humanized" and in turn has the power to "humanize." (The idea of "humanization" was a preoccupation: in "Feeling into Words" Heaney had discussed his own poem "Undine" as an example of "the liberating, humanizing effect of sexual encounter").[124]

This is a notably benign understanding of influence, with little concern about "the element of competition between poet and master, the knowledge that the latter must be confronted although he cannot be outdone."[125] Such benignity is often explicit in Wordsworth's presentation of poetic influence too: as Christopher Ricks notes, in Wordsworth's work invocations of "influence" are frequently "either allusions, or in the immediate vicinity of allusions" and "either given or retain benignant adjectives, such as 'benignant' itself."[126] However, the use of "benignant" does, of course, also suggest at least the possibility of "malignant" influence that has to be fought against ("Competitiveness may be the thing that should be competed with").[127] Indeed, Wordsworth's "Reply to Mathetes" makes it clear he was aware of ways in which the excellence of previous poets might come to exert an oppressive force: contemporary poets might overstate the "typical" general quality of previous literature (since "the large overbalance of worthlessness ... has been swept away"), and weigh the present against the past in its entirety, rather than as a succession of distinct generations; the result could be – as Walter Jackson Bate notes, quoting Ortega y Gasset – that "every age will inevitably feel itself 'empty' in comparison with the past."[128]

Even in "Michael," Heaney's model of the "humanizing" natural landscape, there is a degree of anxiety implicated in the relationship between the natural and the literary, and the "propriety" of that relationship. Susan Eilenberg argues that the poem, with its central image of the house and sheepfold that Luke will not inherit, and the

Fosterage and Poetic Influence

tragic jolt of an inherited debt, "exhibits a guilty anxiety on the subject of the heir."[129] Certainly, the poem might explore or betray guilt about usurpation and undermining. Within the poem itself, there is the fact of Michael's distress being caused by being "bound / In surety for his Brother's Son" (who, despite being "a man / Of an industrious life, and ample means" is "press'd upon" by "unforeseen misfortunes"); and there is also the poet's usurpation of Luke, displacing Michael's son Luke and (poetically) taking possession of a territory that has been forfeited.[130] (Beyond this, in the publication of the second edition of *Lyrical Ballads*, there is Wordsworth's usurpation of Coleridge, "Michael" having taken the place of Coleridge's "Christabel.) More particularly, the application of publishing metaphors to Michael's relationship to the natural world – the "impress" of the natural world on a mind that is "like a book" – seems oddly out of place in a poem that foregrounds the tale as being oral first and foremost. More questions are raised than the poem can hope to answer: do minds and books really "remember" the past in the same way? To what extent can literature equal the natural world in the creation of "pleasurable feeling of blind love" (with all the weight that Wordsworth places on "the grand elementary principle of pleasure")?[131] And, echoing Mary Jacobus's analysis of Book V of *The Prelude*, to what extent does the poem covertly express a fear "that it is not we that write, but writing that writes us"?[132]

Tellingly, in Heaney's discussion of influence in "Michael" this is not the case: what can be read as complex and fraught in "Michael" becomes "companionable and influential" in "The Sense of Place." This is not to say that Heaney does not elsewhere acknowledge the sense of lack of agency that Jacobus reads in *The Prelude*, the possibility of "being written" rather than "writing": this is the same doubt that is expressed in Heaney's "Woodcut" ("Is he a loom or a spool / For his speech? Is he force-fed / Or finding these words?")[133] Rather, Heaney acknowledges such passivity as part of a double-sided, dialogic coin: the Lake District is both "humanized and humanizing." There is then a dialogue between the landscape and the mind, and the relationship (or influence) between the two is not a matter of "passive" inscaping. Instead, "influence" is both a retrospective and prospective act, an internal and external process, a "listening in" which becomes a "speaking out." In terms he will use in "The Makings of a Music" it is "a version of composition as listening, as wise passiveness, a surrender to energies that spring within the centre of the mind, not composition as an active pursuit by the mind's circumference of something already at the centre."[134] Or – as Christopher Ricks comments about allusion – it is "a way of looking before and after, a retrospect that opens up a new prospect."[135] But in "The Sense of Place" Heaney moves beyond this image of influence as a matter of "surrendering" to something already contained within you. There is something willed, forced, and deliberate about this procedure, alongside the suggestion of "passive surrender"; it is a form of "half-creation" as much as perception (to borrow once more from "Tintern Abbey").[136] And it is a process that does not come laden with anxieties about debt and usurpation (as expressed in "Michael"): in Heaney's reading of the poem there is no sense that he feels a "monstrous debt" towards the Lake Poet.

This, as Haughton notes, might seem "monstrous" to some critics; and Heaney himself, as his lecture "The Makings of a Music" suggests, is well aware of how a benign, passive model of influence is at best incomplete.[137] "Feeling into Words" and "The Sense of Place" testify to Heaney's oppositional – or, more positively – dialogic critical mindset: craft vs technique, technique vs tradition, "lived, illiterate, and unconscious" vs "learned, literate, and conscious." If some of these oppositions are clearly weighted (technique above craft, for example) the balance of others is more tremulous: "technique" and "tradition" belong, in "Feeling into Words," to two different approaches to poetry, one auditory-aesthetic, one socio-historical. And in "The Makings of a Music: Reflections on Wordsworth and Yeats," a lecture delivered at Liverpool University in January 1978, Heaney returns to the two poets he had identified with technique and tradition in an attempt to reformulate and explicate this opposition, in a (gendered) metaphorical framework that allows the possibility of resolution.

This possible resolution comes through the lecture's central gambit, a pun on the multiple meanings of "versus": the lecture explores how a series of oppositions – such as Paul Valéry's "*les vers donnés* and *les vers calculés*" or "intellectual baggage" and "instinctual ballast" – may be "combined."[138] Instead of "versus" (opposition), Heaney traces the etymology of "verse" to the image of the poet as ploughman: "'Verse' comes from the Latin *versus* which could mean a line of poetry but could also mean the turn that a ploughman made at the head of the field as he finished one furrow and faced back into another."[139] Poetry, that is, becomes an art of returning (or indeed

Fosterage and Poetic Influence

reflection) rather than antagonistic opposition, and the "reflections" in the title of the lecture also resonate with the echo in the lines Heaney quotes from *The Prelude*: "My own voice cheered me, and, far more, the mind's / Internal echo of the imperfect sound."[140] (This idea of "a poem as a ploughshare that turns time / Up and over" [from the poem "Poets Chair"] will also recur throughout Heaney's work: it is used in the first of the Glanmore Sonnets – "Vowels ploughed into other: opened ground ... Now the good life could be to cross a field / And art a paradigm of earth new from the lathe / Of ploughs"; and then it provides the title to his 1998 collected poems, *Opened Ground*.)[141] This equation of writing and ploughing, and the related image of the boustrophedon – the writing style (used in ancient Greek and other inscriptions) that alternates direction on every line, and which translates as "turning like an ox while ploughing" – can thus also be seen as a guiding metaphor for Heaney's poetic development, with his tendency to return to the same critical and poetic ground, and as a metaphor which enables the combination of opposed forces.[142] As Corcoran argues, comparing Heaney and Muldoon, their "verses take the antagonistic sting from the hostility of opposition, from the word *versus* ('against'), even while recognizing that argument, disputation and competitiveness have their legitimate, even necessary, place in poetry."[143] In the particular context of "The Makings of a Music," the superscription of "return" over "opposition" in the understanding of "versus" allows Heaney to attempt to combine what is otherwise presented as irreconcilable: the influence of Wordsworth and Yeats.

The saving, combining, metaphor is sexual (ploughing has long had such euphemistic connotations). The voice that Heaney ventriloquizes for Wordsworth is a "passive" one, feminine, conciliatory, and attentive (in opposition to Yeats, who is active, masculine, and creative). Borrowing from *Timon of Athens*, Wordsworth is identified as a passive, poetic receiver for whom "poesy is as a gum which oozes / From whence 'tis nourished"; Yeats is someone for whom poetry is forced out of base material, for whom "the fire i' the flint / Shows not till it be struck."[144] The gendering of the two poets is explicit: in a discussion of Yeats's "The Long-Legged Fly," Heaney suggests that "The creative mind is astraddle silence. In my reading, the long-legged fly has a masculine gender and while there is a sense of incubation permeating the whole poem, there is also a sense of intent siring."[145] As Patricia Horton persuasively argues, by gendering their influence as feminine and masculine respectively, Heaney can "limit, absorb and transcend the influence of both, while also leaving the potential to effect some kind of reconciliation in the idea of a sexual union or marriage to be achieved in his own writing."[146]

For obvious and justified reasons, this gendering has been much criticized, leading Heaney to avoid such binary oppositions in later work.[147] Discussing "The Fire i' the Flint" in 2002, Heaney rather defensively notes that "These terms, of course, 'feminine presence' and 'masculine drive' and so on, are now regarded as sexist and suspect and agin' the law somehow. I was basing my distinctions on the biological facts of siring and mothering, you know?"[148] However, if he acknowledged the changing linguistic mores, he was more insistent on the continued value of the underlying distinction between a poetry of "waiting" and of "willful entering": "I used to think that I wasn't a willful writer, that willfulness was somehow agin' the laws of imagination which I took from Wordsworth and Keats and the Romantics: 'The spontaneous overflow of powerful feelings' ... 'If poetry comes not as naturally as leaves to the trees, it had better not come at all.'"[149]

The problems of identifying fixed masculine and feminine characteristics (or poetries) notwithstanding, it is clear that in this distinction in "The Fire i' the Flint" Heaney – unsurprisingly, given that he had written in the bog poems of *North* (1975) of poetry as a sacrifice to the Earth goddess Nerthus – sides with the feminine, "passive" Wordsworth, and the vowels that he had associated with his own "personal and Irish pieties" in the *Listener* article "1972": "I think of the personal and Irish pieties as vowels, and the literary awarenesses nourished on English as consonants. My hope is that the poems will be vocables adequate to my whole experience."[150] The "marriage" in "The Makings of a Music" is another attempt to find such an "adequate" "vocable." The gendered national distinctions from "1972" are not consistently upheld: instead, Heaney associates Wordsworth with "sturdy vowels," and concentrates – for an example of Wordsworth's music – on the word "diurnal" and on the line "Rolled around in earth's diurnal course," claiming that "Unless we can hear the power and dream in the line" we cannot "ever properly hear Wordsworth's music" (one could, however, choose to read those plosive ds as suggesting "sturdy consonants").[151]

What kind of poetic "influence" is being invoked – or fostered – here? Again, in this lecture, influence and poetic authority are based

Heaney's stated aim is "to see how far we can go in seeking the origins" of Wordsworth's and Yeats's "characteristic 'music,'" "to discover their "instinctual ballast," "What kinds of noise assuage him, what kinds of music pleasure or repel him, what messages the receiving stations of his senses are happy to pick up from the world around him and what ones they automatically block out."[152] The ear and not the eye, heart, skin, or spleen is the primary organ of poetry in this understanding.[153] In terms of the earlier distinction made in "Feeling into Words," the lecture approaches both poets from the perspective of a poetry of technique (with its emphasis on the vocal and aesthetic), rather than of tradition (poetry attentive to the historical moment): he stresses that "instinctual ballast" is *not* "intellectual baggage," "the way an individual talent has foraged in the tradition."[154] Heaney does, however, acknowledge the value of such foraging, arguing that "much of the illuminating work on Wordsworth" has come through "tracing and expressing the relevance and significance of ... literary influence," and approvingly remembering W.J. Harvey's reading of the opening lines of *The Prelude* as a reworking of *Paradise Lost* at a lecture while he was a student at Queen's.[155] It is clear, though, that something more than allusion-hunting is desired.

Heaney repeatedly presents Wordsworth as a poet of the musical ear, rather than the book-learned tradition: as a poet listening into (and enchanted by) Nature; as a poet who can then enchant others (and himself) with the sound of his voice; and as a boustrophedonic, pedestrian poet composing aloud while pacing back and forth. Wordsworth, we are told, presents a "version of composition as listening, as a wise passiveness, a surrender to energies that spring within the centre of the mind, not composition as an active pursuit by the mind's circumference of something already at the centre"; he imagines him "on the gravel path, to-ing and fro-ing like a ploughman up and down a field, his voice rising and falling between the measure of his pentameters."[156] Heaney is invoking a continuity of poetic practice stretching back millennia: Wordsworth not only becomes an emblem of that continuous tradition but also manages to relate culture once more to agriculture, to make the poet a worker of the land, like the diviners, thatchers, and farmers of Heaney's first two poetry collections. Wordsworth is, through this image, brought into Heaney's own paternal narratives: he becomes identified with the father in "Follower" who, while ploughing, enacts his own boustrophedonic turn – "with a single pluck // Of reins, the sweating team turned round / And back into the land. His eye / Narrowed and angled at the ground."[157] Even if he has "no spade to follow men" like his father or grandfather (in the famous lines from "Digging"), he can follow in the "ploughing" footsteps of Wordsworth (or Yeats, Frost, Kavanagh, Lowell, Miłosz, and all of those other poetic foster fathers).[158]

This identification with Wordsworth and use of him as an example of wise passiveness is, however, based on an important redirection of Wordsworth's energies, a strategic ethical – and perhaps ideological – misreading of Wordsworth. Heaney's description of Wordsworth's "version of composition as listening" derives from a discussion of a passage, quoted in part above, from Book I of *The Prelude*. This is certainly an image of the poet listening intently to himself: "My own voice cheered me, and, far more, the mind's / Internal echo of the imperfect sound; / To both I listened, drawing from them both / A cheerful confidence in things to come."[159] Despite the emphasis caused by Heaney's selection, Wordsworth is not only listening in, he is also speaking out (as he had been in "Feeling into Words"), in a religious context that Heaney does not acknowledge. Wordsworth describes how he "told," to the "open fields," "A prophesy: poetic numbers came / Spontaneously to clothe in priestly robe / A reno-vated spirit singled out, / Such hope was mine, for holy services."[160] The language is distinctly liturgical, and this passage is a clear exam-ple of Wordsworth treating the natural landscape as the stimulus for (Anglican) religiosity. It is striking that the "speaking out" element of Wordsworth's poetics is now silently elided; the poet's renovated "spirit" has a sacerdotal dimension and sense of vocation that Heaney completely ignores. Instead, Heaney reduces this external, religious stimulation to internal, psychological manifestations, to an internal mesmerism; it is Wordsworth's "mesmerized attention to the echoes and invitations within that constitutes his poetic confidence," and which creates the same effect on the reader, that "kind of sus-pended motion" in which one experiences "a prolonged moment of equilibrium during which we feel ourselves to be conductors of the palpable energies of earth and sky."[161]

This is a compelling description of much of Heaney's own early poetry, in which a tenebrous "suspended motion" is created. However, although he himself suggests that this "moment of equilib-rium" is an experience of "the one life of Joy," which in a poem like "Ruined Cottage" "imbues the music, is intoned by it, and can be

Fosterage and Poetic Influence

apprehended from it," Heaney does not address the same pantheistic divinity as Wordsworth.[162] Rather, in experiencing the "one life" we gain an awareness of our own inner selves; during this experience we "feel ourselves" as a lightening conductor, with the emphasis on the discovery of personal powers rather than on the mediation of the energies of the earth and sky. Where "Feeling into Words" had made communal Wordsworth's personal experience, here the inverse happens: the ability of poetry to have an external, communal effect is subtly replaced by a process of internal exploration and formation.

A similar secularization and re-direction of the energies of the earth and sky occurs in Heaney's description of William and Dorothy lying, listening, on the ground in John's Copse above Dove Cottage (taken from Dorothy's journal entry for 29 April 1802). Dorothy espouses their shared pantheism. They feel "at one" with each other, and with the landscape, and imagine that this is how they will continue after death: "William heard me breathing and rustling now and then but we both lay still and unseen by one another. He thought it would be as sweet thus to lie in the grave, and hear the *peaceful* sounds of the earth and just to know that our dear friends were near."[163] Dorothy's imagination links their breathing, rustling, and listening to the apprehension of death and of being at one with the "one life." Heaney changes the emphasis from what is being listened to (the peaceful sounds of the earth), to the act of listening itself, in doing so redirecting the pantheism of this passage, endowing it with sexual, pagan undertones. The breathing is rendered "erotic," the energies of the experience "chthonic." He suggests that "Dorothy and her brother are as intimate with process here [in the journal entry] as the babes in the wood, and if there is something erotic about the rustling of those leaves, there is something chthonic about the energies fundamental to the whole experience ... The couple listen, they surrender, the noise of the water and the voice of the air minister to them."[164] With the linking of the erotic and the chthonic Heaney seems to be suggesting more his own earlier fascination with bog bodies and fertility rites, in *Wintering Out* (1972) and *North* (1975), than the shared experience described in Dorothy's journal. Heaney offers an erotic reading of Dorothy's words, but then redirects this sexual energy downwards towards the earth below William and Dorothy: the Wordsworths become, to some extent, favoured lovers of the Earth goddess, being prepared for a sacrificial sexual union.

LOVE-ACTS AND KEYBOARDS

"The Makings of a Music" can be seen to mark the highpoint of Wordsworth's influence on Heaney's thinking about poetic composition and the manner in which poets might "foster" each other, or forge themselves in each other's image. In 1974, Heaney had already begun playfully to undermine any identification between himself and the Lake Poet: then he wrote what would become the third of the Glanmore Sonnets in *Field Work* in which his association of himself and his wife Marie with William and Dorothy is quickly rejected: "You're not going to compare us two ... ?"[165] From the late 1970s, Wordsworth becomes less consistently central to Heaney's poetics (this may be related to the fact Heaney tends to focus less on father-figures and models of filiation). Heaney does, however, continue to look for other exemplary poetic "authorities," but these often have a quite different tenor: his relationships with Lowell and Miłosz, say, are the negotiation with peers as well as precursors, and the growing influence of Dante encourages a Virgilian model of pilgrim and spiritual guide, without the filial pressures present in Heaney's own models of "followers."[166] It is not that Heaney's understanding of poetic influence changes utterly; his tendency, for example, to present influence through organic and especially fluvial metaphors, and as a process of healing or salving, persists in later essays and lectures.[167] Thus, in a 1989 essay on translation, "Earning a Rhyme," Heaney argues that "in spite of the real enough influence of ... cultural and political contexts ... the true anxiety and the true motivations of writing are much more inward, much more to do with *freshets* that start unexpectedly in moments of intent concentration and hope."[168] However, other metaphors also become common in Heaney's prose, in which "influence" is less a matter of fluvial informing than of an "imaginative resource" or part of the "inexhaustible literary community chest" (if not quite a "commodity," which can be "bought and sold, or stolen, just like everything else," as in Richard Marggraf Turley's discussion of how Bob Dylan uses Keats).[169]

In the 1985 essay "Envies and Identifications," for example, Heaney argues that "when poets turn to the great masters of the past, they turn to an image of their own creation, one which is likely to be a reflection of their own imaginative needs, their own artistic inclinations and procedures."[170] What is first encountered as "wonder" for the reader can develop into a long-lasting resource: the 1988 "Learning from Eliot" suggests that "what is to be learned from Eliot is the double-edged nature of poetic reality: first encountered as a strange fact of culture, poetry is internalized over the years until it becomes, as they say, second nature."[171] Similarly, in *Stepping Stones* Heaney describes the process in artisanal terms: "one of the gifts of poetry is to extend and bewilder, and another is to deepen and give purchase. The canonical stuff shouldn't be ignored, it's like the hoops on the contemporary barrel."[172] This resourceful model of influence is related, for Heaney, to the Yeatsian capacity for "self-renewal." His "capacity to rekindle the flame of his inspiration at different points of his life," Heaney argues in his selection of Yeats's poems, "appears as a triumphant fulfilment of his own prophetic belief in the mind's indomitable resource"; in the process, Yeats's work makes an "immense contribution ... to our general intellectual and imaginative resource."[173]

There is something "slightly predatory" about this treatment of other poets as resources, as Heaney admits in a discussion of Gerard Manley Hopkins.[174] Most brutally, this appears in Heaney's rewriting of Dante in *Field Work*. In "An Afterwards" Heaney uses the image (which he repeats in his own translation "Ugolino") of Ugolino in the ninth circle of hell "hasped and mounted ... on Archbishop Roger," "tooth in skull, tonguing for brain," as a metaphor for contemporary poets, competing over whose life is "Most dedicated and exemplary": this clearly undermines, as Corcoran argues, "any simply exemplary quality in the words 'dedicated' and 'exemplary.'"[175] Akin to cannibalism, influence is clearly not an inevitable good. The example of other poets can be "salutary," reading poetry can be a "revelation and confirmation" or a "beneficent experience," and poetry itself can be "a consolidating element"; but Heaney is also conscious of the possible emotional and creative dangers of influence.[176] He acknowledges how "stifling" Yeats's might have been (but wasn't); he describes how Auden, in seeking influence, "ached for relation"; and he also quotes Ted Hughes's opinion that "this whole business of influences is mysterious ... Influences just seem to make it more and more unlikely that a poet will write what he alone could write."[177]

The notable thing is that these are not problems Heaney himself faced: the fact that "everything inherits everything" was a burden for Hughes but not generally – in his criticism at least – for Heaney.[178]

How is this the case? How can Heaney maintain faith in the ability of poetry to "corroborate," "clarify, "and "verify," while still offering, in Fiona Stafford's words, "an honest response to genuine complexity"?[179] Stafford emphasizes the importance of memorizing the poems that are influencing you, of internalizing them. The communal, or indeed erotic, aspect may, however, be more important. In Heaney's discussion of Hopkins, the sense of predation is tempered slightly by the understanding that at the centre of the creative process there is "a love-act initiated by the masculine spur of delight" (whether one is entirely comforted by the idea of predation becoming procreation is another matter); this repeats the equation of influence and the "humanizing" effect of sexual encounter in "Feeling into Words."[180] If this feels slightly facetious (or 1970s hippy), it also aligns Heaney with an understanding of influence as a matter of "literary love rather than parricide," in Jonathan Bate's words: an understanding explicitly opposed to Bloom's theories.[181] And it is an understanding of influence that sees the poet not in an isolated, individual battle to the death against the poetic tradition and the burden of the past, but as part of a community (figured here as a loving or sexual relationship): a type of "immortal free-masonry," in Keats's words, or a series of conversations, in Michael Longley's, "with the dead great ones and with the living young."[182]

Heaney locates such an idea of community with the past in the work of Nadezhda Mandelstam, who suggested that "a real community is unshakeable, indubitable, and enduring ... It remains unaffected and whole even when the people united by it are already in their graves."[183] The idea can, however, also be traced back to Wordsworth – one thinks of the girl in "We Are Seven" unrepentantly claiming the continued presence of her dead siblings – or, more broadly, to the uncanny persistences and resurrections of the Gothic. A "communal" approach to the past is not a dismissal of the past's "otherness" or competing ways of approaching it. Instead it is an opening up of what would otherwise be repressed or festering in the present. As such, it is part of the "brave conversation" between contemporaries Corcoran describes, in which "the most painfully difficult matters of cultural authority ... are negotiated at the level of brave articulation and explicitation, rather than suppression or sublimation."[184] The oddity is that not all of these "contemporaries" are alive, and one of the things that has to be faced is their "pastness" (as well as their presence).[185]

So much is clear from the 1985 essay "Place, Pastness, Poems: A Triptych." Heaney suggests that "Language, too, is a time-charged medium": the temporality of language and poetry (the sense that it has "historically evolved") cannot be ignored. "No matter how much," he argues, "the poetic mind may wish to rid itself of temporal attachment and observe only its own pristine operations, its very employment of words draws it into the 'backward and abysm' of common human experience."[186] "Attachment" or the accretion of meaning is consistently troubled in this essay; the past is both given and uncanny. The word "'Old' drifted in the mind and senses," Heaney notes, "when you came upon mossed-over bits of delph or fragments of a clay pipe plugged up with mould. You took such things for granted yet they swam with a strangeness."[187] If all poetry is, as Frost suggests, and Harold Bloom makes explicit, "labyrinthine, not linear," then it is a labyrinth that has temporal as well as spatial dimensions; not least because it is created by a form of intertextual bricolage, with each brick of a different vintage.[188]

Heaney here explores how far the "commonality" of human experience can be stretched. He relies at one point in this essay on the catechistical understanding that your "neighbour ... is all mankind," but "neighbourliness" has always been complicated in Heaney's thinking (one need only think of the "neighbourly murder" in "Funeral Rites" in North).[189] And so elsewhere in "Place, Pastness, Poems: A Triptych" he suggests a shift away from such universalism, and relates the recalibration of poetic tradition to (in effect) postcolonial critiques and writing back of the "centre" (with Eliot, Joyce, and Pound rather forcedly standing in for a "periphery"). "No wonder," he suggests, "that it – the literary past, the tradition – became a category of our thinking at precisely that moment when, politically and culturally, the centre could not hold, when one place could no longer be proved more than another place, when St Louis and Dublin and Wyncote, Pennsylvania could each affirm its rights to it all and Paterson, New Jersey could, with equal and opposite confidence, proclaim an independence of it."[190] The desire to do away with colonial hierarchies, and the centre-periphery dynamic, is clear; however, one must be careful not to replace these with a different form of universalism (Gail McConnell has criticized the way in which Henry Hart reads Heaney's Catholicism as "a form of universalism, which is at once non-political and authentically nationalist") or an absolute insistence on the "local" along such lines.[191] This tendency in Heaney's thinking has been read as a celebration of "local truth," "redemptive localism," or "writ[ing] from your own 'home'" (through such approaches, for Fiona Stafford, a writer can become "a figure of international significance, contributing to the foundation of a better future").[192] Jahan Ramazani is right to strike a note of caution, though, noting that in his Nobel lecture "Heaney is leery, as he puts it, of 'being sentimental or simply fetishizing – as we have learnt to say – the local.'"[193]

What is perhaps important is that each place here – St Louis, Dublin, Wyncote – is able to claim rights on or proclaim independence from "it all," with no sense of inferiority; rather than cultural hierarchy or homogeneity, there is the possibility of infinite variousnesses of being (without one, by virtue of its "locality," being better than another). This variety might be extended to the process by which "the literary past, the tradition – became a category of our thinking" and to the question of whether there might be a distinctive Irish (or Northern Irish) way of creating literary "community" and forging or fostering beneficial, enabling, influential relationships; certainly Edna Longley, Paul Muldoon, Neil Corcoran, Shane Alcobia-Murphy, and Rachel Buxton have all argued for such an approach.[194] For Longley, "the term 'intertextuality' applied to Northern Irish poetry in a special, living sense: not as a theoretical dead letter, but as a creative dynamic working upon mechanisms of tradition and cultural definitions alike" which relies more on "a dispersed collectivity" than "the egotistical sublime."[195] Muldoon extends this beyond the North, and traces an "extraordinary appetite and aptitude for 'intertextuality'" back to the previous generation of Irish writers including Bowen, Beckett, Joyce; it may well be true that across the island of Ireland as a whole there is an obsession with the "irreversible presentness" of the past, rather than its "irreversible pastness."[196] Obliqueness to the English literary tradition is the crucial feature: the need to create both contemporary communities of writers, but also a shared and distinctive literary canon which might be personally and communally sustaining, and which would necessarily operate in a different way than it would for writers in London or Oxford, say (Heaney would often, in a nod to *The Great Gatsby*, write letters from "Oggsford" while professor there).

This is a process of claiming *some* rights on the English lyric, while also acknowledging the richness of an Irish lyric tradition; but it is also the development of literary community and – both more prosaically and crucially – literary friendships. Friendship is, perhaps, the ultimate tonic to Bloomian antagonism, and was a recurring theme of Heaney's criticism. As he notes in *Stepping Stones*, "You wake to different things in yourself and the world just by coming alive in the company of different friends," and he "was as susceptible to the mythic Ted Hughes as to the mordant Seamus Deane. I didn't feel pressured by him, I felt extended, awakened, called upon to take in more of the Northern experience we both shared."[197] Friendship, too, awakens, extends, and opens prospects; and the Wordsworth circle offers Heaney a key example of the importance of friendship to poetic fruition. In his manuscript lecture on *The Prelude*, Heaney identifies the conditions in which Wordsworth's poem can grow: "Through his enlivening and confirming friendship with Coleridge, through the nurture and enhancements of his relationship with his sister Dorothy, his creative powers were opening and asking for some great theme."[198] Wordsworth and Coleridge "found constant intellectual and imaginative excitement and sympathy in one another's company"; only after he met Coleridge did Wordsworth "br[eak] into a new idiom."[199] In place of anxiety about isolation or "eccentricity," friendship leads to a sense of (serious) playful, communal improvisation of a tradition; it leads to poetic growth, ambition, and flexibility. Heaney was far from the first, of course, to foreground the importance of Wordsworth and Coleridge's friendship. However, such examples offer a quick antidote to the antagonistic excesses of Bloom, and also help remind us that Heaney's own poetic career was in large part a succession of supportive, challenging friendships: with Michael McLaverty, Michael and Edna Longley, Derek Mahon, David Hammond, Philip Hobsbaum, Hugh MacDiarmid, Norman MacCaig, Paul Muldoon, Ted Hughes, Robert Lowell, Czesław Miłosz, Helen Vendler, Anne Stevenson (the list could go on for some pages).

This is not just a matter of being avuncular. One of Heaney's repeated images from the 1980s onwards, derived from Osip Mandelstam, is of influence as a "keyboard of classical reference."[200] When it is a communal experience, though, it might be music played by a full orchestra, jazz band, or rag-bag group of session musicians: the making of music, rather than (*a capella*) *a* music. Other poets' work has then at least the potential to be, like Caliban's "noises," "sounds, and sweet airs that give delight and hurt not."[201] As Edna Longley comments about Ciaran Carson, it is "relevant to his aesthetic that, being an exponent and interpreter of Irish traditional music, Carson views 'tradition' as always contemporary, always improvised in the present on a unique occasion, yet transmitted down long, multiple, intricate chains from the past."[202] The musical or theatrical parallels take the isolating sting out of the (Romantic) poet, alone with his or her "original" muse and genius. Fosterage, friendship, collaboration: these are all models of how Heaney negotiates poetic tradition (as they are for Wordsworth). They do not have to be solely optimistic however: there can still be competition, violence, and dissension (as anyone who has been in a band or orchestra will know), but they can lead to a more complex, multivocal, and – perhaps – a more haunting tune.

3

Places and Displacements:
Haunted Ground

REFLECTED AND DIMINISHED

"Yank," an uncollected poem by Heaney published in 1969, recounts a return of the native, but one that is in conversation with Wordsworth's poem "The Brothers" rather than Hardy's novel. There are no reddle men here; indeed, there is nobody at all. The poem was published in *Everyman*, "an annual religio-cultural review" from the Servite Priory in Benburb, County Tyrone – on whose editorial board Heaney sat at the time. "Kennedy," who lives on the mainland, rows an "old man" (the "Yank" of the title) back in a currach to the island he left when he was eighteen years old. The relationship between the two is, from the first, combative: "Kennedy thought he'd test him from the start / And never slackened, but the old arm shot out / Imperiously." The point is that the "Yank" still remembers how to land safely on the island, even after being away for many years: "Good God, man, / Is this your first time on the island?"[1]

The question of how well an emigrant knows or remembers the place in which they grew up is also at the heart of "The Brothers." This poem stages a meeting between the priest of Ennerdale and Leonard, a native of the district returning after twenty years away at sea. They had once been able to assess the landscape as a cultural and social space of shared memory: "We have no need of names and epitaphs; / We talk about the dead by our fire-sides. / And then, for our immortal part, *we* want / No symbols, Sir, to tell us that plain tale."[2] But Leonard, with the intervention of passing years, can no longer trust the accuracy of his remembering: "He had found / Another grave, near which a full half hour / He had remain'd, but, as he gaz'd, there grew / Such a confusion in his memory, / That he began to doubt."[3] Once you are no longer a (naive) inhabitant of place, you are, to some extent, "lost," as Leonard is when he "lifted up his eyes, / And looking round he thought that he perceiv'd / Strange alteration wrought on every side / Among the woods and fields, and that the rocks, / And the eternal hills, themselves were chang'd."[4] The changed landscape is an over-charged metaphor for Leonard's own altered circumstances: the priest's description of two springs that had "bubbled side by side" until one was destroyed by a "rent crag" in a lightning storm is clearly meant to be read as prefiguring, in Wordsworth's drawn-out telling of the history, the revelation of the death of Leonard's brother David, found dead at the foot of "the Pillar."[5] The question remains open, however, as to whether there is actually some (mystical) connection between Leonard's life experience and the landscape he left, but the change is necessarily unsettling: nothing, especially not memory, is "everlasting."

The nostalgic and sentimental view of coherent and generous community suggested by Wordsworth's poem is missing from Heaney's. Here, both arrival and departure are marked by a sense of "diminishment": standing on the shore, Kennedy hears "his voice diminished in his ear."[6] Neither Kennedy nor the old man are "locals"; both are to some extent tourists, lured back not by the hope of community but by a "ghost world" which presents them with an "undisturbed green desolation." The dynamic of "Yank" is not the tension between the naive and the sentimental: rather it is between the living and the dead, the present and the absent. It is a clearance poem, describing a ruined rural landscape imbued with the ghostly presence of the past in the manner of Oliver Goldsmith's "Deserted Village" or (a poem Heaney would later translate) Sorley MacLean's "Hallaig."[7] In place of the crowds who had lined up to cheer the Yank off, there is a dilapidated house, with a mildewed roof, rotten door that rips off its hinges as they enter, and no-one to hear his prayer ("God bless and God rest my father"). The father figure might be absent, but he is also restless: he is faced through a form of tentative, rehearsed embodiment, as the Yank puts out "his arms almost from wall to wall / As if to shoulder an antique yoke."[8] But this measuring of himself against an inherited burden is immediately negated as the old man rejects the verisimilitude of the ruin to his memory: "Our house was a bigger house / than this ... I guess it's caving in." It certainly is by the end of their visit: they leave the door "collapsed" behind them.

Places and Displacements   111

The poem, like the house, is rough and slightly creaky: that Kennedy is "well shocked that sixty years / Unsettled neither certainty nor sand" shows the poem's hand (the shifting relationship between certainty, memory, and landscape) too clearly.[9] Its loose-limbed (Wordsworthian) blank verse does, however, allow for a condensing of narrative combined with numinous, complex dialogue. When the Yank exclaims, "No wonder they all left. There's no life here," the apparent circularity of his thinking does in effect give the possibility of life back to the deserted island: if "life" had been absent before the people departed, then "life" is distinct from human presence and it might exist (in some form or another, desirable or not) in the absence of a population. With the departure of the human residents, however, the memory of the place cannot be retained, and there are multiple ways in which remembering fails. It was "reckoned too dull / For photographs"; the hill, blocking the sky, surely "was never steep as that before"; the measuring of the old man's arm-span to the walls is unsuccessful; and, as they are rowing away, "the unpictured hill" is "reflected and [once more] diminished / In Kennedy's unwatching oarsman's eye." Kennedy and the old man drink "the whiskey" in the ruined cottage in what is, the definite article suggests, a ceremonial, prepared ritual, which turns out to be one of apologetic dejection rather than celebratory homecoming: "I'm sorry, fellow, to have dragged you out / To a place like this."[10]

"Yank," like "The Brothers," is a poem of return that is clearly also a poem of departure, of never needing to go back again: and it expresses the truth that any return to the past risks diminishing or destroying it. Looking backwards is a recurring, and troubling, preoccupation for Heaney throughout the late 1960s and early 1970s: the "backward look" or the "last look" which would record and fix for posterity contains within it the sense of disappearance, or diminution.[11] The poem "Last Look," published in *Outposts* in Spring 1968, imagines a man standing with his back to the road facing onto (across? through?) "the scraggy fields"; to the poet "He could have been ghost already."[12] In "Bachelor Deceased," a poem in memory of Pat McGuckian (a cousin of Heaney's father) published in the *Honest Ulsterman* later that year, the "last look" is that of the bereaved: "I took my last look at him on a dry day / When the cobbles in the yard looked scrubbed as eggs. / And I heard he'd left by the back again // Leaving the door open as ever, the light / Blazing out all night in the empty house."[13] By "Land" (published in

Wintering Out in 1972) the look is clearly that of someone preparing to depart (in "Last Look" it could refer to both the bereaved and the departed): the speaker ritualistically "composed habits for those acres / so that my last look would be / neither gluttonous nor starved. / I was ready to go anywhere."[14] These images will recur throughout Heaney's work. The trope of departure in "Land" is reimagined in Heaney's retellings of the Sweeney myth, and especially the Sweeney Redivivus poems of *Station Island* (and is also interrogated by Paul Muldoon's *Why Brownlee Left*). The encounter with a figure staring out into a field, meanwhile, recurs in "Last Look" in *Station Island* (a complex development of this earlier poem) and "Field of Vision" in *Seeing Things*. The image of the ruined homestead is another that, as we shall see in the next chapter, gains further accretions and resonances in *The Haw Lantern* and *Seeing Things*; Heaney's final collection, *Human Chain*, meanwhile, features a translation of perhaps the most famous Irish poetic "backward look," "Fil súil nglais," Colmcille turning his "grey eye" back to Ireland as he departs for Scotland, never to return.[15]

It would be too easy to read this focus on "last looks" and leavings in biographical terms: Heaney preparing for, and then justifying, his own departure from Northern Ireland. Instead, a broader exploration of dislocation is taking place here, in terms of personal affections and rootedness and also ideas of cultural belonging: one might think of the "Backward Look" of Gaelic culture in *Wintering Out* with its ambiguous relationship to the yellow bittern that escapes over "wall-steads" and disappears into the "gleanings and leavings / in the combs / of a fieldworker's archive."[16] The emphasis on "looking" and rupture in these poems holds, I would argue, the promise of epiphanies: the sense of giving attention and so having something wondrous revealed unto you. However, this is epiphany replayed as threat rather than promise: what the "Yank" discovers is a ghostly absence ("no life" or diminishment) rather than the "overlife" Heaney becomes fond of in his later criticism; the pilgrimage lessens rather than expands the (returning) pilgrim.[17] "Yank" is, then, a form of anti-epiphany, in which the return reveals how much has been lost. "Land," meanwhile, offers a different model: here epiphany might be a trap. As the poet lies with his ear "in this loop of silence," he reminds himself not to be surprised "to find myself snared, swinging / an ear-ring of sharp wire."[18] Presence, belonging, and attentiveness might lead to epiphany; they might also lead to capture.

Heaney does not, in other words, blindly repeat the "bad faith" of a Romantic "return to origins"; rather, he probes and explores the nature of such a return. When you "step through origins," as "Kinship" suggests, you do not find certainty, but a "bog floor" which "shakes" and the "unstopped mouth / of an urn, a moon-drinker, / not to be sounded / by the naked eye": what emerges is an unfathomable depth of peat, the mouth of the death that might, "unstopped," begin to speak, and the threat of being engulfed.[19] When this fear of loss or entrapment is related back to the Wordsworthian trope of landscape-as-memory, something interesting happens. Leonard's discovery in "The Brothers" is that his memory cannot be trusted, in the same way that the landscape cannot be trusted to remain exactly the same (there is "strange alteration" in both). Similarly, the reader of "Yank" is aware of the irony of the claim that sixty years unsettle neither "certainty nor sand" – both are necessarily shifting. Both poems are moving away from the idea of memory-as-revelation, of the perfect retrieval of memories from some internal warehouse (or indeed irruption intact of the past into the present). Instead, "memory" becomes an active process, a form of (half-)creation of the past by the present, a willed encounter: Kennedy and the old man "close with the ghost world that had lured them there," but they are very much ghosts of their own creation.

I have discussed elsewhere how changing models of memory can be traced through Heaney's bog poems (and related to contemporaneous shifts in theories of memory); I focus here, however, on how memory – and in particular the "ghostliness" of memory – serves to disturb any sense of place as being entirely nurturing.[20] Memory, when rendered in "language" as "epitaph," can be, like Wordsworthian "language," a "counter-spirit," "unremittingly and noiselessly at work to derange, to subvert, to lay waste, to vitiate, and to dissolve."[21] This claim comes from the third of Wordsworth's "Essays on Epitaphs," a riposte – like "The Brothers" – to the need for memorialization to take written, linguistic form. An earlier unpublished poem by Heaney, "Obituary," is clearly written in response to Wordsworth's repeated musings on "epitaphs": it ends with the exclamation "Epitaphs are irrelevant / To a grassy grave that boasts no headstone."[22] But this "irrelevance" is ambiguous: it calls into question whether language is or is not necessary for commemoration, whether the dead are being actively remembered or silently forgotten. One of Heaney's touchstones through the 1970s

114 This Strange Loneliness

is Eliot's "Little Gidding" in which the "use of memory" is seen as the "liberation / From the future as well as the past": "See, now they vanish, / The faces and places, with the self which, as it could, loved them, / To become renewed, transfigured, in another pattern."[23] Memory is not, however, a tool; this idea has too much of the "certainty and sand" about it. Perhaps the more pertinent question is what memory is using *us* for, and how it informs that "love of a country" and "attachment to our own field of action" (what Heaney calls "the sense of place"), and the relationship between imagination and place.

THE SENSE OF PLACE

A brief return to "The Sense of Place." Heaney's relationship to his lectures was often slightly antagonistic – in a letter to Michael Longley while working on "The Sense of Place" he describes it as "only a time-waster" – and Heaney was apt to amend, revise, or respond to his lectures and essays in later critical pieces: "The Sense of Place" notably gets displaced by the 1984 lecture "Place and Displacement."[24] "The Sense of Place" presents different ways of responding to the Irish landscape, that "manuscript," as Heaney quotes John Montague, "we have lost the skill to read."[25] Heaney focuses on the work of Patrick Kavanagh, John Hewitt, and Montague himself; and he argues for the existence of two ways in which the land is known and "cherished," one that is "lived, illiterate and unconscious, the other learned, literate and conscious."[26] If there is, once more, a hint of the Schillerian distinction between the naive and the sentimental, there is also an appeal to the metaphysical, spiritual, and religious over the scientific. The place name "Ardee," for example, "succinctly marries the legendary and the local"; elsewhere Heaney pays heed to "a marvellous or a magical view of the world" in which flora has "a religious force, especially if we think of the root of the word in *religare*, to bind fast," and also to a "sacral vision of place."[27]

The overarching aim of the lecture – an aim that has attracted much criticism – is to celebrate a reimagining of the Irish landscape on quasi-mystical, transcendental grounds that are an expression of an immanent or latent Irish "nation." Community and a communal "we" are central to the lecture, with all the attendant ambiguous acts of inclusion and exclusion. Discussing the places that Yeats made famous in his poetry, Heaney suggests that

Places and Displacements

Irrespective of our creed or politics, irrespective of what culture
or subculture may have coloured our individual sensibilities, our
imaginations assent to the stimulus of the names, our sense of
the place is enhanced, our sense of ourselves as inhabitants not
just of a geographical country but of a country of the mind is
cemented. It is this feeling, assenting, equable marriage between
the geographical country and the country of the mind, whether
that country of the mind takes its tone unconsciously from a
shared oral inherited culture, or from a consciously savoured
literary culture, or from both, it is this marriage that constitutes
the sense of place in its richest possible manifestation.[28]

Even the Celtic Twilight is redeemed since "the movement was the
beginning of a discovery of confidence in our own ground, in our
place, in our speech, English and Irish."[29] Kavanagh and Montague
are contrasted, meanwhile, for their differing management of com-
munality and individuality: Kavanagh's place names are "posts" that
"fence out a personal landscape"; Montague's are "sounding lines,
rods to plumb the depths of a shared and diminished culture. They are
redolent not just of his personal life but of the history of his people,
disinherited and dispossessed."[30] John Hewitt's (Protestant) sense of
place, however, is, as was the case in "Feeling into Words," cast in the
terms of a masculine usurpation of feminine belonging and rootedness
(but also a laudable double-vision): "Hewitt is bound to his region not
through the figure of a mythological queen in her aspect as spirit of
the place but through the charter given by a historical king. His vision
is bifocal, not, as in Montague's case, monocular."[31]

In the context of this balancing of Catholic sacrality and Protestant
legalism, within a putatively shared sense of a "country of the mind,"
Heaney introduces his opposition between Wordsworth and the
natural historian Robert Lloyd Praeger. Praeger, from Holywood,
County Down, and from a Unitarian background, co-founded the
monthly *Irish Naturalist* (1892–1924); was director of the National
Library; served as president of the Royal Irish Academy, An Taisce,
the Royal Zoological Society of Ireland, the Dublin Naturalist's Field
Club, and many other societies; and published an extremely popular
autobiographical account of his botanical travels around Ireland,
The Way That I Went, in 1937.[32] It is this last that Heaney criticizes:
he claims Praeger's eye in the book "is regulated by laws of aesthetics, by the disciplines of physical geography, and not, to borrow a

phrase from Wordsworth, by the primary laws of our nature, the laws of feeling."[33] Praeger is missing the "feeling for their place that steadies [Patrick Kavanagh and John Montague] and gives them a point of view"; in other words, Praeger lacks, in Heaney's estimation, what Wordsworth was "perhaps the first man to articulate": "the nurture that becomes available to the feelings through dwelling in one dear perpetual place" (he then suggests that "Michael" presents the image of "active nature, humanized and humanizing").[34] For Heaney, Wordsworth's "laws of feeling" on which this sense of place is based must always have priority over Praeger's "laws of aesthetics" and "disciplines of physical geography."[35]

Heaney's criticism of Praeger rests on the description of the Tyrone countryside in *The Way That I Went*, in which he dismisses the county as a "curiously negative tract," containing the Sperrin Mountains, "among the least inspiring of Irish mountains," and little else.[36] This area is close to home for Heaney – the parish of Bellaghy in which he grew up lies between Lough Neagh ("the only lake to be mentioned in connection with Tyrone") and the Sperrins – and the criticism is apparently felt close to the bone.[37] Heaney, selectively reading Praeger's passage, defends his home-place: "The clue to Praeger's sense of place comes a couple of paragraphs later when he moves into Fermanagh and declares it 'more picturesque and from many points of view more interesting.' His point of view is visual, geological, not like Kavanagh's, emotional and definitive. The Tyrone landscape, for him, is not hallowed by associations that come from growing up and thinking oneself in and back into the place."[38] There is something "parochial" and understandable about Heaney's defence of Tyrone (and Heaney writes elsewhere of Kavanagh as the great defender of the Irish "parish" as a site of value and meaning).[39] In "The Sense of Place," however, Heaney perhaps does Praeger an injustice. Praeger's values were not simply "visual": he was a scientist and generally restricted by the fact that he was writing for the international scientific community; but he was also emotionally, politically, and personally attached to the landscapes he described (and in particular the Irish landscape). As he proudly states in the first paragraph of *The Way That I Went*, "the way that I went was an Irish way ... It was from the beginning a way of flowers and stones and beasts ... we are ourselves creations of nature, and spend our lives amid natural objects."[40]

Praeger also has a shared interest with Heaney in the naming of places, and the complex relationship between name and place. When

Praeger was working "closer to home," as Seán Lysaght has noted, "we get flower names in association with place, where the botanical names are felt to constitute the area's identity."[41] In his lecture, meanwhile, Heaney celebrates the fact that "We are dwellers, we are namers, we are lovers, we make homes and search for our histories," and, importantly, begins the lecture by introducing the genre of *dinnseanchas*.[42] *Dinnseanchas*, or "place-name lore," was a common literary genre in the Middle Irish period that would "interpret the component elements of a name and the traditional lore associated with it in order to access, understand, and proclaim the essence of a specific feature of the environment" and that now offers a sense of how landscape intertwines with "reality," "being," and name.[43] Some of the poems in Heaney's *Wintering Out*, including the well-known "Anahorish" and "Broagh," offer a modern interpretation of this tradition, while in "The Sense of Place" this genre offers a cultural continuity to Heaney's quest for a "country of the mind." This is a shared interest: in his discussion of Tyrone, Praeger himself engages in some basic *dinnseanchas,* tracing back through the etymology of Tyrone to "*Tír Eóghain*, Owen's territory," which "like Inishowen … takes its name from Eóghan or Owen, son of Niall of the Nine Hostages, a great man of the fifth century."[44]

In opposition to Praeger's "aesthetic" approach, Heaney uses Wordsworth to represent a continuous, rooted identification with (and reimagining of) place. Heaney derives this sense of place primarily from "Michael," in which Wordsworth emphasizes the emotional relationship between humanity, or the human person, and nature, suggesting how walking the hills "had impress'd / So many incidents upon [Michael's] mind / Of hardship, skill or courage, joy or fear," and that the fields and hills which "had laid / Strong hold on his affections, were to him / A pleasurable feeling of blind love, / The pleasure which there is in life itself."[45] This is only half the story of "Michael," however: after the death of Michael and his wife, Isabel – with their son Luke fallen into "dissolute" ways and "ignominy and shame" in the city, and having fled "to seek a hiding-place beyond the seas" – their cottage is sold:

The Cottage which was nam'd The Evening Star
Is gone, the ploughshare has been through the ground
On which it stood; great changes have been wrought
In all the neighbourhood, yet the Oak is left

> That grew beside their Door; and the remains
> Of the unfinished Sheep-fold may be seen
> Beside the boisterous brook of Green-head Gill.[46]

Rootedness is valued in "Michael," but with the understanding that uprootedness – "great changes," the turning of the plough – is a constant threat. The emblematic quality of the cottage – "The Evening Star" – exists only in memory; what is left is the oak (a symbol of continuity), and an unfinished Sheepfold. If, as Jonathan Bate argues, "Michael" is "a new kind of pastoral, stripped of the Schillerian 'sentimental,' the sophisticated and self-conscious," the scars of that "stripping" and of the tenuous nature of this pastoral are clearly evident.[47]

The end of "Michael" can be read as an emotional plea to the reader to continue building that idealized, rooted sense of belonging: to follow the star that now only resides within you. Also lurking in the background, however, is the figure of the emigrant Luke, who may or may not one day return, like Leonard in "The Brothers," or Heaney's "Yank." The rootedness, the continuation of that dwelling community, is not certain, and neither is the passing down of knowledge and experience from one generation to another (that positive model of influence outlined in the previous chapter): the son can always reject the inheritance offered by the father, and the younger generation betray the older (as is the case for Michael, "bound in surety for his brother's son," and having to give up "half his substance" to pay his nephew's forfeits).[48]

Even within Heaney's entirely positive reading of the poem there are ways in which he distinguishes and distances himself from Wordsworth. The sense of place Heaney derives from "Michael" is actually a diminution of Michael's own experiences. For Wordsworth the natural landscape, and the quasi-spiritual "Nature," are agents of a deity. In *The Prelude* the natural landscape contains and is worked upon by "spirits" or "Nature," forces which are inherently religious.[49] "Nature" in *The Prelude* inspires and educates the poet, with the end goal of "love": it "first / Peopled my mind with beauteous forms or grand / And made me love them."[50] "Nature" is, in effect, the real presence of God in the natural landscape, and Wordsworthian epiphanies come when "Nature" reveals its divine essence.[51] Alan G. Hill argues that Wordsworth's attitude to Nature shares the emphasis of Comenius's hierarchies in *Pansophiae prodromus* (1639): "Knowledge emulates nature; knowledge imitates nature; knowledge

Places and Displacements

is the daughter of nature. And no less true is the following: there can be no nature without God; nature emulates God; nature is the daughter of God; nature imitates God."[52] By this mystical tradition, when as a boy Michael, for example, "felt the power / Of Nature, by the gentle agency / Of natural objects," he was also feeling the presence of God.[53]

Heaney, however, turns the religious element of Michael's experience into a psychological event (in a manner reminiscent of his rewritings of Wordsworth in *Death of a Naturalist*). For Heaney, the passage as a whole exhibits a "temperate understanding of the relationship between a person and his place, of the way the surface of the earth can be accepted into and be a steadying influence upon the quiet depths of the mind."[54] With a Jungian gesture, Heaney contrasts the "*depths* of the mind" with Wordsworth's "Nature," which is reduced to "the surface of the earth" with no immortal spirit or force at work within it. Heaney, in other places the consummate poet of digging through the "surface of the earth" with his poetic spade, here rejects Wordsworth's religio-mystical relationship with the physical landscape in favour of an emphasis on the psychological and cultural benefits of a "humanized and humanizing" – and not spiritual and spiritualizing – Nature.

This is perhaps an example of the way in which, for Gail McConnell, Heaney's poetics is both attracted to, and moves away from, the redemptive, salvific promises of Christianity.[55] Heaney is at pains, after all, to celebrate the vestigial traces of a "magical view of the world," "a diminished structure of lore and superstition and half-Christian thought and practice," as well as the ability for poetry to give meaning to a place: the names of the Yeatsian poetic landscape, for example, "now live in the imagination, all of them stir us to responses other than the merely visual, all of them are instinct with the spirit of a poet and his poetry."[56] Equally, however, it might suggest Heaney's resistance to a particularly "Protestant" manner of conferring meaning onto the landscape. Michael's spiritual relationship with place becomes, in Heaney's reading, atavistic, cultural, and pastoral; "sense of place" is seen as an act of cultural possession, which has accrued meaning and value over many generations. For Heaney, Michael's relationship with "place," like John Hewitt's, is tendentiously and tentatively based on colonization rather than on birthright or divine sanction; Hewitt's "cherishing of the habitat is symptomatic of his history, and that history is the history of the colonist, who, much like

Wordsworth's Michael, has grown to be native to his fields through the accretions of human memory and human associations."[57]

This "idea of country" shared by Michael and Hewitt is not, clearly, one shared by Heaney, who had spent so much of the earlier lecture celebrating the numinous, mysterious, and sacramental (and who, as Edna Longley argues, tends to use the "superior strengths of nature/nativeness" to oppose the planted bawns of the colonist).[58] Thus, the final gesture of the lecture, to appeal to the "primary laws of our nature" and suggest that "when we look for the history of our sensibilities ... it is to what [Professor J.C. Beckett] called the stable element, the land itself, that we must look for continuity," is one which on its own terms is peculiar, if not tongue-in-cheek.[59] For the "land," in Heaney's poetry, is often a bogland: it is an unstable, "bottomless" landscape; that "quaking sod" which "gives no footing," as Daniel Corkery has it.[60] If the "land itself" is "the terrain of nationalist struggle" (as Kate Trumpener argues about Britain), then in Ireland that struggle inevitably becomes (in Heaney's description of Goya's painting *Riña a garrotazos* in "Summer 1969") "that holmgang / Where two beserks club each other to death / For honour's sake, greaved in a bog, and sinking."[61]

Perhaps, though, it is not "place" but "principle" that is at stake here, what Seamus Deane describes, in his analysis of the French Revolution, as a conflict between Burkean "local attachment" and a Jacobin emphasis on "sympathy" rather than "sensibility." For Deane, Jacobinism takes as its country "the world and its race mankind," and so "devotes the whole strength of its feeling to a principle, not to a place."[62] Jacobin art, with which Deane identifies Wordsworth and Hazlitt, then relies on the belief in the sharing of "common humanity": "Feeling rises in the self but can be transmitted to others. It is thereby generalized or rendered universal. This is the definition of the work of the imagination. Thought so generalized is reason. Feeling and reason are complementary to each other, not opposites. Each entails a communication from the self to others; each is a mode of finding that which is basically human in the writer and in his audience."[63] This is the principle of "humanization" that Heaney lauds in Wordsworth; Praeger and Hewitt fail, in these terms, not because of a lack of attention to local detail, but because of their inability to translate that to a general or universal sense of "common humanity" that combines emotion (feeling) with reason (it is a "sense," rather than an understanding, of place, after all).

Places and Displacements

121

The emphasis on "sharing," rather than claiming possession, is important and suggests a major difference between Heaney's and Wordsworth's poems about place names (or "Poems on the Naming of Places"). Wordsworth's poems grouped under this title in the second volume of the 1800 *Lyrical Ballads* lay claims on the landscape, naming rocks and dells and summits for his friends and family: these are acts of ecolectic possession, marking the landmarks' significance (and claiming them publicly) for a domestic group. There is no anxiety about such acts of possession, although there might be about the liberties that allow them. The fourth poem, "Point Rash-Judgement," commemorates the self-admonishment of Wordsworth and "two beloved friends" (Sara and Samuel Taylor Coleridge) for presumptively judging a man fishing in a lake rather than joining in the harvest: "We all cried out, that he must be indeed / An idle man, who thus could lose a day / Of the mid harvest."[64] The Wordsworths too are bunking off harvest: the privilege of their position almost becomes clear to them and the reader, and the anxiety this causes is buried once more only by the act of naming, and by turning the event into a lesson.

Questions of, and anxieties about, right and ownership are central to Heaney's place name poems in *Wintering Out*, "Anahorish," "Broagh," "Toome." These do not name (or claim) places but, in the manner of *dinnseanchas*, retell a story of how that place name came about. These acts of lexicographical excavation are in part exclusionary: in "Broagh," Heaney famously describes the "last / gh the strangers found / difficult to manage."[65] As Seán Lysaght notes, here Heaney is courting an attitude to "naming and identification" which is "tribal and territorial, implying that the place and its name have a peculiar flavour that can only be savoured and safeguarded by the natives"; Lysaght contrasts this with "The Peninsula" (in *Door into the Dark*), which adopts a "more universal" approach, "taking its cue from geology and natural history, and transcending the confines of sectarian or cultural disputes."[66] Neither of these attitudes to naming is rigid, however: they are both partial, and unsettle each other. "Broagh," for all its exclusion of those "strangers," questions any claim of right. Not only does it enact the particular linguistic mix of Northern Ireland in its end words ("rigs" from Scots, "docken" from Elizabethan English [retained by "colonial lag" in Scottish and Hiberno-English], "pad" from Dutch, "ford" from Norse), but it acknowledges that linguistic mixing also has its political and violent dimensions, and cannot be separated off into a reified ahistorical realm.[67]

Once you highlight etymology and the deep history of language (the fact that language is a "time charged medium"), complex interactions occur. Hearing "*Broagh, / its low tattoo / among the windy boor-trees*," one cannot ignore that "tattoo" in this meaning is a military word, introduced into English from Dutch in the 1680s. Nor does the "boortree" offer much hope. For the rarer linguistic elements, Heaney draws heavily on Professor John Braidwood's 1969 lecture "The Ulster Dialect Lexicon," given while he was a colleague of Heaney's at Queen's; as Braidwood suggests, "in Ulster-Scots an elder-tree is a *bourtree*, and the belief persists around Ballymena that this was the tree of which the Cross was made, its stunting being recalled in the description of the bourtree as 'ever bush and never tree.'"[68] If it is true, in Andrew Murphy's words, that "local naming bears within itself a kind of compressed narrative of local history," and that "Broagh" offers, in Neil Corcoran's words, "a paradigm of a certain kind of inclusiveness" (since the line is not drawn between the communities in Northern Ireland, but around them), the poems also present a compressed narrative of dislocation, rupture, and violence.[69]

Heaney adopts Wordsworth as a model for a sense of place, however, despite all such historical problems with "naming"; and he uses Wordsworth to propose a relationship with the land that is not tied to appropriation or colonialism (despite the "Poems on the Naming of Places"). By introducing a landscape that is viewed primarily as something that is "humanized and humanizing" rather than a place of political contention (atavistically rooted community versus opportunistic colonizer), Heaney suggests the possibility of a relationship with land that is a matter of principle rather than habitation. To hope for the outcome of the end of the lecture, in which "land itself" is a "stable element" below or above political signification, is, as the rest of the lecture (including the association of Wordsworth and Hewitt) makes clear, to place to one side the tendency of humanity to name, claim, and possess land. It is, as the 1978 BBC Radio 4 broadcast "Omphalos" discussed in my introduction suggests, a matter of erotics rather than politics: "Broagh, the Long Rigs, Bell's Hill; Brian's Field, the Round Meadow, the Demesne; each name was a kind of love made to each acre. And saying the names like this distances the places, turns them into what Wordsworth once called a prospect of the mind."[70] The introduction of the "prospect of the mind" suggests how far the relationship to place is part of Heaney's broader utopian projections, of a means of identifying with a place – and creating a "future" – that is not bound by political discord.[71] Even if a resort to the land as the element of continuity is necessarily doomed (is there anything more political than land – or borders – in Ireland?), that does not make it any less valuable for Heaney as the site and aim of utopian hopes, of a personal "country of the mind" that could be separated from geographical and political space.

"THE GLANMORE SONNETS" AND THE RETURN OF THE DEAD

This attempted creation of a distinct, utopian space is of interest to me partly because of how it relates to Heaney's most "Wordsworthian" series of poems, the "Glanmore Sonnets" in *Field Work*. In this sequence, the Heaneys' life in Glanmore is viewed against, and overwrites, the Wordsworths' experience of living in Grasmere: it is a "Seamus Heaney Lives Here" response to his own radio broadcast on Dove Cottage. The poems are explicit about this act of identification: Heaney begins a comparison between himself and Marie and Dorothy and William – "I won't relapse / From this strange loneliness I've brought us to. / Dorothy and William –" – only for his wife to stop him – "she interrupts: / 'You're not going to compare us two...?'"[72] (There might be a nod here also to Beckett's *Waiting for Godot*, when Vladimir exclaims "Christ! What has Christ got to do with it? You're not going to compare yourself to Christ!" and Estragon bathetically responds "All my life I've compared myself to him.")[73]

Heaney's trip to Dove Cottage for *Wordsworth Lived Here* provided the spur for the sequence, and in draft form the Wordsworthian parallel was even more explicit – three sonnets were grouped together as the "Preludes in Glanmore."[74] As Heaney remembers in *Stepping Stones*, the trip to Grasmere was when "the sonnets announced themselves": "There was even a sonnet about a place in Grasmere called the White Moss where Wordsworth used to walk – his moss *bán*; but in the end I didn't think it worked, probably because it was overworking that kind of wordplay."[75] Heaney remembers Glanmore as the "first place where my immediate experience got into my work"; previously his poems had "arisen from memories of older haunts."[76] And this immediacy or spontaneity is, again, framed in Wordsworthian terms: "I knew it was the right place because,

124   This Strange Loneliness

when I was there, I always felt what Wordsworth might have called that 'blessed mood, / In which the affections gently lead us on.'"[77]

The time in Glanmore – and Wordsworth's example – were not, however, solely sustaining or "blessed." Darcy O'Brien describes Heaney's "somber and self-critical mood" in December 1973 during the period in which, as he told O'Brien, he had "been getting a lot out of Wordsworth lately," and it is this sombreness, and the tensions and anxieties that come about from rewriting Wordsworth, and from the relationship between "older haunts" and newer ones, that is of interest to me here.[78] As the first line of the first sonnet suggests, the landscape of the "Glanmore Sonnets" is "opened ground": the poems expose a haunting presence underlying the Edenic surface. The landscape is open to various ghosts – figures from Heaney's childhood, those killed in the Troubles, previous writers – whose presence ultimately unsettles any attempt to consider Glanmore a utopia.[79] "Glanmore is not Grasmere" as Heaney notes in an early version of Sonnet III: "That was a different ministry of fear."[80]

For Heaney, the transition between *North* and *Field Work* was a "turn," a major change of direction signalling and based in the desire not for "a door into the dark, but a door into the light."[81] This transition involved fundamental metrical and vocal changes: Heaney took up a longer, more mellifluous line, the "rhythmic contract of metre and iambic pentameter and long line [which] implies audience," and attempted to use the first-person pronoun to "mean" himself.[82] This changed attitude to the line and to language was, for Heaney, "a shift in trust: a learning to trust to melody, to trust art as reality, to trust artfulness as an affirmation and not to go into self-punishment so much."[83] At the heart of this "trust" was a deliberate change in attitude to literary tradition (and the art-form as a whole) which was based on a greater assertion of belonging, or in the terms of *North*, "rights on / The English lyric."[84] As Neil Corcoran argues, Heaney's use of iambic pentameter in *Field Work* is then a step towards asserting a "right" on the "English lyric," or at least an "open acknowledgement ... of an allegiance to the English lyric tradition."[85]

The "openness" of this acknowledgment is important. *Field Work* features one of the most telling self-revisions of Heaney's career: the phrase "opened ground," which is used as a "siring" metaphor for the colonization of Ireland in "Act of Union" in *North* becomes the "opened ground" of the first and second "Glanmore Sonnets" in

Places and Displacements

Field Work, in which Heaney attempts to catch a "voice" "back off the slug-horn and slow chanter / That might continue, hold, dispel, appease."[86] As that first line of the sonnets – "Vowels ploughed into each other: opened ground" – makes clear, this "opening" is a linguistic and literary metaphor, a way of combining, and crucially revising different voices (the "voice" is, after all, caught "back off" someone else's art).[87] The second sonnet repeats the first line of the first one ("Vowels ploughed into other, opened ground") in a new context: this not only suggests the merging of Irish and English linguistic elements into a single vocable, but it also gives an example of how many different languages might mix successfully. "Continue" and "dispel" derive from Latin, "hold" derives from Old English, and "appease" from French. The separate languages are "ploughed" together, as it were, into the Scots-Irish voice of the "chanter" and the unusual tones of the "slug-horn." The "slug-horn" famously appears in Robert Browning's "Childe Harold to the Dark Tower Came" (where it is inaccurately described as a "trumpet"), in Chatterton's "Battle of Hastings," and also in Hugh MacDiarmid's "Water Music"; it can be traced back to the Irish "sluagh-ghairm," a rallying cry for an army.[88] Here, as elsewhere in Heaney's work (one thinks of the "manifold griefs of chanters and assuaging bows" in "Ballad"), Heaney is incorporating music into his poetry to figure the elegiac and healing power of art.[89]

There are poetic as well as political and autobiographical reasons for a desired new beginning, for "opened ground." *Field Work* emerges, as much criticism has suggested, in part out of the impasse that Heaney felt he had reached in "Exposure" (the final poem in *North*) where he exclaims he has "missed / The once-in-a-lifetime portent, / The comet's pulsing rose."[90] *North* had (on in its own mythological and metaphorical terms) been Heaney's most explicit and direct response to the Troubles, and as such worked and worried through various different ways of attempting to find "images and symbols adequate to our predicament" or "befitting emblems of adversity."[91] Exhaustion is apparent in "Exposure," the exhaustion of inspiration and hope, and the political climate of the late 1970s, with violence continuing after the lull of the IRA's temporary ceasefire in 1975 offered no respite. As the decade wore on, the problem was not only that of trying to find "befitting emblems of adversity," but of trying to find them *again*, of having to repeatedly face a violent conflict that shows no signs of abating.

126 This Strange Loneliness

In the face of this exhaustion, Glanmore, in the phrasing of the sonnets, offers a "haven," and one that might promise a form of "dwelling" of the kind valorized by Heidegger or Ricoeur and based on the realization, in Jonathan Bate's words, that "our world, our home, is not earth but language." [92] Glanmore is a space where Heaney could create his own dwelling in the poetic tradition, through allusion to Dante, Lowell, Kavanagh, Mandelstam, Joyce, Wyatt, Philip Sidney, Shakespeare, and, centrally, Wordsworth. [93] Allusion here is a form of willed encounter. From *North* to *Field Work* the central metaphor for the relationship to past poetry subtly changes: it is no longer a matter of "digging," an excavation that unearths the past as object; instead it is an opening of the ground, and a holding open of it, in a way that allows the dead to rise and "haunt" the present. The first "Glanmore Sonnet" begins, as we have seen, by combining language and landscape in Heaney's newly created haven in Glanmore, by "opening" ground, and ends by welcoming what comes through this opening: "Breasting the mist, in sowers' aprons, / My ghosts come striding into their spring stations. / The dream grain whirls like freakish Easter snows." [94] Czesław Miłosz is one of Heaney's guides here, with his suggestion in "Ars Poetica?" that "Our house is open, there are no keys in the doors / and invisible guests come in and out." [95] More traumatically, so too is Dante, with the visiting or summoning of ghosts in the *Inferno*: this brings with it, as in "An Afterwards," the fear of predation, of Count Ugolino "in the ninth circle" of hell, with his mouth fixed onto Archbishop Ruggieri's head, "tooth in skull, tonguing for brain." [96] Haunting risks becoming "consumption."

Revision, consumption, predation, a holding open of oneself and one's poems to the past: in terms of 1970s poetics these themes take us back to Harold Bloom's *Anxiety of Influence*. Although Heaney's criticism largely opposes Bloom's emphasis on competition and the fight to the death between poets, his poetry is less definitively optimistic. In *The Anxiety of Influence* Bloom depicted poetic influence (and so poetry itself) as a *"misreading of the prior poet, an act of creative correction that is actually and necessarily a misinterpretation,"* so that the *"main tradition of Western poetry"* is *"a history of anxiety and self-saving caricature, of distortion, of perverse, wilful revisionism."* [97] Most pertinent in Bloom's schema, perhaps, is his final "ratio" of influence (*apophrades*, the return of the dead), where if you are an ambitious poet flicking through Bloom you will surely

Places and Displacements 127

quickly stray. Here poets are encouraged to measure themselves (however straight-facedly) against the "last phases of Browning, Yeats, Stevens – all of whom triumphed against old age," and take up the role of "The strong poet [who] peers in the mirror of his fallen precursor and beholds neither the precursor nor himself but a Gnostic double, the dark otherness or antithesis that both he and the precursor longed to be, yet feared to become."[98] For Bloom, *apophrades* acts through deliberately "holding open" one's poetry in ways that accept and change the meaning and influence of other poems: "the poem is now *held* open to the precursor, where once it *was* open, and the uncanny effect is that the new poem's achievement makes it seem to us, not as though the precursor were writing it, but as though the later poet himself had written the precursor's characteristic work."[99]

The problems with Bloom's approach – the reliance on outmoded notions of the family Romance, the apparent chauvinism of the model of masculine poetic struggle, Bloom's blind spots to his own anxious oedipal struggles – have been well documented.[100] Here, however, I am not arguing for the merits or otherwise of Bloom's ideas; instead, I am interested in ways in which Bloom's theory may well itself have influenced how poets (especially those who might view themselves as "strong" poets) understand their relationship with the "tradition." There are issues with this, however. As Corcoran counsels, in a discussion of the presence of what Paul Muldoon refers to as the "ghost Bloom" in the work of Muldoon and Heaney, one should be wary of any straightforward Bloomian reading of their relationship not least because "both Heaney and Muldoon have known the theory for as long as it has been around" and so may have positioned themselves accordingly and knowingly.[101] Muldoon's playful approach to Bloom complicates things even further. In *The End of the Poem* he explores "one aspect of the anxiety of influence on which Harold Bloom does not dwell – namely the attitude of the precursor to the later poet when their lifetimes and careers overlap"; and in 1999, after being asked by a flight attendant if he was Seamus Heaney, he wryly writes to Heaney, "What can it all mean? Is Bloom right after all?"[102] Although Heaney was generally less amenable to Bloom's theories, the "return of the dead," or more precisely the willed encounter with the dead, is the basic metaphor and mechanism of *Field Work*. The "holding open" of a poem "where once it *was* open" – a controlled mediation of influence that verges on uncanny appropriation – is the strategy

128 This Strange Loneliness

of Heaney's revised "opened ground." This is not an imagining of poetic "influence" as something that occurs "naturally." Instead, it is shamanic or magical: the influence of other poets is conjured.

Central to these conjured poets is Wordsworth. Echoes of his work, and his feeling for sound and rhythm, resonate throughout the "Glanmore Sonnets" to the extent that it is unclear whether Heaney is ventriloquizing through Wordsworth or vice versa. These echoes have been well documented in previous criticism: Neil Corcoran notes how in Sonnet II "'sensings, mountings from the hiding places' is Wordsworthian in its participle forms; Thomas Foster argues that "The opening line of Sonnet 6, 'He lived there in the unsayable lights,' is an almost direct transcription of the famous Lucy poem, 'She dwelt among the untrodden ways'"; Elmer Kennedy-Andrews, meanwhile, suggests that Heaney's "Rhyme and rhythm and the use of the highly disciplined sonnet form reflect the ploughman's steady, careful movement. The poetic voice is modelled on Wordsworth's."[103] There are also structural parallels: like the spots of time, sonnets IV, V, and VI trace the significance of the childhood experience for the adult poet's identity. In these poems Heaney is adopting the approach to poetry that he had identified with Wordsworth in "The Sense of Place" and "The Makings of a Music": as a poet of place, and of the "nurture" that comes through "dwelling in one dear perpetual place"; of a "pedestrian" poet, his technique connected to that of the boustrophedon (the traditional system of writing "as the ox ploughs"); and the poet of "wise passiveness," surrendering "to energies that spring within the centre of the mind."[104] In particular, "listening in" is central to Heaney's poetic identity in the "Glanmore Sonnets": in Sonnet IV Heaney remembers how he "used to lie with an ear to the line / For that way, they said, there should come a sound / Escaping ahead, an iron tune."[105] Deborah McLoughlin has shown how Heaney's image of his youthful listening self explicitly echoes Thomas de Quincey's "sketch of Wordsworth's demeanour as he awaited the arrival of the mail coach bringing news of the progress of the Peninsular Campaign" in the *Recollection of the Lake Poets*.[106] Like Wordsworth, Heaney is "in exile, nostalgic for home and youth," linked to the past as well as to the future (listening for the sounds that "escape ahead"), both historian and prophet.[107]

The identification with Wordsworth here is once more a complex negotiation of poetic "authority," of Heaney's need (following Sidney) to "apologize" for poetry and discuss the nature and function of his

Places and Displacements 129

own art.[108] In response to Lowell's translation of Boris Pasternak's "Hamlet" (which ends "To live a life is not to cross a field"), Sonnet I claims that "Now the good life could be to cross a field / And art a paradigm of earth new from the lathe / Of ploughs."[109] If that "earth" is the work of previous poets, however, this can come with some anxiety (in the everyday sense, rather than the Bloomian). If poetry makes of language a "nest," a place to "dwell" (as in the Heideggerian or Batesian model), the apophradic poet is then, on one level, a cuckoo in that nest, with all the anxieties of the interloper. This is a position suggested by the third sonnet, which begins "This evening the cuckoo and the corncrake / (So much, too much) consorted at twilight. / It was all crepuscular and iambic."[110] The association of poet and cuckoo is knowingly ("so much, too much") overblown, suggesting the "unease" that Heaney had felt after completing the first of these sonnets (what would become Sonnet IV) with the "thought that that music, the melodious grace of the English iambic line, was some kind of affront, that it needed to be wrecked; and while I loved the poem, I felt at the time that its sweetness disabled it somehow."[111] The association, and the feeling of permission and grace it offers, is not fully negated, however, and the poem ends with the prospect of an invigorating (Wordsworthian) "corresponding breeze": "a rustling and twig-combing breeze / Refreshes and relents. Is cadences."[112] This breeze, these cadences (like the "ghosts" of the first sonnet) are reinvigorating: they "refresh" and "relent," with the full meanings of make new, make flexible, and even "renew a loan," a "loan" that knowingly – not under influence or duress – the poem holds open. The encounter with the ghosts is thus a peering into a dark that becomes the light and resurrection of the "freakish Easter snows": Heaney's "shift of trust" enables a recognition of previous poets that becomes a "refreshing."

This attempt to open new ground that allows refreshment can be aligned, in Bloomian terms, with the "quest romances of the post-Enlightenment," the quest "to re-beget·one's own self, to become one's own Great Original."[113] The sequence certainly offers various originary metaphors of "re-begetting," returns that promise journeys forward. There is an image of the boustrephedon in Sonnet II, of "Each verse returning like the plough turned round"; and in Sonnet IV, there is a travelling outwards that is a journey back: "Two fields back, in the house, small ripples shook / Silently across our drinking water / (As they are shaking now across my heart) / And

130   This Strange Loneliness

vanished into where they seemed to start."[114] In the early poems in the sequence, this origin is personal, self-centred, and self-implicated, with its location in the "heart" (here in Sonnet IV) or, as V suggests, in a childhood escape: "I fall back to my tree-house and would crouch / Where small buds shoot and flourish in the hush."[115]

What is being proposed in Sonnet V is a return to origins that will be not only ameliorating or healing, but also generative (in the manner his criticism repeatedly strives towards). Often the sequence is read as if this quest has been a success: for Alan Gillis, for example, the sequence is "infused with spring-seasoned affirmation."[116] I would be less positive, however, and suggest that this may be what the sequence sets out to do, but that over its course it falters. In Bloom's (ludicrous) mythopoeic terms, the poet must travel, dually, "the road back to origins" and the "road forward to possibility" and overcome "a demon of continuity" (the "Covering Cherub") whose "baleful charm imprisons the present in the past."[117] Which is to say, as Bloom does, that "Discontinuity is freedom," and any path dependent solely on continuity (or "origins") will not allow the creation of something new.[118] Thus, when the haven that Heaney tries to create in the "Glanmore Sonnets" is threatened (by the thought of "dew on armour and carrion," of meeting something "blood-boltered on the road" in VIII; or a black rat swaying "on the briar like infected fruit" in IX), imagination does not provide the salve; indeed, imagination has perhaps tainted the fruit.[119]

Violence, not repose, is at the heart of the Glanmore sonnets. The "ghosts" of Glanmore are not, after all, solely poetic, and Glanmore is infected and surrounded by a preoccupation with death and, inevitably, the violence of the Troubles. *Field Work* is the most elegiac of Heaney's collections up to this point. Across the volume, there are elegies for Colum McCartney, Sean Armstrong, Sean O'Riada, Robert Lowell, and Francis Ledwidge: omens or deathly (non-literary) visitors, meanwhile, appear in "Triptych," "The Toome Road," "The Badgers," and "The Singer's House"; and Dante lurks around every corner, with the warning – in "Ugolino" – about the poet's "consumption" of reality. This violent, hellish context haunts and finally overpowers "Glanmore Sonnets," precisely as Heaney's art struggles to justify its existence on purely literary terms. In Sonnet IX, Heaney questions his reasons both for moving to Glanmore and for writing poetry. He cannot provide a satisfactory answer. When the black rat unnerves his wife, Heaney asks himself, "Did we come

Places and Displacements

to the wilderness for this?" and caustically and cynically rejects the protections and sanctions of their pastoral retreat.[120] Heaney and his wife are Adam and Eve in the wilderness and not, as they had thought, in Paradise. The rat swaying "on the briar like infected fruit" is the emblem of the fall repeated from *Death of a Naturalist* and carries with it the earlier volume's fear of the natural landscape. The poetic traditions that had implicitly sanctioned Heaney's retreat and offered him a haven cannot help overcome him his fear. In answer to his self-interrogation he replies, "We have our burnished bay tree at the gate, / Classical, hung with the reek of silage / From the next farm, tart-leafed as inwit."[121] Heaney not only desecrates the bay tree – the laurel crown of poetic excellence – by hanging it in silage, but also figures it as a source of guilt, a guilt that once more originates in part in Heaney's reliance on literary allusion. The *Agenbyte of Inwyt* (1340) was a Middle English translation of *Somme des Vices et Vertus* (1279), a French manual of virtues and vices; more pertinently, as Deborah McLoughlin notes, "the phrase 'agenbite of inwit,' meaning 'remorse of conscience,' recurs throughout Joyce's *Ulysses*, and is usually concerned with sexual and familial guilt."[122]

Even Heaney's acknowledgments of remorse, that is, are filtered through the literary tradition; everything reeks of allusion. And it is ultimately not literary tradition that provides respite or a sense of belonging in this sequence but the familial and sexual. In Sonnet X, for all its metaphorical reaching to Lorenzo and Jessica, Diarmuid and Grainne, it is not a literary "refreshing," or return to personal origins, that allows Heaney to discover "respite" in his dream, but the realization of his wife's presence and separateness, in the memory of their "first night," their wedding night.[123] The "strange loneliness" of III (in which Heaney compares them to Dorothy and Wordsworth, then demurs) is "strange" in part because it is not entirely lonely.[124] By Sonnet VIII – with its imperative "Come to me quick, I am upstairs shaking. / My all of you birchwood in lightning" – it is not the "haven" of Glanmore that is providing succour, but his wife; in Corcoran's words, the "poignant memory of human suffering there is countered with the urgent imperative of sexual desire, as if the one could occlude the other."[125] The addressee and focus of the poems (previously Glanmore itself) has changed: where his wife (never named in the sequence) was "she" in Sonnet III, from VIII onwards she is addressed as "you."

This change could be seen as the moment in the sequence – perhaps even in Heaney's career – at which he shifts from desiring a "conventional" pastoral that is "idyllic" or one "founded in reality" to one that is "threatened"; or in which he abandons the "argument" between Edenic Georgic and Utopian Eclogue for a relationship to the natural world (and to origins) that is more than literary.[126] Thus, in IX, the poet does not find an answer to the question "What is my apology for poetry?" but instead chases the rat away, and discovers his wife's face "Haunt[ing] like a new moon glimpsed through tangled glass."[127] By the end of the sequence, their "covenant of flesh" and dewy dreaming faces provide a "respite" which is, as Corcoran argues, "temporary" and "vulnerable."[128] The most important "ghost" haunting the sequence is not, finally, Wordsworth (or any other of the poetic spectres), but the poet's wife. If "firmer ground" is located in the sequence, it is not because of the "opened ground" of Sonnet I (and the ghosts that stride through it), or because of the return to a childhood "tree-house"; the origin that is returned to, and provides "the road forward to possibility" is not found in the poet's imagination, but in his wife's presence, her body.[129] Heaney appears to rely here, as in "Feeling into Words," on the liberating, humanizing effect of the sexual encounter, but there are clear problems with this replacement of literature and the imagination with an objectivized, productive, and ultimately passive female body: the relationship between poetic creation and procreation is uneasy at best; at worst it calls into question whether there is, ultimately, any apology for poetry that could compete with the creation of another human life.

Perhaps the trajectory of a return to origins is *necessarily* self-defeating for Heaney, and more poetic dead-end than return of the dead. In "Yank" the fact that time had "Unsettled neither certainty nor sand" is uncanny and unwelcome: change and disruption are to be expected and are, in their own ways, reassuring. A return to an origin that definitively provides "firmer ground" should be a cause of suspicion and portend a suffocating stasis. Perhaps, in Agata Bielik-Robson's post-Bloomian terms, Heaney is somewhere between the "antithetical" poet for whom "anxiety becomes a mark of *displacement*, a negative defense of one's own singularity which refuses to participate in cosmological orderings" and those "Critics of a Platonizing kind" who believe in "the benevolence of influence which, in the end, only shows us our right place in the great chain of being."[130] For Heaney, influence is both benevolent and displacing: the great chain of being in which you find your place might be best imagined as a shifting bog or a wavering tune.

Muldoon's rewriting of Heaney is always pertinent (and influential on Heaney), and his poem "Why Brownlee Left" undermines Heaney's attempt to reconcile himself to a settled, organic, "naive" sense of place. The "Brownlee" of the poem (with Brownlee here suggesting "brown leas," "opened ground") leaves behind "his pair of black / Horses, like man and wife, / Shifting their weight from foot to / Foot, and gazing into the future"; Brownlee thus abandons the idealized domestic, erotic, and boustrophedonic relationship with the land explored in the "Glanmore Sonnets"; and even the horses he leaves behind are shuffling, impatiently perhaps, on the spot.[131] Certainly, from this point in Heaney's poetry, mobility and transformation, rather than rootedness, will be key: by his next collection, *Station Island* (1984), Heaney has moved off from the idea of a return to origins to the motif of a poetic pilgrimage. Rather than holding a created "home" open and inviting the dead in, he is – developing his interest in Dante from *Field Work* and replacing Bloom's anxiety of influence with Jung's individuation – more intent on meeting the dead face-to-face on the neutral ground of *Station Island*. And in terms of his engagement with Wordsworth, he becomes, as Heaney signals through the titles of lectures, the poet of "Place and Displacement" rather than "the Sense of Place."

PLACE AND DISPLACEMENT

Heaney delivered *Place and Displacement: Recent Poetry of Northern Ireland*, the inaugural Pete Laver memorial lecture, in Grasmere in 1984. Laver, a poet and illustrator as well as librarian at Dove Cottage, had died of a heart attack while walking on Scafell in August the previous year, aged thirty-six.[132] There are various types of loss and "displacement" being dealt with in this lecture: significantly, it was also, as Guinn Batten notes, written just after the death of Heaney's mother.[133] The topic of the lecture is Northern Irish poetry but – unsurprisingly, given the context – Heaney uses the example of Wordsworth as a way of introducing his talk. Despite similarities of theme with his earlier essays, however, the approach Heaney takes to Wordsworth is quite different from that of "Feeling into Words," "The Sense of Place," or "Makings of a Music," and is largely informed by the remarkable shift that had taken place in his critical practice in the early 1980s. This was itself in part encouraged by Heaney's own personal relocation, after taking up a position at

134 This Strange Loneliness

Harvard, which would see him spending a term each year in the United States from January 1982 onwards; it is a change in tack, however, not across the Atlantic, but to the east, to Europe.[134]

Where only one essay in his first collection of prose, *Preoccupations* (1980), discussed Central or Eastern European writers, there is barely a page in the second half of his second essay collection – *The Government of the Tongue* (1986) – on which Heaney does not allude to a European writer, or discuss one directly. In the late 1970s and early 1980s the (moral and artistic) touchstones Heaney most often invokes are Osip and Nadezhda Mandelstam, Czesław Miłosz, and Zbigniew Herbert. These are writers whose work Heaney believes – talking about Nadezhda Mandelstam's autobiography *Hope against Hope* (1970) – has "a different moral and spiritual specific gravity from anything published in the West in the last fifty years."[135] Each bears witness to huge and hugely destructive social, cultural, and political changes in their countries and all attempt, to some extent, to "remember" the ancient, and dis-continuous, traditions of their cultures within current turmoil. Like the boustrophodenic Wordsworth in "The Makings of a Music," or the Wordsworth of "The Sense of Place," they are bearers of cultural tradition; but importantly, they are living through a moment of political or psychological crisis.[136]

Indeed, when Heaney introduces Eastern European writing in his "Current Unstated Assumptions about Poetry" (a talk first given at the Modern Language Association convention of 1979), he does this through his preoccupation with remembering and preserving traditions. Heaney ends the article, after wandering through discussions of the Yugoslavian poet Vasko Popa, and Americans James Wright and Robert Lowell, with Osip Mandelstam's image of a poem as "the funerary boat of the dead Egyptians."[137] In the Egyptian ship of the dead, for Mandelstam, "Everything needed for life is stored in this ship, and nothing is forgotten"; it carries with and preserves all previous life, culture, and experience.[138] This ship is a new guiding metaphor for how poetry "remembers." Previously, through *Wintering Out* and *North*, bogs and moors were Heaney's main repositories of memory and experience (and it is notable that Heaney uses Ted Hughes, whom he had previously celebrated as a fellow pagan, "a haunter of the *pagus*, a heath-dweller, a heathen," to frame his discussion of Popa).[139] The bog, as Heaney suggests to Monie Begley in 1977, was "a kind of Jungian ground or landscape in that it preserved traces of everything that had occurred before.

It had layers of memory."[140] Mandelstam's image of the poem as the Egyptian ship of the dead appears to have confirmed Heaney's instinctive feeling that poetry, like the bog in "Bogland," protects and perpetuates a nation's culture and traditions and is, in effect, a kind of collective unconscious; Mandelstam's image also opened up a world of new poetic icons, symbols, and exemplars.

From these European writers, Heaney develops the image of the poet exiled or persecuted by society who, paradoxically, perpetuates that society's traditions and values (and so offers hope for the future). This had been latent in the self-portrait of "Exposure" (the "wood-kerne // Escaped from the massacre") and evident in his interest in the figure of Sweeney from the early 1970s onwards; in the late 1970s and into the 1980s it becomes an obsession.[141] Heaney returns repeatedly to images of persecuted poets or those who need, physically, to hide their poems in the equivalent of that ship of the dead: Osip Mandelstam on the run as described by his wife Nadezhda in *Hope against Hope* (1970) and *Hope Abandoned* (1972); Anton Chekhov drinking brandy on his first night on the prison-island of Sakhalin; Alexander Kutzenov fearfully burying his poems in jars in his garden under cover of darkness.[142] Heaney (somewhat ambitiously) co-opts Socrates and Jesus into this role-call of persecuted poets, wondering how good Socrates's poetry would have been had he written original work rather than translated the fables of Aesop the night before his execution, and developing the image of Jesus writing in the sand as an metaphor for a poet whose "poetry ... is arbitrary and marks time in every possible sense of that phrase."[143] All these precursors, in broad terms, made Heaney focus more intently on poetry's importance as a counterweight to social and historical pressures; as a result, they radically altered Heaney's relationship with Wordsworth. Thus, in *Place and Displacement*, Heaney rereads Wordsworth's poetry and his "spirit" to reflect the examples of the Eastern European figures. Where previously Wordsworth had represented a "poetry of technique" or a "wise passiveness," distanced from quotidian, political reality, he now becomes a poet in conflict, torn between political or social demands on the one hand and belief in the independence of poetry on the other.

In *Place and Displacement*, the Wordsworth that Heaney presents is a "social" poet writing in the midst of a personal crisis that is intimately bound up with a national crisis, the war with post-Revolutionary France. Heaney suggests that the last books of

The Prelude "worry and circle and ruminate in an effort to discover what had happened to him in the 1790s when a passion for liberty and human regeneration, embodied for Wordsworth in the fact of the French Revolution, came into conflict with other essential constituents of his being founded upon the land and love of England."[144] Wordsworth is torn by his sense of places, or senses of place: rather than being able to dwell, he "is displaced from his own affections by a vision of the good that is located elsewhere."[145] Where previously binary divisions had been figured through separate poets or threads (Yeats and Wordsworth, technique and craft), now they are internalized, as they were for Mandelstam, Herbert, Miłosz, Socrates, and Jesus: Heaney's interest in "inner émigrés" is belatedly mapped onto Wordsworth.[146]

The purpose of this internalization is to allow for the possibility of (Jungian) individuation, a process in which consciousness can overcome irreducible and unresolvable conflict. Individuation, as Jung conceived it, resolves an opposition between the conscious and the unconscious in order to facilitate a journey towards unity, a unified self.[147] It is the process by which the unconscious is "recognized as a co-determining factor along with the conscious"; poetically, it is the spiritual journey through which one becomes a "personality," as a result of which "the centre of gravity of the total personality shifts its position. It is no longer in the ego, which is merely the centre of consciousness, but in the hypothetical point between conscious and unconscious. This new centre might be called the self."[148] In *Place and Displacement*, Heaney describes a case study in Anthony Storr's introduction to Jung's psychology in which a patient faced with "what appeared to be an insoluble conflict, solved it by 'outgrowing' it, by developing a 'new level of consciousness' through a certain 'detachment of [his] emotions.'"[149] This becomes a model for the writer's personal individuation, through "the appeasement of the achieved poem," in which the location of "the roots of one's identity in the ethnic and liturgical habits of one's group" is replaced by a "liberated moment, when the lyric discovers its buoyant completion, when the timeless formal pleasure comes to its fullness and exhaustion, in those moments of self-justification and self-obliteration the poet makes contact with the plane of consciousness where he is at once intensified in his being and detached from his predicaments."[150] This is not Heaney supporting the transcendental claims of art-for-art's sake, however, but arguing for a "profound relation ... between poetic technique and historical situation," which, in the Northern Irish case, avoids being an evasion of the "actual conditions" through a "concern with poetry": "the purely poetic force of the words is the guarantee of a commitment which need not apologize for not taking up the cudgels since it is raising a baton to attune discords which the cudgels are creating."[151]

Heaney's main focus for this notion of an "individuated" poetic voice is on Northern Irish poetry, but for an example of a poem that offers a mix of the "diagnostic, therapeutic and didactic" in the face of psychic displacement, he turns to *The Prelude*. "Wordsworth's case," he argues, "is symptomatic of the historical moment, but it is not paraded as being representative: the pressure of the poem's occasion launches it beyond allegory and exemplum."[152] In a tendentious act of identification, Heaney equates Wordsworth's position with that of his own peers:

> Like the disaffected Wordsworth, the Northern Irish writers I wish to discuss take the strain of being in two places at once, of needing to accommodate two opposing conditions of truthfulness simultaneously ... They belong to a place that is patently riven by notions of belonging to other places. Each person in Ulster lives first in the Ulster of the actual present, and then in one or other Ulster of the mind. The Nationalist will wince at the Union Jack and "God Save the Queen" as tokens of his place in the world, he will withhold assent from the solidarities implicit in these emblems rather as Wordsworth withheld assent from the congregation's prayers for the success of the English armies. Yet, like Wordsworth among his patriotic neighbours, the northern Nationalist conducts his daily social life among Unionist neighbours for whom these emblems have pious and passionate force, and to whom his nationalist principles, his hankering for a different flag and different anthem, are as traitorous as Wordsworth's revolutionary sympathies.[153]

There is an individuating sleight-of-hand here, in the introduction of "two opposing conditions of truthfulness" rather than two opposing conditions of "truth." Conflict is avoided through an opaque and slippery acknowledgment of necessary difference: to focus on "truthfulness" is to emphasize subjective position rather than objective "truth"; and though the Nationalist "hankering for a different

138   This Strange Loneliness

flag and different anthem" is "*as* traitorous as Wordsworth's revolutionary sympathies," it is unclear whether this suggests they are traitorous in the same manner or to the same degree. Indeed, the lecture depends on an opaque gesture towards an individuated (and hence currently unknowable) "beyond": the idea of *The Prelude* being "beyond allegory and exemplum."[154] In *Place and Displacement*, that is, Heaney appropriates Wordsworth for a wider-reaching discussion of how poetry can respond to historical circumstance and yet still retain its own "truthfulness" (rather than historically circumscribed or defined truth).

As such, Heaney is, as Hugh Haughton has noted, for once also keeping pace with contemporary trends in Wordsworthian criticism.[155] The notion of "displacement" had appeared in Geoffrey Hartman's and Jerome McGann's work on Wordsworth, and David Simpson had published in 1983 his *Wordsworth's Historical Imagination: The Poetry of Displacement*. However, where McGann and Simpson differ over whether the "displacement" of history into poetry is an evasion of or engagement with history, for Heaney the question is how the "achieved poem," like "Wordsworth's idea of 'the good place'" might "be seen as a product of trauma, a strategy for psychic survival, rather than evasion."[156] This is, as Lucy Newlyn glosses, also an archetypally Romantic gesture, "a displacement from the political or sociocultural plane (events, times, circumstances, and places) onto the imaginative plane (subjective impressions, personal illusions, psychic defences, transcendental aspirations)."[157] "Heaney," as Michael O'Neill argues, "finds heartening the very thing that some recent critics have found reason to fault: Wordsworth's turn to and use of poetry to describe 'a consciousness coming together through the effort of articulating its conflict and crises.' This formulation might describe much of Heaney's own efforts to articulate conflict yet in doing so to heal trauma."[158] The differences with Wordsworth need, however, to be stressed. Where Wordsworth desired, crucially, a "good place" to enable a "reconciliation with nature," psychic healing, and an end to "alienation" (in M.H. Abrams's understanding), Heaney proposes the "release" and "appeasement of the achieved poem"; if any "unity" is to be achieved, it is on the abstracted (individuated) plane of art.[159] The hope of Heaney's prose is that this might be achievable; the lesson of his poetry is that this must remain only a hope.

Places and Displacements

SUBTERRANEAN STREAMS:
STATION ISLAND AND *THE PRELUDE*

One of the central themes of *Place and Displacement* (as in *The Prelude*) is thus the attempt to heal the emotional and psychological rift caused by a sense of "displacement," of not belonging. This rift had been broached as early as "Yank," but in *Station Island* the problems of trying to salve the wounds it has caused come to a head. In *Station Island*, Heaney has not fully left behind an attachment to place; he has not, like Muldoon's Brownlee, mysteriously "left." This departure is, however, rehearsed in the collection through the figure of Sweeney, the mad king from the Irish *Buile Suibhne*, half-man half-bird, who is fated to journey the treetops of Ireland and Gaelic Scotland without the hope of a permanent, settled home; and it is also explored through the peripatetic mode of pilgrimage rather than the boustrephedon. By the end of *Station Island* Heaney accepts pilgrimage not as a redemptive end in itself, but rather as a stepping stone, a stage in what will later become a restless, uprooted exile, figured through Diogenes in the wilderness in *The Haw Lantern*, endlessly searching for "one just man."[160]

This process had been long in the making. Heaney had never been a "naive" poet: from the beginning, the "naturalist" had been dead. What happens after *Field Work* is a shift in how he attempts to be a "sentimental" poet, searching for "lost nature" or justice or truth or reality: either by exploring in depth one "dear, perpetual place," or by constantly moving, passing between places, times, and traditions. This is the difference between exploring one poetic tradition and moving between many different traditions, with a more concerted engagement with the Gaelic tradition (particularly in his translations of *Buile Suibhne* and Brian Merriman's *Cúirt an Mheán Oíche*), "classical" literature (whether it be his translations of Dante, Sophocles, or *Beowulf*, or the hybridizing combination of Ovid and Merriman in *The Midnight Court*), and – once more – Eastern European writers. The trouble for Heaney in *Station Island* (as in *Place and Displacement*) is how to negotiate between these different poetic traditions when a Heideggeran model of "dwelling" no longer suffices; his preferred mode is a strange meeting of hybridity and individuation.

Many of Heaney's poems and theoretical positions can broadly be seen to be "hybrid" in the way described by Homi Bhabha. They present (within an "encounter," colonial or otherwise) "the trace of what is disavowed," not through repression, but by repeating it "as something *different*" and in so doing disturbing "the visibility of the colonial presence and mak[ing] the recognition of its authority problematic."[161] Or, as Heaney put it in a 1973 interview, they take "the English lyric and make it eat stuff that is has never eaten before."[162] Thus, the "Glanmore Sonnets," for example, turn the questions of the English sonnet tradition (such as "What is my apology for poetry?") back on that tradition, and reveal the difficulties those questions pose for it. By *Station Island*, the possibility of combining vowels (associated with "the personal and Irish pieties") and consonants ("the literary awarenesses nourished on English") into "vocables adequate to [his] whole existence" has been exploded. In *Field Work* "vowels" were "ploughed into other" and the ground overturned, opened, made raw.[163] In *Station Island*, instead of this ploughed interspersing of self and other, the comingling of apparently opposed forces, there is the transcendence of difference and conflict; a transcendence once more enabled by Jungian individuation.

Thus, in "Making Strange," the narrator juxtaposes two distinct cultures and relationships to the land: that of the "travelled" Jamaican-American poet Louis Simpson and an old – "bewildered" – acquaintance of Heaney's from the Derry countryside (based on his own father), who stand in respectively for cosmopolitan sophistication and rural groundedness.[164] The narrator stands between the two, one with "travelled intelligence / and tawny containment, his speech like the twang of a bowstring" and the other "unshorn and bewildered / in the tubs of his wellingtons."[165] (There is perhaps self-allusion here: Neil Corcoran notes how the cows in "The Strand at Lough Beg" in *Field Work* are described as turning their "unbewildered gaze" as if to express "their mournful lack of surprise at anything we might do to them.")[166] The narrator does not "resolve" this opposition, but steps above it: he proposes to become both "adept" and "dialect," to be in-between, double, chameleon, belonging provisionally to both of these worlds but not fully to either.[167] Heaney had toyed with previously with idea of being "adept": in "England's Difficulty" in *Stations* he describes how he "moved like a double agent among the big concepts" and "An adept at banter, he crossed the lines with carefully enunciated passwords, manned every speech with checkpoints and reported back to nobody."[168] By *Station Island* the quality of being "adept" (associated with the "travelled" poet) suggests not the act of being a "double-agent" but

Places and Displacements   141

being a *homo sacer*, one whose knowledge sets them apart, marks them as being both within and outside the "tribe" (which then means they can be used as a sacrificial victim). This sense of impending exclusion or exile is explored in the "Sweeney Redivivus" poems in *Station Island* and in "The King of the Ditchbacks," where the poet is once more a "rich young man // leaving everything he had / for a migrant solitude."[169] Again, this repeats a motif from *Stations*: in "The Wanderer," the poet is already by this stage contemplating the "rich young man" he once was, but "who could tell you now of flittings, night-vigils, let-downs, women's cried out eyes" and yet still "would not renegue on this migrant solitude."[170]

This is not only to say that *Station Island* returns to, rewrites, and perhaps completes *Stations* (as the names suggest, and various critics have explored), but also that departure is not a singular event in Heaney's poetry, but an ongoing process. Heaney values "becoming" adept rather than "being" adept; "migrant solitude" is a desirable state of mind (with an echo, once more, of that "utter solitude" in *The Prelude* that leads to the "holy calm" that then enables a "prospect in [the] mind") but perhaps only with the sense of displacement, of "migration."[171] This also repeats and completes an earlier poem of Heaney's: in the 1960s he had used lines from *The Prelude* as an epigraph to an unpublished poem, "In Glenelly Valley" ("And I was taught to feel, perhaps too much, / The self-sufficing power of solitude"). [172] This poem seems to offer a less flattering picture of someone who is both in and outside of a community, who is "touched by God." The poet gives a lift to some children who advise against him helping a (somewhat clichéd) "old woman" who was "clutching a black cat / To her bosom. Wore a black dress and a wide hat": a young girl's diagnosis is that "she's dotin,' head's cut"; Heaney drives off, "wrecking a hill-crazed dream."[173] Heaney is well aware of the risks of being outside the community, and of how one's "migrant solitude" (self-celebrated and chosen or otherwise) might be perceived; by *Station Island* he is willing to accept those risks, to place himself outside the protection of the tribe.

"Making Strange" is of interest for my purposes because of the way in which it once more negotiates with Romantic antecedents: the Schillerian naive and sentimental, the trope of "natural inspiration," and the typical guilt-ridden Wordsworthian meeting on the public highway with a rural figure who symbolizes either social and political decay or Wordsworth's own self-indulgence. "Making Strange"

142 This Strange Loneliness

does not present a first-person encounter, as Wordsworth's poems tend to; the poet is here in part a bystander, a mediator, and as such is able to limit and control the disturbing potential of the meeting. It is not a "Strange Meeting," an encounter with the *unheimlich*, the guiltily raised dead, as in Wilfred Owen's poem of the same name or as in the "Glanmore Sonnets," but a meeting in which Heaney himself can "make strange" all that he knew (the zinc huts, the puddles, the stones). This phrase combines the dialect senses of acting in an unfriendly manner or as if surprised (towards his own people), and of "behaving oddly," like a child unintelligible to his parents.[174] So, the narrator decides to "love the cut of this travelled one / and call [the field] also the cornfield of Boaz": Heaney alters the landscape through the biblical allusion, to suggest that he is like Ruth amid the alien corn (an allusion that could use shared knowledge of the Bible tale to bridge the gap between his two interlocutors).[175]

The allusion to Ruth offers one path towards the transcendence of difference; the "cunning middle voice" coming "out of the field across the road" that impels the poet to be "adept" and "dialect" offers another.[176] The "middle voice" of ancient Greek is somewhere between the active and the passive, suggesting some form of self-reflexivity; this is less important, however, than the voice's point of origin. It could be seen to originate in the Romantic figure for poetic inspiration located in ecological nature, the "blessing in this gentle breeze / That blows from the green fields" at the beginning of *The Prelude*, Shelley's West Wind, or the "desultry breeze" of Coleridge's "Eolian Harp."[177] The "cunning middle voice" is also, however, a contorted echo of another version of this natural voice in "Making Strange," the "wind coming past the zinc hut."[178] This "cunning middle voice" actually advises the poet to "go beyond" Romantic rootedness, to "Go beyond what's reliable / in all that keeps pleading and pleading, / these eyes and puddles and stones."[179] In Heaney's hands the trope of Romantic inspiration undermines itself, deconstructs itself, and offers a way forward: the poet is engaged in "departures" he "cannot go back on" (the "cunning" might then be that of a voyaging, not a homecoming, Odysseus).

The "cunning middle voice" is one instance of a freshening, invigorating speech (often associated with breezes or breathing) that runs through much of *Station Island*, encouraging the poet to set sail. In the first section of "The Loaning," for example, a "wind shifting in the hedge was like / an old one's whistling speech."[180] The association

Places and Displacements 143

of the wind and speech is important. Both can be listened into for admonitory (or inspiring) messages; and in this manner the third section of "The Loaning" repeats and modifies the epiphanic "listening-in" of Wordsworth's "There Was a Boy." When the "boy" is imitating the owls on the banks of Windermere, the owls fall silent, and he hangs listening into a sudden silence; in this silence, "a gentle shock of mild surprize / Has carried far into his heart the voice / Of mountain torrents."[181] Heaney repeats and modifies this image of the startled poet listening into an absence, in a celebration of auditory attentiveness:

> Stand still. You can hear
> everything going on. High-tension cables
> singing above cattle, tractors, barking dogs,
> juggernauts changing gear a mile away.
> And always the surface noise of the earth
> you didn't know you'd heard till a twig snapped
> and a blackbird's startled volubility
> stopped short.[182]

The "surface noise of the earth" is only noticed in the absence of the blackbird's song, after it has "stopped short." Where Wordsworth's "boy" becomes aware of the sounds of the natural landscape, for Heaney, those sounds are pluperfect: they "had been heard." It is possible to read this in ecological terms, with the twig snapping under the synecdochic weight of standing in for the whole process of deforestation.[183] Heaney's poem is odder than this, however, in its use of symbolic shorthand.

In "The Loaning" the image that disturbs the Wordsworthian motif of the poet listening into the natural landscape is drawn from *Sweeney Astray*, Heaney's translation of *Buile Suibhne*: a "blackbird's startled volubility / stopped short."[184] In *Sweeney Astray*, while Sweeney is relating some of his own hardships, he tells how he is wracked by a bird's irrational fears, and how he is "startled then / by the startled woodcock / or a blackbird's sudden / volubility."[185] Heaney is, I would suggest, making a rather hazy association between the Gaelic tradition and a (disappearing) natural environment. The Irish language, like the "blackbird's startled volubility," has been "stopped short" or curtailed: the "old one's whistling speech" in the first section of "The Loaning" is then, perhaps, not a whistling *English* speech, but that of

144   This Strange Loneliness

a language consigned to a "limbo of lost words." One question that arises is whether English, or any language, can present "everything going on": the answer is, necessarily, no.

The idea that what you might listen into is already gone undermines any tendency to create stable or fixed definitions. Patricia Horton argues that the "cunning middle voice" in "Making Strange" can unite child and adult, feminine and masculine, country and city only if these binary oppositions have fixed and unchanging relationships.[186] This is not true to *Station Island*, however; these poems tend to be more of a meeting of "winds," "speeches," or "voices" – that "shifting" wind in the hedge – than of rooted forces or ideologies. The attempt is to envisage a world where everything is "flux" (and flux will become one of Heaney's key words). The "loaning" provides such a location: a "loaning" is a lane, a by-road, or an open uncultivated piece of ground near a farmhouse or village, on which the cows are milked.[187] In Heaney's poem it is unclaimed nature, a place between the social world and a ghostly, linguistic world, a "limbo," in which everything is in permanent transition. Words flutter "above iron bedsteads"; men talking in the kitchen turn into trees in the twilight (hovering between day and night); and in each of the three sections the narrator finds himself caught in-between the dead and the living.[188] The concrete becomes abstract, the body becomes the soul. "Words" leave the social, rural environment that had previously been the basis of much of Heaney's poetry – they fly into the loaning "from raftered sheds and crossroads, / from the shelter of gable ends and turned-up carts."[189] The words, indeed, lose their ability to refer, to recreate concrete objects, and become disconnected from their speakers, taking on a life (or death) of their own. The poet sees them "streaming out of birch-white throats / and fluttering above iron bedsteads" and then settling in the natural landscape, "in the uvulae of stones / and the soft lungs of the hawthorn."[190] This is a linguistic death – the words flutter above bedsteads "until the soul would leave the body" – but it is also life: the limbo of lost words inspires the poet; in the loaning, he feels a sense of poetic vocation.[191] The poet knows "why from the beginning / the loaning breathed on me, breathed even now / in a shiver of beaded gossamers / and the spit blood of a last few haws and rose-hips."[192] Heaney's poetry cannot reach the implied heights of "Exposure" in which the poet feels he has missed the "comet's pulsing rose."[193] Nonetheless, his art does have a purpose. It expresses the frissons

Places and Displacements

and tremors that link language and experience ("a shiver of beaded gossamers") and the bitter defeats of life ("the spit blood of a last few haws and rose-hips"), in the face of absence and loss.

"The Loaning" does not end where it began but strays far from a Romantic or Gaelic natural landscape of dwelling or embodiment, to imagine a peculiar interrogation scene, via a classical hell. The voices shifting or whistling in the hedge also include, by tentative allusion, those of Osip Mandelstam and Dante. Mandelstam's poem 358 (written while in exile in Voronezh on 21–22 January 1937) enables the narrative structure of the third section of "The Loaning." In the first two stanzas of Mandelstam's poem the act of listening to the rustling of the world around you (Mandelstam's is a cityscape rather than natural landscape) leads to a recollection of Dante:

> I hear, I hear the first ice
> rustling under the bridges,
> and I think of drunkenness swimming
> radiant above our heads.
>
> From stagnant stairs, from squares
> flanked with jagged palaces
> Dante's exhausted lips
> more resonantly sang
> his circling Florence.[194]

Heaney follows Mandelstam's pattern. After hearing the twig snap, the poet remembers that "When Dante snapped a twig in the bleeding wood / a voice sighed out of blood that bubbled up / like sap at the end of green sticks on a fire."[195] Heaney is alluding to Canto XIII of the *Inferno* in which Dante discovers the souls of suicides trapped within trees; Dante's incarcerated suicide, Pier delle Vigne, was "accused of treachery, blinded, and thrown into prison, where he committed suicide."[196] Dante's image of the suicides in the trees offers an origin for the image of the voices (and the mouths) in the trees in "The Loaning." Dante's "tired lips" in Mandelstam's poem become Heaney's suggestion that "When you are tired or terrified / your voice slips back into its old first place / and makes the sound your shades make there," substituting the more abstract "voice" for Mandelstam's "lips," and also perhaps incorporating Mandelstam "tired or terrified" in the Gulag into his image of Dante.[197]

146 This Strange Loneliness

As well as empathy with these "shades" there is also guilty, but unspecific, self-accusation here. The poet empathizes with Dante, who snaps the twig and in doing so torments delle Vigne; he identifies, in other words, with both the tortured and the torturer. When Dante's "tree-prison" metamorphoses into a modern prison cell, Heaney imagines the interrogator preparing himself for the torture he is about to commit: "the interrogator steels his *introibo* / the light motes blaze, a blood-red cigarette / startles the shades, screeching and beseeching."[198] "Introibo" invokes the beginning of the Latin mass, "Introibo ad Altare Dei" ("I will go in to the Altar of God"): by using only the subject-verb combination "I will go in" Heaney places a heavy, empathetic, emphasis on the "I." "Introibo ad Altare Dei" famously appears in the first chapter of Joyce's *Ulysses*, when Buck Mulligan play-acts the role of the priest as he goes about his morning ablutions: there is something of the act or posture about Heaney's use of the "introibo" as well. The staginess of this self-accusation perhaps over-balances the poem. Certainly, neither the first nor third sections survived the cut when Heaney came to making selections for *Opened Ground*; only the second section of the poem was included. This is, in isolation, a comparatively straightforward spot of time in which Heaney remembers "Big voices in the womanless kitchen" as night fell, whose talk came "down / to *Aye* and *Aye* again."[199] There is a sense of vocal affirmation that can be conjured through the willed operation of memory: "I closed my eyes / to make the light motes stream behind them / and my head went airy, my chair rode / high and low among branches and the wind / stirred up a rookery in the next long *Aye*."[200] The "light motes" are shorthand for the thickening of space through the operation of memory; the final section of the poem, however, interrogates the ability to conjure, encounter, and relive the past in this way, to "stir up a rookery" (in a way that Heaney obviously felt was not entirely successful).

Perhaps the tone of the final lines, with those ghosts "screeching and beseeching," serves too much to undermine the trajectory of the title poem, "Station Island," with its own staged encounters with and interrogations of and by the past. When Joyce is given the final word, this – though not the whole story of the poem – does make explicit the sense of departure and new possibility that Heaney had been proposing throughout the collection:

Places and Displacements 147

"Keep at a tangent.
When they make the circle wide, it's time to swim

out on your own and fill the element
with signatures on your own frequency,
echo soundings, searches, probes, allurements,

elver-gleams in the dark of the whole sea."[201]

(This is advice that Michael McLaverty had already dispensed in *North*.) "The Loaning" suggests that those "soundings," searches, "probes" might not be as innocent as the shade of Joyce might hope; but "Station Island" (and the collection as a whole) proposes that one has to keep at a tangent nonetheless, and make the departure in full knowledge of the risks that come with it.

LICKING POETIC BEING INTO SHAPE

The departure from the romanticized landscapes of "Making Strange" and "The Loaning" also marks a growing distance between Heaney's poetry and Wordsworth's. It is not a complete break, however, but more that of the two rivers flowing alongside one another (to borrow the filial image from "The Brothers"), one now tends to flow underground, or to have been chopped – in the image from Heaney's "Sandpit" used in the introduction – into the "brick" which could be used to build a "new estate."[202] Heaney not only swims out on his own, but also creates his own waterways. Even if the influence of Wordsworth may be largely hidden in Heaney's later poetry, however, it can still be traced in the building blocks he uses, in the generative impulses (that "bedhead thumping quickly") that resonate and ripple through time, and especially in those gables, which are now no longer ruined, but which are "alive" with communication and symbolism.

Heaney does not, for one, abandon the central Wordsworthian image of the influential "river of imagination": the idea that natural landscape can *flow* into the individual imagination persists, although it is subject to some major adjustments and anxieties. Two years after the publication of *Station Island* Heaney wrote the foreword for the anthology *A Portrait of the Artist as a Young Girl*, a collection of accounts by nine Irish women writers (Maeve Binchy, Clare Boylan, Polly Devlin, Jennifer Johnston, Molly Keane, Mary Lavin, Joan Lingard, Dervla Murphy, and Edna O'Brien) about their childhoods and the growth of their artistic imagination. For Heaney, relying on the etymological basis of "invention" in "discovery," these are examples of the process whereby "The invention of a narrative for one's childhood is … to some extent a creative discovery of the self": instead of the idea of an authentic or authenticating "origin," he is proposing a constructed and "creative" relationship with one's own past.[203] His model for this is Wordsworth and his imagining of the Derwent. "One of my favourite inventions of this kind," he suggests, "is William Wordsworth's image of the River Derwent as a maternal tongue which licked his poetic being into shape. The river ran past the end of the garden of the house where he was born in Cockermouth, and its noise flowed along his dreams and infused his infant attention with messages of the power and beauties of the natural world."[204] The idea of the river "maternally" licking Wordsworth into shape may suggest a level of anxiety and usurpation that Heaney himself felt, as a male poet using another canonical male poet to frame and introduce the work of nine women writers: he is certainly conscious of the politically gendered "edge to the book, insofar as it constitutes a spirited displacement of the aura of maleness which still tends to surround that hallowed word, 'artist.'"[205]

But there is a tension between the desire to hallow that word "artist" and the awareness of the slight pomposity of Wordsworth's (and by extension his own) egotistic assumptions of artistic right and centrality. "If none of the contributors to this volume is as absolute (or vain) as Wordsworth," he argues, "in assuming that the whole cosmos was just waiting for her arrival to start ministering to her imagination, each one nevertheless has something individual and persuasive to add to that great deposit of evidence which shows childhood to be the great forcing house of artistic talent."[206] (To some extent "individual" female perspective still struggles here against "universal" male norms; it is another male Romantic figure – Keats, and his idea of "schooling an intelligence into a soul" – who provides Heaney's other touchstone.) Heaney is, nevertheless, conscious of the absolutism and vanity of Wordsworth's position. The wholehearted celebration of the "humanized and humanizing" active nature that Heaney had read into "Michael" is still there in his depiction of the River Derwent infusing Wordsworth's "infant attention with messages of the power and beauties of the natural world." It has undergone its own "displacement," however, and the privileged "aura of maleness" that surrounds the treatment of the natural landscape as a nurturing "mother-figure" (as part of that still gendered idea of the "artist") comes in for the gentlest "good-natured and salutary" scrutiny, alongside other features of the life of the artist: "the way in which concessions to innate temperament have to be balanced against the will to change, the whole delicate and crucial negotiation between the unconscious and self-consciousness, between the deliberate and arbitrary."[207] Wordsworth is once more a model of "negotiation," but not one that can be wholeheartedly embraced. This suggests that Wordsworth might, from this point in Heaney's career, become a problem that needs to be dealt with, understood, or "outgrown"; remarkably, though, he still provides a crucial example of how such outgrowing, such transcendence, might come about.

4

The Necessity of an Idea of Transcendence

UNSELFISH SELF-CULTIVATION

In 1982, Heaney was invited to give the commencement address at Fordham University, a private Catholic research university in New York City. Instead of a speech, he read a long poem that, among other things, repeats and reinforces the liberal defence of education he had espoused in the 1960s. In "Verses for a Fordham Commencement" Heaney sets himself the task of composing, in a Robert Burns-inspired "Standard Habbie" stanza, "A formal ode for graduates / On learning and how it relates / To life, how it disseminates / Sweetness and light."[1] The Arnoldian notion of education disseminating "sweetness and light" may have been the poem's starting point, but it does not stand unopposed. The poem acknowledges how poetry "was put severely to the test / In recent years / By guns in streets, bombs on the tracks / Human flesh in plastic sacks," but argues, nevertheless, that "understanding civilizes, / Wakens responsibilities, / Promotes ideas of peace and justice /And demotes vengeance." "History," as Heaney suggests, "implies equation / Between the good and education. / An unselfish self-cultivation / Is the ideal."[2]

In this instance, underlying the defence of art is a restatement of elements of Wordsworth's *Prelude* and his Preface to *Lyrical Ballads*. "Solitude" is, for Wordsworth, the basic condition of inspiration. "How gracious, how benign, is Solitude," he exclaims in *The Prelude* Book IV; in the boat-stealing incident, meanwhile, the "darkness, call it solitude / Or blank desertion" that hangs over the poet's brain marks the working of "a dim and undetermined sense / Of unknown modes of being."[3] In Heaney's manifesto poem this

The Necessity of an Idea of Transcendence

blankness becomes the "illiterate solitude" which "Is the first place where the true and good / Awakens in us."[4] The problem for Heaney is the legitimacy of ideas such as "the true and good" or, indeed, the "imagination." He comments that he approaches the word "imagination" with "some unease" because "it can sound slight and airy ... A bubble word":

> Yet while I'm wary
> I realize
>
> All need its salutary power.
> All men and women must beware
> Who would deny it
> And go against their childhood's grain
> And dry up like earth parched for rain.
> They'll grow mechanical and then
> No drug or diet
>
> No health-farm, clinic, yoga course,
> No mantra *om*, no *Star Wars* force
> Will compensate
> For what is lost when the mind divides.[5]

"Salutary" here echoes Wordsworth's claim for "Simon Lee" in the Preface to *Lyrical Ballads* when he says he aimed to place his reader "in the way of receiving from ordinary moral sensations another and more salutary impression than we are accustomed to receive from them."[6] It is not that health farms, yoga, and *Star Wars* are not good for you, but that you will need the power of the combining, transforming imagination to make them so, and to stop you becoming "mechanical": even when that imagination is structured and bound (or enabled) by the limits of what is, after all, a strict poetic form. More broadly, the fear and risks of mental "division," and what the poetic imagination can do to combat this, will preoccupy Heaney over the next few years.

There is a greater range and pointedness to his defence of poetry – and his comparisons with other forms of culture, high and low – than had often been the case. On a biographical level, this extended range is no surprise: by 1982 Heaney had completed the unlikely progression from Ballymurphy to Carysfort to Harvard, with the attendant shift in public profile and expectation. And the particular occasion, the commencement address, encouraged an engagement with contemporary culture and popular and esoteric threads of therapy and well-being (the strange yoking together of yoga, health-farms, clinics, and the "*Star Wars* force") in ways that his time in Dublin had not. However, this platform also simply allowed him a greater audience for concerns that he had regularly explored throughout the 1970s and early 1980s, in particular his continued interest in learning and educational thinking. Fittingly, for this address, this interest tended to focus on the balance between different types of poetic and artistic "freedom" on the one hand, and social responsibility on the other. In a quotation from Wordsworth's "Ode: Intimations of Immortality" that Heaney used repeatedly in his scripts for *Explorations*, a 1970s BBC NI Schools radio series, from infancy onwards "shades of the prison house begin to close" upon us, through the accumulation of "experience ... the walls of responsibility that sooner or later hem in the freedoms of childhood."[7] Much of his writing about education is an attempt to sustain these "freedoms" as long as possible, and to celebrate the (salutary) imagination that helps avoid the dry, mechanical thinking of adulthood, without straying into escapism or "selfish self-cultivation": however, it does also question whether this liberation should best be seen as a matter of being reborn, revived, or led astray.

A BASKET OF EELS

While pursuing a career as a freelance writer and broadcaster in the early 1970s, Heaney wrote a series of reviews for the *Education Times*, a magazine edited by John Horgan for the *Irish Times* and launched in April 1973.[8] The aim of the magazine was to "help create," as an editorial entitled "Education and Community" argues, "an organic and dynamic unity in the whole sphere of education"; its foundational beliefs were that "few things matter more to a community than the quality of the educational system" and, with a cross-border approach, that "the search for a better and fairer system is a matter of common concern, in Northern Ireland just as much as in the Republic."[9] The Arnoldian force was strong in the reviews Heaney wrote, starting with his contribution to the first issue, "Poetic Sweetness and Light in the Classroom." Here he discussed *Poiemata*, "readings in poetry and prose edited by Desmond

The Necessity of an Idea of Transcendence   153

Egan and Gerard Rice," and *Focus*, an anthology of fifty poems, with analysis, edited by Egan (once more) and Eugene Watters. *Poiemata* is welcomed as a book that shows the editors' "excellent and wide-ranging" taste, "from Longfellow to Lorca, Ben Jonson to James Joyce, from epigram to haiku, from folksong to fiction," but Heaney's reaction to *Focus* also reveals how far it falls short of his own critical standards.[10]

Egan and Watters have, according to Heaney, "a certain verve and appetite for reading but too often lack decorum, discipline and elementary information."[11] In particular, their analysis of Yeats's "Among Schoolchildren" is held up as "incredible, an amazing and unwitting joke"; it is "porridge, and rather short on scholarship, too." As an example, Heaney presents a series of sentences which veer towards the incomprehensible: "He is a bit vague about spelling – when he writes 'solider' he is inclined to see 'soldier' ... Seems he played some Irish sport (taws) and properly chastised a King of Kings." As Heaney suggests, "when the chirpy tone turns on a great poem like 'Among School Children' it is not only inadequate but uniquely inaccurate ... No amount of coy disclaiming can excuse this kind of thing."[12] (Heaney will subsequently offer an account of Yeats's poem and its importance as a model for education that will, on one level, redress Egan and Walter's failings.)

Despite the critical inadequacies of the editors, however, Heaney lauds their desire to make the canon more accessible and less forbidding. Indeed, in "Poetic Sweetness and Light in the Classroom" two distinct responsibilities compete: the need to defend and respect poetry as an art form and helping the child reader as far as possible to understand it. There is, in other words, a pragmatic, teacherly strain to this review which also runs through Heaney's other pieces for the *Education Times*. Discussing Alan Garner's 1973 fantasy novel *Red Shift*, inspired by Welsh mythology and history, Heaney is effusive in his praise for the novel's artistry, comparing its "complexity" and "cool deliberation" to that of the Book of Kells, and praising the way it "weaves the tensions of narrative, the resources of history and myth, and the suggestiveness of the English language into a pattern as live and shifting as a basket of eels."[13] However, he is wary – not "out of desire to withhold praise from the book but to insist on the tough literary fibre of the writing" – that it might exceed the ability of the (expected) teenage readership.[14] Similarly, in a review of Auden's *Thank You, Fog*, the anthology *Poetry Introduction 3* and

Randall Jarrell's *Third Book of Criticism*, Heaney wonders about the audience for poetry reviewing, and the critic's obligations to that audience: "For whom does one review poetry? For the editor? The librarians? The 'general reader'? For the one person in ten thousand for whom poetry is 'a feeling and an appetite'?"[15] Although he quotes Jarrell on how "terribly queer, terribly risky" reviewing is, with its requirement, in Heaney's words, to continue "describing, evaluating and fixing" poetry, this does not stop him "fixing" Auden's "high table insouciance," "high class doodling," and "relaxed camp" (while still lauding him as the "adroitest of makers").[16] Auden is found wanting for his lack of moral, didactic seriousness: Jarrell's criticism, on the other hand, is praised for speaking "with clarity, as literate, receptive, slightly puzzled representative of the reader" and for the way in which his book "proves the discipline both valuable and delightful ... It's all enhancing stuff and there's nothing risky about recommending it warmly."[17] "Enhancing," that is, unlike Auden's "doodling," or Egan and Walter's "porridge."

In these reviews Arnoldian conviction about the moral role of literature and the literary critic meets the concerns of a professional educator and writer: the importance of literature per se goes hand in hand with an awareness of the difficulties of using literature as a tool for moral enhancement in the classroom. To attend to these distinct concerns, Heaney will eventually propose as a model the memorization of poems. One of his "aims" while head of the English Department at Carysfort College, as he comments in a 1981 interview with John Haffenden, was to "get these girls [trainee teachers] to read about twelve to twenty poems a year"; then, "over three years they may know within themselves about thirty or forty poems. That seems to me to be quite a large achievement."[18] This is not a "profitless memorizing," Leavis's criticism of earlier – unscientific – ways of teaching poetry.[19] Instead it is an "internalization" of poetry that contributes not only to "the definition of the culture, and the redefinition of it" but also opens "the students into trust in their own personality, into some kind of freedom and cultivation."[20]

There is the trace here once more of Jungian psychology: the student's personal journey inwards enables a form of individuation or search for "completion." That "unity" is the end point of memorization is made explicit in comments Heaney makes to Siobhan McSweeney in 1981 for her *Crane Bag* article "The Poet's Picture of Education," when he argues that "The ultimate justification for

The Necessity of an Idea of Transcendence   155

memorisation is a unity in your own life" and that "When you learn poetry you get a sense of rhythm, you get an inwardness with the language, you get a possession of it and if, in practice, the thing often seems like a mauling and a diminishing, in the end, to have memorised something is a possession and an enriching one. Even if you're never, as it were, going to use those things again, they are capillaries, back into the original parts of yourself and I think for the whole personality, the more linkages there are between one stage and another, the better you are psychically."[21] This sense that the self can be constructed through memorized poems (through other people's words), and that this is a model for psychic health, suggests, as McSweeney notes, a "preoccupation with romantic individualism and liberal humanism" that Heaney shared (among the Irish poets McSweeney interviewed) with Michael Longley, Eavan Boland, Paul Muldoon, and Brendan Kennelly.[22]

The question does arise, however, of what the relationship between the "romantic individual" and the memorized poems will be (whether the example of Wordsworth or Yeats in "The Fire i' the Flint" might be more fitting) and whether there is an irresoluble conflict between individualism and this self-formation through the absorption of texts, words, and lessons. The only "dissenting voice" to the liberal assumptions shared by the interviewees was Seamus Deane, who warned that "what literature teaches is mastery – first over language, over oneself," but that this is not "the same thing as being civilized. Modern literature sponsors forms of violence, obscenity, threat and sometimes heroicizes these."[23] Such a view of language, and concerns about how it is used, had pervaded Heaney's own poetry from *Death of a Naturalist* onwards (with its emphasis on mastering fear through language, and the violence latent in the natural world). Heaney avoids such concerns here, however, by focusing resolutely on the self in terms of completion ("self-fulfilment, self-refinement … self-betterment") rather than mastery; Heaney continues to avow, however contingently and tenuously, faith in literature's ability to be liberating rather than controlling.

THE SHAKY LOCAL VOICE OF EDUCATION

The belief in a desirable "unity" in one's life, and in natural growth and nourishment, also underlies *Among Schoolchildren*, Heaney's fullest discussion of education.[24] This lecture does not depend on the "inwardness" Heaney had lauded to McSweeney; rather, it proposes a pattern whereby poetry is seen to work on three different levels, which can be understood as the personal, the social, and the visionary.[25] Heaney goes beyond the idea of education as "self-fulfilment, self-refinement," and "self-betterment," and also a faith in the social function of education (the pursuit of truth and justice), to argue for a transcendental imaginative sphere where the ultimate benefits of self-development will be felt. The first stage of education presented here is the experience that Heaney gestured towards in "The Play Way," the process of individual self-discovery in which one is "enabled and freed into some new independence, readied for commitment and truly active selfhood."[26] The second stage is "a matter of sympathetic recognition," preparing the student for a social role, enabling "him" "to feel that he is an integral part of the community deriving satisfaction from his full participation in the common life."[27] There are risks involved in such an education: its point could be, to borrow David Lloyd's comments on the political function of literature, "not only to suggest the possibility of transcending conflict, but to do so by excluding (or integrating) difference."[28] For Heaney, however, the dangers involved in "excluding" difference may be avoided through a mode of thinking which is "munificent ... energetic and delightful" as well as "non-sectarian." This is brought about by the third stage of the educational process, a quest for a redemptive poetic imagination.[29] In this, the teacher has the responsibility "to reveal to himself and to others the vitality of his inner personal world, and to testify to its fundamental value" and the "duty of explicating the world in which the citizen lives" while "divesting oneself of the world."[30]

The relationship between these different stages is complex and ambiguous, and they are not entirely distinct. The "transcendental" effect of poetry can work upon the personal and the social, for example; and the emphasis on a transcendental separateness of poetry to "life," history, or society does not negate the fact that it can operate within the personal or social consciousness. In this way *Among Schoolchildren* precedes *Place and Displacement* in its aim to advocate for the value of poetry as ethical and active in this social world, while also claiming poetry's "extraordinary" status as something set apart and subject to its own "conditions of truthfulness."[31] As such it repeats, but then outstrips, a lesson Heaney had learned from *The Prelude*, that "the fundamental revolution had to take place within

The Necessity of an Idea of Transcendence   157

the individual sensibility before it could be realized in society."[32] There is necessarily something "beyond" even those social concerns: poetry – and education – can work to create a space in which we can "go beyond our normal cognitive bounds" (the means of "going beyond" is implicitly that of Jungian individuation).

Heaney adduces as an example of how such a mode of thinking is possible the last stanza of Yeats's "Among Schoolchildren." He argues that this stanza, "one of the high watermarks of poetry," suggests "the necessity of an idea of transcendence" and "an impatience with the limitations of systems, a yearning to be completely fulfilled at all levels of our being," to reach a place "which is not the absence of activity but is, on the contrary, the continuous realisation of all the activities of which we are capable."[33] As he had in his Fordham commencement poem, Heaney aims to "give witness to ... the good force of imagination, to the practice and function of art and in particular, literary art, and the way that art and its practice can refract and compose the tensions of the world."[34] What Egan and Watters had railed against in Yeats's poem – the ambiguity, "density," and difficulty – is precisely the educational point, since the last stanza of the poem presents a "solid," alluring mysteriousness. For Heaney, this stanza offers "a guarantee of our human capacity to outstrip the routine world, the borders of ideology, and the conditionings of history," and the poem as a whole is a vision "of harmony and fulfilment, of a natural and effortless richness of being, a vision, in fact, of a paradisal place ... where the earthly conflicts between flesh and spirit, beauty, truth, effort and ease, will and temperament, are all elided and assumed into harmony and unity."[35]

"Among Schoolchildren," that is, undoes the fall, presenting a vision of a paradise in which conflict and division are resolved, on terms that transcend the rational. This, however, Heaney acknowledges as only a vision or "idea": as has frequently been noted, Heaney claims not that transcendence is possible, but that we have "the necessity of an idea of transcendence." As John Dennison argues, "what is realized in the work of art is the knowing construction of a redemption otherwise held to be impossible."[36] Dennison is wrong to suggest, however, this is "as much confession as affirmation" on Heaney's part (unless one is of the opinion that transcendence is possible, and should be more stridently argued for).[37] Rather, one of the strengths of Heaney's position is its effortful, "artificial" suggestion of the worth of poetry: poetry is not inherently or "naturally" a "good," but a personal, social, moral "good" that has to be repeatedly argued for and recreated in each instance, and despite the knowledge that there is no absolute truth or measure. Indeed, the stamina of Heaney's repeated advocacy of "the Romantic doctrine of poetry's self-vivifying, self-vindicating truthfulness" and the necessity and value "of an idea of transcendence" in spite of the constant possibility of nihilism and nothingness beyond this world is perhaps what is most impressive.[38] Eugene O'Brien relates Heaney's argument here to Blanchot's idea of the "space of literature" in which there is "a restless unity" that allows "different aspects of meaning to coexist and influence."[39] "Unity" is perhaps more obviously "restless" in Heaney's later thinking, however: here the dominant metaphor is "elision" and "assumption" into "harmony and unity"; there is an almost anxious desire to control, absorb, or negate unruly elements.[40] The crucial point for Heaney is – as in his earlier approaches to education – the acceptance and coexistence of apparently irreconcilable tensions (deriving from the personal, social, or poetic, say), and the possibility of a liberation in which one "divest[s] oneself of the world" but is paradoxically still active in it.[41]

This paradoxical divesting is enabled by what Heaney calls, in a conversation with William Carleton in section II of "Station Island," the "shaky local voice of education": a recognition that we should focus on the local and immediate, but do so with knowledge of their "shakiness," their impermanence.[42] Certainly, Heaney's own approach in *Among Schoolchildren* is primarily "local" and autobiographical, uncovering his own developing understanding of the political, sectarian, and linguistic divisions within Northern Ireland, and using this rootedness as a ground on which to seek "unity."[43] He views his time as a student at Queen's as a clash of cultures: "far from the elegances of Oscar Wilde and the profundities of Shakespeare, I was acting with the Bellaghy Dramatic Society in plays about 1798 ... Far from discussing the Victorian loss of faith, I was driving my mother to evening devotions in the 'chapel' or looking for my name in a list of 'adorers' at the exposition of the Blessed Sacrament."[44] The rhetorical questions this provokes (and which I quoted in the introduction) are slightly stagey: "Was I two persons or one? Was I extending myself or breaking myself apart? Was I being led out or led away?" What is being staged is the development of a central part of Heaney's approach to identity, the ability to combine rather than eliminate, to choose "both/and" rather than "either/or."[45] The

The Necessity of an Idea of Transcendence 159

"shaky local voice of education" does not have to be opposed to the canonical education he received at university, but rather, through attentiveness to language and to the different connotations and power structures of language, can transform it into something even more meaningful. Thus, as Heaney argues, the discovery that the word "lachtar" (a flock of young chickens) was a survival from Irish into the English of Derry suggested "a concept of identity that was enlarging and releasing and would eventually help me to relate my literary education with the heritage of the home ground" in poems like "Broagh"; crucially, however, this is not a case of replacing a "myth of alien superiority" with "the myth of native superiority" but allowing different levels of identity (different types of "truthfulness") to have their say.[46]

The tundish scene in Joyce's *Portrait of the Artist as a Young Man* is once more Heaney's guide for how to escape these "myths."[47] There, Stephen Dedalus discovers that the word "tundish," far from being an othering marker of Irish identity, suggests the deep connectedness of Ireland with elements of an English language past that has been forgotten in England. For Stephen, in Heaney's words, "What had seemed disabling and provincial is suddenly found to be corroborating and fundamental and potentially universal."[48] This provides liberation from prescriptive and narrow forms of identity: "If [Stephen] has gone to the trouble of freeing his mind from the net of the English myth, he is also intent on deconstructing the prescriptive myth of Irishness which was burgeoning in his youth and which survives in various sympathetic and unsympathetic forms to this day."[49] While dancing around one "prescriptive myth" here, Heaney is perhaps espousing another: the belief that an "ampler dimension exists, an ideal of divesting oneself of the world" or that (as he quotes Derek Mahon) "The ideal future / Shines out of our better nature."[50] This "ampler dimension" is the "mode of dream and revelation" in which "we go beyond our normal cognitive bounds and sense a new element where we are not alien but liberated, more alive to ourselves, more drawn out, more educated."[51] While it would be wrong simply to read this "ampler dimension" in terms of a (post-)Catholic reverence or respect for the transcendent, it does bespeak a humanist trust in human capability, and the inexplicable role that the unconscious – personal, and perhaps collective – might play. We can see how far Heaney has travelled from someone like R.F. Mackenzie, for whom "an awareness of continuity, of a fourth dimension, time" can "[fill] out and [amplify] the picture of life on earth, so that [pupils] get the hang of things."[52] "Amplification" now leads, for Heaney, not only to a greater sense of the past and its continuity with the present – that which you can get a grip on or hang of – but also to an idealized (and slightly airy) sense of the possibilities of the future, a world that is beyond the "social realm," but which you can then use to understand that realm.

BE WISE AND CHEERFUL?

What – apart from the Romantic hangover of the "necessity of an idea of transcendence" – does this all have to do with Wordsworth? When Heaney repeats this tripartite structure three years later to offer a model of poetic maturation, his touchstone is not Yeats's "Among Schoolchildren" but Wordsworth's "There Was a Boy." This comes during "The Indefatigable Hoof-Taps," Heaney's 1986 T.S. Eliot Memorial lecture in which he measures Sylvia Plath's poetry against a Wordsworthian idea of an educative poetry that expands one's horizons (the Wordsworth here is implicitly that of *Place and Displacement*, the authoritative poetic figure who had faced and overcome personal and social crisis). A quest for "unity" – across the ages – is once more central to the lecture. Heaney appeals to "the deep humanity of the achieved poem, its access to an evolutionary racial ear"; he draws on Eliot's "auditory imagination" once more as a means of providing continuity between the present and a submerged, subconscious past (which can also be the platform for a shift to the impersonal). The auditory imagination "not only unites for the poet the most ancient and most civilized mentalities; it also unites reader and poet and poem in an experience of enlargement, of getting beyond the confines of the first person singular, of widening the lens of receptivity until it reaches and is reached by the world beyond the self."[53] The ultimate point, for Heaney, is that poetry must (once more) go "beyond ego to become the voice of something more than autobiography," and that we must also go beyond social concerns as we seek out "poetic insight."[54]

For the "three degrees of poetic achievement" that underwrite this search, Heaney offers Wordsworth's "There Was a Boy" as a metaphorical structure.[55] This is the famous description of a young boy hooting to the owls on Lake Windermere and discovering the "solemn imagery" of "the visible scene" when the birds fall silent.[56]

The Necessity of an Idea of Transcendence 161

As Heaney reads the passage, "The first task of the poet … is to learn to entwine his or her hands so that the whistle comes out right" – it is for her own pleasure, and for no other reason. The second, social, stage comes when the boy and the owls are whistling back and forth to each other: "this represents the poetry of relation, of ripple-and-wave effect upon audience."[57] The final stage of development is the achievement of poetic insight, or knowledge. This goes beyond social concerns, to the point, in the language of Heaney's lecture "The Murmur of Malvern" (which parallels this lecture in many respects), that poetry passes "the stage of self-questioning, self-exposure, self-healing, to become a common resource."[58] The boy cannot communicate with the owls but instead discovers something more fundamental: he "stands open like an eye or an ear, he becomes imprinted with all the melodies and hieroglyphs of the world; the workings of the active universe, to use another phrase from *The Prelude*, are echoed far inside him" and then there is a sense of "the poem as a gift arising or descending beyond the poet's control, where direct contact is established with the image-cellar, the dream-bank, the word-hoard, the truthcave."[59] (This lecture was first delivered in 1986; Heaney's emphasis on "the poem as gift" might be a defiant response to David Lloyd's odd criticism the previous year of Heaney's tendency, while seeing language "primarily as *naming*," to treat "poems as gifts, involving no labor on the part of the poet.")[60]

Against the benchmark derived from "There Was a Boy," Heaney finds Plath lacking for the extent to which her life "infiltrates" her work. Heaney's concern, and the reason why he invokes Wordsworth, is the extent to which poems can and should be free from the circumstances of the poet's life: in his conclusion, he defers to the 1802 Preface to *Lyrical Ballads*, the "finest" account "of the problematic relation between artistic excellence and truth, between Ariel and Prospero, between poetry as impulse and poetry as criticism of life."[61] Admirably, for Heaney, Plath's poems demonstrate the truth of Wordsworth's formulation that "all good poetry is the spontaneous overflow of powerful feelings," and it is because of the powerful feelings in Plath's poetry (the way her poems "are also clearly acts of her being, words from which … power streams") that Heaney feels they "already belong to the tradition."[62] However, Heaney implies the best poetry surpasses such "powerful feelings," and the problem with Plath's poetry is that her life intrudes excessively into her work. Although Heaney finds nothing *"poetically* flawed" in her work, he believes that "the greatest work occurs when a certain self-forgetfulness is attained, or at least a fullness of self-possession denied to Sylvia Plath": Plath's poetry is too obviously involved, and too emotional; she fails "to go beyond ego."[63]

Where Plath is criticized, Wordsworth is lauded: he offers an ideal of how poets should live as well as write. "Wordsworth," Heaney argues, "declares that what counts is the quality, intensity and breadth of the poet's concerns between the moments of writing, the gravity and purity of the mind's appetites and applications between moments of inspiration. This is what determines the ultimate human value of the act of writing poetry. That act remains free, self-governing, self-seeking, but the worth of the booty it brings back from its raid upon the inarticulate will depend upon the emotional capacity, intellectual resource and general civilization which the articulate poet maintains between the raids."[64] Although poems are free and self-governing, their worth depends on the poet's diligence and, as it were, his or her intellectual commitment (perhaps the "unselfish" aspect Heaney had celebrated at Fordham). Heaney is presenting a poetic that depends on "purity" and "gravity," a poetic that is moral and ethically efficacious and that, like a poetic equivalent of the quest for the Holy Grail or the philosopher's stone, involves a search for insight and knowledge. This is reminiscent of *Among Schoolchildren*, where Heaney had advocated "the kind of poetry ... in which the poem's absolute business is an unconceding pursuit of poetic insight and poetic knowledge" (and for which Heaney chose as models Mandelstam, Socrates, and Jesus).[65]

There are problems, however, with how Heaney develops and uses his model. In his parabolizing of Wordsworth, Heaney repeats the image of the poet "listening in," enchanted, to the natural landscape that had appeared in "The Makings of a Music"; again, however, he creatively misreads Wordsworth's poem.[66] Wordsworth's is ostensibly an elegy for lost childhood: to include it in the 1805 *Prelude* the poet changes it from the first to the third person, kills off the Boy, and places the meditating narrator at the boy's graveside. This elegiac sense of loss is nowhere apparent in Heaney's reading. Furthermore, he equates the boy's communion with the natural world (the replying owls) with a "social" poetry, a call and response with other people, stripping it of its (quasi-religious) sense of isolation and solitude. Similarly, in the third stage of the poetic achievement Heaney slips

The Necessity of an Idea of Transcendence 163

rather too easily from the quasi-pantheistic, quasi-Wordsworthian terms ("the workings of the active universe") to his own etymological, psychological, or cultural terms. Wordsworth's poem suggests that the boy receives an external pantheistic stimulus. During the moments of silence

> a gentle shock of mild surprize
> Has carried far into his heart the voice
> Of mountain torrents, or the visible scene
> Would enter unawares into his mind,
> With all its solemn imagery, its rocks,
> Its woods, and that uncertain heaven, receiv'd
> Into the bosom of the steady lake.[67]

Heaney replaces the "solemn imagery" of the visible scene with his own favourite metaphors for the hidden places from which poems arise, "the image-cellar, the dream-bank, the word-hoard, the truth-cave." These are all enclosed images, metaphors for something hidden within: they flow from the poet's subconscious into his or her conscious, not from the external world into the poet's mind. As in Heaney's previous redirections of Wordsworth's energy, where Wordsworth was looking for a religious truth just beyond his skills of description, Heaney discovers the psychological (and cultural) operations of a poet composing. Wordsworth's religious truth becomes Heaney's poetic truth; religious "spirit" becomes poetic "psyche" and cultural memory.

If he misreads Wordsworth, he also does Plath an injustice. There is the continuation of his earlier gendered approach to poetry (as had been developed in "Fire i' the Flint"), and here his "version of the feminine" causes problems, as Brearton notes, for how he discusses a female poet. He does not acknowledge, for example, that "self-forgetfulness" might be a "luxury denied the female poet struggling to express female subjectivity"; his sense of the "greatest work" tends to foreground the freedoms and (self-)possessions inherited by male poets.[68] It is also odd, as Haughton comments, that Heaney objects to Plath's "dominant theme of self-discovery and self-definition" given the centrality of this to Wordsworth's *Prelude*; as he notes, "Plath's ferocious theater of envies and identifications" perhaps "represents a threat to Heaney's more benign project."[69] This is perhaps not ultimately that surprising. It is against Heaney's (didactic)

164 This Strange Loneliness

liberal humanism that Plath (unlike Wordsworth) is found wanting. Elsewhere Heaney comes to a similar judgment against Philip Larkin, suggesting, in "The Main of Light," that Larkin would repudiate "the Pedlar's advice to Wordsworth in 'The Ruined Cottage' where, having told of the long sufferings of Margaret, he bids the poet 'be wise and cheerful.'"[70] Larkin does not work towards what Heaney later identifies as "the goal of life on earth, and of poetry as a vital factor in the achievement of that goal, [which] is what Yeats called in 'Under Ben Bulben' the 'profane perfection of mankind'": his poetry (perhaps like Plath) does not opt "for the condition of overlife" nor rebel "at limit."[71] The distinction between Wordsworth and Plath perhaps rests, fundamentally, on the (banal) point that one espoused optimism and cheerfulness in the face of suffering, one did not.

These are not, however, Heaney's final words on Plath or "There Was a Boy": as is often the case, he later revises his earlier criticisms. He returns to Plath's poetry, for example, in a *Sunday Times* article in 1999 to highlight instead the "kinetic effect" of her work, the way it "has a carry-over effect in life."[72] And he also later takes a more nuanced view to his reading of "There Was a Boy": in a 1993 *Poetry Review* article he celebrates Robert Frost's "The Most of It" as a "bit of Romantic revision, Frost's sceptical retort to Wordsworth's answering owls."[73] This skepticism is necessary. There is a hint of poetic quietism in the Pedlar's injunction to be "wise and cheerful," or in the celebration of "overlife" or "the gravity and purity of the mind's appetites and applications between moments of inspiration"; the concerns of the social, everyday world can be transcended through cheerfulness or the pursuit of an oxymoronic "profane perfection." Such optimism is incredibly hard to maintain, and is undermined somewhat by Heaney's most public instance of advocacy for Wordsworth's work, published between "The Indefatigable Hoof-Taps" and these later revisions – his introduction to the 1988 Faber selection of the older poet's work: this had begun the process of tempering and contextualizing any celebration of the transcendent and the "cheerful."[74]

Heaney's introduction to the *Essential Wordsworth* does not open new ground; instead it reads like an assemblage of his previous versions of the Lake poet. He praises Wordsworth as an archetypal poet in whom "emotional susceptibility, intellectual force, psychological acuteness, political awareness, artistic self-knowledge, and bardic representativeness are ... truly and resolutely combined";

The Necessity of an Idea of Transcendence 165

"Wordsworthian," meanwhile, is defined as "Democratic, even republican," "visionary," "philosophic," "cathartic," and "salutary."[75] Wordsworth once more provides a model for how one strives towards unity or fulfillment through an exploration of the mysterious or "uncanny": the "one big truth" Wordsworth knew by his late twenties, Heaney argues, was that the "uncanny moments" of childhood "were not only the foundation of his sensibility, but the clue to his fulfilled identity."[76] This truth, and his "indispensable" role as the "finder and keeper of the self-as-subject," underpins his achievement, the "largest and most securely founded in the canon of native English poetry since Milton": thus, when Heaney chooses to use *Finders Keepers* as the title for his collected criticism, he is aligning himself with Wordsworth (as well as the broad lyric genre of the "self-as-subject").[77] Heaney does not, however, entirely downplay Wordsworth's "role as 'loser and weeper'"; this "essential" Wordsworth is once more a psychologically and emotionally displaced figure, attempting to individuate his way towards resolution, and succeeding.[78] If Wordsworth did, indeed, fulfill the "Yeatsian" task of "hammering his thoughts into unity," then his poems can only "communicate such an impression of wholeness and depth" because they "arrived as the hard-earned reward of resolved crisis"; a crisis from which he was "helped back towards his characteristic mental 'chearfulness' by two indispensable soul-guides," Dorothy and Coleridge.[79]

Heaney's introduction traces the same movement towards fulfillment, transcendence, and unity as *Place and Displacement*. He has to balance this, however, with another, less salutary, narrative: by the nature of the book, he has to consider Wordsworth's life as a whole, rather than sketching out the curtailed epiphany of an abbreviated biography. For the first time in Heaney's writing, Wordsworth is also a poet, ultimately, of disappointment. Heaney introduces, with no aim of dispelling, the "general impression that as the years proceeded Wordsworth became more an institution than an individual," an impression "reinforced by the sonorous expatiation of his later poetry and the roll call of his offices and associations – friend of the aristocracy, Distributor of Stamps for Westmoreland, Poet Laureate."[80] For Wordsworth, having "lost the path that should have kept leading more confidently and deeply inward," his destiny becomes an acting out of the moral of "Ode: Intimations of Immortality," in which he has "to endure and try to make sense of the ebb of his powers and the flight of his vision."[81]

There is clearly, however, an impulse in Heaney's introduction to account generously even for Wordsworth's later years, for his "discipline of maintaining equanimity in the face of loss," and the "habit of patience" which found reward "in masterpieces of disappointment like the 'Immortality Ode' and 'Elegiac Stanzas.'"[82] This is a work of critical pruning of the kind Heaney later imagines will happen to Hugh MacDiarmid as it had to Wordsworth: "the second phase of his career will be rendered down to a series of self-contained, self-sustaining passages of genuine poetry."[83] The overall lesson is that the search for unity, resolution, and salvation can never be fulfilled. Instead, it is the search itself – and the moments of tremulous tension that it brings – that is important: "As a poet, he was always at his best while struggling to become a whole person, to reconcile the sense of incoherence and disappointment forced upon him by time and circumstance with those intimations of harmonious communion promised by his childhood visions, and seemingly ratified by his glimpse of a society atremble at the moment of revolution."[84] If Heaney appeals, as in *Place and Displacement*, to a Jungian sense of individuation, then he does so in the knowledge that, as the "Ode: Intimations of Immortality" suggests, any sense of "harmonious communion" may also be a glory passed away from the earth.

A TENDER HAZE OR LUMINOUS MIST

With Heaney, there is often a dovetailing between the concerns of his criticism and the insights of his poems. Poems open ground that the criticism then explores; or, less generously, the criticism argues for a poetics that justifies or predicts his poetic method. From *Among Schoolchildren* through "The Indefatigable Hoof-Taps" to Heaney's introduction to Wordsworth's poems, there is a shift from a desire for the transcendental or poetic (that which outstrips social and political conditions) to the realization that the "struggle to become a whole person, to reconcile the sense of incoherence and disappointment" with "intimations of harmonious communion" might be an impossible quest (but valuable nevertheless in its quixotic persistence). It is no surprise then that a similar shift – from a desire for the transcendent to a presentiment of failed transcendence – can also be traced in his poetry, between *Station Island* (1984) and *The Haw Lantern* (1987): and, as in his prose, the failure of transcendence is not a cause for defeat or despair.

The Necessity of an Idea of Transcendence 167

The Haw Lantern repeats and negates many of the images and tropes of *Station Island*, rejecting the possibility of a poetic plane "other" to the social and human world (and so the poet's ability to exist "in-between" these worlds). Instead of the central trope of the poet as a sacrificial or penitential figure who helps salve political or social rupture, in *The Haw Lantern* there is rumination on loss and silence in which the tense negotiation is between presence and absence (rather than the social and the poetic). Poetry is made, as in "Hailstones," "out of the melt of the real thing / smarting into its absence."[85] This is a collection of intense existential introspection, in part spurred by the death of both of Heaney's parents: various poems brood over the nature of the voids they have left, and are made particularly fraught by the rejection (signalled at the end of "Station Island") of the possibility of an omniscient God who can offer guidance, redemption, and, especially, everlasting life. This rejection does not provoke an amoral stance, however – quite the contrary. The poetic imagination finds renewed impetus as the haws that breathed inspiration on the poet in "The Loaning" mutate into the haw lantern with which Diogenes judges people in the title poem "The Haw Lantern": voids become sources of illumination.

How Heaney imagines trees, for example, changes from *Station Island* (and *Sweeney Astray*). Earlier, they were used as poetic hiding-places ("My hidebound boundary tree. My tree of knowledge. / My thick-tapped, soft-fledged, airy listening post"), sites of dislocation and mystification ("The old trees were nowhere, / the hedges thin as penwork"), or as shorthand for the Gaelic literary tradition (with the association between the Gaelic alphabet and trees).[86] In *The Haw Lantern* almost all of the trees have been felled (an exception is the haw in the title poem, "burning out of season ... a small light for small people").[87] In the final "Clearances" sonnet, written in memory of his mother, a chestnut tree, which was Heaney's "coeval," no longer exists, and Heaney imagines "walking round and round a space / *Utterly empty, utterly a source*."[88] The same lines had been applied to the body of a dead dog in section III of "Station Island" (itself a delayed reappearance of the image from the short story "There's Rosemary"); there, though, the "source" is "like the idea of sound; // like an absence stationed in the swamp-fed air."[89] Unlike the "bad carcass and scrags of hair" of the dog, however, the tree has transmogrified, diffusing a sense of peace, "Its heft and hush become a bright nowhere, / A soul ramifying and forever / Silent, beyond silence listened for."[90] "Clearances" suggests the pantheism of "There Was a Boy," when the boy "hangs listening" into a silence and hears the "voice / Of mountain torrents": out of the silence comes the apprehension of a beneficial universal spirit.[91] What Wordsworth's boy discovers to be a presence, however, Heaney experiences as a "bright nowhere."

When he theorizes this imaginative transformation in "The Placeless Heaven" (a lecture delivered at Kavanagh's Yearly in November 1985), Heaney describes how "In my mind's eye I saw [the tree] as a kind of luminous emptiness, a warp and waver of light"; the tree is no longer a "living symbol of being rooted in the native ground," but instead a symbol of "preparing to be unrooted, to be spirited away into some transparent, yet indigenous afterlife. The new place was all idea."[92] This does not lend itself, as in the first of Wordsworth's "Essays upon Epitaphs," to a mystifying nostalgia with respect to the past, the idea that "The character of a deceased friend or beloved kinsman is not seen, no – nor ought to be seen, otherwise than as a tree through a tender haze or a luminous mist, that spiritualises and beautifies it."[93] Although Heaney's work expresses a similar sentiment to Wordsworth's claim that such spiritualizing "*is* truth, and of the highest order ... it is truth hallowed by love," it is also anxious about the aestheticization of death (and especially violent death). One of Heaney's most famous self-accusations comes in "Station Island," when the ghost of his cousin Colum McCartney charges him with "whitewash[ing] ugliness" and using Dante's *Purgatorio* to "saccharin[e]" his death in the poem "The Strand at Lough Beg": Heaney is accused "indirectly," while the "Protestant who shot me through the head" is accused directly.[94] The poems in *The Haw Lantern*, as a result, try to focus on death and loss, and to pay homage, without a reliance on the "saccharine" or the unduly hazy or misty.

"Clearances viii," for example, pictures the moment of his mother's death: "The space we stood around had been emptied / Into us to keep, it penetrated / Clearances that suddenly stood open. / High cries were felled and a pure change happened."[95] This does not suggest that our essence is diffused among our acquaintances at death (that we become, in W.H. Auden's elegy for Yeats, our "admirers") or that a "tender haze" intervenes; the emptying of space is also a diffusion of emptiness (a clearance which can perhaps be reimagined, memorialized, or worshipped).[96] This is a "pure change," a

The Necessity of an Idea of Transcendence 169

purifying, a passing of responsibility, and a starting anew; and it is ghosted (that "change," the space that is "utterly empty") by Yeats's "Easter 1916" where all is "changed, changed utterly."[97] As in Yeats's poem, there is an effort at assuaging, at salving wounds. The breathy *h* and *sh* sounds of the felled tree's "heft and hush" reassure and comfort, and soften the violent *k* and *t* of the felling of the tree: "I heard the hatchet's differentiated / Accurate cut, the crack, the sigh / And collapse of what luxuriated / Through the shocked tips and wreckage of it all."[98] In both cases, however, the space can only be "kept," be a "source," because of its absence: they are only *eutopias* because they are *utopias*; it is the utter emptiness that is, perhaps strangely, fortifying, or generative.[99]

This is because there is a feeling here of having passed through a traumatic test or examination, of moving on to an aftermath that may be deflationary or euphoric. Such tests are repeated throughout *The Haw Lantern*. In the title poem, the haws of "The Loaning" become the haw lantern of "the roaming shape of Diogenes / with his lantern, seeking one just man; / so you end up scrutinized from behind the haw." Diogenes is a projection, a manifestation of breath pluming "in the frost," of "small people, / wanting no more from them but that they keep / the wick of self-respect from dying out." And there is nobility, as well as disappointment, in undergoing the scrutiny and being found wanting, as Diogenes "scans you, then moves on."[100] In "From the Frontier of Writing" this scrutiny is figured as passing through a checkpoint: even though at first the poet feels "a little emptier, a little spent ... subjugated, yes, and obedient," he is "arraigned yet freed" as the checkpoint recedes behind him "like tree shadows into the polished windscreen."[101]

The image of the haws changes because Heaney's focus shifts from poetic inspiration to "witnessing" and to ethical (self-)judgment. As the emphasis on individuation in *Place and Displacement* and *Among Schoolchildren* suggests, Heaney's poetry often negotiates between two different views of cultural identity: one which posits a (pre-existing) communal identity into which the poet can tap, and another which suggests a much more fragmented and disaffected identity, born out of discontinuities, ruptures, and disappointments, a fragmented identity which the poet witnesses (or testifies to). This second is a form of cultural identity not based on a given past, but on an imagined future: as Stuart Hall argues, it is "a matter of 'becoming' as well as of 'being.' It belongs to the future as much as to the past. It is not something which already exists, transcending place, time, history and culture."[102] In later collections Heaney will explore such an identity through images of tentative, shimmering flux (of "shakiness" or "restlessness"); in *The Haw Lantern* he sets about deconstructing any reliable notion of the transcendent, moving from an exploration of being to one of becoming.

Heaney turns away from the idea of a hypothetical ahistorical plane to which one can escape, and instead positions himself in liminal spaces, from which he can write back to the "real world" in a parabolizing (and at times sermonizing) manner. He writes, astraddle, "From the Frontier of Writing," "From the Republic of Conscience," "From the Land of the Unspoken," and "From the Canton of Expectation"; and he constructs and deconstructs a "Parable Island" and "Mud Vision." In each, the "unreal" world visited is based on some element of twentieth-century (Irish) existence, and the relationship between both "worlds" is seen primarily in terms of frontiers and border crossings: there is a constant dialectic between "homecoming" and "exile." In "From the Republic of Conscience," the poet is called upon "when I got home / to consider myself a representative / and to speak on their behalf in my own tongue."[103] In "From the Land of the Unspoken," the "silent" people's exile "among the speech-ridden" began before anyone can remember; they have always been and always will be a "dispersed people."[104] The poet here is not an inspired, transcendent figure resolving the divisions of society, but a witness of a fragmented and disaffected world.

In part Heaney reaffirms the idea that the world is itself "text," constituted first and foremost by language, and never fully intelligible. This idea had been evoked in "The Loaning" and "The King of the Ditchbacks" in *Station Island*, where the poet discovers the "limbo of lost words" and "a dark morse / along the bank."[105] In "Alphabets" in *The Haw Lantern*, however, Heaney rather programmatically (as the Phi Beta Kappa poem at Harvard in 1984, it was for a programmatic occasion) traces how his ability to describe the natural landscape parallels his linguistic development. His first encounter with symbol-forming ("A shadow his father makes with his joined hands / And thumbs and fingers nibbles on the wall / Like a rabbit's head") develops into the a-b-c, and then into the Latin, Irish, and Greek languages and scripts he learned at school and university.[106] As with the early poems of *Death of a Naturalist*, developing

The Necessity of an Idea of Transcendence 171

linguistic skill leads to developing mastery of the world (and a synecdochic relationship between the two): many of the languages are figured through natural and agricultural images – "a swan's neck and a swan's back" for the number 2, Irish being like trees "The lines of script like briars coiled in ditches," and Latin a ploughman with a "team of quills."[107] This is the "mastery" and control that Seamus Deane had expressed wariness about; in "Alphabets," though, it is a matter of wonder. The end point of this linguistic journey is also its origin: like the astronaut who "sees all he has sprung from, / The risen, aqueous, singular, lucent O / Like a magnified and buoyant ovum," Heaney returns to an image of his own potential, pre-literate self "All agog at the plasterer on his ladder / Skimming our gable and writing our name there / With his trowel point, letter by strange letter."[108] This could be seen as the multiple, and multi-linguistic, adult selves being neatly contained within the "lucent O," the limitless potential of the ovum, in a way that annuls any conflict between the linguistic inheritances (especially because it moves from the concrete – the plasterer's trowel – to the abstract symbol of the Earth in its entirety).

Banally, the entire earth is the "potential" space here, and there is no historical tension or even interplay between the languages. Where this could potentially have offered up a multiplicity of meanings, and of, in Steven Matthews's words, "densely incrowding times and voices which the text can only struggle to contain," the whole direction of Heaney's thought is here against it; instead he presupposes a closed circle of historical inevitability in which the child has little chance of changing the course of his future (and no desire to change it).[109] "Alphabets," then, presents a sanitized version of history through English, Irish, Latin, and Greek that is clearly problematic, as is the rooting of each of these in the land or "natural" landscape. Any transition between languages as history (either personal or cultural) develops is then seen as being a natural process, one of (inevitable) evolution; this is the opposite of the historically nuanced *dinnseanchas* poems in *Wintering Out*. The problem here is similar to one that can be read into the parables in this collection: that they repeatedly reinforce the idea that the poet – when he has "Conscience," when he is "Unspoken," and so on – can elide difference, can create and validate a unified whole, whether it be a unified self or text.

However, these poems also seem to be working against themselves, pulling in an opposite direction. If they are working towards

172   This Strange Loneliness

a foreclosed, unified self, a "lucent O," they are also heading not towards an utterance that will represent this (a great "I am"), but towards silence. In "From the Land of the Unspoken," for example, silence itself becomes the (necessarily) absent language of "true" meaning. Here "unspoken assumptions have the force / of revelation," and any attempt to communicate this meaning will fail: "whoever is the first of us to seek / assent and votes in a rich democracy / will be the last of us and have killed our language?"[110] The optimism of "Alphabets" is quite undone. It is tempting to use postcolonial ideas of lost "authenticity" here: Dennis Lee's suggestion, for example, that for Canadian writers "the *words* of home are silent ... Try to speak the words of your home and you will discover – if you are a colonial – that you do not know them ... To reflect is to fall silent, discovering that your authentic space does not have words."[111] Notably, though, the spaces Heaney creates in *The Haw Lantern* may not have words and may be "empty," but they also tend to be occupied by weighty symbols: silent, but meaningful, stones. A moment of communication in "From the Land of the Unspoken," for example, comes when the poet and his fellow "citizen" are "pretending to be absorbed in a display / of absolutely silent quernstones": physical objects turned into pure, significant (and unproblematic) symbols.[112] In "The Stone Verdict," meanwhile, Heaney desires that the last heavenly judgment on his father take the form of a pile of stones – it should be "like the judgement of Hermes, / God of the stone heap, where the stones were verdicts / Cast solidly at his feet."[113] These rocks may be "hermetic," devoted to Hermes, god of boundaries and psychopomp, messenger of the gods; however, their messages, their verdicts, are wordless.[114] As Helen Vendler notes, this image derives from W.K.C. Guthrie's *The Greeks and Their Gods*, and the acquittal of Hermes (who had killed Argos) being delivered by the gods casting their voting-pebbles at his feet, and so building a heap of stones around him: the powerful silence of this "verdict" is fitting for Heaney's father, "whose silent integrity was mistrustful of speech."[115] Thus, Heaney wants his father's "apotheosis," his cairn, to be "maybe a gate-pillar / Or a tumbled wallstead where hogweed earths the silence" and where language would destroy the possibility of communion: "somebody will break at last to say, 'Here / His spirit lingers,' and will have said too much."[116] Silence is the guarantor of connection across the grave; when the silence is broken, the "spirit" is gone.

The Necessity of an Idea of Transcendence 173

DISAPPEARING VISIONS

The cairn, the "tumbled wallstead," the possibility of a "spirit" lingering in silence: this is, once more, Wordsworthian territory.[117] Wordsworth, on a basic level, repeatedly uses piles of rocks on a hillside to evoke the memory of some "absent" person, their spirit enshrined there and persistent in the plants that flourish in the stones. In "The Ruined Cottage," for example, the narrator traces in the ruins of the cottage "That secret spirit of humanity / Which, mid the calm oblivious tendencies / Of nature, 'mid her plants, her weeds and flowers, / And silent overgrowings, still survived."[118] Within the silence of the ruins, the "secret spirit of humanity" survives (and so there is some form of persistent hope). It is such a hope of continuation, permanence, and even eternity that Heaney desires in "The Stone Verdict" but cannot express: it must remain as an unspoken potentiality. This image of a cairn, of a spiritualized ruin, is the last element of a dynamic which presents multiple voices but presupposes the ability of a single unifying voice to incorporate or comment on them; and which simultaneously opposes the modern world to an imaginary ideal, spiritual, and previous "other" world. It is a gesture towards the possibility of a spiritual, yet also secular, world, which might redeem and revitalize the "soullessness" of twentieth-century Ireland: the hope for redemption is, however, made manifest only to be absolutely deflated in Heaney's poem "The Mud Vision," the end point of this dream of the visionary.

The "Mud Vision" of the title occurs in a modern Ireland that is sophisticated, soulless, and empty, a land that has rejected the possibility of epiphany and a meaning for existence: it is a poem of "spacelessness" rather than space.[119] The central thrust of the poem is somewhat reactionary. Contemporary Ireland is founded on a lack: writing and art are in the hands of "menu-writers / And punks with aerosol sprays"; religion is slogan and abandoned symbol ("Statues with exposed hearts and barbed-wire crowns / Still stood in alcoves") or reduced to a disembodied media message ("Satellite link-ups / Wafted over us the blessings of popes"); and traditional culture has become solely superficial – they have "screentested / Our first native models and the last of the mummers."[120] All the vestiges of the modern world are rejected as disconnected, disconnecting, disengaged, and disengaging; the poet tells how "We sleepwalked / The line between panic and formulae," "Watching ourselves at a distance, advantaged / And airy as a man on a springboard / Who keeps limbering up because the man cannot dive."[121] There is no possibility of creation here; any potential is necessarily stymied.

The mud vision of the title promises redemption, to provide a unifying element, to create spiritual and mystical possibility out of the secular and muddy materials of the "real" world. It is an epiphany located in a lost centre of the world, in "the foggy midlands," and like the "lucent O" and "ovum" in "Alphabets," it too is a circle ("a gossamer wheel, concentric with its own hub / Of nebulous dirt") full of potential.[122] Unlike the ovum, however, it is also full of mud: it is "silt," a "trembling corolla" causing a "fuzz," "a smudge," "mould in the verbena," "a light / Furrow-breath on the pillow."[123] What it offers is a complete system of belief, a closed esoteric circle of meaning, which will stand in for the absent single and unifying truth of "God." The onlookers "were vouchsafed / Original clay, transfigured and spinning"; that is, they are offered an Adam, a spiritually created physical manifestation, "sullied yet lucent" as it were, which they can claim as their own (unlike the distant "heard of" "sun standing still and the sun / That changed colour").[124] Its nebulousness, its "sulliedness" is important: it is not a revelation of the divine, but a muddying of it.

As such, "The Mud Vision" undermines the Wordsworthian epiphanic structure in which an imaginatively nourishing apprehension of the infinite is developed from a close and personal contact with the natural landscape. The mud vision does not bring lasting contact with the infinite, and does not ultimately encourage the imagination, but judgment. It is presumed to be "a test / That would prove us beyond expectation"; however, they "lived, of course, to learn the folly of that."[125] As with the test in "The Haw Lantern," the best that can be hoped for is to be "cleared" and left (in a post-coital manner) "a little emptier, a little spent."[126] "The Mud Vision" proposes a different type of "clearance," however. When the vision departs it leaves a Wordsworthian landscape, a ruin like those of "Michael" or "The Ruined Cottage": "One day it was gone and the east gable / Where its trembling corolla had balanced / Was starkly a ruin again, with dandelions / Blowing high up on the ledges, and moss / That slumbered on through its increase."[127] Looking back in *Stepping Stones*, Heaney would locate his own adult experience of "visionary moments" akin to those in Wordsworth's "Ode: Intimations of Immortality" at a "gable": "Out in the country, on

The Necessity of an Idea of Transcendence 175

starlit nights in Glanmore, pissing at the gable of the house, I had the usual reveries of immensity."[128] In "The Mud Vision," however, as the gable becomes a ruin it is now doubly an absence: absent of human life and also of the epiphany experienced there. The vision has been reduced to the finite terms and temporalities of the natural world: its "corolla" has been replaced by dandelion clocks. The image of "slumber[ing] on through its increase" echoes (once more) "A Slumber Did My Spirit Seal," where the departed "Lucy" no longer feels the "touch of earthly years" but is instead "Roll'd round in earth's diurnal course / With rocks and stones and trees."[129] That such eternal "slumbering" and the touch of the earthly no longer appears to suffice is perhaps in part because "The Mud Vision" is more clearly anxious than Wordsworth's poem about what underlies the vision, about its authenticity and efficacy, and about the extent to which it is a performance rather than an (epiphanic) experience.

Anxiety about the visionary is perhaps due to the fact that behind Heaney's poem there isn't a pantheistic life force, but a historical precedent: the apparitions of the Virgin Mary in a hawthorn bush in Ardboe on an almost nightly basis between August and December 1954, and the phenomenon these caused. In a *Paris Review* interview in 1997, Heaney remembers at the time "feeling this huge sense of animation and focus and expectation and skepticism all at once. It was a current that flowed in and flowed out of this one little place, which was as a matter of fact the place my wife comes from, Ardboe, on the shores of Lough Neagh. And even though I did not believe that the mother of God had stood there on a hawthorn bush at the end of a local garden, I was tuned in to the animation. So that memory of a community centered and expectant and alive to vision is behind the poem."[130] (As Heaney notes, the memory of this "vision" combines with a work of art created on the side of the Guinness storehouse in Dublin, "by the English artist Richard Long, a big flower-face on a wall, made up entirely of muddy handprints. It began as a set of six or eight petals of mud and then moved out and out concentrically until it became this huge sullied rose window.") For Heaney, the poem negotiates his understanding of Ireland as a country with "a religious subconscious but a secular destiny," and it is the nature of that destiny, the aftermath of the experience, rather than the content of the emptied-out epiphany – Virgin Mary or muddy handprints – that is ultimately important. In the final three lines the poet speaks out of the poem: "You could say we survived. So say that, and watch

176   This Strange Loneliness

us / Who had our chance to be mud-men, convinced and estranged, / Figure in our own eyes for the eyes of the world."[131] What "survives" is not the "secret spirit of humanity," as in "The Ruined Cottage," but the poem itself, the "convinced and estranged" performance of epiphany and of muddy authenticity: a "figuring" in which meaning is bestowed by the "eyes of the world" as well as "our own eyes."

The Wordsworthian idea of an eternal infusing spirit is used as a metaphor not for the vision it stimulated, but – at most – for the poem that encapsulated the vision. Jonathan Bate suggests that "'The Ruined Cottage' proposes that the survival of humanity comes with nature's mastery over the edifices of civilisation": "The Mud Vision" might, on the other hand, propose that the survival of humanity comes with poetry's, or the imagination's, mastery over these edifices, in spite of the "experts" with their "*post factum* jabber" and "big explanations."[132] This is just a "figuring," however, a pose not unlike that of the man "on a springboard / Who keeps limbering up because the man cannot dive": there is nothing authenticating or essential at the heart of the vision. If this is a secularization of the Romantic transcendental vision, it is one that is dubious about the moral and ethical values of the secular world. The "muddiness" is the problem, the desire to hold on to the land or the soil as the element of continuity. In *Seeing Things*, Heaney will talk about learning to "walk on air / against my better judgement": this is the ability to step off the springboard, but not fall, to become Hercules rather than Antaeus. This "airiness" is what is worked towards in *The Haw Lantern*, especially in "The Disappearing Island." The poet describes how "The island broke beneath us like a wave. // The land sustaining us seemed to hold firm / Only when we embraced it *in extremis*. / All I believe that happened there was vision."[133] "All" is doubled here: it might mean everything or nothing, or both. Vision then stands in for, and becomes, reality: as Seamus Deane notes, "it is the actual that becomes the product rather than the precondition of the vision."[134] *All* that we have is vision: and here, unlike "The Mud Vision," that is a cause for celebration; the visionary allows the land to "hold firm."

There is, I would suggest, a passage in Wordsworth which informs this shift to a trust in, and reliance, on the "visionary": it is drawn from the famous note to "Ode: Intimations of Immortality" that Wordsworth dictated to Isabella Fenwick, and gives emotional and intellectual depth to Wordsworth's experience of the "sublime." Wordsworth comments:

The Necessity of an Idea of Transcendence 177

> I used to brood over the stories of Enoch and Elijah, and almost to persuade myself that, whatever might become of others, I should be translated, in something of the same way, to heaven. With a feeling congenial to this, I was often unable to think of external things as having external existence, and I communed with all that I saw as something not apart from but inherent in my own immaterial nature. Many times, while going to school have I grasped at a wall of [sic] tree to recall myself from this abyss of idealism to the reality. At that time I was afraid of such processes. In later periods of life I have deplored, as we all have reason to do, a subjugation of the opposite character and have rejoiced over the remembrances, as is expressed in the lines "obstinate questionings &c."[135]

(The quotation from the "Ode" continues "obstinate questionings / Of sense and outward things, / Fallings from us, vanishings.")[136] Wordsworth presents us with a trope of "translation" – in the religious sense of being "carried across" to heaven – and of the dissolution of the real world (halted only by physically grasping it). Further, Wordsworth's relationship to this "abyss of idealism" changes over time; he comes to rejoice in flux and uncertainty, the present-participled fluidity of "questionings," (and "fallings" and "vanishings"). Jonathan Wordsworth notes "the sense of the endlessness of the present participle" in Wordsworth's poetry, and especially how the *stepping* in "'Stepping Westward' has become a guarantee of never-reaching, and therefore of never sinking into stasis and death – never *needing* rebirth."[137] In the "Ode" the present participles guarantee both the endlessness of the external and our inability ever to reach or know it – the outward things are eternal "fallings from us."

Heaney's "Disappearing Island" repeats this sense of eternal motion. The dissolution of the island can only be halted by physical contact (embracing) at the moment of death, the moment of "translation" to heaven. There is something tremulous about this physical contact. There are two present participles in the poem – "Disappearing" in the title, and "sustaining" (in the image of the "land sustaining us") – which work directly against each other. There is a balance that is not static, but is a constant give and take, an eternal flow. The land is disappearing and, paradoxically, because of this it is sustaining the people on it: the disappearance of the island is what guarantees its existence. The "real world," if it exists, is revealed to be in constant flux, constantly renewing and changing itself through contact with the visionary.[138] The view *in extremis*, from the point of death, that Heaney adopts in this poem is, as Helen Vendler comments, "an almost posthumous perspective" from which the poet can define the "transcendent" and the "real" "as the obverse and reverse of a single perception."[139] This perspective is part of an ongoing tendency across Heaney's career to link the poetic imagination and death (and the dead); imagination is used to face the dead and ultimately to commune, or converse with the dead. However, it also suggests that there is something deathly about the visionary, a crisis in the "idea of transcendence." If Heaney is really writing from the "border" of vision, and the border of death, what can be seen there, beyond the limits? What is the relationship between time and eternity that would allow you to see "beyond"? And what language can be used for this?

Heaney's perspective is a development of the problem that Wordsworth had faced in "Ode: Intimations of Immortality" (and in his comments on the poem). Wordsworth's crisis is retrospective rather than originative: it is based on the loss of the visionary power of childhood ("whither is fled the visionary gleam?"). Wordsworth could, however, retain even as a trace memory from childhood the possibility of transcendence, of a Kantian sublime which, as Hart notes, will "raise the forces of the soul above the height of vulgar commonplace, and discover within us a power of resistance of quite another kind, which gives us courage to be able to measure ourselves against the seeming omnipotence of nature."[140] By *The Haw Lantern*, however, Heaney cannot subscribe to such a notion of the "sublime" or transcendent – even the language is suspect – and even "an idea of transcendence" risks having its power sapped by post-factum jabber, media commentary, the touch of mundane reality. To invoke terms such as the "*sublime*" or "*inspiration, vision, apocalypse, imagination, the daemonic*," or "*transcendence*" has always been, as Thomas Weiskel argues, "to beg many questions; yet the terms are indispensable, for the data of experience cannot be authenticated or even recognized without implicit acts of metaphor."[141] The main lesson of "The Mud Vision," then, is that the language of the visionary is both irrevocably tainted – muddied – and nevertheless necessary.

The Necessity of an Idea of Transcendence 179

SEEING *SEEING THINGS*

How, given the problems with the "visionary," can Heaney develop a (Kantian or Wordsworthian) "power of resistance" that helps him measure himself against omnipotence or nothingness? Perhaps only through a fundamental reframing – or fudging – of the question of the epiphanic.[142] Heaney's next collection, *Seeing Things*, is his most focused exploration of ambivalent potential, and of the possibility of separating the idea of "epiphany" as an act of imaginative transfiguration from the need for there to be something beyond this world that is "revealed." The epiphanic experience (rather than what is revealed) is celebrated as an end in itself. The title poem alludes to the Joycean epiphany (with its emphasis on "claritas" or "radiance") in its second section – "*Claritas*. The dry-eyed Latin word / Is perfect for the carved stone of the water" – and this emphasis on an intensely focused (and dry-eyed) re-envisioning of a world that is both fixed and fluid, solid and liquid, stone and water, is replayed throughout the collection.[143]

Seeing Things presents the movement, in Elmer Kennedy-Andrews's words, from "the archaeological and excavatory to the aerial and ornithological, from earth to air, darkness to light."[144] This is paralleled by a shift, from *Field Work* onwards, towards the visual, to "recurrent images," as Seamus Deane notes, "of eye, needle, notch, the infinitesimally small opening through which the actual flows, as through an isthmus, into the visionary."[145] However, the shift is not simply from earth to air, from archeology to vision, or to a more subjective, self-reflexive verse. Air might supplant earth, but water is the most bountiful element in *Seeing Things*: seas, rivers, and fishing hold strong sway in Heaney's poetic landscapes and seascapes. Part of the attraction of the visual is also that of hydraulics. The experience of *claritas* in "Seeing Things" is not just of light but of "lightness of being," of being buoyed up and escaping the "Heaviness of being."[146] It is a "lightening" that can be provided by water as well as by light.

So, when Heaney comes to rewrite "The Mud Vision" (a union of the visionary and the visceral) the vision now unites water and light. In "Lightenings i" Heaney extracts the image of the ruin from "The Mud Vision," strips it of any "lingering spirit," and bathes it in rain and a dazzling, estranging light. The image of the ruin is in

This Strange Loneliness

flux, constantly affected by and flitting between ever-changing light and shadow ("shifting brilliancies"). There is interplay between a concrete, "bare wallstead" and cold hearth and the cold clear light that shines on it, doubled in the reflection from a puddle:

Shifting brilliances. Then winter light
In a doorway, and on the stone doorstep
A beggar shivering in silhouette.

So the particular judgement might be set:
Bare wallstead and a cold hearth rained into –
Bright puddle where the soul-free cloud-life roams.[147]

The half-rhymes "light" and "silhouette" balance each other, but in a relationship characterized by movement (the present participles are "shifting" and "shivering") not stasis. This contrasts sharply with the image of the "set" "particular judgement" which opens the second stanza, and indeed this set judgment is undermined and dissipated by the balancing of the "bare wallstead" and the "bright puddle where the soul-free cloud-life roams." What Vendler calls the "Christian fiction of the 'particular judgement' – when one is judged, alone, exposed to the gaze of God, after death" – is rejected.[148] There is no lingering spirit here: the cloud-life metamorphosing the set scene is doubly "soul-free," free of souls and free like a soul. The poem is an epiphany of absence: Heaney discovers an "old truth dawning: there is no next-time-round": "after the commanded journey, what? / Nothing magnificent, nothing unknown. / A gazing out from far away, alone."[149] Rather than being attenuating, this realization is energizing, uplifting. What is left is "Unroofed scope. Knowledge-freshening wind"; the final participle, "freshening," reinvigorates the earlier "shifting."[150]

Here, there is indeed a "restless" energy to Heaney's seeing. This is not a visionary poem, but one that hovers, in terms Heaney borrows from Zbigniew Herbert in his lecture "The Atlas of Civilisation," between "Two glances: one visionary, the other observant."[151] The noumenal powers of the visionary are here applied to the concrete, phenomenological world: depending on the stress Heaney is either *seeing* things or seeing *things*; taken together, he is of course doing both. "Observant," however, still retains a religious *frisson*, the hint of "observance," of paying attention to religious rites and rituals: in

The Necessity of an Idea of Transcendence 181

its careful attention, the poem retains what John Burnside has called "secular / agnostic sacrality," but its focus is resolutely on this world, not a transcendent other-place.[152]

This has often been read as Heaney negotiating his Romantic inheritance: veering between "a field of force" and a "field of vision," or "a neo-romantic visionary poetry" and "a humbler *choisiste* writing," "re-inspecting the phenomenal world in the aftermath of death," exploring "a quasi-visionary insight, or numinous *frisson*, 'seeing things' with Wordsworthian imagination," or adopting a posture of "wise passivity, an acceptance that we cannot conjure or manipulate the marvelous into appearing but only hold ourselves open to its arrival."[153] Ted Hughes, for one, saw the clear influence of Wordsworth on the "Squarings" poems in particular: "Made me think of *The Prelude*, in the ranging self-reassessment, the lifting of sacred moments, with ordinary gestures, into the pattern of the liturgy, and in the ways the whole thing is a self-rededication, a realigning of yourself, to 'the vows made for you'"; however, with a nod to Eliot he also calls the sequence Heaney's "Quartet."[154]

The way in which this collection builds on (but then departs from) the Wordsworthian example is of course important to me here (and will be discussed shortly); but perhaps more so is the general way in which "seeing things" becomes an ethical, as well as an aesthetic, action, a "moral and political imperative."[155] In *The Cure at Troy* (Heaney's 1991 version of Sophocles' *Philoctetes*), when Neoptolemus tells Philoctetes to "stop just licking your wounds. Start seeing things," the instruction suggests Philoctetes is to become ethically active, he is to work "for a good thing."[156] This is not the pose of the pilgrim from *Station Island*, or even Diogenes in *The Haw Lantern*, but that of a witness who is attentive to and testifies about the nature of reality, and political and social conditions, but who is not actually bound by these conditions. As such it is a form of spectral or ghostly witnessing that is focused not on the infinite or the divine, but – from the brink – on the everyday world: indeed, in retrospect, this appears to mark the development of Heaney's final position on the afterlife, the claim that he will repeat, through Wordsworth, in *Stepping Stones*, that "it is on this earth 'we find our happiness, or not at all.'"[157]

Using the perspective *in extremis* as a way to witness "this earth" might then, as Terence Brown argues, enable art to overcome any guilt of escapism and "rest easy in a kind of chastened delight, knowing of its own untrammelled possibility," while not agonizing too much over the fact of mortality.[158] A later poem, "The Turnip-Snedder," in *District and Circle* can be read as an affectionate (if gristly) pastiche of such a perspective, with the life cycle of turnips standing in for that of humans: "'This is the way that God sees life,' / it said, 'from seedling-braird to snedder' ... 'This is the turnip-cycle,' / as it dropped its raw sliced mess / bucketful by glistering bucketful.'"[159] In *Seeing Things*, however, even this level of displaced gristliness is avoided in the exploration of death: what Helen Vendler presents as "unignorable annihilation" is approached with a comparative lightness.[160]

In "Lightenings vii," for example, Heaney remembers how "at parties in renowned old age" Hardy "imagined himself a ghost / And circulated with that new perspective"; this develops the image of Hardy in the previous poem, experimenting "with infinity" by pretending to be dead in a field of sheep.[161] (It is probably only a coincidence, but Hardy shared this interest in a ghostly perspective with Wordsworth: as Frances Ferguson notes, Wordsworth believed that a person could be a "*spectator ab extra* not only to other human beings but also to himself" and so found "Achilles an appealing character because he was able to imagine his own death."[162]) For Wordsworth, Hardy, and Heaney, this exploration of death and infinity was, fundamentally, fortifying. The shift in perspective renders the border between time and eternity fluid and generative; it also means that meaning can be narrated onto death, and that the nothingness of death can to some extent be controlled or averted by being imagined or "told."

Thus, in the first part of "Seeing Things," Heaney adopts the role of a *spectator ab extra* on a boat trip to Inishbofin and becomes aware of the precariousness of their position: "It was as if I looked from another boat / Sailing through air, far up, and could see / How riskily we fared into the morning."[163] The distinction is not here between appearance and reality, but as in *The Haw Lantern* between appearance and disappearance, a coming into presence and a fading into nothingness.[164] This coming into presence is permitted through the creation of a story-world. In the third part of "Seeing Things," when Heaney recalls his father almost drowning in a river, he mixes two different temporal perspectives. The actual events – his father's horse rearing and falling into the river with his cart, sprayer, and hat – are subject to the normal experience of time, our transient experience that shuttles us from oblivion to oblivion. These events

The Necessity of an Idea of Transcendence 183

are, however, set within a fairy tale narrative which begins "Once upon a time," ends "happily ever after," and depicts an afternoon marked out in time only by the throwing of "stones / At a bird on the shed roof."[165] The brush with death thus provides a link between the transient and the eternal, the real and the imaginary: it interrupts our experience of time (that relationship between the subject and time that Christopher Salvesen defines as "memory").[166] Heaney's father is imagined endlessly (because of the present participle) "tumbling off the world" with his horse, cart, and sprayer; and so the memory is itself rendered timeless, located in an eternal present.[167] At stake here is the extent to which memory (and indeed poetry) provides some means of stopping time: can the "deer of time" be slain, as Edwin Muir suggests, or at least chased from the woods for as long as the poet or poem lives, as Sorley MacLean hopes in "Hallaig"?[168] As Heaney's father walks "With his damp footprints out of the river," can these footprints persist in memory, for all that his "ghosthood" is already "immanent"?[169] (By "The Strand" in *The Spirit Level* these footprints will be refigured as "The dotted line my father's ashplant made / On Sandymount Strand" and the answer is definitive: the line "Is something else the tide won't wash away.")[170]

The question of what will dissolve and what won't is raised repeatedly in *Seeing Things*; this question is associated with probing what role the doubled vision – part observation, part re-imagination – plays. In "Field of Vision," for example, Heaney remembers an old woman who had sat for years staring straight ahead "Out the window at sycamore trees unleafing / And leafing at the far end of the lane."[171] From her he gets "an education / Of the sort you got across a well-braced gate," when you "could see // Deeper into the country than you expected" and so "the field behind the hedge" grows "more distinctly strange as you kept standing / Focused and drawn in by what barred the way."[172] The concrete details – the "whitewashed pillars," the gate that is "lean, clean, iron, roadside" – dissolve, become abstract, grow "strange." The gate is a border of vision here: and as it bars the way it focuses our attention and draws it in. It does not, however, provide a definite limit or meaning to the vision; all that is promised is the continuous process of "unleafing" and "leafing." The poem does not propose that the imagination, or the act of observation, can relieve or assuage the old woman's physical suffering; worryingly, though, it does use her as the basis of a moral lesson ("an education") in a manner similar to Wordsworth's

184 This Strange Loneliness

encounter with the impoverished angler in "Point Rash-Judgement" or the leech gatherer in "Resolution and Independence." This "strange" view across a barred gate will be repeated in "Out of Shot" in *District and Circle*: here, the thought process progresses from "inspecting livestock," to the "distant Viking *vik* / of Wicklow Bay," and from there to a news report of a donkey "Loosed from a cart" by mortar fire in a bazaar, "wandering out of shot / Lost to its owner, lost for its sunlit hills."[173] In both "Field of Vision" and "Out of Shot," once more, the question of what is actually *beyond* that gate is unanswerable: the more one looks at it, the "stranger" it gets.

In *Seeing Things* it is generally the visionary that dissolves, in a way that confirms the importance of the "real." When Heaney alludes to Henry Vaughan to ask the question "*All gone into the world of light?*" in "Settings xliv," the poem answers: "Perhaps / As we read the line sheer forms do crowd / The starry vestibule. Otherwise // They do not."[174] Vaughan's statement ("They are all gone into the world of light! / And I alone sit ling'ring here") is turned into a question, but then also deferred and rendered metaphorical. The "lucent O" of "Alphabets" is reworked as Heaney admits that there is nothing outside the phenomenological world: "What lucency survives / Is blanched as worms on nightlines I would lift, / Ungratified if always well prepared // For the nothing there – which was only what had been there."[175] Heaney argues that if the "moment of admission of *All gone*" is "more like a caught line snapping," the loss of the eternal makes one more aware of the passing of time, of how "eddies swirl a dead leaf past in silence / Swifter (it seems) than the water's passage."[176] Similarly, the title poem, despite the appearance of a supernatural force, paradoxically reaffirms the importance of the natural world. Describing the intricately carved stonework on a cathedral façade, Heaney comments that "in that utter visibility / The stone's alive with what's invisible"; crucially, however, this is "Like the zig-zag hieroglyph for life itself," rather than a hieroglyph for anything beyond this life.[177]

Throughout *Seeing Things* Heaney plays with this relationship between the "utterly visible" and the "invisible," creating structures that hint at something beyond this world only to deliver us, ultimately, back to the phenomenological world. The most notable structure comes in "Squarings," a web or net of forty-four poems divided into four stanzas of three lines each, reminiscent of the *terza rima* form; the sequence is further split into four subsections,

The Necessity of an Idea of Transcendence · 185

creating the geometrical or mathematical shape 4x12x12.[178] This can be seen as a "field of force" in which meaning is generated by interactions and relationships across the sequence as a whole rather than in poems in isolation.[179] However, this reliance on interactions and relationship (rather than the single word, image, item, or poem) is also evident in Heaney's tendency towards lists in the collection, to include (at times almost banal) fragments of reality: "sunlight, turfsmoke, seagulls, boatslip, diesel" in "Seeing Things"; "Bare flags. Pump water. Winter evening cold" in "Scrabble"; "scythe and axe and hedge-clippers ... Poker, scuttle, tongs, a gravel-rake" in "The Cot"; and "*Perpetuum mobile*. Sheer pirouette. / Tumblers. Jongleurs. Ring-a-rosies" in "Wheels within Wheels."[180]

Nothing "transcendental" seeps through these fragmented lists, nothing hovers just behind the visible, unless it is imagined. Missing are verbs that would bring concrete massive reality to life: the world *is* but does not do, and requires the energizing power of the poetic imagination. In "The Settle Bed," for example, Heaney realizes that the he does not have to be weighed down utterly by "inheritance." The bed, and the world it symbolizes, is leaden and heavy, made almost entirely of past-participles, verbs or nouns operating as adjectives: "Willed down," "waited for," "trunk-hasped," "painted," "cribbed," "seasoned," "unkindled," "shuttered," "chimed," "planked," "car-goed." Even this, though, can be transformed: "whatever is given // Can always be reimagined, however four-square, / Plank-thick, hull-stupid and out of its time / It happens to be."[181]

The role of the imagination is then that outlined for poetry in "The Government of the Tongue": since it exists "in the rift between what is going to happen and whatever we would wish to happen, poetry holds attention for a space, functions not as distraction but as pure concentration, a focus where our power to concentrate is concentrated back on ourselves."[182] Poetry offers a way of transforming the given and the historical. In the oft-quoted example from *The Cure at Troy*, it offers a space in which "The longed-for tidal wave / Of justice can rise up, / And hope and history rhyme" – where "hope" is taken in the sense outlined by Vaclav Havel as "not the expectation that things will turn out successfully, but the conviction that something is worth working for, however it turns out" (ethical action, however quixotic, is more important than success).[183] Or, in a "revision of the Platonic schema," as Heaney argues in "The Government of the Tongue," art "remains promissory rather than obligatory":

186 This Strange Loneliness

it "is not an inferior reflection of some ordained heavenly system but a rehearsal of it in earthly terms; art does not trace the given map of a better reality but improvises an inspired sketch of it."[184] In improvising a future, art takes the blockish materials of the present and places them in new alignment, or indeed discovers the impermanence and transience in all things. But, like Jesus's writing in the sand, it offers "a break with the usual life but not an absconding from it. Poetry, like the writing, is arbitrary and marks time in every possible sense of that phrase."[185] And, as a comment in "Sounding Auden" suggests, how a poem "marks time" might be by "float[ing] adjacent to, parallel to, the historical moment. What happens to us as readers when we board the poem depends upon the kind of relation it displays towards our historical life."[186]

This approach to poetry renders its effects subjective and individual: each person's "historical life" will inform the meaning of the poem quite differently. But this is all to the point. There is an improvisational quality to a poem's ethical dimensions, a floatiness and airiness that paradoxically gives it heft. This is most evident in "Lightenings viii," a poem based on the Irish *Annals of Clonmacnoise*, which trace the history of Ireland "from the earliest period to A.D. 1408," and include the brief note that, in 744 "There were shipes seen in the skyes with their men this yeare."[187] Heaney turns this into a parable for the imagination, and for how poetry floats alongside the "historical." A ship gets snagged on the altar of Clonmacnoise monastery:

> A crewman shinned and grappled down the rope
> And struggled to release it. But in vain.
> "This man can't bear our life here and will drown,"
>
> The abbot said, "unless we help him." So
> They did, the freed ship sailed, and the man climbed back
> Out of the marvellous as he had known it.[188]

The real and the "marvellous" are balanced here, allowed to intermingle, but not to impose meaning on the other. For the crewman the monks are "the marvellous"; the abbot, meanwhile, discovers the heaviness of their own being, realizing that "This man can't bear our life here and will drown."[189] For both, the other is vision, a break from the ordinary that cannot be explained and yet illuminates their

The Necessity of an Idea of Transcendence   187

everyday existence: but what is marvellous is inherently contingent and subjective, dependent on what each has "known" as reality. This is a moment, as Heaney's 1995 lecture "Further Language" will suggest, in which the creative spirit is "at its most venturesome" and so "establishes a plane from which we can get new bearings on ourselves and take the measure of our segmentedness and instabilities"; a moment in which the "complications and contradictions of history, politics, culture, fidelity, hostility, inner division, challenge, and change get themselves gathered in words and become available to writer and reader as a mode of self-knowledge."[190]

THE OFFING

Gathered, perhaps, but also cast off. The experience in the Clonmacnoise poem is ineffable and excessive; it is beyond our comprehension. Robert Frost's poem "Birches" provides the key image here: Frost pictures a boy who "always kept his poise / To the top branches, climbing carefully / With the same pains you use to fill a cup / Up to the brim, and even beyond the brim."[191] There are repeated instances of "brimming over" in *Seeing Things*, when meaning overflows our ability to understand or contain it. In "A Retrospect," for example, "Everything ran into water-colour. /The skyline was full up to the lip / As if the earth were going to brim over."[192] (This is a poem imagining a timeless existence into which history, figured as a flowing river, overflows: "at one place, the swim and flow / From hidden springs made a river in the road.") Elsewhere, in "Settings xxiv," while describing a "Deserted harbour stillness" with its "Fullness. Shimmer" Heaney ends by suggesting that there "air and ocean" are "known as antecedents / Of each other," and exist "In apposition with / Omnipresence, equilibrium, brim."[193] Knowledge itself here seems "shimmering" and impermanent: the dynamic flux of air and water seems to propel the last line from the Latin "Omnipresence" and "equilibrium" to the Anglo-Saxon "brim," the flow of cultural history brings out excess and plenitude. Equilibrium is not static, but a constant activity, a give and take always threatening to spill over. If there are echoes of Romantic images of the imagination – Coleridge's favoured image of the spring, say, or the transmogrification of this into the "the abounding glittering jet" in Yeats's "Ancestral Houses" (from "Meditations in Time of Civil War") – there is also a slightly different emphasis.[194] What is important is not the imagination's "effortless, ever-self-renewing abundance" but the way in which it finds itself having to encapsulate a fluid, constantly brimming sense of multiple possibilities.[195] It is the joyous apprehension of the complex plenitude of life, rather than a circumscribed historical existence on the one hand or an escapist desire for transcendence on the other, that *Seeing Things* ultimately espouses.

The difference can be seen in how Heaney reworks the resolved opposition from "Making Strange" – between "being adept and dialect" – in "Casting and Gathering." Here, in another angling metaphor (there are two fishermen on opposite banks casting and gathering, and the poem is dedicated to Ted Hughes, a skilled fisherman), Heaney attempts to hold two contradictory truths in balance. The contrast is between a strict self-consciousness that would stay vigilant and brittle and a relaxed willingness to "Go with it!"; and also between a traditional folk-wisdom of self-mockery ("You are not worth tuppence. / But neither is anybody") and a more libertarian attitude to the future and the world (to "Give and swerve").[196] This is figured through sound: the "*hush* / And *lush*" of the casting, and the "speeded-up corncrake, / A sharp ratcheting" of the gathering. Both fishermen make both sounds, "when one man casts, the other gathers / And then *vice versa*, without changing sides": and so it is possible to both "love hushed air" and "trust contrariness."[197]

This resolves the dilemma Heaney faced, when writing *Field Work*, of being attracted to, but distrusting, the melodious line. The experience of "Casting and Gathering" is, avowedly, not a matter of understanding, of "seeing" or "knowing"; instead the emphasis is on "love" and "trust." The poem can be seen to embody Coleridge's comment on the poetic mind that "As soon as it is fixed on one image, it becomes understanding; but while it is unfixed and wavering between them [different images], attaching itself permanently to none, it is imagination," but with the caveat that this "wavering" (in terms drawn from Emmanuel Lévinas) is itself an ethical position.[198] For Lévinas, "the idea of the Infinite" is to be found in one's "responsibility for the Other," and especially in the unknowability of the other: ethics then becomes a matter of (possibly "bewildered") love, rather than the imposition of meaning or value.[199] The ideal treatment of other people is one that combines love and unintelligibility; it is like Heaney's memory of "John Dologhan, the best milker ever // To come about the place," in "Montana" in *Electric Light*, in which "a bright path // Opened between us like a recognition / That made no sense."[200]

The Necessity of an Idea of Transcendence   189

In place of "sense" or "knowing" (with all their connotation of mastery and control), the collection aims towards – as in "Casting and Gathering" – "love" and the feeling of release (the instruction to "give and swerve"). These combine, in complicated ways, with the remembrance of the dead, the dead who are both beloved presence and source of light. For example, in "Scrabble" (the first of the "Glanmore Revisited" sonnets), written in memory of Heaney's archeologist friend Tom Delaney, "love" is "Taken for granted like any other word / That was chanced on and allowed within the rules"; but where Delaney is remembered through love, his experience of death is imagined as the word "scrabble" itself: "Intransitive. Meaning to scratch or rake at something hard. / Which is what he hears. Our scraping, clinking tools."[201] The verb is intransitive: there is no possible connection between the living and dead. As in "Seeing Things," the temporal dimension of death is different, our activities are present participles, "scraping" and "clinking," while death presents a continuity of past, present, and future; it is "remembered ... half-imagined" and also "foretold." It is almost as if the yoke of time has been slipped, as if memory ceases to function, or be necessary, as you awaken into an eternity of presence. Thus, in "The Ash Plant," when Heaney imagines his father at the moment of his death, "he is like a sentry // Forgotten and unable to remember / The whys and wherefores of his lofty station"; but this forgetting is also a "wakening" in which he is "relieved yet in position, / Disencumbered as a breaking comber."[202] Death is a "lightening," the removal of a burden, as well as an illumination. The afterlife in "Lightening v" is "flimsy," but thus also as manoeuvrable as a skiff; and in "Lightening xii," the last of these poems, "lightening" is described as "A phenomenal instant when the spirit flares / With pure exhilaration before death," as well as "the usual sense of alleviation, / Illumination."[203] Crossing the border into death you feel the tug of the tide, the lifting of the boats, the spirit flaring.

But beyond this border? As *Seeing Things* has repeatedly suggested, we cannot know: therefore, this is where *it* ends, on the border, in the "offing." In "Squarings xi" Heaney describes the "offing" as "The visible sea at a distance from the shore / Or beyond the anchoring grounds."[204] This is a space of immanence, flux, and flitting suggestiveness; there is the permanent sense of something about to come into being: "The emptier it stood, the more compelled / The eye that scanned it. / But once you turned your back on it, your back // Was suddenly all eyes like Argus's."[205] What cannot be seen can be sensed:

190   This Strange Loneliness

the offing is "Untrespassed still, and yet somehow vacated // As if a lambent troop that exercised / On the borders of your vision had withdrawn / Behind the skyline to manoeuvre and regroup."[206] The "borders of vision" is the title of a 1982 work on William Wordsworth by Jonathan Wordsworth and the offing here is a reconfiguration of the mountainous space listened into in "There Was a Boy": but rather than the "visible scene" that "would enter unawares into his mind," in "Squarings xi" there is the sense of the visionary withdrawing, rather than entering, of the lambent and lucent receding beyond our sight, as happens in the "Immortality Ode."

There is something slightly ominous about the offing here (with the militarism of "troop," and the possibility that the "lambent" contains the "lambeg") which is removed in the final poem of the collection. Here, "sixth sense" is used as the basis for the afterlife, as the offing presents itself as a staging post between the past and the future and becomes at once prospect and retrospect:

> Strange how things in the offing, once they're sensed,
> Convert to things foreknown;
> And how what's come upon is manifest
>
> Only in light of what has been gone through.
> Seventh heaven may be
> The whole truth of a sixth sense come to pass.[207]

At the end of the poem Heaney imagines that, bathed by light "on the road beyond Coleraine / Where wind got saltier," "That day I'll be in step with what escaped me." Following Ted Hughes's suggestion that this sequence is Heaney's "Quartet," the attitude towards time here appears to be as solemn and non-linear as Eliot's in "Burnt Norton," where he intones "Time present and time past / Are both perhaps present in time future, / And time future contained in time past."[208] (It is also reminiscent of Heidegger's claim that "Maintaining myself alongside my past in running ahead I have time.")[209] Lost past and possible future walk "in step" with the present, but only here, in the offing, at the very border of existence.

In *The Redress of Poetry*, Heaney suggests that the role of poetry is to give the offing a sense of lambent possibility: poetry "enters our field of vision and animates our physical and intelligent being"; its redress is best exemplified when "the spirit is called extravagantly

The Necessity of an Idea of Transcendence   191

beyond the course that the usual life plots for it, when outcry or rhapsody is wrung from it as it flies in upon some unexpected image of its own solitude and distinctness."[210] God-less solitude in the universe brings also the freedom of individuality: poetry helps you transcend the usual life, either in "outcry or rhapsody" (it is not all bathed light); and this is adequate compensation for the realization that "there is no next-time-round."[211] The absence of an afterlife also, perhaps paradoxically, underpins the power and value of poetry. In his introduction to *The Redress of Poetry*, after clarifying *The Haw Lantern*'s main theme of poetry "crossing from the domain of the matter-of-fact into the domain of the imagined," Heaney turns to Wordsworth's Preface to *Lyrical Ballads* as an authority for the fact that "poetry does not need to invoke a god to sanction its workings."[212] Instead, poetry's

> truth, as William Wordsworth asserted, does not stand upon "external testimony but [is] carried live into the heart by passion; truth which is its own testimony, which gives competence and confidence to the tribunal to which it appeals, and receives them from that same tribunal." Admittedly, Wordsworth is not very specific about the composition of that ultimate tribunal and its seat is anyhow likely to have been moved nowadays from "the heart" to some more theoretically secure address; but it nevertheless survives as the tribunal whose reality all responsible poetry depends upon and the one through which its redress is mediated.[213]

Few of Wordsworth's contemporaries would have been uncertain of the composition of such an "ultimate tribunal"; but Heaney, making claims for the distinctive truthfulness of poetry and religion, is on vaguer and more suggestive ground. Although we might desire a more "theoretically secure address" for poetry's truth, that security is not possible: poetry is its own tribunal, for it cannot rely on anything else. Therefore, its role comes through its ability to tell the "truth" about the world, or witness the world, even while knowing that there is no external validation of that "truth"; it is, at best, a "condition of truthfulness."

This is not to label Heaney a poet of the post-truth age, or to suggest he was able to believe blindly in a poetic vocation or objectivity, or even to claim that he is a witness to what Jerome McGann calls the "last and final illusion" of Romanticism, the belief that "it can expose or even that it has uncovered its illusions and false consciousness, that it has finally arrived at the Truth" (and so has "locate[d] the goal of human pursuits, needs, and desires in Ideal space").[214] Rather, the strength of Heaney's mature work comes in the absolute recognition that this is an illusion, that we need "an idea of transcendence" – and perhaps even more importantly a *feeling* of transcendence – rather than transcendence itself: marvels are to be "credited" precisely for their airiness, their flimsiness.[215] "False consciousness" can never be uncovered, if only because we can never know what might be shimmering in the offing (and distorting our vision). It is clear, once more, why Heaney is so drawn to Eliot's description of the "use of memory" in "Little Gidding," where he claims it is "For liberation – not less of love but expanding / Of love beyond desire, and so liberation / From the future as well as the past." "History," Eliot notes, "may be servitude, / History may be freedom. See, now they vanish, / The faces and places, with the self which, as it could, loved them, / To become renewed, transfigured, in another pattern."[216] The act of transfiguring history, of renewing it, is an "expanding / Of love beyond desire." Memory (or indeed poetry) can then offer liberation from historically bound notions of "freedom" and "servitude"; it offers a different order of freedom, a different type of truthfulness.

Thomas Docherty sees Heaney's work as a secular continuation of the liberal humanist project (in ways that echo "Little Gidding"): he points to the sense that "The unenlightened religious sphere of the social was to be replaced by a metaphorical thinking in which I see myself in the other subjects of history among whom I am condemned to live; and poetry was to enable such a meeting between free subjects."[217] As Heaney's next collection, *The Spirit Level*, would make clear – in ways that *Seeing Things* generally avoided – this "freedom" also entailed political and ethical responsibilities in the world that poetry could illuminate. History was not just to be encouraged to "vanish" as one disappears into the offing; rather, in *The Spirit Level* the perspective returns to being one based in "attachment to our own field of action," to "social historical and political contingencies," informed but not bound by the perspective from the border of death.[218]

SPIRIT LEVELS

Where much of Heaney's work in the 1980s and early 1990s focused on ideas and feelings of transcendence and poetic "liberation," *The Spirit Level* asks instead what happens *after* liberation. The sense

The Necessity of an Idea of Transcendence   193

of "lightened" poetic freedom that was developed in *Seeing Things* is paralleled in *The Spirit Level* by a political liberation from violence (there was an IRA ceasefire in 1994, and a subsequent ceasefire of most loyalist paramilitary groups, although many of the poems in the collection were written before this point) and also a general theme of personal (and even religious) release.[219] This release is evoked most clearly in "After the Liberation," the last section of "To a Dutch Potter in Ireland," where the poet celebrates what it means "To have lived it through and now to be free to give / Utterance, body and soul."[220] The context for the poem is post-World War Two Holland rather than Northern Ireland: Sonja Landweer, to whom the poem is addressed, had lived through the Nazi occupation of Holland (during which her father was killed). There is a sense that in both contexts the liberation offers a form of new beginning, a reward for having "lived it through," and of having avoided not just death but also the destruction of a sense of self. The three-part phrase "Utterance, body and soul," read literally, suggests the "liberation" allows for free speech, personal freedom, and religious tolerance.[221] This entails, in part, the reclamation of facets of one's identity that may previously have been disallowed. Thus in "Tollund," Heaney's reworking of his own "The Tollund Man," Heaney and a companion find themselves in Jutland to be "Ourselves again, free-willed again, not bad": "ourselves again" is a liberating reinterpretation of the Irish "Sinn Fein" (we ourselves), which had been appropriated, of course, by the political wing of the Provisional IRA in a way that tended towards "an obscurantist isolationism and an atavism."[222] "Tollund" offers the possibility that Irish cultural nationalism can be redefined in ways that enable greater interaction with other communities and cultures.

In the lecture "Frontiers of Writing" (delivered at Oxford in November 1993), Heaney describes the double bind in which constitutional nationalists in Northern Ireland found themselves during the 1980s, in respect to the dirty protests and hunger strikes in the Maze prison. "As the Thatcher administration remained unmoved in the face of the deaths," Heaney remembers, "and the cortèges kept winding from the prison gates to the local graves, there began to be something almost unseemly about the scruple which prevented a show of support for the hunger strikers' immediate claims – a support withheld because logically it would have been taken as an endorsement of the violent means and programmes of the Provisional IRA.

194 This Strange Loneliness

Such caution had produced only silence, and now the silence was by default appearing like assent to the triumphalist, implacable handling of the affair by the Thatcher cabinet."[223] By the composition of the poems in *The Spirit Level* the political climate had changed sufficiently (due to the attitude of the non-Thatcher cabinet and the Provisional IRA) for Heaney to offer support to the political process without being seen to implicitly endorse or condemn the Provisional IRA's campaign. So much is suggested in "Mint" where there is a new-found willingness to address directly the political situation, without being perceived as taking sides, while also acknowledging that an earlier lack of attention was itself a cause for self-accusation: "Let the smells of mint go heady and defenceless / Like inmates liberated in that yard. / Like the disregarded ones we turned against / Because we'd failed them by our disregard."[224] As with "ourselves again," in "Mint" Heaney is reclaiming not just a universal sense of an "imperturbable" life, but also the ability to engage with an Irish cultural nationalism: in this case through the mint's emblematic green.[225]

This is not, however, subscription to a political doctrine. Heaney is consistent in arguing – as he did in the 1986 lecture "The Regional Forecast," in terms that repeat those of *Among Schoolchildren* – that "The writer's task will ultimately be visionary rather than social; the human rather than the national dream is his or her responsibility" and so they will be led to "not just a simple programme of cultural nationalism but something more detached and vigilant."[226] As such, these poems do not present a programmatic, definitive identity, but rather, as Heaney will later say of the 1998 Belfast Agreement, aim to "hold a space open" which allows for a recalibration, a re-evaluation of the past and the present.[227] For my purposes, it is important that this "space" is, in "To a Dutch Potter in Ireland" and "Mint," imagined as a refiguring of the "ruined gable-end" that had provided the location for "The Mud Vision." In "To a Dutch Potter in Ireland" "ruins" are overgrown with rye, and life has persisted despite the war, and there is a sense of a turning of the seasons, of a new beginning: "Omnipresent, imperturbable, / Is the life that death springs from. / And complaint is wrong, the slightest complaint at all, / Now that the rye crop waves beside the ruins."[228] Similarly, the "Mint," which "looked like a clump of small dusty nettles / Growing wild at the gable of the house," offers the promise of rebirth – it "spelled promise / And newness in the back yard of our life" – although it is not itself new, but a dogged survivor, "As if something callow yet

The Necessity of an Idea of Transcendence   195

tenacious / Sauntered in green alleys and grew rife."[229] Where the best that could be hoped in "The Mud Vision" is to "survive," by "Mint" there is the possibility of greater optimism, of a cultural victory over militant tendencies: the "gable-end" is not a ruin on which the transcendental appears, but is somewhere that "tenacious" life can once more grow "rife."

"Mint," in other words, is yet another figuration of rebirth, that recurring spasm in Heaney's work: it suggests the possibility of a renewed origin or source of poetic energy and meaning, a carry-over from the past which through its "tenacity" allows us to reimagine the future. Similarly, in "Mycenae Lookout," the theory poem of *The Spirit Level* (and one which also provides the title of Heaney's selected prose, *Finders Keepers*), Heaney writes his earlier preoccupation with wells and pumps into his reimaging of the aftermath of the Trojan War. Heaney pictures an "old lifeline leading up / and down from the Acropolis" to the "well at Athens"; this lifeline is, portentously, "the ladder of the future / and the past, besieger and besieged, / the treadmill of assault // turned waterwheel."[230] The memory of a violent past gets turned into the promise of a peaceful future: "treadmill of assault" turned into waterwheel standing in for the clichéd sword turned into ploughshare. The ladder then becomes a source of personal redemption: the "men puddling at the source // through tawny mud" come back "deeper in themselves for having been there, / like discharged soldiers testing the safe ground, // finders, keepers, seers of fresh water" (how different the return here is to those of the "Yank" or "The Backward Look").[231]

There is perhaps a Wordsworthian quality to this renewed faith in the return to a "source." Wordsworth was, after all, the primary English language poet of childhood, of a faith in a "first creative sensibility" unsubdued by the "the regular action of the world," as he claims in *The Prelude*; and he is, as Heaney had noted in the *Essential Wordsworth*, the "finder and keeper of the self-as-subject."[232] But if this is the case, in Heaney's work the self that is used as source or as subject is always historically situated. In "The Redress of Poetry," for example, Heaney theorizes the relationship between the poet and the historical moment in ways that illuminate "Mint" and "Mycenae Lookout." Here, Heaney proposes that "if our given experience is a labyrinth, its impassibility can still be countered by the poet's imagining some equivalent of the labyrinth"; the poet's work then "does not intervene in the actual but by offering consciousness a chance

196 This Strange Loneliness

to recognize its predicaments, foreknow its capacities and rehearse its comebacks in all kinds of venturesome ways, it does constitute a beneficent event, for poet and audience alike."[233] The relationship between poetry and history is one of "foreknowledge," "rehearsal," and "comeback" (in ways that rework the out-of-timeness of death in *Seeing Things*): the redress of poetry, as Heaney argues, offers "a sensation both of arrival and of prospect, so that one does indeed seem to 'recover a past' and 'prefigure a future,' and thereby to complete the circle of one's being."[234]

The Wordsworthian notion of the "prospect," which had been informing Heaney's mental landscape since the early 1970s, reappears here at a crucial moment, at the beginning of Heaney's late poetics. The experience of poetry is the ecstatic moment of self-abnegation and self-realization, one in which the "circle of one's being" is completed, or – as in "The Poet's Chair," where Socrates (as he is in the *Crito*) is waiting for the ship to return from the shrine of Apollo and so for his execution – in which "for the moment everything's an ache / Deferred, foreknown, imagined and most real."[235] This ability to foreknow the future is morally fortifying. When Heaney moves from this image of Socrates to an image of himself as a child watching his father ploughing, the child-poet is "all foreknowledge. / Of the poem as a ploughshare that turns time / Up and over ... Of being here for good in every sense."[236] This ethical determination is the result, as Andrew Murphy comments, of a "dogged, compromised optimism," an optimism that remains all too aware of what has gone before it, and yet despite this still continues to hope.[237] And it is an optimism founded on intervention rather than passive observance. The central gesture of *The Spirit Level* is that of upsetting the balance, of "weighing in" "against your better judgement." It is, in the words of Simone Weil that Heaney uses in "The Redress of Poetry," based in a recognition that "obedience to the force of gravity" is the "greatest sin" and that "If we know in what way society is unbalanced, we must do what we can to add weight to the lighter scale ... we must have formed a conception of equilibrium and be ever ready to change sides like justice, 'that fugitive from the camp of conquerors.'"[238]

One way of "adding weight" is explored, aptly, in "Weighing In," a poem which proceeds from the image of a 56 lb. weight balanced "Against another one placed on a weighbridge – / On a well-adjusted, freshly greased weighbridge – / And everything trembled,

The Necessity of an Idea of Transcendence   197

flowed with give and take."[239] Where in *Seeing Things* this sense of "give and take," of tremulous possibility, would have been sufficient, here it is found ethically wanting. Instead, Heaney rejects the principle it suggests of

> bearing, bearing up
> And bearing out, just having to
>
> Balance the intolerable in others
> Against our own, having to abide
> Whatever we settled for and settled into
>
> Against our better judgement.[240]

This principle of balancing (or bearing witness) is no longer enough: as the "Cassandra" section of "Mycenae Lookout" suggests, there is "No such thing / as innocent / bystanding."[241] The poem's caustic retort to the idea of balancing (and to Yeats's introduction to the *Oxford Book of Modern Verse*) is that "Passive / Suffering makes the world go round."[242] Balancing the tremulous give and take of the weights is only sufficient in an "unearthly" world that is otherwise just, a world in which "The scales ride steady and the angel's strain / Prolongs itself at an unearthly pitch."[243] In our imperfect world, however, "settling" only offers endless and cyclical suffering. So Heaney desires to upset the balance, to "Prophecy, give scandal, cast the stone" because "every now and then, just weighing in / Is what it must come down to, and without // Any self-exculpation or self-pity."[244] Chivalry is not enough anymore; what is necessary is dirtier: "At this stage only foul play cleans the slate."[245]

This is *not* the only option, however. In "The Gravel Walks," it is not weighty political commitment, but, once more, airiness that is trusted to provide poetic redemption. In "Weighing In" the "principle of bearing, bearing up / and bearing out" comes "Against our better judgement"; in the ethics of "The Gravel Walks" we are encouraged to oppose or disobey our "better judgement" that would have us weigh in, and to engage in "foul play." After delineating an "eternity" of gravel, and mulling over the different possible historical uses of these "Gems for the undeluded," Heaney ends on an artistic, musical (and so weightless) version of gravel: "So walk on air against your better judgement / Establishing yourself somewhere in between /

Those solid batches mixed with grey cement / And a tune called 'The Gravel Walks' that conjures green."[246] The answer is, once more, to be "in between" the concrete and the musical, the real and the ethereal. As such this poem could almost sit comfortably alongside those of *Station Island*, *The Haw Lantern*, and *Seeing Things*. The difference here is in the last word, "green," with its hint and hope of rebirth and renewal (of cultural nationalism). The gesture here is not towards the transcendental but to the cultural: rather than a transcendent epiphany, what the poem imagines, in the end, is a world made both airy and weighty by a work of art that can transform the gritty and stonelike, but like them might – possibly – endure.

5

"Total Play and Truth in Earnest": Heaney's Late Style

LATE IN THE DAY

I wanted to fish with a fly and just never stayed at it long enough to learn to cast, so that effort fizzled out too. But inside my sixty-eight year old arm there's a totally enlivened twelve-year-old one, feeling the bite. And that's enough for a lifetime of poems. That, and the memory of being out with Barrie [Cooke] on the Nore and once with Ted [Hughes] in Devon. Fleetness of water, stillness of air, stealthiness of action. Spots of time.[1]

Perhaps surprisingly, given the frequency with which he used images of fishing, Seamus Heaney was never a skilled angler: as he told Dennis O'Driscoll, despite a "wild longing to own a proper fishing rod" when he was a boy, from his teens onwards he was "on a riverbank hardly more than a dozen times."[2] Fishing nevertheless offered him a sense of nostalgia, of a road not travelled, and an inner store of memories: it could be both a source for his poetry and a metaphor for it. The childhood muscle-memory of "feeling the bite" persists in his arm (the child is father of the man, after all); and poetry is recast as the recovery of moments that were fleet, still, and stealthy; it is not the number of those moments but their quality that matters. This passage, with its retrospective glance and emphasis on persistence (especially the persistence of the child in the man), is, this chapter argues, illuminative of Heaney's late poetics in numerous ways. It reasserts the relationship between one's earliest memories and the present day; it generously acknowledges friends and influences on both sides of the Irish Sea (memories of fishing on the Nore and in

Devon being equally cherished); it tips an understated nod to Wordsworth in the identification of "spots of time" as the basis for poetry (and even identity); and, perhaps most importantly, it celebrates the sense of being "enlivened" and of taking pleasure in physical experience (or the memory of it). It is a poetics which suggests that one memory, one "spot of time," can sustain a "lifetime of poems" if treated with enough care and delight.

The Spirit Level, as Helen Vendler has commented, celebrates a "stoic" poetry: a poetry of "keeping going" and of "sitting at one's work, standing forgetful of self in a parental protectiveness, going about perennial motions, bearing one's blindness or one's widowhood without letting them sap one's vitality, and singing, like Caedmon, in the intervals between one's duties"; this stoicism is double-edged, however, as it represents "the virtue of middle age, when one's progress is at best horizontal, and the future can hold only a decline."[3] From *The Spirit Level* onwards this decline is faced head-on, and responded to defiantly and occasionally joyously, with a sense of the compensations poetry might bring, as well as the responsibilities it must live up to. Where much of Heaney's early poetry was to some extent written "in the margins" of *The Prelude*, his late work has as its exemplar Wordsworth's "Ode: Intimations of Immortality from Recollections of Early Childhood," a product of the "years that bring the philosophic mind," during which the poet "will grieve not" for what is lost, but "rather find / Strength in what remains behind."[4] The search continues – in spite of personal loss, the sense of being past the high excitement of one's life, and the inevitability of death – for a fortifying "strength" in poetry.

Heaney's late work presents a combination of dogged persistence, valedictory restatement, and celebratory reaffirmation. The emphasis veers sometimes between "survival" and "freedom" – "let all things go free that have survived" as the poet instructs us in "Mint" in *The Spirit Level* – but also, in Heaney's consideration of "lateness," a feeling (once more) of unexpected, joyous "release."[5] "Late in the Day" in *Electric Light*, for example, combines the image of "a monk of Clonard" (as described in William Wilde's *Beauties of the Boyne*) whose pen, when the candle had gone out, "Feathered itself with a miraculous light / So he could go on working," with a memory of his friend the author David Thomson in a urinous reworking of Wordsworth's "I wandered lonely as a cloud." Heaney says that, "late now in the day," he needs the "likes" of the monk's quill:

freshets and rivulets
Starting from nowhere, capillaries of joy

Frittered and flittering like the scimitar
Of cowpiss in the wind that David Thomson
Flashed on my inner eye from the murky byre
Where he imagined himself a cow let out in spring

Smelling green weed, up to his hips in grass.[6]

This is a desire for new inspiration, which will be self-generating rather than forced (with, as in "Mint," the possibility of "green" new beginnings): it will also bring joyous "lifeblood" that is – positively – insubstantial (flittering) and excessive (frittered). Wordsworth's remembered daffodils "flash upon that inward eye / Which is the bliss of solitude" and fill his heart with pleasure. Heaney's poem, meanwhile, characteristically makes Wordsworth's golden vision "murky" while also drawing on the remembered resources of childhood ("The glee of boyhood still alive and kicking / In the tattered stick man I would meet and read / A lifetime later") to give praise for the possibility of future releases and escapes: the man is "glad of another chance to believe his luck."[7]

Not only the lateness of the day (or Thomson's lateness) is suggested here; Heaney is also imagining the late stage of his own career. If the consideration of "last things" involves the sense of things slipping away or being let loose, "late style" is the boon that comes from such liberation. To mark the eightieth birthday of Brian Friel, the playwright and Heaney's long-time friend and co-director of the Field Day Company, Heaney published a prose acrostic based on Friel's name. In "L" he chooses (alongside love and language) the word "'late,' as in 'Late Style'": "that final stage of freedom and mastery when technique is second nature, knowledge of life seems to brim over and there is an uncanny sureness, an ability to give seemingly spontaneous yet entirely authoritative expression to old matters in a new way, a readiness to take risks and trust that the audience will follow. Late flowerings of this sort are among the things of Brian's I find most thrilling ... They have an uncanny fluidity and airiness about them, at once total play and the truth in earnest."[8] That "late style" might bring "freedom and mastery" and "uncanny fluidity and airiness" can also be read as optimistic self-appraisal,

202   This Strange Loneliness

a recognition of the fluidity and airiness that entered his work in *Seeing Things* and continues in poems such as "Perch" in *Electric Light* (this describes the fish as being "on air // That is water" and "on hold / In the everything flows and steady go of the world").[9] There are certainly none of the reservations that Seamus Deane had expressed about "mastery." Rather, there is an acknowledgment of status (as both affirmation and challenge). The passage reaffirms the importance of artistic friendship and community to Heaney; he comments that he felt that Friel had admitted him to a "guild of makers" when he sent Heaney a letter after the publication of *Death of a Naturalist*, and so given him "an honour to be cherished and a standard to be lived up to ever since."[10] And it also suggests the hope for a "late flowering" of Heaney's own.

In this chapter, I explore Wordsworth's role in Heaney's "late style," how he continues to celebrate him as a formative influence and grapple with him as a cautionary example. Unsurprisingly, in Heaney's late work, as he comes to look back over and give shape to his career as a whole, many of his preoccupations are held up to the light once more, many of his favoured themes reappear. As part of this process, Heaney's previous negotiations with Wordsworth evolve: these include the relationship between poetry and education, the restatement of liberal humanism, the reworking of the spot of time, and even the image of the ruined wallstead. But these are, as his comments on Friel suggest, reinvigorated by "riskiness," especially a spiritual riskiness that had begun after the death of his parents. This is the willingness to use what he called in an interview with Karl Miller in 2000 the "baby language" of his faith, words which his "secular education had taught [him] to be afraid of, words like 'soul' and 'spirit'": "I felt that this dimension of reality, which I had in a sense schooled myself out of, must be risked somehow."[11] To describe Heaney's poetry in *The Spirit Level*, and afterwards, as solely a "stoic" celebration of persistence, one that aims at most to avoid "the slightest complaint," would be to ignore this emotional pull towards the joyful, celebratory, unexpected, and risky. Heaney has an even greater tendency in his late work to use the language of transcendence and of the spiritual, even if there is no divine presence to underpin these; what is required are artistic, rather than religious, defences. In his late style, Heaney is not a plodding Sisyphus or earthbound Antaeus, but a poet of "excess," of "extraness," and of pleasure; he is also

Heaney's Late Style 203

one who generously acknowledges the role of earlier poets – and his peers – in the formulation of a poetry which can help us both endure and enjoy life.

"THIS CAN GO ON, MY GOD!"

In a 1991 lecture, "On Poetry and Professing," Heaney suggests that "The good of literature and of music is first and foremost in the thing itself and their first principle is that which William Wordsworth called in his Preface to *Lyrical Ballads* 'the grand elementary principle of pleasure,' the kind of pleasure about which the language itself prompts us to say, 'It did me good.'"[12] "Pleasure" had come to have a particular weight in Heaney's critical comments. Speaking on BBC Radio about *The Haw Lantern* in 1987, Heaney had suggested that "There's nothing wrong with taking pleasure in it [writing] or with what Mandelstam calls 'the truancy of writing.' There's nothing wrong with the absconding from life that writing represents. In fact, it is what writing is for."[13] The following year, in an interview with Rand Brandes, he reiterates that "in poetry just being useful is a bigger sin that just being pleasurable"; he also lauds Stanislaw Baranczak's critical book on Zbigniew Herbert for its "Johnsonian desire to find in literature a fortification as well as a distraction," its "combination of prudence and pleasure."[14]

Wordsworth's Preface gives some intellectual substance to this pleasure seeking. In the Preface, his principle that the poet works under the "necessity of giving immediate pleasure" derives from a belief that "it is a task light and easy to him who looks at the world in the spirit of love: further, it is a homage paid to the native and naked dignity of man, to the grand elementary principle of pleasure, by which he knows, and feels, and lives, and moves."[15] For Wordsworth, "pleasure" is the basis for all sympathy and all knowledge; however painful these may be, there will always be an element of pleasure underlying them. Wordsworth's sense of delight and love is slightly different from Heaney's understanding of this "principle," even if for both it is fundamentally fortifying and heartening; where Wordsworth appeals to dignity and the spirit of love, Heaney celebrates the beneficial effect of "the language itself." The difference is once more between an ideology with a religious underpinning, and one that depends – even shakily – on a liberal humanist understanding of culture and that upholds the belief that literature "does you

204   This Strange Loneliness

good" even as it acknowledges the deep flaws in this argument. For Heaney turns to Wordsworth's pleasure principle in "On Professing and Poetry" immediately after he acknowledges the problems with such a position in the face of "the historical fact of the Holocaust: what good is a devotion to and an appreciation of the beautiful, the question goes, if some of the most cultivated people in a most cultivated nation could authorize mass killings and attend a Mozart concert on the same evening?"[16] (In his Nobel lecture Heaney will repeat this theme, more bluntly: "Only the very stupid or the very deprived can any longer help knowing that the documents of civilization have been written in blood and tears, blood and tears no less real for being very remote."[17]) "On Professing and Poetry" searches for a way of defending such humanism, and a belief in "civilization." It begins with a reminiscence of Michael McLaverty asking Heaney, as he was teaching a class at Ballymurphy, "when you look at the photograph of a rugby team in the newspaper, don't you always know immediately from the look of the players' faces which ones of them have studied poetry?"[18] Heaney can't rely on playful physiognomy as a justification for poetry, but he is clear about the desire to find *some* justification: "if it is a delusion and a danger to expect poetry and music to do too much, it is a diminishment of them and a derogation to ignore what they can do," he insists, and turns to a slightly unconvincing celebration of "pleasure" as a fortification and end in itself as an example of the "good" they can do.[19]

This is Heaney's own form of *non serviam*, a refusal to accept either moral ineffectualness or the historical circumspection of art, to follow the tendency to read imaginative literature (as he had earlier argued in "Extending the Alphabet") "simply and solely as a function of an oppressive discourse, or as a reprehensible masking."[20] It is also, in part, another intervention in the long-running argument he had been having with himself about the role of poetry and of a cultural humanist education. Where *Among Schoolchildren* and the other lectures discussed in the previous chapters had proposed a transcendent role for poetry, there is from the 1990s onwards a critical equivalent to the "weighing in" of *The Spirit Level*, a greater need for poetry to have an active role within historical circumstances, in the face of "oppressive discourses" or the challenges to "civilization." Heaney's argument will now revolve around the belief, in the words of Samuel Johnson that he alludes to in his Oxford essay on Elizabeth Bishop, that "the only end of writing is to enable the readers better to enjoy life, or better to endure it."[21] The question is whether "enjoying" life is sufficient, whether one should accede to the "grand elementary principle of pleasure," or go "beyond" it, to search for something "extra," something that will help us to "endure." "There are times," Heaney suggests in his Nobel lecture, "when we want the poem to be not only pleasurably right but compellingly wise, not only a surprising variation played upon the world, but a re-tuning of the world itself." Wordsworth is one of the examples, along with Anna Akhmatova, that Heaney gives as "proof that poetry can be equal to *and* true at the same time"; Orpheus, meanwhile, provides a mythological counterpart to these poets.[22]

In "Dylan the Durable," one of the lectures Heaney gave as Oxford Professor of Poetry, he finds fault with Dylan Thomas's "Fern Hill" (in contrast to Wordsworth's "Immortality Ode") because it "is as if Orpheus, grown older, had reneged on his larger task, that of testing the power of his lyre against the gods of the underworld and wresting life back out of death, and had gone back instead to his younger, happier if less world-saving task of casting musical spells upon the whole of nature."[23] The "pleasurable" task ("casting musical spells" on nature) is secondary to the larger task of "wresting life back out of death": this, moreover, is the responsibility of middle and old age. If there is a journey "beyond the pleasure principle" here, it is not quite the same as Freud's, which involved attention to instincts that seek to "restore an earlier state of things."[24] In Heaney's "returns" and restorations, as with Wordsworth's in *The Prelude*, there is no going back: they are aware of diminishment and ultimate failure and yet continue "the Orphic effort to haul life back up the slope against all the odds."[25]

The last major development of Heaney's critical picture of Wordsworth, developed in his Oxford lectures, will be his re-creation of the lake poet as an Orphic figure who can combine pleasure, accuracy, wisdom, truth, moral heft, and (for all his apparent sombreness) a sense of surprise and "excess." This involves a critical reworking of Keats's idea that poetry should "surprise by fine excess."[26] In the lecture "Speranza in Reading" Heaney suggests that poetry "justifies its readers' trust and vindicates itself by setting its 'fine excess' in the balance against all of life's inadequacies, desolations and atrocities."[27] In "Extending the Alphabet," meanwhile, Heaney relates this directly to Wordsworth's work. "Even a poem as tonally sombre as, say, 'Tintern Abbey,'" Heaney argues, "is doing something surprising and excessive,

206　This Strange Loneliness

getting further back and deeper in than the poet knew it would, the poet being nevertheless still ready to go with it, to rise to the rhythmic and rhetorical occasion"; despite its sombreness, "Tintern Abbey" can "surprise" by "outstripping the reader's expectation."[28] Such arguments had been prefigured somewhat in Heaney's introduction to the *Essential Wordsworth*, when he had noted that the "almost geological sobriety" of some of Wordsworth's early poems ("Tintern Abbey" included) makes it easy to "forget that they are the work of a young man."[29] By "Extending the Alphabet," though, it is not Wordsworth's youth but his exuberance that is important.

This will be confirmed in Heaney's later turns to Wordsworth. Speaking to Harry Thomas in 2002, Heaney suggests that "what distinguishes poetry is a more-than-enoughness, that it's always more, that poetry goes beyond what's merely necessary. It's an extraness."[30] Heaney introduces this emphasis on extraness in part as a rewriting of his own earlier gendered opposition between "waiting" and "willful" characterizations of poetry: the "'feminine presence' and 'masculine drive'" which "are now regarded as sexist and suspect and agin' the law somehow."[31] Where Wordsworth had previously been associated with a "feminine" form of poetry, he is now recast as being "exulting" rather than "oozing." Heaney offers the (slightly back-handed) praise that "even somebody like Wordsworth, whom I tend to think of as the great grey poet, has a more-than-enoughness":

> You think of "Tintern Abbey" and you suddenly realize, this poem is extraordinary! It keeps coming, it's full of fresh starts, and you can feel Wordsworth exulting and going with it. It wasn't written before it was written, so to speak. We tend to think of it as being there like a mountain, a serenity, a monument. But it's a poem of excitement! It was written, my God, when he was twenty-eight or twenty-nine ... twenty-eight! There's the scene and then there's the exultation of memory and then there's the extraness of suddenly understanding himself at this moment, and then after that there's Dorothy, and then there's the sense that *this can go on, my God!* He's beginning to see that nature is a system of amplifying reality, and he is a part of it. There is discovery.[32]

Far from being passively responsive, the Wordsworth Heaney imagines now is one of explosive "fine excess," a poet who presents (as Philip Sidney would recommend) a "*forcibleness*, his translation of the Greek word *Energeia*, energy."[33] Wordsworth is recast as a poet of amplifying energy, of surging tumult: this involves, ultimately, "discovery," the shock of the new, as well as the reaffirmation of the ("serene") known. Heaney finds in this combination of solidity and of exultation, these "fresh starts," a way, ultimately, to combine the Johnsonian requirement for poetry to help one enjoy or endure life. Heaney, as ever, settles on a "nevertheless," a both/and, in his faith that poetry's importance lies both in its "pleasureableness" and its ability to fortify: that the poem "can go on, my God" is testament to its endurance and its excessiveness.

RIPPLING INWARDS

The crucial thing for Heaney is that this is true not just of a poem, but also the individual human life. When Heaney notes of Wordsworth in "Tintern Abbey" that he's "beginning to see that nature is a system of amplifying reality" we are once more in the territory of the educational sublime: the discovery in the natural landscape of something "beyond," something "excessive," which takes you out of yourself.[34] The feeling of "extraness" or "furthering" which is so fundamental to Heaney's late poetics is also central to his late thinking on education, in a way that recalls but outstrips the argument made in *Among Schoolchildren*. In a speech he gave at the University of Pennsylvania commencement ceremony in 2000, for example, Heaney places the graduating students in a position he had previously imagined himself in as a poet: "You stand at a boundary. Behind you is your natural habitat, as it were, the ground of your creaturely being, the old haunts where you were nurtured; in front of you is a less knowable prospect of invitation and challenge, the testing ground of your possibilities. You stand between whatever binds you to your past and whatever might be unbounded in your future."[35] Past "binds" might become future "unboundedness." This is not a case of "divesting oneself of the world" as in *Among Schoolchildren*, but rather imagining that world anew, of trying to create one's own prospects, with "prospect" here straying close to the phenomenological "projects" of Maurice Merleau-Ponty, which would unsettle our habit of "thinking that all of this [the man-made] exists necessarily and unshakeably."[36] This approach might be slightly generic: by the nature of the occasion, most commencement addresses tend to have a futural dimension, to engage in a bit of "prospecting."

208 This Strange Loneliness

But importantly such futurity does not deny the "binds ... to the past," the old haunts and "ground ... of creaturely being." There is a sense in which the imagination is not all-conquering but is also, to some extent, grounded and limited. It is not simply the case, as "The Settle Bed" in *Seeing Things* had suggested, that "whatever is given // Can always be reimagined, however four-square, / Plank-thick, hull-stupid and out of its time / It happens to be."[37] Rather, as "The Bookcase" in *Electric Light* (2001) notes, the future itself is in some way "bounded": the bookcase "turns on a druggy hinge, its load / Divulging into a future perfect tense"; each future moment is one that at some point *will have* happened, and this knowledge limits the extent to which it can be liberatingly reimagined.[38] The past and the future are, in other words, bound to each other in ways that we cannot foretell or deny: the sixty-eight-year-old arm still has "a totally enlivened twelve-year-old one, feeling the bite" inside it. This has various implications for personal growth, self-discovery, and education; these appear most clearly when the idea of education as "amplification" merges with what Edna Longley calls Heaney's "favourite geometry of centre and circle."[39]

This geometry can be traced back as far as the early uncollected poem "Fisher" (1964), where poetry is imagined (once more) as similar to angling: the poet "cast[s] a line baited with metre / And images ripple, words scatter."[40] It has also appeared at various points in this book already: in the "ripple-and-wave" effect Heaney identifies in "There Was a Boy," in "the Indefatigable Hoof-Taps," and in the "small ripples" shaking across his heart in the fourth "Glanmore Sonnet." Heaney's most famous use of this image, however, comes in his Nobel lecture, where he imagines a ripple of water in a bucket in his childhood and argues that "poetry can make an order as true to the impact of external reality and as sensitive to the inner laws of the poet's being as the ripples that rippled in and rippled out across the water in that scullery bucket fifty years ago."[41]

Throughout these examples, the "rippling" suggests a form of psychological and emotional growth that combines continuity with expansive discovery. Heaney also uses it this way in an interview with John Quinn in 1997, when he relates it to his own (self-)education. He describes being his "own pupil" when he began teaching, and widening his knowledge and "learning a lot through simply having to prepare courses": "I still come back to the image of the ripple which moves outwards but in some way is still the same ripple. It contains other things, other experiences, other ripples, but there is a concentric element to it, as there is to human growth. Within yourself there is always the little self who was there from the beginning. I suppose the purpose of the writing I have done has been to make a wholeness out of all those moves and differences to get the first place and the ultimate place into some kind of alignment."[42] If there is a desire to unify all the "moves and differences" that are the result of education, there is also apparent here an attraction to the pre-literate "little self" (the "pre-reflective stare / All agog" as he describes it in "Alphabets").[43] Heaney strays close to "restorative nostalgia" here, a nostalgia that could concretize and purify memories, to "rebuild [a] lost home" and recover wholeness, but which risks creating a hollow shell of that "wholeness."[44] In "Fretwork," a discussion of his translation of *Beowulf* (and Octavio Paz's opposition to Saussurean semiotics), Heaney uses the idea of increasing contact (with "other tribes, trade with other nations, invasion by bigger empires, conversion to other faiths, education in other cultures") to suggest that "the writer's longing can be understood as a nostalgia for the original undifferentiated linguistic home."[45] This nostalgia threatens complexity, difference, and nuance, offering instead an incredible "pre-lapsarian, philological Big Rock Candy Mountain" (as Heaney describes it in the lecture "Further Language").[46] Heaney still appears to be struggling with Antaeus, the figure for rootedness with which he self-identified in *North*, until he is "graip[ed]" by Hercules "out of his element / into a dream of loss / and origins."[47]

This is, however, something of a straw man. The nostalgia of "Fretwork" is entirely at odds with the "extraness" Heaney had recently come to embrace. Generally, for late Heaney, change is to be embraced rather than lamented, and is seen as entailing a development and complication, rather than a desertion, of one's origins. Where in *Among Schoolchildren* Heaney had relied on Joyce to elucidate his complex sense of displacement from the English language (and how this impinges on any ability to seek an Ur-language), by the mid-1990s one of his favourite touchstones was the Australian poet Vincent Buckley. In the 1995 lecture "Further Language," Heaney notes that in a passage in Buckley's autobiography "where he is remembering his own education, Buckley writes: 'Language is an entry to further language.' And in the same context he proclaims, 'I never thought of Shakespeare, or of any great writer, as a gateway to anything but puzzled delight.'"[48] Political or postcolonial considerations, that is, are subordinate to the "delight" of literature. Repeating these terms in an interview with John Brown in 2002, Heaney suggests that "further language" is not a departure from but a return to origins, an "increment of inwardness" rather than a "displacement": "I suppose I eventually tuned the further language to the first note. Or better say it tuned itself. I'm conscious, all the same, that some of the recent work I've done in criticism and translation grows out of that old vernacular stuff that's always there, deep down."[49] The diverging ripples, that is, do not displace you from your "centre," but paradoxically can carry you deeper into yourself.[50] Importantly, there is open-endedness here, rather than conclusion or unity: our guide might be the unnamed speaker in "The Fragment" in *Electric Light* who asks (responding to lines from *Beowulf*) "Since when … Are the first line and last line of any poem / Where the poem begins and ends?"[51]

It is the sense of amplification and discovery (as well as fortification) that is once more important: the exultation of realizing that one can "go on" probing inwards while developing outwards. The ability to outstrip the conditions that constrain you comes dialogically through a process of re-entering one's own depths, of being "at home and away in [oneself]," as he puts it in his interview with John Brown, or of allowing "every linguistic link and chink and loophole to bring me through to something uncensored, some gleam of half-extinguished thought flaring up."[52] In this process, poetry and education are again substantially the same: "I suppose I would still put trust in education, a liberal education, as they say, a humanist education. To quote Frost again: education changed the plane of regard. It helps you to get a new look at yourself."[53] Frost is one guiding light; Wordsworth is another. When pressed on his own poetic influences (or in Brown's words "havens"), Heaney describes Wordsworth in terms of this being "home and away," of growing up to, and growing up with:

> Wordsworth I just gradually grew up to. He has always been a mountain on the horizon. Wordsworth helps you think about poetry as a way of taking the measure of yourself and the world, and yourself-in-the-world. He has such range. There's a wildness in a poem like "Loud Is the Vale" that opens you up to your aloneness and the vastness you inhabit; and then you have a more serene mysteriousness at the end of "The Ruined Cottage,"

in that image of tall grass and weeds. Hard to beat. Durable, as you say. The thing you learn, I suppose, is that for poetry to matter, the amount of it you know isn't as important as the meaning any small bit of it can gather up over a lifetime.[54]

Durability and "amplification" through persistence are central here: meaning accumulates on one place, quotation, or idea, and helps you take the "measure of yourself and the world, and yourself-in-the-world." In an evocation of his own argument, Heaney moves from natural imagery (the "mountain on the horizon") to the existential phrasing of "yourself-in-the-world": knowledge changes, becomes more sophisticated, and turns back in on itself, informing itself.

ENLIGHTENMENT AND ITS DISCONTENTS

Meaning also accumulates and evolves in Heaney's criticism. It is remarkable how consistent (or, to be less generous, repetitive) Heaney's prose of the 2000s is in its preoccupations, arguments, and insistences: the focus on "durability," say, or changes of perspective, or "endurance," appear repeatedly. This is perhaps a mark of the sheer pressure Heaney faced, after the Nobel Prize, for "copy," whether it be journalistic, academic, or poetic; however, this tendency towards repeating and recycling oneself might itself be testament to how the accumulation of meaning still provides growth and development, and might still help "fortify the spirit against the ruin."[55] This suggestion comes from one of Heaney's last in-depth discussions of education, the 2003 lecture "Bags of Enlightenment," which outlines the different motivations and rationale behind the two school anthologies he edited with Ted Hughes.[56] Where *The Rattle Bag* (1982) presented poetry as an "ad hoc enrichment," with an emphasis on "unexpectedness," *The School Bag* (1997) – in line with Heaney's focus on the accretion of meaning – views poetry "as a body of literature that can be approached deliberately and consciously, in order to understand its inner relations and development, the way it is always growing up yet seeming to stand still."[57] By *The School Bag* what is important is "the value that attaches to a few poems intimately experienced and well-remembered": "Such a poem can come to feel like a pre-natal possession, a guarantee of inwardness and a link to origin."[58]

This view reiterates the sense of being "home" and "away," of delving into original possessions to enable future development and growth, but with an added apostolic, rather than simply social, dimension: in an allusion to Matthew 19:24, such poems can lead the reader into the "kingdom of rightness." This "rightness" is a matter of psychic cohesion more than of religious plenitude, however; as Heaney suggests, they "proceeded in the faith that the aural and oral pleasures of poetry, the satisfactions of recognition and repetition, constitute an experience of rightness that can make the whole physical and psychic system feel more in tune with itself."[59] And, once more, Heaney argues for, but goes beyond, Wordsworth's "grand elementary principle of pleasure": "devotion to that principle did not entail an abandonment of the reality principle. Far from it."[60] Instead, "pleasure" is valued in part because it allows us to survive "desolation": "poetry should also be taught in all its seriousness and extensiveness because it encompasses the desolations of reality, and remains an indispensable part of the equipment we need in the human survival kit."[61]

Heaney once more refuses his own invitation here to discuss Wordsworth and Freud, to compare their "pleasure principles" or "reality principles," or their desire to "restore an earlier state of things" and their lamenting that to do so is impossible.[62] Freud simply appears of little interest to Heaney: Wordsworth has more to teach about childhood, and its importance for adulthood. Thus, when talking about education for the foreword to the 2003 *Childhood and Its Discontents: The First Seamus Heaney Lectures* (a series of lectures on education, edited by Joseph Dunne and James Kelly), Heaney unpicks the echo of Freud's *Civilisation and Its Discontents* in the book's title to emphasize Wordsworth's place as an influential thinker about childhood. Heaney notes that a "century before Freud (whose name, strangely, is little mentioned in the course of these discussions), Wordsworth announced that the child was father to the man. Although he did not name it, he had in fact located the unconscious as a powerful determining factor in the individual's sense of identity and purpose."[63] Heaney's own returns to his psychic origins are, this suggests, not a matter of understanding and healing trauma, but of drawing sustenance, as well as a unified sense of self, that taps into an older source than Freud's sexual psychodramas. Wordsworth, Heaney argues, possessed "a sophisticated grasp of contemporary psychological theories about consciousness

Heaney's Late Style

and identity" and so formulated "the notion that the experience of beauty and fear in early childhood had a formative and positive effect on the adult person's capacities"; thus, Heaney notes, "as a conception, it has proved remarkably durable."[64]

Durable too is Wordsworth's ability to help us answer central psychological and moral questions. Heaney lauds him for broaching "Questions of happiness ... how can the human creature be fitted for life in the modern world? Questions of adaptation: how do our traditional ideas and our moral being square with new social conditions which keep arriving at ever greater speed ...? Questions about one's answerability to or for human suffering."[65] And the answers that Heaney proposes to these questions come from *The Prelude* ("one of the most important documents in the history of ... the virtual child"):

> When he made an inquisition of himself in his late twenties, Wordsworth remembered how the emotional sympathies of the pre-pubertal boy had been enlarged by living in unmediated relationship with the cloudscapes and mountainsides and lake surfaces of Cumberland. Equally he remembered that the country people he dwelt among showed no signs of either personal affectation or class distinction, and realised that this rural society had convinced him of the natural dignity and equality of human beings. And he was convinced that his moral sense had been fostered and confirmed by what we would now call the projection of his guilt feelings upon the landscape: when, for example, he stole out on a rowing expedition in another person's boat, the overshadowing cliff seemed to stalk him in a minatory fashion, as if it were some huge conscience enforcer coming after him across the water.[66]

For Heaney, the "continuing usefulness of the Wordsworthian paradigm" presented in the boat-stealing incident comes through the action, primarily, of fear, which "pointed to the reality of an unknown and scaresome dimension beyond us, but ... also suggested that as human beings we were still fit to bear this reality, were even braced by it and certainly the better for facing it."[67] As was the case in *Death of a Naturalist* some forty years earlier, it is fear, and how fear reveals the unknown sublime, that is the basis for moral development, fosterage, and, ultimately, fortification.

214   This Strange Loneliness

If this is Heaney now engaging in finger-work on his keyboard of reference (and it has this air), it also testifies to the way in which Heaney's earliest reading of Wordsworth – the epiphanic moments of "education" – have continued to persist across Heaney's poetics. They do not simply contribute to the makeup of his mental landscape but provide the prospecting metaphor for how he could hope to extend and amplify his own – or his readers' – psychic territory. This has practical, political consequences in Heaney's late poetry. To show this, I revisit part of Heaney's own childhood territory, and how it too suggests "the reality of an unknown and [perhaps not just] scaresome dimension beyond us," and in particular, the way that Heaney returns to, and reworks, the Wordsworthian epiphany in his poetry. The location for this is Toomebridge.

AT TOOMEBRIDGE

As Heaney relates in the 2004 lecture "Title Deeds: Translating a Classic," at Toomebridge in 1981 the coffin of Francis Hughes – one of ten Republican hunger strikers – was delivered by an armoured British Army convoy to the funeral procession comprising Hughes's friends, family, neighbours, and supporters.[68] For Heaney this confrontation at Toomebridge was an assertion on the community's part of their *dúchas*, a term he defines via the Irish writer and critic Monsignor Brendan Devlin (who, like Heaney, attended St Columb's in Derry, and who would be the principal celebrant at Heaney's funeral). "In an effort to explain it in English," Devlin notes, "the Royal Irish Academy's dictionary of the common old Gaelic languages uses such terms as 'inheritance, patrimony; native place or land; connection, affinity or attachment due to descent or long-standing; inherited instinct or natural tendency.' It is all of these things and, besides, the elevation of them to a kind of ideal of the spirit, an enduring value amid the change and the erosion of all human things."[69] *Dúchas*, in other words, derives from attachment to surroundings and continuity with the past: it is the understanding of "where we come from," in all possible senses, not just in terms of familial or community ties or local rootedness – it also allows access to a wider sense of cultural "inheritance." The context of this anecdote and definition in "Title Deeds" is a discussion of Heaney's *Burial at Thebes* (his 2004 version of Sophocles' *Antigone*), and Heaney identifies Devlin's definition of *dúchas* with his

Heaney's Late Style

own reading of the classics, and how they provide consciousness with "co-ordinates … ways of locating ourselves in cultural as well as geographical space."[70] For Heaney, the classics too are part of his *dúchas*, one of the means by which he can displace and relocate himself: they add nuance and complexity to what he calls in "Electric Light" "The very 'there-you-are-and-where-are-you?' // Of poetry itself."[71]

"At Toomebridge," also published in *Electric Light*, can be read as an exploration of how different aspects of Heaney's *dúchas* interact. It is another spot of time, a moment of revelation in which the present is opened up and occupied, unexpectedly, by an apprehension of the past. It is also a place where history thickens into perception, where multiple pasts jostle and compete. As such it is a site of "chronotopic sedimentation," in Ian Duncan's words, on which different histories have been overlaid and which, as a result, threaten or promise to destabilize the present.[72] This is achieved through the accumulation of adverbial phrases, a layering of "wheres." Here is the poem in full:

At Toomebridge

Where the flat water
Came pouring over the weir out of Lough Neagh
As if it had reached an edge of the flat earth
And fallen shining to the continuous
Present of the Bann.
Where the checkpoint used to be.
Where the rebel boy was hanged in '98.
Where negative ions in the open air
Are poetry to me. As once before
The slime and silver of the fattened eel.[73]

While the title physically locates the poem in place and in the (presumed) present, the fourfold repetition of "where" presents a developing historical, and personal, "sense" of place, while also calling into question how we are to apprehend or understand "place." Repetition, as ever, might undermine as much as reassure, and uncertainty is accentuated by the other adverbial phrases that structure the poem, "As if" and "As once before": there is a lot of ambiguity about just *how* the shifts between metaphorical or historical contexts might function.

This Strange Loneliness

What is of interest to me is how there is a personal trajectory implied in the poem, a tracing of how Heaney's own career and life have developed. This trajectory was absent from the poem when it was first published in 1998. The earlier version repeats the phrase "The year two thousand": it is futural, looking ahead two years to (the apocalyptic) millennium, with the sense that the "continuous / Present of the Bann" is overcome by a "Mud Vision"-esque glimpse of "the sky above" which "Was hurdle and hurdler all at once, / The furl of inner light in the overspill / Axle and portal and crystal as the warp / Those words make in the mind: / 'The year two thousand.'"[74] In the face of such millennial timescales, the poem ends with a throwaway gesture: "Where the rebel boy / Was hanged on the bridge in 1798. / Where poetry can take it and can leave it." By *Electric Light*, though, this has become an internalized reflection: "Where negative ions in the open air / Are poetry to me." This change, and the poem as a whole, are revealing of how Heaney's understanding of the epiphanic, and its relationship to place, has developed; in this reading (perhaps slight over-reading) it can be seen as part of his ongoing dialogue with a Wordsworthian sublime.

The first phrase ("Where the flat water / Came pouring over the weir out of Lough Neagh") is a descriptive, mimetic scene-setter: the enjambment enacts the water flowing over the weir out of Lough Neagh into the Bann – a build-up is released as the water comes pouring out. This places us among the sexually suggestive spurting and flowing images from some of Heaney's earliest work, the pump of "Mossbawn" or the dammed release of "Undine." Unusually for Heaney, however, the water in this image is "flat"; it is rendered two-dimensional, superficial, a mirror with no depth. One could argue that what is (at least temporarily) hidden by this flatness is Heaney's own poetic history with the lough, the "Lough Neagh Sequence" published in *Door into the Dark*. This sense of a hidden history is emphasized by the second adverbial element, in which the water is reflectively "shining": "As if it had reached an edge of the flat earth / And fallen shining to the continuous / Present of the Bann." The allegorical, metaphorical, sidestepping "as if" is used in a fashion similar to "The King of the Ditchbacks" in *Station Island* to displace the poem from the natural landscape, and to postulate an imaginative – and fallacious – parallel realm (the "flat earth"). Here, the parallel is between the water "pouring over the weir" and the water "fallen shining": the first of these is a completed physical process, the second a metaphysical and poetic conceit; it also involves a discovery of greater knowledge and capaciousness (more than the two dimensions of the flat earth).

As the first chapter discussed, "falling" was central to the epiphanies of *Death of a Naturalist*, in part as a means of gaining knowledge of oneself and the world around you; Heaney employs the past participle "fallen" in this manner here. The "fall" brings a jolt of realization, an epiphany: the past participle "fallen" is followed immediately by the present participle "shining" and the concept of the "continuous / Present of the Bann." This echoes Heaney's introduction to his own translation of *Beowulf*: *Beowulf*'s "narrative elements," he argues, "may belong to a previous age but as a work of art it lives in its own continuous present, equal to our knowledge of reality in the present time."[75] The sense of a "continuous present" involves, as Heaney comments in an interview with Karl Miller, the ability to move "between a deep past and what is going on around us," and so enables us (in an allusion to Eliot's version of "tradition") to establish a "kind of coherence ... some stay against confusion."[76] The word "shining" itself creates, like the Wordsworthian present participles of the "Immortality Ode," a sense of "continuousness," of endless luminescence and process, of never reaching or dying. Thus, the poem offers a metaphorical ("As if") discovery of an endless, ahistorical luminescence within the natural landscape, a discovery located in the lost historical past of the past perfect tense ("as if it had ... fallen shining"), the discovery of a form of persistent, aesthetic (and at least proto-religious) space-time. Were this the end of the poem it would stand as a (shorthand) version of a Wordsworthian epiphany, in which knowledge of the infinite is discovered through interaction with the natural landscape; it is not, though, the end of the poem.

Instead, there is an abrupt shift away from the natural (and present) towards a political or historical past: "Where the checkpoint used to be." Recent Irish history irrupts into the sense of the Bann's continuous present. This is, however, also a recognition that it *is* history and not the present political climate. The checkpoint, crucially, is no longer there: we are now, as was suggested slightly prematurely in *The Spirit Level* but now confirmed, in the period of an aftermath to the "checkpoints" of the Troubles. With the irruption of the historical into the natural setting, however, there is no returning to the innocent and ecstatic appreciation of the landscape that the first two

218   This Strange Loneliness

lines offered: there is no escaping the awareness of history once it is upon you. Instead, we are taken further into the history of colonial oppression, to "Where the rebel boy was hanged in '98." We are returned to the United Irishmen Rebellion of 1798, led by Wolfe Tone, which had been the subject of another early Heaney poem, "Requiem for the Croppies" in *Door into the Dark*. The specific reference is to Roddy McCorley, who was hanged at Toomebridge a couple of years after the rebellion, in 1800.[77] This is tapping into a cultural nationalist memory, in which the past is not only more distant but also more heroic, with the mythic resonance of "'98." There is tribal grievance here, but no agent present: the "boy," passively, "was hanged," with an air of apparent inevitability. This might recognize passive suffering; but it might also suggest a cult of martyrdom, or indeed the passivity and futility of such a cult.

That it is "'98" is relevant in another way. Heaney's *dúchas* stretches also to cover Wordsworth and Coleridge's *annus mirabilis*, the year in which the main part of the *Lyrical Ballads* was composed, and in which Wordsworth started on *The Prelude*. Behind the passive suffering of the "rebel boy," and even behind the shadowy agency of the British army, lies, perhaps at many removes, the memory of the English poets, a memory that may feed into the next phrase: "Where negative ions in the open air / Are poetry to me." Heaney steps back from the natural and historical setting of the poem and turns his attention to the process of composing poetry itself. From remembering "'98" Heaney moves on to present the synthesis of the natural and the historical in the poetic. "The open air" is infused with the "negative ions" of … what? The violent history of Northern Ireland? Keatsian negative capability? Heaney rarely uses scientific concepts or vocabulary in his work and, as such, the etymology of ion is important. "Ion" comes from the Greek, meaning "something that goes," suggesting the malleability and mobility of the particles. And they are in "open air": more than the usual pat significance of the "open air" of the countryside, this phrase suggests in this context that the air is open because it is no longer blocked. There is no longer a checkpoint at Toomebridge; you can pass and breathe freely; the ions are free to "be" poetry. Here, poetry *is* (and does not just come out of) the interaction between history and freedom (especially the freedom to write); perhaps it can thus also celebrate hope, life, and endurance in the face of historical reality, and "all of life's inadequacies, desolations and atrocities."[78] This makes sense of the words

Heaney's Late Style 219

of Heaney's earlier version of "At Toomebridge": poetry "can take it and can leave it" inasmuch as it can take historical strain and yet can also leave history behind.

This is not, however, poetry in the abstract, but a self-inwoven return to Heaney's own work. "As once before / The slime and silver of the fattened eel" alludes to "A Lough Neagh Sequence," which had focused on the lives and annual cycles of the eels and eel fishermen (a topic which would be taken up once more in "Eelworks" in *Human Chain*).[79] "As once before" introduces both similarity and difference (as once before *but no longer*); and what is important is the relationship between the present and the past, poetry and history (the way, as Heaney had suggested in "Further Language," that the "complications and contradictions of history, politics, culture, fidelity, hostility, inner division, challenge, and change get themselves gathered in words and become available to writer and reader as a mode of self-knowledge").[80] "Slime and silver" suggests the interest in natural decay and abjection and the archeological poking into mud that characterized Heaney's early poetry. This was, however, always a historical obsession, a retrospect that was, ultimately, horrifying. In the "Vision" section of "A Lough Neagh Sequence," for example, Heaney imagines a cable of eels crossing the land to reach the water as a physical manifestation of the warning that he had been given as a child that a cable of lice would drag him into the water if his hair wasn't "fine combed"; and the poem ends with a horrid realization of this fear: "Phosphorescent, sinewed slime / Continued at his feet. Time / Confirmed the horrid cable."[81] By "At Toomebridge," this cable into the past is no longer horrid: the negative ions can be transmuted to poetry; the slime is balanced against the "silver." This poem stands as a reflection on the historical imagination as much as on Toomebridge itself: what can be gained from dipping into the self, and into history, suggests a fattened possibility, a shining (yet slimy) luminescence. Yet it is not – after the revisions – millennial or otherwise religious: strength comes from introspection, from history, from the natural landscape, but not from a "sky above" that is "hurdle and hurdler all at once."

TRANSLATING *DÚCHAS*

This is not the only "epiphany" in *Electric Light*: indeed, the collection repeatedly presents such stolen, lambent moments in which poetry is drawn from the natural or everyday world; moments, in

220 This Strange Loneliness

the terms of "The Clothes Shrine," in which the "Drag of the workaday" can be "Made light of and got through / As usual, brilliantly."[82] If there is a turn to the eclogic in this collection (in "Bann Valley Eclogue" – a translation of Virgil, Eclogue IX – and "Glanmore Eclogue"), there is also a return to the Greater Romantic Lyric, that "in-out-in" structure of enlightenment and discovery. "Ballynahinch Lake," for example, is almost a textbook example of such a poem. The poet and (presumably) his wife stop and park beside the lake in Connemara, where "a captivating brightness held and opened / And the utter mountain mirrored in the lake /. Entered us like a wedge knocked sweetly home / Into core timber"; the echoes of Wordsworth's "There Was a Boy," in which the "visible scene" entered "unawares into his mind / With all its solemn imagery," are clear.[83] The central epiphany of "Ballynahinch Lake" (the "out" in the "in-out-in") comes from seeing a pair of waterbirds taking off. What is important is their physical struggle, their weightiness: they are "no rafter-skimming souls / Translating in and out of the house of life / But air-heavers, far heavier than the air."[84] The experience is, ultimately, affirming, if unsettling; it is as if "something in us had unhoused itself," and when "she" bent to turn the key in the ignition "her driver's brow ... shook a little as the ignition fired."[85] Something has indeed changed, and been "fired"; the world is less stable, less settled in some way. There is, as the epigraph from Leopardi's "Il Sabato del Villaggio" suggests, an acknowledgment that this is only a temporary season of pleasure: "Godi, fanciullo mio; stato soave, / Stagion lieta è cotesta" [Be happy, my little boy; a sweet state / A joyful time is this].[86] In Leopardi's poem, after the "Saturday" of childhood comes, necessarily, the "Sunday" of adulthood, anxiety, and sadness.

It is telling that the word "epiphany" appears in *Electric Light*, in "Out of the Bag." The poem's conceit is that Heaney and his siblings had not been born, but delivered in "Doctor Kerlin's bag." While thinking about childbirth and "delivery" Heaney describes realizing that Epidaurus was a sanatorium: "A site of incubation, where 'incubation' / Was technical and ritual, meaning sleep / When epiphany occurred and you met the god ... "[87] Epiphany is here a divine event, but also a human one, as natural, and mysterious, as sleep or birth (or rebirth). Epiphanies like these can only be celebrated, not explored: the anxieties about the "real world" and the world of the numinous or the imaginary expressed in *Seeing Things*

Heaney's Late Style

and *The Spirit Level* are to some extent avoided. As "The Known World" asks and answers: "How does the real get into the made up? / Ask me an easier one."[88] This poem goes on to explore one of Heaney's own "spots of time," the experience of being part of a Greek Orthodox pilgrimage in Macedonia, and apparently presents his own "notebook" notes, and then an unreal or unreliable memory: "I had been there, I knew this, but was still / Haunted by it as by an unread dream."[89] Even one's own past experience, that is, is "an unread dream": our pasts are haunting revelations hidden in (and never fully disclosed by) epiphany.

The breadth of reference here is important: epiphanies are as much a matter of cultural encounter, of reading Leopardi – or in "Out of the Bag" Peter Levi or Robert Graves – as they are of experiences in the natural world. *Electric Light* acknowledges how the limits of Heaney's cultural hinterland have been extended over the course of his life. Poems such as "Known World," "The Little Canticles of Asturias," or "Sonnets from Hellas" depict, in self-aware fashion, the globe-trotting of a world-famous poet; others ("Montana," "Out of the Bag," "The Loose Box," "Turpin Song," "The Border Campaign," "Vitruviana") trouble over – in the by now familiar Heaney manner – the adult poet's relationship with his early childhood and development. And just as "At Toomebridge" hinted at different resonances to "'98," the elegies and poems written "in memory" in the second part of the collection acknowledge different types of allegiance: to Ted Hughes, Joseph Brodsky, Zbigniew Herbert, Sorley Maclean, Iain Crichton Smith, Norman MacCaig, George Mackay Brown, Rory Kavanagh, and Mary O Muirithe. In the words of "Into Arcadia," the first of the "Sonnets from Hellas," Heaney describes himself "subsisting between eclogue and translation," between a (literary) rural rootedness and a "travelling between."[90] However, the "eclogue" is itself a "translation," which has been made central to the English literary tradition: it too is testament to that fact that what you are rooted in can be extended; the foreign, external, or other, can grow to become home soil, *dúchas*, or point of origin.

Such flexing and reshaping of his *dúchas* had long been one of the reasons Heaney had turned to translation. As Clíona Ní Ríordáin argues, Heaney's versions of *Buile Suibhne* and *Philoctetes* – *Sweeney Astray* (1983) and *The Cure at Troy* (1991) – were "written to set the old colonial roof echoing" and "the original text" is thus "a filter used to make a statement about the ongoing political situation

222   This Strange Loneliness

in Northern Ireland."[91] *The Midnight Verdict* (1993), on the other hand, tries to find illuminating parallels (and disjunctions) between Latin and Irish "classics," placing alongside each other the narrative of Orpheus in Ovid's *Metamorphosis* and an extract from Brian Merriman's 1780 *Cúirt an Mheán Oíche*. This is a validation of the importance of Irish politics and culture on the one hand, and self-identification with Sweeney, Merriman, Sophocles, and Ovid on the other; both a rooting in Irish culture and history and an opening out of that history in constructive dialogue with literatures beyond the English. This dimension of translation is most fully discussed in Heaney's introduction to his *Beowulf*. There he argues that putting a "bawn" (derived from the Irish *bábhún*, it is the defensive wall round an Irish tower, such as at Bellaghy Bawn in Heaney's home village) into *Beowulf* "seems one way for an Irish poet to come to terms with that complex history of conquest and colony, absorption and resistance, integrity and antagonism, a history that has to be clearly acknowledged by all concerned in order to render it ever more 'willable forward / again and again and again.'"[92] There is a postcolonial leaning to this, but also a desire not to be limited by the colonial past. Heaney links his own linguistic heritage to the Old English of the poem through the word "thole" ("the Old English word meaning 'to suffer,' the word þolian"), and suggests that on meeting "thole" in *Beowulf* he felt an equivalent of Osip Mandelstam's "nostalgia for world culture."[93] This is nostalgia not for a settled past, but for "some unpartitioned linguistic country, a region where one's language would not be simply a badge of ethnicity or a matter of cultural preference or an official imposition, but an entry [once more] into further language."[94] The righting of historical wrongs is not the only dynamic here. Although, as Andrew Murphy argues, for Heaney "a willingness to reimagine history's potential" provides an alternative to "grinding, cyclical destruction," there also needs to be – as "The Tollund Man in Springtime" suggests – a recognition that "'The soul exceeds its circumstances.' Yes. / History not to be granted the last word / Or the first claim ... "[95]

BRITANNICNESS

This desire for an "unpartitioned linguistic country" may itself seem like the nostalgia for a "pre-lapsarian, philological Big Rock Candy Mountain" Heaney had rejected in "Further Language," with its

Heaney's Late Style

rejection of the claims of "history" (or indeed ideology) in favour of unity or wholeness.[96] That this is a prospective "furthering" rather than a "puddling at the source" is, however, important. It allows for the accumulation of meaning, significance, and resonance, and is, I would argue, once more based on an example derived from Wordsworth. Heaney's wrestling with Wordsworth through the 1970s and 1980s was one of the key ways in which he explored his "rights" on the English lyric, on the complexities of his multiple inheritances, without, in the words of *Among Schoolchildren*, replacing a "myth of alien superiority by the myth of native superiority." By *Electric Light* and *Beowulf*, different historical moments and cultural forces tend to merge together in a single text, or at a single location. The central image is of a localized, thickened, and complex presentiment of history: in other words, a "spot of time" that is experienced – with all the caveats of their scaresome, sublime, and horrifying nature – as a matter of "surprise" or, in Vincent Buckley's terms, "puzzled delight."[97] That Buckley was speaking of Shakespeare is to the point; this way of understanding the colonial legacy of English culture is fundamentally enabling, rather than disabling – it permits an enjoyment of the culture alongside a historical resettling.

The practice of historical "revisioning" is crucial. Although Heaney rarely presents his engagement with Wordsworth in such terms (other than, in an early form, in *Place and Displacement*), their relationship can be seen as an example of a complicating "archipelagic" or "four nations" way of looking at these islands, that shifts the perspectives on the relationships between the islands and nations (away from an Anglo-centric view) while acknowledging the myriad ways in which they are deeply connected.[98] Certainly, Heaney's repeated negotiations with Wordsworth come primarily in conversations with other British and Irish poets – Yeats, Kavanagh, Joyce, Hewitt, Burns, MacDiarmid, Clare – in ways that help us reimagine the literary constitution of these islands. In other words, while how Heaney reads Wordsworth is based on a continuous aesthetic kinship, it is also responsive to changes in the cultural and politico-cultural relationships between the Republic of Ireland, Northern Ireland, England, Scotland, Wales, and the abstraction of "Britain"; and to some extent Heaney's prose writings can be seen as purposeful interventions in that process of change and evolution.

This is, for example, one of the motivations behind Wordsworth being used as a touchstone for his discussion of Hugh MacDiarmid in "Tradition and an Individual Talent": the arc of comparison is between the Lake District and MacDiarmid's various "peripheral" points in Scotland (Langholm, Montrose, Whalsay, and Biggar) without recourse to a metropolitan centre. It takes a more political turn, meanwhile, when Heaney uses the Habbie Simpson stanza form, predominantly associated with Robert Burns, in his 1983 "Open Letter," to complain about his inclusion in Blake Morrison and Andrew Motion's *Penguin Book of Contemporary British Poetry*. Perhaps paradoxically – unless viewed from an archipelagic perspective that acknowledges Scottish resistance to any London-centric cultural bias – he uses a Scottish poetic form to assert his Irishness ("my passport's green") rather than Britishness.[99] In "The Regional Forecast" he complicates this playful identification with Scotland further, celebrating the way that "the new awareness created by translations and communications" can help us "find co-ordinates to establish (if necessary) a second literary home-from-home. The satellite picture can make Scotland look as sea-girt as Greece, and we might just get a fresh sense of what is happening in Scottish poetry if we thought of the work of, say, Norman MacCaig in relation to the work of somebody like Yannos Ritsos."[100] There is an ambiguity about whether the Scottish poet MacCaig is part of Heaney's "home" or his "home-from-home" (and Heaney then goes on to mention the Scots Iain Crichton Smith and Sorley MacLean alongside Derek Mahon, Paul Muldoon – and then Les Murray and Derek Walcott); there are different types of identification going on, which mark kinship on non-national, and geographically complicated, lines.[101]

The change of perspective to that of the satellite picture is characteristic. What ultimately links these poets "in these various regional, post-colonial or off-centre situations" is that they "have long ago been freed to throw away the cracked looking-glass of the servant and to scan the world through the cunningly arranged and easily manoeuvreable periscope of their submerged sensibility."[102] This overrides any limiting, overly rooted, perspectives. Thus, for example, in the 2000 lecture "The Pathos of Things," when Heaney explores the relationship between Japanese verse, the English pastoral tradition, and Old Irish poetry, he takes in – on his way – discussions of *The Prelude*, Pound, T.E. Hulme, and Matthew Arnold, with reference to the Irish and Northern Irish poets Derek Mahon, Michael Longley, Paul Muldoon, Cathal Ó Searcaigh, and Michael Hartnett, as well as Iain Crichton Smith.[103] "Irishness" or "Britishness" are, in other words, unnecessarily limiting frames of reference; instead we should aim to hope, as Heaney argues in a discussion of Louis MacNeice in "Frontiers of Writing" (1993), for "the evolution of a political order, one tolerant of difference and capable of metamorphoses within all the multivalent possibilities of Irishness, Britishness, Europeanness, planetariness, creatureliness, whatever."[104] Where John Dennison censoriously reads this "whatever" as a "vacuous generalization," it is more profitably seen as recognition that the terms we use to interpret the world are themselves contingent and transient (what, after all, could follow from "creatureliness" except the exhaustion of categories – carbon-basedness? atomness?)[105] The desire for such an open-ended attitude can be seen as a desire for respect, sympathy, and acknowledgment for all life; a desire that could perhaps ultimately be encompassed by another of Heaney's preoccupations, "neighbourliness."

In both *The Spirit Level* and *Electric Light*, first in "An Invocation," a poem for Hugh MacDiarmid, and then in "Ten Glosses," Heaney asks himself the catechistical question: "Who is my neighbour? My neighbour is all mankind."[106] That MacDiarmid is the spur for this repeated celebration of "all mankind" is telling. Heaney places him on Shetland, where he wrote "On a Raised Beach," his masterful attempt to find a language that could encompass the unknowable otherness of the natural world, and could combine a universal perspective with the haptic sense of the rocks under his touch. More mundanely, MacDiarmid is from the neighbouring islands. This gesture acknowledges that the relationship of "neighbours" (even "each neighbourly murder" described in "Funeral Rites" in *North*) exists necessarily within a much larger context, and combines a recognition of difference as well as closeness.[107] Heaney answers his own question in "An Invocation" with the instruction "And if you won't incline, endure / At an embraced distance. Be the wee / Contrary stormcock that you always were": better not to yield, but to be contrary, to endure, and to "embrace" distance.[108]

Part of the political purpose of Heaney's Nobel lecture is to argue for the importance and plurality of traditions, for an "embraced distance" on the national level. As he argues, there is an ongoing partition of the island of Ireland between "British and Irish jurisdictions" and of "affections in Northern Ireland between the British and Irish heritages"; but he hopes that this partition will "become a bit more like the net on a tennis court, a demarcation allowing for agile give-and-take, for encounter and contending, prefiguring

226   This Strange Loneliness

a future where the vitality that flowed in the beginning from those bracing words 'enemy' and 'allies' might finally derive from a less binary and altogether less binding vocabulary."[109] From 1998 onwards, however, following the Good Friday Agreement and the subsequent reshaping of the political geography of these islands, Heaney becomes more explicit in his support for an archipelagic – even "post-national" – approach to history and cultural history. In the 2001 lecture "Through-Other Places, Through-Other Times: The Irish Poet and Britain," for example, Heaney sees a fluid, salubrious potential encapsulated in the word "Britannic" (for which he draws on the work of the historian Hugh Kearney). "Britannic," in contradistinction to "British," "works more like a cultural wake-up call and gestures not only towards the cultural past but also towards an imaginable future. Without insistence or contention, 'Britannic' is a reminder of much that the term 'British' managed to occlude. 'Britannic' allows equal status on the island of Britain to Celt and Saxon, to Scoti and Cymri, to Maldon and Tintagel, to *Beowulf* and the *Gododdin*, and so it begins to repair some of the damage done by the imperial, othering power of 'British.'"[110] Heaney espouses, as a means towards such a "Britannic" approach that can comprehend "the triple heritage of Irish, Scottish, and English traditions that compound and complicate the cultural and political life of contemporary Ulster," the perspective of the "through-other."[111] As he explains, in a discussion of W.R. Rodgers, "'Through-other' is a compound in common use in Ulster, meaning physically untidy or mentally confused, and appropriately enough it echoes the Irish-language expression *tri na cheile*, meaning things mixed up among themselves"; this he proposes (with perhaps a tongue half in his cheek) as an alternative to postcolonial approaches: "In the post-colonial phase of our criticism and cultural studies, we have heard much about 'the other,' but perhaps the moment of the through-other should now be proclaimed, if only because it seems to have arrived."[112]

Edna Longley argues that Heaney relies heavily on an idea of faith or "fidelity" in this essay, making fidelity "a principle that carries [Louis] MacNeice over what appears stretched and fissured terrain" rather than seeing "MacNeice's inheritance, affections and predilections ... as constitutive, mutually complicating, an epitome of archipelagic cultural and poetic dynamics."[113] However, this should be no surprise: much of Heaney's poetic ultimately depends on and reasserts a faith in intangible notions such as "good," "continuity," or "art." The idea of a "Britannic melting pot" or support for "mobile mongrel islanders" itself requires a great leap of "faith," particularly – as the years since Heaney's death have shown – since the "British Isles" are still riven by suspicions and by blithe misunderstandings of the shared history and identity of the islands: the continued difficulty of many politicians to comprehend the nature of the border between Northern Ireland and the Republic (let alone the importance of the Good Friday Agreement) testifies to this.[114] Heaney's own formulation of *dúchas* is precisely what Longley finds missing: that "constitutive, mutually complicating," and diverse understanding of "inheritance, affections and predilections." *Dúchas* would, in the words of Norquay and Smith, "acknowledge the desire to belong, which pulls us into identifications with geographical and historical spaces, and recognise that this desire still holds possibilities of allegiances that may be empowering and enlightening."[115]

What was useful for Heaney was the extension of ideas of belonging, neighbourliness, and national responsibility beyond the "nation," and beyond any disempowering and limiting focus on relationships within these islands, that went together with the recognition of the validity, importance, and sovereignty of an Irish perspective that could shuck off any colonial or imperial hangover. Talking about his support for the Lisbon Treaty in an interview in January 2010, for example, he mentions Robert Emmet's "famous speech from the dock where he asks that his epitaph not be written until his country 'takes her place among the nations of the earth'" and argues that "Ireland, thanks to membership in the EU over the previous three and a half decades, had indeed taken her place and ... her independence and sovereignty had been newly established and acknowledged. One important result of joining the European Union, for example, was a lessening of concern about the older union with Britain."[116]

APT ADMONISHMENT

Heaney's late invocations of Wordsworth must be read in the light of his re-evaluation of the bonds between Ireland and Britain. Paradoxically, though, since Wordsworth is treated primarily as part of Heaney's own personal inheritance, and not a colonial imposition, their relationship appears to solidify, rather than loosen or lessen: to complicate things further, the archipelagic (or peripheral) bonds are not that limpidly straightforward. Heaney's 2000 introduction to

228   This Strange Loneliness

David Thomson's *The People of the Sea* is an example of this complex re-evaluation of the relationship between Ireland and the constituent parts of Britain.[117] Thomson's book is a reflective account of his travels around the Highlands and islands of Scotland and the West of Ireland in search of stories involving seals and selkies: it tends not towards the loose Celtic Twilight treatment of the myths, however, but to a timeless "Homeric somberness," in Heaney's words, that delights through its "absence of nostalgia" ("nostalgia" here has a hint of the Twilight about it, not the allure of "world culture").[118] As such, the book validates the stories of the western (Celtic) seaboard, taking them on their own terms, and not presenting them for the consumption of a metropolitan (English) readership; Heaney's own discussion, however, is not as straightforwardly "marginal" in its perspective.

The two touchstones Heaney uses are the Orkney poet Edwin Muir and Wordsworth's "Solitary Reaper." The two poets had been associated, in Heaney's 1989 essay "Edwin Muir," with "prospects," with the ability to create images which "dwell in two places at one time."[119] Similarly, Muir here once more upholds a "sense of the need for a renewed covenant with all life and a respect for its sacredness," inspired by the threat of nuclear destruction; "The Solitary Reaper" also enables access to another mode of understanding.[120] Heaney quotes from the poem (one of "the most haunting lyrics in the English language"):

Whate'er the theme, the Maiden sang
As if her song could have no ending;
I saw her singing at her work,
And o'er the sickle bending; –
I listened, motionless and still;
And, as I mounted up the hill,
The music in my heart I bore,
Long after it was heard no more.

This famous stanza is like a spell that keeps time, in two senses: it keeps the metrical beat of the octosyllabic line, and it also manages to shift into the eternal present of song-time an incident that might otherwise have remained part of the accidental record … The chance words of Thomas Wilkinson's *Tour of Scotland* [which Wordsworth relied upon] have been magicked into the domain of the eternally recurrent, the once-upon-a-time world of story, where the strains of "no ending" and "still" and "more" echo and overflow above the brim of the usual.[121]

The poem, as Heaney notes, was "written after a tour in Scotland and is about the experience of listening to one of the local people express herself unforgettably in her native Gaelic." Unforgettably, but also unintelligibly. Heaney, like Wordsworth, treats the song as pure, meaningless music (the song can only have "no ending" if you are unable to follow its own narrative flow). The cultural ignorance of Wordsworth (and Wilkinson) is almost being repeated here. Why doesn't Wordsworth's speaker ask his guide what the girl is singing? Why doesn't Heaney acknowledge that the incident might already be in "the eternal present of song-time" (since it is, itself, a song)?

Heaney and Wordsworth both laud the sombre exoticism of the encounter, rather than the sombre or joyful content of the song or tale itself. If this act of exoticization is treated generously, it suggests how Heaney prefers (as in Edward Thomas's "As the Team's Head-Brass," Elizabeth Bishop's "At the Fishhouses," or Wordsworth's "Resolution and Independence") for "content" to be "dreamt through, as it were, rather than dumped down."[122] It is peculiar, though, given his own knowledge of Irish and own advocacy of the Gaelic poet Sorley MacLean, that Heaney's eye and ear align with those of Wordsworth, the tourist, rather than with the singing girl. This is not an isolated case: similar exoticism is at play when Heaney comes to translate "Hallaig," MacLean's hallucinatory poem about the clearances on the Isle of Raasay. What attracts Heaney is the uncanny, trance-like nature of MacLean's work, and the manner in which his voice "had a certain bardic weirdness that sounded both stricken and enraptured. Whether you were listening to him or reading him on the page, you were led into an uncanny zone, somewhere between the land of heart's desire and a waste land created by history – a felt history that stretched from the Highland clearances to the Spanish civil war and the world war it ushered in."[123] This is stretching credibility somewhat, as to the specific details of the "felt history" that a "voice" can convey: it is hard to see how any "voice" in English, in comparison, could invoke by aural means alone a "felt history" of the Napoleonic wars, the death of Victoria, and Chamberlain's appeasement. Relating MacLean to Orpheus, "the singer who enchants all nature," does, however, make some sense. This comparison does not deny the meaningful content of MacLean's work (or that of the reaping girl), but does allow for something beyond the rational: MacLean's "Hallaig" then appears "a dividend paid to MacLean by his lyric muse because, in Yeats's words, he had not 'broken up his lines to weep.' His Orphic gift had survived the test of awakening to the nightmare of history."[124] The music is not cut off from the happenings of the world; it is, rather, in Archibald MacLeish's words that Heaney uses in his Nobel lecture, "equal" to them. What Heaney is hoping to do in his translation is "what Yeats wanted rhythm to do in poetry: prolong the moment of contemplation." This is subtly different from Wordsworth's emotion recollected in tranquility: instead of the loss and diminishment necessarily present in Wordsworth's formulation, there is a held-open space, a continuing access to another world, another experience.

"Encounters" with something beyond the rational or intelligible, such as Wordsworth's with the reaping girl, are important in Heaney's late work and they are clear developments of the poems written with a view of the "offing" in *Seeing Things*. These encounters are, crucially, conscious of their own presumptions, and of their responsibility towards who is encountered. The Wordsworthian model for this is not "The Solitary Reaper" but, as "Apt Admonishment: Wordsworth as an Example" (Heaney's last extended discussion of Wordsworth's poetry) makes clear, the poem "Resolution and Independence."[125] Heaney had previously used the querying title "Yeats as an Example?"; here there are fewer doubts. In this lecture, Heaney is exploring what he terms "poetic recognition scenes," "meetings where the poet comes face to face with something or someone in the outer world recognized as vital to the poet's inner creative life, and accounts of these meetings represent some of the highest achievements in the art. When a practitioner describes an encounter with a living or dead master, or an equivalent moment of epiphany, something fundamental is usually at stake, often having to do with poetic vocation itself."[126] These meetings are familiar from Heaney's own poetry (the ghosts of *Field Work* or *Station Island*, say) and are fundamental to the development of his interest in fosterage and individuation. They are, on a biographical level, "crucial events in the growth or reorientation of the poet's mind" while also being, on the mythic level, "evidence of a close encounter between the poet and the muse."[127]

They are also, however, similar to the uncanny encounter of "The Solitary Reaper" (or MacLean's "Hallaig"). In the modern era (Heaney's comparison is with Hesiod), they are "occasions when the poet has been, as it were, unhomed, has experienced the *unheimlich*."[128] Even in these encounters, however, the poet receives "a renewed sense of election, surer in his or her vocation," and the experience is usually "unexpected and out of the ordinary, in spite of the fact that it occurs in the normal course of events, in the everyday world. A strange thing happens. A spot of time becomes a spot of the timeless, becomes, in effect, one of 'the hiding places of [the poet's] power.'"[129] What is happening here is both summation and return full-circle. Heaney is reworking his own "Feeling into Words" (this is explicitly acknowledged later in the lecture), but he is also acknowledging how the spot of time he adopted from Wordsworth has become the main medium for exploring the unknown in his own late poetry. Through the poet's attention the "spot of time becomes a spot of the timeless," and the historic moment points towards – necessarily without fully revealing – something beyond its own bounds.

Although Dante, Eliot, Lawrence, and Hughes are all discussed here in terms of such access to the timeless, Heaney ultimately focuses on Wordsworth. "Resolution and Independence" is, for Heaney, an example of how "the achievement of a true poem is a way of establishing self-worth in a world that does not necessarily regard poetry as being of any great worth in itself."[130] Heaney compares Wordsworth's poem with Dorothy's diary account of the same encounter with a leech gatherer (this is a technique Heaney had also used in his comparison with the Fenwick notes used in "Feeling into Words" and with Wilkinson's prose account in his discussion of "The Solitary Reaper"). What distinguishes William's leech-gatherer from Dorothy's is an "aura of strangeness, this sense that the figure is not a sociological specimen being observed and presented as a symptom of an ill-divided society, but rather somebody who has entered the poet's consciousness as a dream presence, an emanation or, to employ Wordsworth's own word again, an 'admonition.'"[131] The important thing, drawing on Wordsworth's own prose, is that he "traces primary laws, rather than dictates them, the law in this case being the one that says human beings, given the right conditions, have an immense and heartbreaking capacity for dignified endurance; and furthermore, to witness such endurance helps the rest of us also to endure."[132] Heaney is, to some extent, trying to strip away from Wordsworth the centuries of criticism and interpretation – "Before Freud comes along to define the uncanny, before Joyce fixes

232   This Strange Loneliness

upon his notion of the epiphany, before Lawrence puts his trust in
the promptings of his creatureliness rather than the voices of his
education" – to reimagine his bridging of "the gap between the quotidian and the visionary worlds" on his own terms, the terms of
endurance, a "new and haunting acoustic," and, pre-eminently, "apt
admonishment."[133]

Heaney is, in part, rehearsing the earlier lessons of his own poems.
A similar encounter had been presented in "Field of Vision" in
Seeing Things, for example, when the poet remembers a "woman
who sat for years / In a wheelchair, looking straight ahead / Out the
window" and receives from their face-to-face meeting "an education
/ Of the sort you got across a well-braced gate."[134] In both there is
an image of endurance – "she never lamented once and she never /
Carried a spare ounce of emotional weight" – but in "Resolution
and Independence" there is also a resistance to that poetic gaze
that would focus, interpret, and clarify. The leech-gatherer's words
become unintelligible: "The Old Man still stood talking by my side;
/ But now his voice to me was like a stream / Scarce heard; nor
word from word could I divide; / And the whole Body of the man
did seem / Like one whom I had met with in a dream."[135] In "Apt
Admonishment," Heaney identifies the Tollund Man as his own
equivalent of the leech-gatherer, and the encounter between them
one in which "there was something familiar between us yet something that was also estranging and luminous"; there is also an echo
here of the meeting in "Montana" which involved a "recognition /
That made no sense."[136] Heaney stresses, however, what continues
beyond this encounter, the idea that writing a poem can "lead the
writer out of himself or herself, provide an experience of estrangement, and then resituate him or her in the usual life, bemused, as it
were, as if for a moment the gift for uttering truth had been possessed."[137] "Resolution and Independence," then, is an instance "of
something constant in the poetic life, something indeed that is indispensable to it. Call it apt admonishment, call it contact with the
hiding places, call it inspiration, call it the staying power of lyric,
call it the bringing of memories that are luminous into the relatively
dark world, call it what you like, but be sure it is what a poet's inner
faith and freedom depends upon."[138] This is, substantially, a reaffirmation of the claims made in "Feeling into Words," and developed
over three decades, about poetry's reliance on the unknown and on
memory, on "hiding places." But at the end of those three decades

of development, there is also an emphasis on the trance-like, the enduring, and the admonishing; poetry is not ultimately an act of "mastery" but one of humility, of accepting the unknowable limits of inspiration, as well as a celebration of the joy it can bring.

VISIONARY OBSTINACY

Such humility may, indeed, involve recognition of some of the issues with Wordsworth as an example, of the admonishment as well as the encouragement he offers. Wordsworth's poetry clearly offers models of endurance in the face of loss, not just in "Resolution and Independence" but also in "Michael" and "Old Man Travelling" as well as, in slightly different forms, in "Ode: Intimations of Immortality" and "Tintern Abbey." In "Tintern Abbey," for example, the poet describes how his mind "revives" "not only with the sense / Of present pleasure, but with pleasing thoughts / That in this moment there is life and food / For future years."[139] This is, once more, a "prospect of the mind," if the word prospect is understood, as Fiona Stafford argues, to imply "both distance and future possibility" and "an active assessment of the capacities of the landscape, rather than a retreat into a lair, sunlit or otherwise."[140] But it is also a prospect that acknowledges those future years will bring diminishment: "Tintern Abbey," balancing between retrospect ("Five years have past") and prospect, hopes for any sense of loss to be counterweighted by the accumulation of "pleasant" memories.[141] Similarly, in "Ode: Intimations on Immortality" the knowledge that "there hath past away a glory from the earth" is not utterly succumbed to; the sense that even "in our embers / Is something that doth live" offers recompense, and just "The thought of our past years in me doth breed / Perpetual benedictions."[142] Even the trace of what has passed is a blessing, and the ability to celebrate this is an example of what Heaney describes in *Stepping Stones* as "visionary obstinacy" (in a discussion of Miłosz's refusal to abandon the "Christian humanist wager"): "you could argue that there's something analogous to Miłosz's deployment of the full orchestra after Auschwitz in Wordsworth's response to the loss of visionary gleam in his great 'Ode': it was only when the gleam had fled that Wordsworth opened all the gorgeous stops."[143]

The celebration of "visionary obstinacy," of the opening of the stops, is necessary because for any poet responding to Wordsworth as an example, the most compelling cautionary tale comes not,

234

ultimately, from his poems but from his life. Jonathan Bate, in his attempt to reclaim Wordsworth's importance as a "nature poet" above all else, argues that "most people know two facts about Wordsworth, that he wrote about daffodils and that he lived in the Lake District."[144] I would add that if people know a third fact about him, it is that the younger (attractive, radical, exciting) Wordsworth is followed inexorably by the older (conservative, didactic, moralizing) Wordsworth, stumbling behind him, changing his meaning: the Wordsworth who, as George Bornstein comments, "forsook his original poetic vision by growing every more prosaic and didactic."[145] Shelley's accusation in "To Wordsworth," that the older poet had abandoned his radicalism, deserting "honoured poverty" and "songs consecrate to truth and liberty," stuck.[146]

Thus, for twentieth-century poets and critics there was no escaping the fact that the "example" of Wordsworth was tainted (or rendered slightly ludicrous) by his later years. He became, in Bornstein's words, "a ruined hulk warning of the rocks."[147] For Dylan Thomas he suggested caprine "decay": "But why Wordsworth?" he asked Pamela Hansford Johnson in a letter on 15 October 1933, "Why quote that decay? Shelley I can understand, but old Father William was a human nannygoat with a pantheistic obsession."[148] For Yeats, meanwhile, Wordsworth was "the one great poet who, after brief blossom, was cut and sawn into planks of obvious utility."[149] Certainly, he offered him a particular warning as he pondered his own later years. "A poet," Yeats commented, "when he is growing old, will ask himself if he cannot keep his mask and his vision without new bitterness, new disappointment ... He will buy perhaps some small old house, where, like Ariosto, he can dig his garden, and think that in the return of birds and leaves, or moon and sun, and in the evening flight of the rooks he may awake out of vision. Then he will remember Wordsworth withering into eighty years, honoured and empty-witted, and climb to some waste room and find, forgotten there by youth, some bitter crust."[150] The different examples offered by Yeats and Wordsworth are particularly instructive. In Alasdair Macrae's words, where "Wordsworth stagnated as a poet, Yeats enjoyed amazing aggrandizement in the second half of his career," producing, as Corcoran notes, "some of his greatest work in, and about, old age."[151] In contrast, as Hugh Haughton has argued, "the prospect of finding himself in a Rydal Mount of his own must occasionally [have given Heaney] pause."[152] This may have been especially true after Paul Muldoon had associated Heaney in "Madoc – A Mystery" not with Wordsworth but – worse – Southey.[153]

Heaney was not immune to concerns about being too closely associated with Wordsworth, that "great grey poet": from the *Essential Wordsworth* in 1988 he had been discussing "the ebb" of Wordsworth's "powers and the flight of his vision."[154] However, by turning the question "Yeats as an Example?" into the affirmative "Apt Admonishment: Wordsworth as an Example," Heaney implicitly gives an answer to this. He asserts that Wordsworth can still be a fortifying presence and that there is much to be learned from him: he continues to hold faith in the project of the early Wordsworth and to celebrate whatever could be salvaged from his later oeuvre. Discussing Hugh MacDiarmid in one of the lectures in *The Redress of Poetry*, Heaney had predicted that "sooner or later, however, what happened to Wordsworth will happen to MacDiarmid: the second phase of his career will be rendered down to a series of self-contained, self-sustaining passages of genuine poetry."[155] Heaney's own selection of Wordsworth's work was part of this process of "rendering down," although it too subscribes to the idea of the Lake poet's precipitous decline. Only four of the fifty poems in the *Essential Wordsworth* were composed after 1807 – "Surprised by Joy," "Lines (Composed at Grasmere)," "XXIV After-Thought" from *The River Duddon*, and the "Extempore Effusion upon the Death of James Hogg" – but this last, in particular, Heaney repeatedly advocates. (In *Stepping Stones* he compares Ted Hughes's *Birthday Letters* to "other big late-career sequences" like Wordsworth's "Ecclesiastical Sonnets" and Lowell's "Notebook" and – unsurprisingly – decides Hughes's "more than holds its own.")[156]

This is not to say that Heaney ignores Wordsworth's later poetry, but that he approaches it with selective tact. If, in the case of Wordsworth, those passages of "genuine poetry" are few and far between, that does not mean they are not worth celebrating. Thus, although in *Stepping Stones* he draws a distinction between poets like Yeats (and R.S. Thomas and Miłosz) – as poets who exemplify "scepticism and stamina" – and Wordsworth, as a poet who has "settled for the run of his own mill," he also stresses that "the unforeseen" can still surprisingly arrive:

> in certain great poets – Yeats, Shakespeare, Stevens, Miłosz –
> you sense an ongoing opening of consciousness as they age, a
> deepening and clarifying and even a simplifying of receptivity to

236   This Strange Loneliness

what might be awaiting on the farther shore. It's like those rare summer evenings when the sky clears rather than darkens. No poet can avoid hoping for that kind of old age. But equally no poet can forget Wordsworth's loss of grip or Eliot's alibis in the theatre. Still, everybody should also remember Wordsworth's marvellous rally in a poem like "Extempore Effusion," the one in memory of James Hogg, the Ettrick Shepherd. There's no rule.[157]

Heaney acknowledges Wordsworth's decline but opts to stress what achievements can still be acknowledged in his later work; his response to Wordsworth, and to other poets, is measured, generous, and humane, with any criticism assuaged through playful (and playfully clichéd) metaphor ("the run of the mill"). Indeed, it is almost paternalistic, as if here in *Stepping Stones* Heaney is not so much anxious foster-son seeing his own decline in the example of a poetic-foster-father, but rather a protective custodian of Wordsworth's legacy.

Heaney identified this role, in a 2010 interview, with artists in general: artists "are custodians of what has been preserved, we hold it in trust and should hand it on" and it is "the function of the art to make whatever it deals with – whether it be matters past or present, painful or pastoral – 'safe, as we read it, from change.'"[158] Underlying this is a firm reassertion of (a small 'c' conservative) belief in culture, in the slow and careful development of human civilization over time, in the good of what is passed on from generation to generation. When asked in *Stepping Stones* if he can recall any "visionary moments" akin to Wordsworth's "Ode" that came from later than his childhood, Heaney first undermines any accusation of pretention by talking about how "the usual reveries of immensity" usually came as he was "pissing at the gable of the house" in Glanmore. However, he then remembers standing on a balcony at Berkeley and places his "own epiphany" against the "apocalyptic vision" of his contemporaries Allen Ginsberg and Gary Snyder: "The bricks were already warm in the sun, it was clear and summery and light-drenched; you could see the white terraces and tower blocks of San Francisco across the bay and the green traces of trees and gardens in between, and I had this visitation of – well, I don't know what to call it … Humanist joy? Awe? A tremendous sense of what human beings had achieved on earth. Something akin to Wordsworth's revelation on Westminster Bridge."[159] Wordsworth, in his revelation, looks out over London which "doth like a garment wear / The beauty of the morning," wonders at the sun "steep[ing]" beautifully in its "first splendour," and exclaims "Ne'er saw I, never felt, a calm so deep! / The river glideth at his own sweet will: / Dear God! the very houses seem asleep; / And all that mighty heart is lying still!"[160] This is a "calm" of contained energy, of potential, of power held in check and reserve; and despite the "Dear God!" it is, as Heaney suggests, a humanist joy, a wonder at the world created by and for humans. It is, again, a "prospect in the mind," one in which there is a numinous, deeply felt connection between inner and outer realities, between the perceived energy of the world outside us and our own "hearts" and imaginations, a sense of shared, overabundant "life."

This memory of a joyful, awed, humanist optimism in the face of "apocalypse" is characteristic of Heaney's late attention to Wordsworth. On the one hand, it is a weighing in on behalf of the humanist cause, reasserting the value of culture and poetry: what he describes in a speech on the acceptance of the Cunninghame Medal in 2008 as "the extra dimension which life attains not only from the study of literature but from its composition" (which is itself in part based on his belief that "poetry, which William Wordsworth once described as 'the breath and finer spirit of all knowledge'" contributes to "natural knowledge").[161] And on the other, it is an example of his own trust in the accretion of meaning, in the value of long-held memories and knowledge, if they are carefully attended to and nourished. As he argues in *Stepping Stones*, the Wordsworthian "early-in-life experience" is crucial, but needs to be located and encouraged: "It's like a culture at the bottom of a jar, although it doesn't grow, I think, or help anything else to grow unless you find a way to reach it and touch it."[162]

The overall sense from *Stepping Stones* is of a cumulative legacy, a "definite long-term influence" whereby "the grip I got on poems like 'Michael' and 'Resolution and Independence,' the deep familiarity with the Preface to *Lyrical Ballads*, stood to me for the rest of my life."[163] That idea of "formation" and familiarity is itself part of Wordsworth's influence on Heaney:

> The essential for doing a poem is either entrancement or focus, which equals enjoyment ... What is important for the doer is the quality of the attention, the "habits of meditation" Wordsworth spoke about. In his Preface to the *Lyrical Ballads* – a document still full of wisdom about how the thing works – Wordsworth

238   This Strange Loneliness

says, "I believe that my habits of meditation have so formed my
feelings, as that my descriptions of such objects as strongly excite
those feelings, will be found to carry along with them a *purpose*."
That would be my feeling: agonizing over those things – how to
live properly, I mean – is worthwhile because it forms your "habits of meditation," your frame of mind, your disposition, your
temperament.[164]

Wordsworth is acknowledged as central to Heaney's own formation,
to the habits that have helped develop his disposition, his temperament, and as one of the mainstays in Heaney's own ethical self-questioning. This risks, however, turning Heaney's late engagement with
Wordsworth into a staid affair, a matter of dutiful rehearsal, reassertion, when it is often more mischievous, more playful. Heaney
gently acknowledges the issues with Wordsworth's work, the times
it can be ploddingly pedestrian rather than epiphanically immediate:
Heaney's own "Postscript," as he notes, "could have been given a
long Wordsworthian title, something like, 'Memorial of a Tour by
Motorcar with Friends in the West of Ireland,' but that would mis-
represent the sudden, speedy feel of it."[165] At its best, though, Wordsworth's poetry is still felt to be swiftly responsive and alive to the
surprise and wonder of the world; he can still provide, especially in
his extempore effusions, "'a timely utterance' that gave relief." [166]

A PULSE IN THE TIMBERED GRIPS

What is clear throughout *Stepping Stones* is the way in which thinking about Wordsworth's work has helped to form Heaney's "temperament" and informs his poetry both on the level of content, form, and
structure but also in a more trance-like, subconscious, or subterranean
manner (with the suggestion that poetry needs either "entrancement
or focus"). To end, I look at how this influence manifested in two
poems from *District and Circle*, "A Scuttle for Dorothy Wordsworth"
and "Wordsworth's Skates," and then discuss some of the implications of the image of "grip": the "grip" which Wordsworth had helped
Heaney get on the world, which Wordsworth himself risked losing,
and which is released at the end of *Human Chain*.

"A Scuttle for Dorothy Wordsworth" is published in *District and
Circle* alongside another "gift" poem, "A Stove Lid for W.H. Auden,"
under the title "Home Fires." Heaney had been offering such poetic

Heaney's Late Style

"gifts" since at least "A Peacock's Feather" (subtitled "for Daisy Garnett") which was published in *The Haw Lantern* but composed in 1972; by *Station Island*, and with the poems "A Hazel Stick for Catherine Ann" and "A Kite for Michael and Christopher," the recipients' names are included in the title, and the act of bestowing, rather than just the object itself, is foregrounded. Such gifts are clearly important to Heaney: *Human Chain*, and so his collected oeuvre as a whole, ends on "A Kite for Aibhín." Where "A Stove Lid for W.H. Auden" is an act of mock-heroic domestication of Auden (with the stove lid standing in for the Shield of Achilles), "A Scuttle for Dorothy Wordsworth" can be read as an affectionate recognition of his own – and William's – tendency to use Dorothy's journals as combustible material: the lecture "Apt Admonishment," the most recent of these examples, was delivered in 2006, a year after the poem had first appeared in *Irish Pages*.

"A Scuttle for Dorothy Wordsworth" is formed of two vignettes (in two sextet stanzas). The first, an image of "Dorothy young" shovelling a pile of coals "Carted by one Thomas Ashburner" (the appropriateness of whose name "Goes unremarked" because of Dorothy's toothache) is based on her entries in the *Grasmere Journal*. On 30 August 1800 (dated the 28th by Dorothy), for example, she remarks, "Thomas Ashburner brought us our 8th cart of coals since May 17th."[167] Strangely, Heaney foregrounds and changes Dorothy's pain. In her journal for this day, she has a headache (after reading "a little of Boswell's Life of Johnson") and lies down in the orchard; in Heaney's poem, she has toothache, "every jolt and jag" of which "Backstabs her through her wrist-bone, neck-bone, jaw-bone."[168] The 30th of August 1800 is otherwise a relatively standard day in the Grasmere life of the Wordsworths, aside from one hint of the ominous passing of time. John and William bathed together (after William had "finished his Inscription of the Pathway, then walked in the wood"); later they rowed down the lake (which was stirred by breezes). "We looked at Rydale," Dorothy writes, "which was soft, chearful, and beautiful. We then went to peep into Langdale. The Pikes were very grand. We walked back to the view of Rydale, which was now a dark mirror. We rowed home over a lake still as glass, and then went to George Mackareth's to hire a horse for John. A fine moonlight night. The beauty of the moon was startling as it rose to us over Loughrigg Fell."[169] Rydale turns from being "soft, chearful, and beautiful" into being "a dark mirror"; the lake "still as glass" suggests a visibility, but also – given it is night – the invisibility of infinite blackness. So too in Heaney's poem, there is a dark reflection: "Dorothy young" turns into "Dorothy old," "doting at the flicker / In a brass companion set, all the companions / Gone or let go, their footfalls on the road / Unlistened for."[170] There is a playing with tenses, though, that allows the poem to end with a sense of prospect: the footfalls "sounded once as plump / As the dropping shut of the flap-board scuttle-lid / The minute she'd stacked the grate for their arrival."[171] The simile allows us to move into the storybook world of an eternally possible future, an arrival that can always be hoped for, even if in reality the companions are all "gone or let go" and all that is left is the "companion set." There is a redemption here of Dorothy in old age, a generous act of translating her from her "dotage" into a realm of youthful possibility. Whether or not it makes up for once more turning her and her journal into material is another matter. Certainly, another Northern Irish poet, Sinéad Morrissey, begins "1801," her own reworking of Dorothy's diaries, from a more propitious point ("A beautiful cloudless morning. My toothache better") to end on a more convincing prospect of future renewal:

I almost said *dear, look*. Either moonlight on Grasmere –
like herrings! –
or the new moon holding the old moon in its arms.[172]

In Morrissey's poem, it is William who is "pale as a basin, exhausted with altering"; Dorothy is not consigned (however affectionately) to her dotage.

"Wordsworth's Skates," like "A Scuttle for Dorothy Wordsworth," juxtaposes decay with life, age with youth. The poem is a *via negativa*, rejecting mundane causes for a scratch ("A star") in a window – "Slate scrape. / Bird or branch?" – to settle on an image that is also a personal memory: "the whet and scud of steel on placid ice."[173] This recalls the lines from Wordsworth's *Prelude* he remembered learning by heart in primary school: "All shod with steel, / We hiss'd along the polished ice."[174] It is *not* the skates in their present state that is important, "Not the bootless runners lying toppled / In dust in a display case, / Their bindings perished" (even though this was a visual detail Heaney was keen to include in *William Wordsworth Lived Here*).[175] What is cherished is their re-imagined former glory, their movement and life; although it alludes to *The Prelude*, the poem's reaching after

Heaney's Late Style

the energy and movement of youth is also suggestive of the fading epiphanies of "Ode: Intimations of Immortality." The passage of time that would render the "polished ice" "placid," and the boots themselves "decayed," is to be refused: instead what is imagined is the "reel of them on frozen Windermere / As he flashed from the clutch of earth along its curve / and left it scored."[176] Heaney's memory here goes awry: as Erica McFarlane notes, "it was almost certainly Esthwaite water, near Hawkshead, where he went to school, on which Wordsworth skated as a child, not the much larger Windermere, which is further afield and rarely freezes."[177] However, this poem is not really one of memory or description (even that description which is "revelation"), but rather of pure marvel: of being "marvellously yourself" as one of the "Ten Glosses" in *Electric Light* suggests.[178] The marvel comes in the reeling of the skates on the ice, and how their "flashing" (their "verb, pure verb") leaves the world scored. The boots in their present decayed form are not what is retained: it is, paradoxically, their mark left on ice that melted centuries ago; it exists in that "continuous present" Heaney had sought for, even if – in actuality – having existed only fleetingly. Where Dorothy is left with the prospect of "arrival," William (although never actually named in the poem, aside from one "he") is given a form of departure. The skates (and by extension the skater, and the poem itself) are allowed to escape from "the clutch of the earth": this offers a fitting farewell to a poet who had fostered Heaney's own risky airiness.

This is not quite the end, however. Biddings of farewell have even greater weight in *Human Chain*, the collection Heaney published in 2010, having come through a stroke in 2006. He recognizes that these poems are the product of a period that could not have been hoped for or expected and has to be celebrated as such: the endurance and "extra"-ness Heaney had frequently espoused takes on a particular poignancy. The opening poem, "'Had I not been Awake,'" replays Heaney's stroke "in allegory" and, as Nick Laird notes, creates a "tenor of uncertainty and precariousness."[179] However, in spite of the sense of Heaney's being got up "the whole of me a-patter," and it being "A courier blast that there and then / Lapsed ordinary," there is still resistance to diminishment: "But not ever / After. And not now."[180] There is, in other words, a determined stoical persistence in this collection once more: the realization of physical decline, as suggested in "The Butts," but the need "for all that / To keep working."[181]

242   This Strange Loneliness

Such persistence is, however, acknowledged as necessarily temporary and part of an inevitable circle of life. In "Route 110," for example, the poet sees himself, on a journey back into his memories, as being in the "age of ghosts," "Needy and ever needier for translation," and then, ultimately, preparing for the "age of births."[182] Being there is not, though, a cause for despair. The inevitability of death and decline is offset by the feeling of being part of a chain of being, part of a community in the broadest sense. Any freedom experienced is one that frees you into, rather than out of, communal bonds. Thus, in the title poem the passing of sacks of food along a human chain is celebrated for its sense of release (again, however temporary), but also as entailing an awareness of mutual reliance, of communal strain: "Nothing surpassed // That quick unburdening, backbreak's truest payback, / A letting go which will not come again. / Or it will, once. And for all."[183] The "miraculous" in this collection is not the ability to meet the divine, or to recreate oneself *ex nihilo*; rather, it is the continuity created by bonds of community, affection, and companionship – "neighbourliness" experienced in small acts of generosity and love. Thus the miracle in "Miracle," another parabolizing of his stroke, is "Not the one who takes up his bed and walks / But the ones who have known him all along / and carry him in – ..."[184] The "humanist joy" celebrated in *Stepping Stones* is here felt on a much more intimate level, as a response to human touch rather than to panoramic vistas.

In part this merging of a sense of communal reliance and of personal "release" is the culmination of one of Heaney's repeated late wordplays, the idea of "grip." The uncollected 2007 sequence "Cutaways," which combines Heaney's earlier images of the ploughman, charioteer, and water-diviner, ends with his father placing his hand on the poet's, "to guide the plough, / Each slither of the share, each stone it hit / Registered like a pulse in the timbered grips."[185] These lines are recycled in "Chanson d'Aventure" in *Human Chain*, in Heaney's description of "Doing physio in the corridor, holding up /As if once more I'd found myself in step // Between two shafts, another's hand on mine, / Each slither of the share, each stone it hit / Registered like a pulse in the timbered grips."[186] This continues Heaney's emphasis on the haptic, on the beneficial effect of the felt and handled world. At the end of "The Tollund Man in Springtime" in *District and Circle*, the bog body tells how "As a man would, cutting turf, / I straightened, spat on my hands, felt benefit / And spirited myself into the street."[187]

In "A Shiver," meanwhile, he asks, "does it do you good," when swinging a sledgehammer, "To have known it in your bones, directable, / Withholdable at will, / A first blow that could make air of a wall, / A last one so unanswerably landed / The staked earth quailed and shivered in the handle?"[188] The answer, throughout *Human Chain*, appears to be "yes": the holding on to the world, the *amplitude* that comes in handles, in grips, is to be cherished.

The collection as a whole, however, is balanced between the desire to maintain a grip and the knowledge that at some point there will be a final "letting go" (as Clair Wills notes, the collection is both a continuation of Heaney's "sustained engagement with the Romantic belief in memory as a means of recovering community and human solidarity in solitude" and a recognition of "Belatedness," that "There are some things for which poetry is too late").[189] Death is not faced in this book with a simplistic stoicism. In "The Baler" the joyous image of "the giddied-up race of a tractor / At the end of the day / Last-lapping a hayfield" is balanced, if not undermined, by that of the painter Derek Hill, near the end of his life, saying that "He could bear no longer to watch // The sun going down / And asking please to be put / With his back to the window."[190] But precisely because of this acknowledgment of a bleak refusal to face death (or the future or the passing of time), the humour of Heaney's "Loughanure," written in memoriam another painter friend, Colin Middleton, takes on a particular edge. Here Heaney repeats the painter's pose that he had parodied decades earlier in "The Boule Miche of the North," the story

Of how he'd turn away from the motif,

Spread his legs, bend low, then look between them
For the mystery of the hard and fast
To be unveiled, his inverted face contorting

Like an arse-kisser's in some vision of the damned
Until he'd straighten, turn back, cock an eye
And stand with the brush at arm's length, readying.[191]

That unexpected Wordsworthian gerund, the "readying" rather than the "readied," places the memory in the realm of permanent presence, of potential and prospect: but it does so in a knowingly and seriously comedic, rather than a stoically pious, manner.

244   This Strange Loneliness

Human Chain as a whole is itself a "readying" for the final moment of release prophesied in "'Had I been awake'" and "Human Chain": a form of "last look."[192] The penultimate poem, "In the Attic," begins with an allusion to Jim Hawkins "aloft in the cross-trees / Of *Hispaniola*," in a nod to his childhood love of Stevenson's *Treasure Island* (and in particular the double death of Israel Hands, "being both shot and drowned").[193] In the final stanzas his own blanking on names and "uncertainty on stairs" becomes the "lightheadedness" of a cabin boy on the rigging, "As the memorable bottoms out / Into the irretrievable, // It's not that I can't imagine still / That slight untoward rupture and world-tilt / As a wind freshened and the anchor weighed."[194] This is an evocation of the "uplift" that poetry can provide, the sense of adventure that has "an uncanny fluidity and airiness" while being "at once total play and the truth in earnest."[195] David Wheatley notes that Heaney gives us "only 'the good news' about poetry in a spirit of Arnoldian uplift but baulk[s] at anything more uncomfortable"; Heaney, Wheatley suggests, comes from a "position of unmistakably Leavisite vitalism. Writing is on the side of 'life' or, in the Heaneyesque coinage, 'overlife,' and anything failing to muster the necessary good cheer in its defence stands self-condemned of treachery and desertion."[196] So be it. Heaney would likely approve of M.H. Abrams's suggestion that for Arnold and Leavis the chief values were "life, love, liberty, hope, and joy," with "Life ... itself the highest good, the residence and measure of other goods."[197] But it is not that Heaney simply "baulk[s] at anything more uncomfortable" than "good cheer"; his emphasis on "life" as that which is to be celebrated, or that it is "on this earth 'we find our happiness, or not at all,'" comes with a recognition of pain, suffering, diminishment, and loss, a knowledge that what sustains us might itself become irretrievable.[198]

What Heaney learned from Wordsworth developed and accreted, as this book has shown, over his lifelong engagement with the English poet. Wordsworth's emphasis on childhood education and the individual child's "fosterage" in the natural landscape provided an epiphanic model that Heaney could turn to when exploring the individual's experience of the world, with all its mysteries, uncertainties, and anxieties. This then fed into and complicated Heaney's repeated agonizing over the role of poetry in the world and the difficult status of culture and civilization when a liberal humanist approach can no longer be taken for granted or accepted unquestioningly. And it was precisely in his repeated returns to Wordsworth, to the accretion of different layers

Heaney's Late Style   245

of complicating meaning, that Wordsworth's work provided a model for poetry's worth, for the benefits of durability, of familiar touch and contact, for the reassurance of the known, and the ability – with joyous surprise – to reimagine it, to outstrip one's historical conditions (or at least dream a "prospect" in which this is possible), and exceed the bounds of one's own limitation, decay, or loss of grip: one can always return to one's childhood, one's origins, and start again.

Heaney's poetic oeuvre ends on just such a joyfully defiant celebration of "overlife" or excess. In the final poem in *Human Chain*, "A Kite for Aibhín" (after Giovanni Pascoli's "L'Aquilone"), the string on the kite "breaks and – separate, elate - // The kite takes off, itself alone, a windfall."[199] This is an "unspooling," Heaney returning to his "first hill in the world," Anahorish Hill, but it is also an "uplift" ("elate" suggests a "raising") in which the kite (and by implication Heaney too) is let go, to be supported by that "Air from another life and time and place."[200] There is, typically, a sense of the unexpected gift and also a gesture to the future: the poem, like the kite, is "a windfall" which may someday land again. However, if this suggests the possibility of an afterlife, or "another life," of a new adventure beginning, this is gently rejected in Heaney's final poem, "In Time," written in 2013 and published after his death. Its timeliness, rather than its imagining of "another life and time and place" is crucial. Like Wordsworth in "Tintern Abbey" imagining Dorothy's return to that spot after his own death, Heaney addresses Síofra, his granddaughter, seeing her "years from now / (More years than I'll be allowed) / Your toddler wobbles gone, / A sure and grown woman."[201] Ghosting himself, Heaney describes dancing with Síofra, feeling once more "the power / I first felt come up through / Our cement floor long ago," earthed like Antaeus, "here for real." Imbued with the sense that it is "on this earth 'we find our happiness, or not at all,'" this last poem combines a rootedness in the real with the belief that poetry nevertheless "keeps time," and can hold open a space in which one can playfully, but seriously, break out from the everyday in a final careful, light-footing:

> An oratorio
> Would be just the thing for you:
> Energy, balance, outbreak
> At play for their own sake
> But for now we foot it lightly,
> In time, and silently.[202]

Notes

INTRODUCTION

1 O'Driscoll, *Stepping Stones*, 35.
2 Heaney, "Editor's Note," *Soundings '72*; Heaney, *Preoccupations*, 141; Heaney and Hass, *Sounding Lines*.
3 See Batten, "Heaney's Wordsworth and the Poetics of Displacement," 185.
4 Wordsworth, *The Prelude*, 1805: XI, 258–78. The 1850 *Prelude* has "renovating" for "vivifying."
5 Ibid., V, 466–73.
6 Ibid., V, 483.
7 Heaney, *Preoccupations*, 69; Corcoran, "Heaney and Yeats," 169.
8 O'Driscoll, *Stepping Stones*, 34.
9 Ibid., 404. Corcoran also finds it "odd that Seamus Heaney never wrote about Keats, who was surely almost – to use a Heaneyism – as deeply water-marked into this poet's sensibility as Wordsworth": Corcoran, "The Melt of the Real Thing," 15.
10 Wordsworth, *Poems in Two Volumes*, 1983, 74, 71.
11 Heaney, *Preoccupations*, 68; Ricks, *Allusion to the Poets*, 91; Beer, "Coleridge and Wordsworth," 197. For a wide-ranging discussion of water imagery in Heaney's work, see Allen, "Seamus Heaney and Water."
12 Wordsworth, *The Prelude*, 1805: XIII, 171–84; Abrams, *Natural Supernaturalism*, 118.
13 Heaney, *Station Island*, 55.
14 "My Heart Leaps Up when I Behold": Wordsworth, *Poems in Two Volumes*, 206.
15 Heaney, "There's Rosemary," 30.

248 Notes to pages 7–11

16 Ibid., 31. Richard Rankin Russell identifies a possible earlier echo of Wordsworth in the poem "Reaping in Heat," published in the Autumn 1959 issue of the Queen's student magazine *Q*, which "imagines a scene that resembles Wordsworth's 'The Reaper'": Russell, *Seamus Heaney*, 29.

17 *Hamlet* IV: 5: Shakespeare, *The Norton Shakespeare*.

18 Heaney, "The Seductive Muse," 6.

19 Heaney, *Preoccupations*, 20.

20 Heaney, *The Spirit Level*, 12; O'Driscoll, *Stepping Stones*, 475, quoting Wordsworth, *The Prelude*, 1805: X, 727.

21 Heaney, "Envies and Identifications," 5. Such critical self-revelation is discussed in Swann, "The Poet as Critic," 361, and Wheatley, "Professing Poetry," 126. As Wheatley notes, "Heaney's criticism is often at its most revealing when he pronounces on artists in the similar position of having to reconcile the claims of common human justice and the more unrelenting logic of art."

22 Coughlan, "Bog Queens," 200. Italics in original. In response to Coughlan, Guinn Batten argues that Heaney might offer "a fresh and appealing understanding of the way that masculine forms of embodiment may, contrary to expectation, identify with the maternal body": Batten, "Heaney's Wordsworth and the Poetics of Displacement," 179.

23 Heaney, *Preoccupations*, 17–18.

24 Joyce, *Ulysses*, 7, 526.

25 Hartman, *Wordsworth's Poetry*, 212; Hartman, "On Traumatic Knowledge," 552.

26 See Ross, "In Search of Enabling Light," 121n30, and Makdisi, *Romantic Imperialism*, 52.

27 Wordsworth, *The Prelude*, 1805: II, 367–71.

28 The 1799 *Prelude*, published for the first time some five years after Heaney was lecturing, also has "a prospect in my mind," and "I forgot / The agency of sight" instead of the more striking "bodily eyes": Ibid., 1799: II, 399. I draw on different versions of the *Prelude* at different points in this study, to reflect Heaney's own usage.

29 Ibid., 1805: II, 371–7.

30 Ibid., 1805: II, 377–92.

31 Ibid., 1805: II, 395.

32 Heaney, *Finders Keepers*, 251.

33 Ibid., 251–2.

34 Wordsworth, *The Prelude*, 1805: X, 692–3.

35 Ibid., 1805: X, 685–6 and 723–7.

36 O'Driscoll, *Stepping Stones*, 100.

Notes to pages 11–16

37 Wordsworth, *The Prelude*, 1805: X, 966–70.
38 Abrams, *Natural Supernaturalism*, 430–31.
39 O'Brien, "Seamus Heaney and William Wordsworth," 187.
40 Ibid., 187.
41 Ibid., 194.
42 Heaney, "The Pathos of Things." O'Brien died in 1998; Heaney subsequently wrote an introduction to O'Brien's fictionalized account of his own childhood: Heaney, "Introduction," *A Way of Life, Like Any Other*.
43 Brown, *In the Chair*, 77.
44 O'Driscoll, *Stepping Stones*, 404. See "Reading," in Heaney, *Preoccupations*, 21–4, (first published as Heaney, "Seamus Heaney Recalls"), "Rhymes" (Heaney, *Preoccupations*, 24–7), and O'Driscoll, *Stepping Stones*, 34, for further discussions of his earliest reading.
45 Corcoran, "Heaney and Yeats," 165.
46 O'Neill, *The All-Sustaining Air*, 137.
47 Brown, *In the Chair*, 77; O'Driscoll, *Stepping Stones*, 386, 466.
48 Haughton, "Power and Hiding Places," 64.
49 Horton, "A Truly Uninvited Shade," 23.
50 Ibid.
51 Among the most notable discussions of their relationship, in chronological order, are O'Brien, "Seamus Heaney and William Wordsworth"; Corcoran, *The Poetry of Seamus Heaney*; Swann, "The Poet as Critic"; Andrews, *The Poetry of Seamus Heaney*; Roe, "Wordsworth at the Flax-Dam"; Hart, *Seamus Heaney*; Lysaght, "Contrasting Natures"; Vendler, *Seamus Heaney*; Dentith, "Heaney and Walcott"; Horton, "Romantic Intersections"; Horton, "A Truly Uninvited Shade"; Longley, *Poetry & Posterity*; Kinsella, "Poet to Poet"; Ross, "In Search of Enabling Light"; O'Neill, *The All-Sustaining Air*; Batten, "Heaney's Wordsworth and the Poetics of Displacement"; Larrissy, "Seamus Heaney and Romanticism"; Russell, *Seamus Heaney's Regions*. Among more recent studies, Cavanagh, *Professing Poetry*; McConnell, *Northern Irish Poetry and Theology*; and Dennison, *Seamus Heaney and the Adequacy of Poetry* have been particularly useful, as have O'Donoghue, *The Cambridge Companion to Seamus Heaney*, and Brandes and Durkan, *Seamus Heaney*.
52 Haughton, "Power and Hiding Places," 66, 64. Haughton's essay is, as he acknowledges, in part the fruit of conversations with Michael Kinsella, who had completed his thesis on "Heaney's Wordsworth" under Haughton's supervision, in 2003: ibid., 100n29.
53 Batten, "Heaney's Wordsworth and the Poetics of Displacement," 187.
54 Ibid., 183, 180, 190.

250 Notes to pages 17–21

55 For a useful overview of the development of Irish Studies, see Kirkland, "Towards a Disciplinary History of Irish Studies."

56 Haughton, "Power and Hiding Places," 64.

57 The work of Eugene O'Brien extensively maps Heaney onto contemporary literary critical trends: see O'Brien, *Creating Irelands of the Mind*; *Searches for Answers*; *Seamus Heaney as Aesthetic Thinker*.

58 Bate, *Romantic Ecology*, 6. Liu, *Wordsworth: The Sense of History*, 18–19.

59 Longley, *The Living Stream*, 266.

60 Horton, "A Truly Uninvited Shade," 23.

61 Lloyd, "Pap for the Dispossessed," 325.

62 Brown, *In the Chair*, 92; Longley, *Poetry & Posterity*, 237. See Alcobia-Murphy, *Sympathetic Ink*, 97–101 for a discussion of various possible meanings of "politics" in the Northern Irish context, especially how Longley's position evolves; see also Morrissey, "Against All Rhyme and Reason" for a defence (against Conor O'Callaghan) of political poetry as not being only "the last resort of the truly talentless."

63 Crotty, "The Context of Heaney's Reception," 50. See also Janus, "Mnemosyne and the Mislaid Pen," 56; O'Brien, *Seamus Heaney as Aesthetic Thinker*, 179, McDonald, "Faiths and Fidelities," 6.

64 Heaney, *The Government of the Tongue*, 45.

65 De Man, *The Rhetoric of Romanticism*, 50.

66 Andrews, *The Poetry of Seamus Heaney*, 15–16.

67 See Cook, *Against Coercion*, 104. Cook offers the example of Amerindian writers alluding in English; she is in part responding to Butler, "Repossessing the Past," 83.

68 Joyce, *A Portrait of the Artist as a Young Man*, 205. See, for example, Heaney, *Among Schoolchildren*, 12. Heaney's response to Joyce is often discussed in the criticism: see, for example, Corcoran, *The Poetry of Seamus Heaney*, 121–4; Longley, *The Living Stream*, 166; Longley, *Poetry & Posterity*, 97; O'Brien, *Creating Irelands of the Mind*, 67–8; Alcobia-Murphy, *Sympathetic Ink*, 223; Foster, "Crediting Marvels," 214.

69 Bornstein, *Transformations of Romanticism*, 56.

70 Kavanagh, *Collected Pruse*, 268–9 quoted in Longley, *The Living Stream*, 208.

71 Stafford, *Starting Lines*, 36; Stafford, pages 34–5, offers a judicious negotiation of the intricate interstices of nationality and literary tradition.

72 O'Neill, *The All-Sustaining Air*, 133, 135.

73 Ibid., 24, 2, 122.

Notes to pages 22–4 251

74 Ibid., 10. O'Neill is developing on points made by Larrissy, *Romanticism and Postmodernism*, 3. It is tempting to argue for Heaney as a "Post-Romantic" poet, rather than yet another "last" Romantic, with this "post" having a relationship, ill-defined though it may be, to the "posts" in postmodernism, poststructuralism, postcolonialism, and post-secularism; however, his own impatience with such labels discourages this. In his poem in memoriam Ted Hughes, "On His Work in the English Tongue," he suggests that Hughes is "Post-this, post-that, post-the other, yet in the end / Not past a thing": Heaney, *Electric Light*, 61.

75 Wright, *Representing the National Landscape in Irish Romanticism*, 2. Karen O'Brien had argued for such subsuming in "later seventeenth- and eighteenth-century georgics" in England: O'Brien, "Imperial Georgic," 161.

76 Heaney, *Preoccupations*, 41.

77 Lloyd, "Pap for the Dispossessed," 322, 320.

78 Heaney, *The Redress of Poetry*, 198. See Heaney, "Adroitest of Makers," 17: "all these are authentic works, Janus-faced as poems should be, looking in to the self and out through the form." See also Heaney, *Preoccupations*, 50. Metaphors for such doubleness and dislocation (and resolution) are too frequent in Heaney's prose to permit extended discussion here, but have been frequently broached in the criticism. See, for example, Andrews, *The Poetry of Seamus Heaney*, 13; Foster, "The Poetry of Seamus Heaney," 36; Cavanagh, *Professing Poetry*, 34; and Wheatley, "Professing Poetry," 126.

79 O'Neill, *The All-Sustaining Air*, 131.

80 Heaney, "An Open Letter," 24. Heaney, *Preoccupations*, 34.

81 Heaney, *Among Schoolchildren*, 8, 9.

82 See Longley, *Poetry & Posterity*, 99. Some of these limits have been sketched out already by Nicholas Roe and Seán Lysaght: see Roe, "Wordsworth at the Flax-Dam," 169, 170. See also Horton, "Time That Was Extra," 23.

83 Heaney, *Field Work*, 35.

84 Heaney, *Today Programme*. See also "Earning a Rhyme" (1989) where Heaney celebrates Wordsworth, along with Donne, Dryden, Eliot, and Synge, for their attempts "to refresh the language of English literature" and their return "to the spoken idiom": Heaney, "Earning a Rhyme," 95, and Heaney, *Finders Keepers*, 60.

85 Heaney, *Front Row*.

86 Heaney, *Preoccupations*, 13; Heaney, *Finders Keepers*, x. "How with this rage ... " appears in Heaney, *Preoccupations*, 57, 33, and Heaney,

252 Notes to pages 24–7

"Editor's Note" to *Soundings '72*, 6, where there was already a defiant but also weary element to his defence of poetry: "I am tired of speculations about the relation of the poet's work to the workings of the world he inhabits, and finally I disagree that 'poetry makes nothing happen.'"

87 O'Donoghue, "Introduction," 1. See Brearton, *The Great War in Irish Poetry*, 250. See Cavanagh, *Professing Poetry*, 45, for a discussion of the anxiety behind this repeated questioning, and Dennison, *Seamus Heaney and the Adequacy of Poetry*, 10, for the limited range of meanings of "adequacy" that Heaney employs.

88 Heaney, *Preoccupations*, 41. Heaney, *Field Work*, 41.

89 Wordsworth, *Poems in Two Volumes*, 128. Adam Potkay argues for a return to an ethical approach to Wordsworth's poetry after the historicist approaches of the last few decades by restating the importance of these questions in "Resolution and Independence": see Potkay, *Wordsworth's Ethics*, 204.

90 O'Driscoll, *Stepping Stones*, 383.

91 Ibid., 304. See also Heaney, "Further Language," 12, and Heaney, "Bags of Enlightenment," 4.

92 Dennison, *Seamus Heaney and the Adequacy of Poetry*, 117. Dennison's book as a whole discusses the evolution of "late humanism" or post-Christian humanism across Heaney's career.

93 Heaney, *District and Circle*, 51.

94 O'Driscoll, *Stepping Stones*, 318.

95 McConnell, *Northern Irish Poetry and Theology*, 118–19; Brownlee, "The Untranscendent Vision."

96 McConnell, *Northern Irish Poetry and Theology*, 22, 54, 55.

97 See "Settings xiii" in Heaney, *Seeing Things*, 69. See also Foster, "Crediting Marvels"; Dennison, *Seamus Heaney and the Adequacy of Poetry*, 7; McConnell, *Northern Irish Poetry and Theology*, 84.7; McConnell, *Northern Irish Poetry and Theology*, 84."

98 O'Driscoll, *Stepping Stones*, 475, quoting Wordsworth, *The Prelude*, 1805: X, 727; ibid., 1805: III, 128.

99 There has been good deal of valuable work done in recent years clarifying the dynamics of Heaney's critical prose. Notable contributions include Longley, "Heaney – Poet as Critic"; Swann, "The Poet as Critic"; McDonald, "Seamus Heaney as Critic"; Wheatley, "Professing Poetry"; Cavanagh, *Professing Poetry*; Dennison, *Seamus Heaney and the Adequacy of Poetry*; O'Brien, *Seamus Heaney as Aesthetic Thinker*; Flynn, "Radically Necessary."

Notes to pages 28–34   253

100 Heaney, *Station Island*, 55. See Wordsworth, *The Prelude*, 1805: XIII,
171–84. For Wordsworth, the imagination is described as a stream that
emerges from a "place of birth / in its blind cavern," travels to "light /
And open day," disappears from sight "bewildered and engulfed" only to
rise "once more / With strength, reflecting in its solemn breast / The
works of man and face of human life"; ultimately from its "progress" we
draw "The feeling of life endless, the one thought / By which we live,
infinity and God."
101 O'Driscoll, *Stepping Stones*, 372.

CHAPTER ONE

1 O'Driscoll, *Stepping Stones*, 71.
2 Corcoran discusses Heaney's faith in "fortification" at length: Corcoran,
The Poetry of Seamus Heaney, 83–92.
3 Heaney, "The Gentle Flame," 7–8.
4 Ibid., 3.
5 Ibid.
6 Heaney, "Field Work Manuscripts," 10.
7 Corcoran, *Seamus Heaney*, 20.
8 Holt, *How Children Fail*; Taylor, *Experiments in Education at Sevenoaks*;
Jackson, *English Versus Examinations*; MacKenzie, *Escape from the
Classroom*.
9 Heaney, "Kicking Against the Code," 748. *English Versus Examinations*
is a volume of essays derived in part from the journal *The Use of English*,
which "for the past 25 years [had] been publishing reports on underground reform and experiment."
10 Heaney would later praise the work of Maria Montessori, a pioneer in
progressive educational approaches: Heaney, *Among Schoolchildren*, 6.
11 Heaney, "Evangelists," 55. See Heaney, *Preoccupations*, 47.
12 Heaney, "Lecture on Composition."
13 Heaney, "Evangelists," 54–5.
14 MacKenzie, *Escape from the Classroom*, 112.
15 Ibid., 88
16 Ibid.
17 Heaney, *Wintering Out*, 14.
18 Heaney, "Kicking Against the Code," 748.
19 Heaney, "Confessions and Histories," 21.
20 Quinn, *My Education*, 166.

254   Notes to pages 34–8

21 Wordsworth, *Early Poems and Fragments*, 358: 43–4; Wordsworth, *The Prose Works of William Wordsworth*, 3:295. In 1826 Wordsworth also condemned anything that could be described as "Education without Religion": see W.W. to Lord Lonsdale, 15 May 1826 in Wordsworth and Wordsworth, *The Letters of William and Dorothy Wordsworth*, V, 447. For a full discussion of Wordsworth's attitudes to education and schooling in general, see Boyson, *Wordsworth and the Enlightenment Idea of Pleasure*, 178–9; and Pointon, *Wordsworth and Education*. For more on Wordsworth's own primary education, see Thompson, *Wordsworth's Hawkshead*.

22 See, for example, Deane, *Strange Country*, 6.

23 Wordsworth and Wordsworth, *The Letters of William and Dorothy Wordsworth*, III, 249–50.

24 Ibid., 251.

25 Bell, *An Experiment in Education*, 5, 7.

26 Gottfried, *Matthew Arnold and the Romantics*, 12.

27 W.W. to Francis Wrangham, 2 October 1808: Wordsworth and Wordsworth, *The Letters of William and Dorothy Wordsworth*, III, 269–70.

28 W.W. to Christopher Wordsworth, 1 January 1819: ibid., III, 513.

29 W.W. to Mary Wordsworth, 9–13 May 1812: ibid., VIII, 64–5.

30 W.W. to Thomas Poole, 13 March 1815: ibid., IV, 210.

31 Wordsworth, *The Excursion*, IX, 258–63.

32 Ibid., 294–303.

33 See Moorman, *William Wordsworth: The Later Years*, 178; Hickey, *Impure Conceits*, 118.

34 Letter to Hugh James Rose, 11 December 1828: Wordsworth and Wordsworth, *The Letters of William and Dorothy Wordsworth*, IV, 685–6.

35 John Wordsworth and Dorothy Wordsworth to Francis Merewether, 6 June 1831: ibid., V, 390.

36 As Alan G. Hill argues, this places Rousseau within a tradition stretching back to Aristotle: Hill, "Wordsworth, Comenius and the Art of Education."

37 Rousseau, *Émile, ou, De l'éducation*, 1.

38 Wordsworth and Wordsworth, *The Letters of William and Dorothy Wordsworth*, I, 222. See Newlyn, *William and Dorothy Wordsworth*, 52.

39 Jacobus, "The Art of Managing Books," 216; Wordsworth, *The Prelude*, 1805: V, 220–2.

40 Wordsworth and Coleridge, *Lyrical Ballads*, 113. See also Boyson, *Wordsworth and the Enlightenment Idea of Pleasure*.

Notes to pages 38–41 255

41 Wordsworth and Coleridge, *Lyrical Ballads*, 103–4.
42 Ibid., 149.
43 Ibid., 148.
44 Ibid., 149–50.
45 Ibid., 149.
46 Schiller, "On Naïve and Sentimental Poetry," 191: "The poets are every-where, by their very definition, the *guardians* of nature ... They will either *be* nature, or they will *seek* lost nature," italics in the original.
47 As Lucy Newlyn argues, "Hartley's account of mental process chimed with their exalted views of memory as a *creative* function, as well as reinforcing their belief in environmental influence": Newlyn, *William and Dorothy Wordsworth*, 52, italics in original. See also "David Hartley."
48 Wordsworth, *The Prelude*, 1799: I, 130; 1805: I, 428; 1850: I, 401.
49 Heaney, *Preoccupations*, 65.
50 Wordsworth, *The Prelude*, 1850: I, 364–5, 382–5. I quote from the 1850 *Prelude* here as the only version Heaney would have known when preparing his lecture on the poem in the 1960s. See Wolfson, "Wordsworth's Craft," 112; Stafford, *Local Attachments*, 116. Michael Cavanagh relates these moments to Heaney's sense of "equilibrium," outlined in *The Redress of Poetry* as "a temporary state in which both sides rest, and their mutual antagonism permits itself to be seen for what it is": Cavanagh, *Professing Poetry*, 71.
51 Wordsworth, *The Prelude*, 1850: I, 398–400.
52 Heaney, "The Prelude," 6. A holograph manuscript of this lecture is held in the archives at Emory University. It is undated but would appear to be a university lecture from Heaney's time at Queen's: certainly, it anticipates many of the arguments and readings made in "Feeling into Words" (1974; published in *Preoccupations*) but without the idiosyncratic critical and theoretical apparatus Heaney employs there.
53 Wordsworth and Coleridge, *Lyrical Ballads*, 178.
54 Ibid., 241.
55 Ibid., 242.
56 Bloom, *A Map of Misreading*, 95.
57 Abrams, *The Correspondent Breeze*, 78. Abrams' "Structure and Style in the Greater Romantic Lyric" was first published in 1965.
58 Abrams, *The Correspondent Breeze*, 76–7.
59 Bornstein, *Transformations of Romanticism*, 50–1, 52. For reworkings of Abrams and Bornstein's formulation, see O'Neill, *The All-Sustaining Air*, 85. A related focus on "vertiginous estrangement" can be found in Kermode, *The Sense of an Ending*, 168–9.

256   Notes to pages 41–4

60 For more on "helical" or spiraling models of poetic return, see Abrams, *Natural Supernaturalism*, 193.

61 Wordsworth and Wordsworth, *The Letters of William and Dorothy Wordsworth*, III, 195.

62 Butler, "Poetry 1798–1807," 53; Reiman, *The Romantics Reviewed*.

63 Wordsworth and Wordsworth, *The Letters of William and Dorothy Wordsworth*, III, 194–5.

64 Wordsworth and Coleridge, *Lyrical Ballads*, 178. See Ellis, *Wordsworth, Freud, and the Spots of Time*, 114–15.

65 Heaney, *Death of a Naturalist*, 45, italics in original. The poem was originally published in the journal *Outposts* and collected with minor typographical revisions in *Death of a Naturalist*; it does not appear in Heaney's later selections of his work (see Heaney, "The Play Way.")

66 Heaney, *Death of a Naturalist*, 45.

67 Ibid.

68 In *Among Schoolchildren*, his extended celebration of the art of teaching, Heaney suggests that "The Latin root of the verb 'to educate' is *educare*, to lead or bring or draw out, and our notions of education to a large extent centre upon this etymological core": Heaney, *Among Schoolchildren*, 6. It can be argued that "education" is derived rather from *educere* (to bring up or rear, train or mold), rather than *educare* (to lead or draw out): see Craft, "Education for Diversity."

69 Heaney, *Death of a Naturalist*, 45; Eliot, *The Complete Poems and Plays*, 61; Cuda, "The Use of Memory," 154.

70 Heaney, *Death of a Naturalist*, 11.

71 Heaney, "The Singing Classes," 17. This was written on the closure of Carysfort Teacher Training College and published in *Education Today* in 1993.

72 Gottfried, *Matthew Arnold and the Romantics*, 12. Frye, "The Drunken Boat," 16–17. See also Bornstein, *Transformations of Romanticism*, 13.

73 Heaney, "Untitled: Script for Explorations," 3–4, quoted in Russell, *Seamus Heaney's Regions*, 80–1. See Heaney, "For Joy and for Fun."

74 Ramazani, *Poetry of Mourning*, 336–7. See also Andrews, *The Poetry of Seamus Heaney*, 27. Dillon Johnston argues that in "Heaney's vertical quest, striking inward and downward," the concern is primarily "onto-logical and epistemological rather than aesthetic": Johnston, "Irish Poetry after Joyce (Heaney and Kavanagh)," 205–6.

75 Coincidentally, the epigraph to Holbrook's book is from Eliot's "East Coker," and includes a phrase that Heaney will use often in his criticism: "a raid on the inarticulate / With shabby equipment always deteriorating /

Notes to pages 44–6 257

In the general mess of imprecision of feeling, / Undisciplined squads of emotion": Eliot, *The Complete Poems and Plays*, 182; Heaney, *Preoccupations*, 47; Heaney, *The Government of the Tongue*, 169.

76 Heaney, "Educating the Epsilons," 11.

77 Ibid., 10.

78 Ibid.

79 Ibid.

80 Holbrook, *English for the Rejected*, 10, emphasis in original. Wordsworth appears once in Holbrook's book, when he describes a "little girl," Rose, "bravely making her way towards an acceptance of the greatest loss, as Wordsworth does in his sonnet 'Surpris'd by Joy,' and finding for herself hope and confidence in the 'continuity of life'": ibid., 251.

81 Heaney, "Educating the Epsilons," 10. Wordsworth and Coleridge, *Lyrical Ballads*, 307, 289n11.

82 Heaney, "The Seductive Muse," 5.

83 Wordsworth, *The Prelude*, 1850: I, 398–400; Wordsworth, *Poems in Two Volumes*, 185.

84 "The Ministry of Fear" in *North* (1975) and "Alphabets" in *The Haw Lantern* (1987) do figure the continuity of the poet from child-pupil to adult-lecturer, but from a perspective that emphasizes personal growth and learning. In contrast, there are numerous classroom or school scenes in Heaney's work which reimagine the child's perspective. These include "Kernes" (Heaney, *Stations*, 14); Heaney, "Five Derry Glosses," 71; "The Schoolbag" (Heaney, *Seeing Things*, 30); Heaney, "The Singing Classes"; "A Present from Mr Pause" (a prose poem which describes, in the context of boarding school "the uselessness of that time and much time since") (Heaney, "From 'Private Excursions,'" 42); "The Border Campaign," "The Real Names," "Bodies and Souls," and "Clonmany to Ahascragh" (Heaney, *Electric Light*, 18, 45–50, 73–4, 75–6); "Senior Infants" and "The Lagans Road" (Heaney, *District and Circle*, 29–33, 36–7); "Album," "Hermit Songs" (which reworks "The Singing Classes"), and "Lick the Pencil" (Heaney, *Human Chain*, 4–5, 74–9, 80–1). His primary school teachers make various appearances in his poetry, including Miss Walls in "Death of a Naturalist" (Heaney, *Death of a Naturalist*, 5), "Master Murphy" (Heaney, *Station Island*, 72), "The Sally Rod" (the first section of "Senior Infants" in Heaney, *District and Circle*, 29), and Heaney, "Cutaways." For a discussion of how Heaney's poems fit into an Irish tradition of "classroom scenes," including those of Yeats and Joyce, see McDiarmid, "Heaney and the Politics of the Classroom." For discussions

258   Notes to pages 46–8

of schoolroom scenes in Joyce and Yeats, see Bizot, "Mastering the
Colonizer's Tongue"; Rickard, "Stephen Dedalus among Schoolchildren."

85 Heaney, "Writer and Teacher." The original is italicized throughout.

86 Heaney frequently discussed his friendship with McLaverty: see Heaney,
"Are You Doing Any Poetry with Them?"; Heaney, *Finders Keepers*,
67–70; Heaney, "Michael McLaverty," 31; Heaney, "Introduction to
Collected Short Stories by Michael McLaverty," xiii; Heaney, *A Tribute to
Michael McLaverty*. McLaverty also is the subject of, or appears in,
"Fosterage" (*North*), "Station Island," and the 1969 poem "An Evening at
Killard." See Parker, *Seamus Heaney*, 29–30; Hillan, "Wintered into
Wisdom: Michael McLaverty, Seamus Heaney, and the Northern Word-
Hoard"; Hillan, "Michael McLaverty, Seamus Heaney and the Writerly
Bond." An exhibition about their friendship was held at the Seamus
Heaney HomePlace in 2017.

87 See Parker, *Seamus Heaney*, 26. Ciaran Carson comments how for one
"pundit ... the Act had made potentially good carpenters and plumbers
into bad poets": Carson, *The Star Factory*, 104.

88 Heaney, *Finders Keepers*, 67; O'Driscoll, *Stepping Stones*, 70.

89 Quinn, *My Education*, 175.

90 Heaney, "The Boule Miche of the North," 19. The central image of this
vignette is of a painter turning away and looking back at their subject
through their legs; as I later discuss, this is repeated in "Loughanure," his
sequence in memory of the painter Colin Middleton (Heaney, *Human
Chain*, 63). Heaney's interest in "liberation" crystallizes from the early
1970s onwards around Eliot's suggestion in "Little Gidding" that the "use
of memory" is "liberation / From the future as well as the past": Eliot, *The
Complete Poems and Plays*, 195. See Dennison, *Seamus Heaney and the
Adequacy of Poetry*, 44–5; Cuda, "The Use of Memory," 157–9.

91 Brandes, "Seamus Heaney's Working Titles," 21.

92 Hart, *Seamus Heaney*, 26.

93 Bacon, *The Advancement of Learning and New Atlantis*, II, V.I. Another of
Bacon's images resonates with Heaney's poetics of the 1970s, particularly
the lectures "Feeling into Words" and "*Fire i' the Flint*" (both published in
Preoccupations): Bacon suggests that it would be good to divide natural
philosophy "into the mine and the furnace, and to make two professions
or occupations of natural philosophers – some to be pioneers and some
smiths; some to dig, and some to refine and hammer": Ibid., II, VII.I.

94 Wordsworth, *The Prelude*, 1805: I, 306; Ricks, "Review of Death of a
Naturalist," 23; Andrews, *The Poetry of Seamus Heaney*, 24.

Notes to pages 48–52

95 Stafford, *Local Attachments*, 34. For other discussions of Wordsworth's influence on *Death of a Naturalist*, see Roe, "Wordsworth at the Flax-Dam"; Haughton, "Power and Hiding Places," 89–92.

96 Corcoran, *The Poetry of Seamus Heaney*, 5–7.

97 Allison, "Seamus Heaney and the Romantic Image," 198–201. John Desmond argues that in such moments "Heaney keeps a firm foothold in both the historical milieu and in the vertical, transcendent dimension of reality he learned in his early Catholic training, and in so doing he resists being encapsulated within a purely historical-cultural framework": Desmond, *Gravity and Grace*, 12.

98 Heaney, *Death of a Naturalist*, 5.

99 Ibid., 6.

100 See Buxton, *Robert Frost and Northern Irish Poetry*, 48. She quotes a letter from Heaney of 19 February 2000: "Frost helped me to think about poetry, how it linguifies things, if you'll excuse the expression."

101 Heaney, *Death of a Naturalist*, 5–6.

102 Ibid., 7. Fran Brearton links the rats recurring throughout this collection to cultural memories of the First World War: Brearton, *The Great War in Irish Poetry*, 228.

103 Andrews, *The Poetry of Seamus Heaney*, 24–5.

104 Heaney, *Death of a Naturalist*, 8.

105 Haffenden, *Viewpoints*, 69. See Davis, "Door into the Dark," 29; Brearton, "Heaney and the Feminine," 84.

106 Heaney, *Death of a Naturalist*, 40.

107 Clutterbuck, "Pilot and Stray in One," 106–7.

108 Andrews, *The Poetry of Seamus Heaney*, 25.

109 Heaney, *Death of a Naturalist*, 46. In later, optimistic, returns to this idea, Heaney presents this as poetry allowing for a sense of a "fuller life," "an overbrimming, totally resourceful expressiveness": Heaney, *The Redress of Poetry*, xvii.

110 See Heaney, "An Advancement of Learning." For an extensive discussion of Heaney's revision process for this poem, see Crowder, "Seamus Heaney's Revisions for 'Death of a Naturalist,'" 103–6.

111 Andrews, *The Poetry of Seamus Heaney*, 26.

112 Hart, *Seamus Heaney*, 103.

113 Heaney, *North*, 65; Stevens, *The Collected Poems of Wallace Stevens*, 344.

114 Hartman, *Wordsworth's Poetry*, 185. See Nichols, *The Poetics of Epiphany*, 4.

260 Notes to pages 52–4

115 Nichols, *The Poetics of Epiphany*, 3–5; Abrams, *Natural Supernaturalism*, 421. The widespread use of "epiphany" has not met with universal approval: see Ellis, *Wordsworth, Freud, and the Spots of Time*, 6.

116 Joyce, *Stephen Hero*, 211. See Abrams, *Natural Supernaturalism*, 421; Nichols, *The Poetics of Epiphany*, 11–12. Haecceity links Joyce's epiphanies and Hopkins's notion of "inscape": see Kearney, *Navigations*, 134.

117 Frye, *A Study of English Romanticism*, 158.

118 Tobin, *Passage to the Center*, 175. See Longley, *Poetry & Posterity*, 100: "In 'Death of a Naturalist' how to conceive 'Nature' in adult terms is left open at the moment of fallen knowledge." Paul Hamilton argues that the Romantic trope of sublimity recasts "failures of understanding as the successful symbolic expression of something greater than understanding": Hamilton, "From Sublimity to Indeterminacy," 13.

119 Hart, *Seamus Heaney*, 22, 11.

120 Heaney, *Death of a Naturalist*, 29.

121 Lerner, *Domestic Interior and Other Poems*, 30. Buxton notes that "Laurence Lerner was, [Seamus] Deane declares, an 'outstanding teacher,' one who 'reordered the local tyranny in our minds, by showing us how deeply interjected the sour hegemony of our sectarianism had become'": Buxton, *Robert Frost and Northern Irish Poetry*, 44–5; quoting Deane, "The Famous Seamus," 62–3e.

122 For a useful discussion of the Irish Catholic strain of the Gothic, see Wright, *Representing the National Landscape in Irish Romanticism*, 49.

123 Heaney, *The Government of the Tongue*, 131. "Lowell's Command" was originally published in *Salmagundi* in 1988

124 Hulme, *Selected Writings*, 71; Cooke, "Harriet Cooke Talked to the Poet Seamus Heaney," 8.

125 For further discussions of Heaney's complex relationship to Catholicism and Protestantism, see Dentith, "Heaney and Walcott," 92; Longley, *Poetry & Posterity*, 100, 305.

126 McConnell, *Northern Irish Poetry and Theology*, 84; Wimsatt, *The Verbal Icon*, 231. Peter McDonald notes that "The poetry in which Heaney has tried to register a kind of secular faith is not always his strongest": McDonald, "Faiths and Fidelities," 12.

127 Heaney, *Preoccupations*, 46–7.

128 Heaney, "Two Voices," 8. The title is complexly allusive. It suggests Eliot's "three voices of poetry" (Eliot appears in this essay), and perhaps also a critique of Heaney by David Lloyd published the previous year in the magazine *Ariel*: Lloyd, "The Two Voices of Seamus Heaney's *North*." But as Patrick Crotty has suggested to me, it also has a Wordsworthian echo,

Notes to pages 54–9

to his "Thought of a Briton on the Subjugation of Switzerland" ("Two Voices are there, one is of the sea, / One of the mountains; each a mighty Voice ...") and J.K. Stephen's parody of it, "A Sonnett" ("Two Voices are there, one is of the deep ... The other of an old, half-witted sheep ... And Wordsworth – both are thine!"): Wordsworth, *Poems in Two Volumes*, 164; Stephen, *Lapsus Calami*, 83.

129 Heaney, "Two Voices," 8.

130 Gillis, "The Modern Irish Sonnet," 584, 586. Helen Vendler argues that Muldoon's sonnets seemed "impressively constructed but too often had a hole in the middle where the feeling should be": Vendler, "Anglo-Celtic Attitudes," 58.

131 Heaney, "Violence and Repose," 13.

132 Ibid.

133 Ibid.

134 Ibid.

135 Heaney, "January Review: The Arts In Ireland." In a later letter to Deane, Heaney feared that he was himself "neglecting the silence, or neglecting to graze on it": Heaney, "Letter to Seamus Deane."

136 Dennison, *Seamus Heaney and the Adequacy of Poetry*, 62.

137 This can be related to what Christopher Ricks terms the Romantic "self-inwoven or reflexive simile" which "describes something both as itself and as something external to it which it could not possibly be": see Ricks, *The Force of Poetry*, 34; Batten, "Heaney's Wordsworth and the Poetics of Displacement," 181.

138 Dennison, *Seamus Heaney and the Adequacy of Poetry*, 62, 92.

139 Heaney, *Stations*, 3.

140 Ibid. In a letter to Michael Longley, Heaney makes it clear that his prose poems hadn't been influenced by John Montague's: Heaney, "Letter to Michael Longley," March 1975.

141 Wordsworth, *The Prelude*, 1805: I, 305–9; Heaney, "Stations Drafts," 3.

142 Heaney, "Two Poems." This is stated in an early version of "Glanmore Sonnet III" composed at the same time as *Stations* and published in *Prospice* magazine in 1976

143 Makdisi, *Romantic Imperialism*, 21, 45–69.

144 Wordsworth, *The Prelude*, 1805: XI, 258–64. As Fiona Stafford has noted, in the 1799 version, these spots of time have "a fructifying virtue": Stafford, *Local Attachments*, 305n9.

145 Wordsworth, *The Prelude*, 1805: XI, 270–2.

146 Ibid., 1805: XI, 265–8.

147 Ibid., 1805: XI, 262–3.

262 Notes to pages 59–65

148 Ibid., 1805: XI, 308–10.
149 Ibid., 1805: XI, 372–5.
150 Ibid., 1805: XI, 384–8.
151 Ibid., 1799: I, 284–7. There is no parallel passage in later versions of *The Prelude*.
152 Heaney, *Stations*, 3.
153 Heaney, "Autobiographical Borings," A2.
154 Heaney, *Stations*, 3. Heaney would also use the prose poem form to explore the sectarian structuring of his childhood in "One Christmas Day in the Morning": Heaney, *District and Circle*, 31–2.
155 Heaney, *Stations*, 20.
156 Ibid., 13. This is an allusion to the first stanza of the well-known English recusant hymn "Faith of Our Fathers," written by Frederick W. Farber: "Faith of our fathers, living still, / In spite of dungeon, fire and sword; / O how our hearts beat high with joy / Whenever we hear that glorious Word!": see Oratory of St Philip Neri, London, *The Catholic Hymn Book*, 315.
157 Heaney, "Stations Drafts." These phrases are from a draft poem, "Oral English": crossed through is another possible title, "Finding a Voice."
158 Heaney, *Stations*, 16.
159 Heaney, "Autobiographical Borings," A2; Heaney, *Stations*, 14.
160 Heaney, *Stations*, 4, italics added.
161 Stevenson, "Stations," 50.
162 Heaney, *Stations*, 4.
163 Haughton, "Power and Hiding Places," 82; Haffenden, *Viewpoints*, 68.
164 Heaney, *Stations*, 8. This image is reworked in "The Toome Road," Heaney, *Field Work*, 15.
165 Ibid., 13.
166 Ó Cadha, "Pattern."
167 Heaney, *Stations*, 23.
168 Wordsworth, *The Prelude*, 1805: IV, 468, 474–8; 1850: IV, 434.
169 Heaney, *Stations*, 12. For Heaney's childhood love of Stevenson, see Heaney, "Seamus Heaney Recalls," 7; reprinted in Heaney, *Preoccupations*, 23.
170 Heaney, *Stations*, 15.
171 Coleridge, *Samuel Taylor Coleridge*, 104; Shelley, *The Poems of Shelley*, 3:364.
172 Wordsworth and Coleridge, *Lyrical Ballads*, 199; Heaney, *Stations*, 15.
173 Heaney, "Woodcut," 4.
174 Heaney, "Stations Drafts."
175 Muldoon, *New Weather*, 21.
176 Heaney, *The Spirit Level*, 40.

Notes to pages 66–71

CHAPTER TWO

1 Heaney, "The Prelude," 7.
2 Cook, *Against Coercion*, 104.
3 See Matthews, *Yeats as Precursor*, 36, 1–2; Wheatley, "Professing Poetry," 129; Newlyn, Foreword, x; Mandelstam, "Conversation about Dante," 45.
4 O'Neill, *The All-Sustaining Air*, 11; see also Buxton, *Robert Frost and Northern Irish Poetry*, 15. For a Bloomian reading of Heaney's influences, see Johnston, "Irish Influence and Confluence in Heaney's Poetry," 151; Wheatley, "Professing Poetry," meanwhile, presents Heaney as a "strong critic."
5 Hart, *Seamus Heaney*, 123; "Getting Along Seamus-ly"; Cavanagh, *Professing Poetry*, 20. For "the anxiety of authorship," see Gilbert and Gubar, *The Madwoman in the Attic*, 48–9.
6 Heaney, "Place, Pastness, Poems," 38.
7 Gottfried, *Matthew Arnold and the Romantics*, 28; Eliot, *The Use of Poetry and the Use of Criticism*, 111.
8 Heaney, *Preoccupations*, 62; Lau, *Keats's Paradise Lost*.
9 Heaney, "The Prelude." 7. He refers to Wordsworth, *The Prelude*, 1805: III, 260–94. From the passage he quotes, Heaney omits references to Newton and – in allusion – to Cincinnatus ("Dictators at the plough") presumably to emphasize Wordsworth's poetic predecessors.
10 Wordsworth, *The Prelude*, 1805: III, 260–77.
11 Heaney, "Interview with Frank Kinahan," 410.
12 Heaney, *Finders Keepers*, 33–4; see also Heaney, "The Power of T.S. Eliot."
13 Eliot, *Selected Prose of T.S. Eliot*, 38.
14 Arnold, *Essays on English Literature*, 116.
15 Heaney, *Preoccupations*, 136.
16 Corcoran, *Poets of Modern Ireland*, 96–7.
17 See Horton, "A Truly Uninvited Shade," 23.
18 Heaney, *Preoccupations*, 195.
19 O'Brien, *Seamus Heaney as Aesthetic Thinker*, 90.
20 Heaney, *Preoccupations*, 195.
21 Ibid., 196; Eliot, *The Use of Poetry and the Use of Criticism*, 118–19. Heaney draws on the concept of the "auditory imagination" at length in the 1976 lecture "Englands of the Mind"; he also traces his reading of it back to his time as a student at Queen's: Heaney, *Preoccupations*, 150. See also Cavanagh, *Professing Poetry*, 4.
22 Heaney, *Preoccupations*, 195.
23 Eliot, *Selected Prose of T.S. Eliot*, 38.

264 Notes to pages 72–8

24 Heaney, *Preoccupations*, 196.
25 Ibid., 197–8.
26 Haughton, "The Irish Poet as Critic," 527.
27 For a discussion of Heaney's attentiveness to "audience," see Lavan, "Heaney and the Audience."
28 Wilson, "William Wordsworth Lived Here"; Kinsella, "Poet to Poet," 200. Michael Kinsella provides an annotated transcript of this broadcast in his unpublished PhD thesis, "Poet to Poet: Heaney's Wordsworth," 220–7. Since the broadcast is more difficult to access than this transcript, I refer to Kinsella's thesis throughout.
29 Kinsella, "Poet to Poet," 220.
30 Haughton, "Power and Hiding Places," 62; Heaney, "Envies and Identifications."
31 Kinsella, "Poet to Poet," 223. Kinsella suggests that the change from coal to peat might be "more in keeping with [Heaney's] own semi-autobiographical poems at the time."
32 Ibid., 224.
33 Ibid.
34 Ibid., 224–5.
35 Ibid., 225.
36 Ibid., 222. As Kinsella notes, "natural forms" is an allusion to *The Prelude* 1805: III, 124 or 1850: III, 130.
37 Ibid., 221, 223.
38 Ibid., 221–2.
39 Ibid., 225.
40 Ibid., 226–7; Wordsworth and Coleridge, *Lyrical Ballads*, 290.
41 Wordsworth, *The Prelude*, 1805: XI, 335–42.
42 Kinsella, "Poet to Poet," 234.
43 Heaney, *Preoccupations*, 41.
44 Alcobia-Murphy, *Sympathetic Ink*, 142.
45 Heaney, *Preoccupations*, 46.
46 Ibid., 45. The image of the radio dial is repeated in Heaney's Nobel lecture, "Crediting Poetry"; indeed, many ideas touched on "Feeling into Words" inform Heaney's prose over the next four decades. For a comparison of "Feeling into Words" and "Crediting Poetry," see Haughton, "Power and Hiding Places," 70. The image of turning the "wireless knob" and being able to roam "at will the stations of the world" also appears in "Electric Light": Heaney, *Electric Light*, 81.
47 Heaney, *Preoccupations*, 43.
48 Ibid., 46, 43, 54.

Notes to pages 78–81

49 Ibid., 44.
50 Ibid., 45. Joyce, *A Portrait of the Artist as a Young Man*, 205. The phrase "a shy soul fretting and all that" is also a self–allusion to one of Heaney's *Stations* that shares the title "Incertus": Heaney, *Stations*, 24. See Dennison, *Seamus Heaney and the Adequacy of Poetry*, 20–1.
51 Heaney, *The Government of the Tongue*, 109. Heaney's desire for "authority" has been much discussed: see McDonald, "The Poet and 'The Finished Man,'" 99; Corcoran, *The Poetry of Seamus Heaney*, 225; Corcoran, *Poets of Modern Ireland*, 95–120; Alcobia-Murphy, *Sympathetic Ink*, 142–75; Wheatley, "Professing Poetry," 124.
52 Heaney, *Preoccupations*, 57. Heaney may at this point have been aware of Wallace Stevens's brief comments about this Shakespearean question in *The Necessary Angel*; certainly, Heaney later takes one of his own repeated critical motifs – the idea of the "nobility of poetry" as "a violence from within that protects us from a violence without" – from this essay: see Heaney, "Yeats's Nobility," ii; Heaney, *The Redress of Poetry*, 1; Stevens, *The Necessary Angel*, 34, 36.
53 Heaney, *Preoccupations*, 56–7.
54 The 1850 version is less personal and more universal, describing the "hiding-places of *man's* power" rather than "my power" (emphasis added): Wordsworth, *The Prelude*, 1850: XII, 279.
55 Ibid., 1805: XI, 333–5.
56 Cavanagh, *Professing Poetry*, 24, 29.
57 Haughton, "Power and Hiding Places," 69.
58 Edna Longley, for example, highlights the assumption made in the lecture of a singular, nationalist reading of the Easter Rising: Longley, *The Living Stream*, 71–2.
59 Wordsworth, *The Prelude*, 1805: XI, 328–33.
60 Ibid., 1805: XI, 335–42.
61 Heaney, *Preoccupations*, 47.
62 See Heaney, "Evangelists," 55; Heaney, "Lecture on Composition."
63 Eliot, "Professional, Or," 61; Cook, *Against Coercion*, 249.
64 Stead, *The New Poetic*, 124–5. For a useful discussion of Eliot's response to Wordsworth, see O'Neill, *The All-Sustaining Air*, 81; as O'Neill notes, "Eliot fulfils Wordsworth as much as he revises him."
65 Brown, *In the Chair*, 77. See Heaney, Editor's Note, 1974, 5: "[a poet's] technique is his poetic personality, his natural accent, not a voice imitated from those poets who have influenced and educated him. Technique matures as the young poet discovers his proper subjects, as he gradually realizes that the self is all he has to work towards and out of. Technique

266 Notes to pages 81–8

can be meticulous with language, it can be reckless, spendthrift, even clumsy – but it must always be authentic."

66 Bate, *John Keats*, 124.

67 Eliot, *The Complete Poems and Plays*, 195.

68 Heaney, *Preoccupations*, 47–8.

69 Ibid., 51.

70 Ibid.

71 Ibid.

72 Ibid., 50. Wordsworth, *Lyrical Ballads, and Other Poems, 1797–1800*, 350.

73 Heaney, *Preoccupations*, 50.

74 Ibid.

75 Ibid., 60.

76 Batten, "Heaney's Wordsworth and the Poetics of Displacement," 183; Heaney, *Preoccupations*, 52.

77 Heaney, "Interview with Mike Murphy," 93.

78 Batten, "Heaney's Wordsworth and the Poetics of Displacement," 179.

79 Ibid., 178–9.

80 Wordsworth, *The Prelude*, 1805: I, 305–9; Heaney, *North*, 56.

81 Andrews, *The Poetry of Seamus Heaney*, 109.

82 Yeats, *Autobiographies*, 14; Heaney, *Preoccupations*, 62.

83 Hughes, "Representation in Modern Irish Poetry," 82.

84 Haughton, "Power and Hiding Places," 62, 71.

85 Parker, *Seamus Heaney*, 168. Parker is discussing the third Glanmore Sonnet, which is dealt with in the next chapter.

86 Heaney, "Field Work Manuscripts," 15.

87 Heaney, *Preoccupations*, 63; Wordsworth, *The Prelude*, 1805: I, 388–9. As Heaney makes clear in "Chekhov on Sakhalin" (*Station Island*) and "Chekhov, Nero and a Knocker" (*The Government of the Tongue*), this is a reference to Chekhov's self-imposed exile to the prison island of Sakhalin.

88 Heaney, *North*, 59.

89 Keats, *Keats's Poetry and Prose*, 461.

90 Lloyd, "Pap for the Dispossessed," 321–2.

91 Wordsworth, *The Prelude*, 1805: I, 307–9.

92 Quinn, *My Education*, 166. As Heaney has said in interview, "My father grew up with three bachelor uncles, men who were in the cattle trade in a fairly substantial way, traveling back and forward to markets in the north of England, and it was from them that he learned the cattle trade. So the house where he spent his formative years was a place where there were no

Notes to pages 88–91   267

women, a place where the style was undemonstrative and stoical. All that affected him and, of course, it came through to us in his presence and his personality": Cole, "The Art of Poetry, No.75."

93 Heaney, *The Haw Lantern*, 2.

94 Heaney, *North*, 65.

95 Heaney, *Station Island*, 92–3.

96 Heaney, *Seeing Things*, 50. A further example comes in *Stepping Stones* when Heaney describes how Tom Flanagan in Berkeley "turned into a sort of literary foster father to me" and especially gave him a "far more charged-up sense of Yeats and Joyce, for example, and of the whole Irish consequence": O'Driscoll, *Stepping Stones*, 142–3. Jonathan Allison gives valuable insights into the drafting process of "Fosterage," and the relationship between the quotidian, the visionary, and political violence in manuscript versions of the poem: see Allison, "'Friendship's Garland' and the Manuscripts of Seamus Heaney's 'Fosterage.'"

97 Joyce, *A Portrait of the Artist as a Young Man*, 105.

98 Kelly, *A Guide to Early Irish Law*, 413. More on the institution of fosterage in Ireland can be found in Kelly, 86–92. A comparative outline of the international uses of fosterage can be found in Gwynn, "Fosterage."

99 See Ní Chonaill, "Fosterage," 29; Parkes, "Fosterage, Kinship and Legend," 359–61.

100 Samuel Ferguson's Celtic Twilight poem *Congal* (1872) mentions the foster relationship between Congal and the High King of Ireland, Domnal, who had sought refuge with Congal's maternal grandfather Eochaid Buie in Scotland, on "Alba's hospitable shore": Ferguson, *The Poems of Samuel Ferguson*, 265.

101 Parkes, "Celtic Fosterage," 368n19.

102 Ibid., 368. This quotes Hardiman, "A Statute Enacted in Kilkenny, A.D. 1367," 10f.

103 See Parkes, "Fosterage, Kinship and Legend," 605–8.

104 Trumpener, *Bardic Nationalism*, 200, 197.

105 Heaney, *The Haw Lantern*, 5.

106 Heaney, *Finders Keepers*, 55.

107 Ibid., 56.

108 Ibid.

109 Alcobia-Murphy, *Sympathetic Ink*, 111. This quotes Heaney, "Something to Write Home About," 631.

110 Muldoon, *Why Brownlee Left*, 38, 47; Bloom, *The Anxiety of Influence*, 64. See also Kendall, *Paul Muldoon*, 84; Muldoon, *The End of the Poem*, 46; Corcoran, *Poets of Modern Ireland*, 130. Corcoran usefully traces

268   Notes to pages 91–4

Bloomian echoes in Muldoon's poetry, and Muldoon's early comments
about Bloom's theories: Ibid., 124–33. See also Morrissey, "And Fostered
Me and Sent Me Out." The argument here draws on Mackay, "The End of
'Home.'"

111 Muldoon, *Why Brownlee Left*, 47. As Tim Kendall suggests, "'Foster's
pool-hall' is an updated version of Mael Dúin's 'fosterage' and, like its
source (and like much else in *Why Brownlee Left*), 'Immram' is concerned
with 'pedigree,' particularly on the paternal side": Kendall, *Paul Muldoon*,
84. See also Clair Wills and Edna Longley on the related poem
"Immrama," also in *Why Brownlee Left*, which in Longley's words
"impugns not only any mythologized purity of family stock, but doctrines
of such purity": Longley, *The Living Stream*, 170; Wills, *Reading Paul
Muldoon*, 80.

112 Muldoon, *Why Brownlee Left*, 38.

113 Heaney, "Out of London: Ulster's Troubles," 23.

114 Heaney, *Death of a Naturalist*, 5. Haughton reads this first line as ending
"with that loaded Wordsworthian word 'heart'": Haughton, "Power and
Hiding Places," 90.

115 Heaney, *Wintering Out*, 47; Heaney, "Winter Seeds."

116 Heaney, *Field Work*, 13.

117 Heaney, *North*, 36. Guinn Batten relates Heaney's figuration of alteration
and return to Romantic uses of spirals: Batten, "Heaney's Wordsworth
and the Poetics of Displacement."

118 Heaney, *Preoccupations*, 44, 50; Wordsworth, *The Prelude*, 1805: I, 43.

119 Heaney, *Preoccupations*, 145.

120 Ibid.

121 Ibid.; Wordsworth and Coleridge, *Lyrical Ballads*, 272–3.

122 Bate, *Shakespeare and the English Romantic Imagination*, 22. This quotes
Russell and Winterbottom, *Ancient Literary Criticism*, 475–6. Bate
develops the ideas of M.H. Abrams and Walter Jackson Bate: see Bate, *The
Burden of the Past and the English Poet*, 128.

123 This might be a case, as Edna Longley argues, of Heaney's romanticism
"read[ing] other romanticisms literally (and then [being] read literally
itself)": see Longley, *Poetry & Posterity*, 83. As Lucy Newlyn argues, the
"streamy ... unwilled fluidity" of Associationism could explain not only
the influential relationship between the environment and the memory, but
also "memory's communal power," and provide a justification for
Wordsworth's – and Coleridge's – belief in a communal way of living:
Newlyn, *William and Dorothy Wordsworth*, 45, 32.

124 Heaney, *Preoccupations*, 53.

Notes to pages 94–7

125 Bate, *Shakespeare and the English Romantic Imagination*, 22.
126 Ricks, *Allusion to the Poets*, 84.
127 Ibid., 84–5.
128 Bate, *The Burden of the Past and the English Poet*, 70–1. This quotes Wordsworth's "Reply to Mathetes": Wordsworth, *The Prose Works of William Wordsworth*, 2:9.
129 Eilenberg, *Strange Power of Speech*, 93, 88.
130 Wordsworth and Coleridge, *Lyrical Ballads*, 277.
131 Ibid., 272–3, 301. For an extended discussion of "pleasure" in Wordsworth's work, see Boyson, *Wordsworth and the Enlightenment Idea of Pleasure*. Rosie Lavan notes how both Seamus Heaney and Seamus Deane associate education with pleasure: Lavan, "Explorations: Seamus Heaney and Education," 54, 56.
132 Jacobus, "The Art of Managing Books," 216.
133 Heaney, "Woodcut," 4. Peter McDonald probes the exclusionary relationship between propriety and property in Heaney's *Open Letter* (1983) – in particular his "deep design / To be at home / In my own place and dwell within / Its proper name" – in ways parallel to Eilenberg's discussion of "Michael": McDonald, *Mistaken Identities*, 195.
134 Heaney, *Preoccupations*, 63.
135 Ricks, *Allusion to the Poets*, 86. For a discussion of the allusions within Wordsworth's lines "what half-create / and what perceive," see ibid., 109–15.
136 Wordsworth and Coleridge, *Lyrical Ballads*, 159. As Corcoran notes, "'half-' prefixing an adjective or an adverb is a not uncommon Heaney usage ... and sometimes seems to signal an almost embarrassed tentativeness, in which the impulse to proffer is virtually equalled by the desire to withhold": Corcoran, *Poets of Modern Ireland*, 98.
137 "To many people, Heaney's keenness to acknowledge his debt to the patenter of the 'Romantic Ideology' and incarnation of Keats's 'Egotistical Sublime' might even have something monstrous about it": Haughton, "Power and Hiding Places," 63.
138 Heaney, *Preoccupations*, 61.
139 Ibid., 65.
140 Ibid., 63. Wordsworth, *The Prelude*, 1805: I, 64–5; 1850: I, 55–6.
141 Heaney, *The Spirit Level*, 47; Heaney, *Field Work*, 33.
142 Foster, "Crediting Marvels," 210. Talking about Heaney's later work, Foster argues that "Heaney can now revise previous versions of his earlier self in order to insert and inscribe awareness of the later self, such is his confidence in his persona, and it quietly implies a poetic destiny. Later still,

270   Notes to pages 97–102

in 'Desfina' from *Electric Light*, Greek roads are 'looped like boustrophedon'": see Heaney, *Electric Light*, 43.

143 Corcoran, *Poets of Modern Ireland*, 135.

144 *Timon of Athens* I:I: 23–5: Shakespeare, *The Norton Shakespeare*, 2581.
Heaney, *Preoccupations*, 79. See Swann, "The Poet as Critic," 367. Heaney
had discussed the passage from *Timon of Athens* previously – in the 1974
lecture on Gerald Manley Hopkins "The Fire i' the Flint" – but did not
associate it there with Wordsworth and Yeats.

145 Heaney, *Preoccupations*, 78.

146 Horton, "A Truly Uninvited Shade," 18.

147 See Brearton, "Heaney and the Feminine" for an overview of the
substantial body of feminist criticism of Heaney's work.

148 Thomas, *Talking with Poets*, 52.

149 Ibid., 52–3.

150 Heaney, *Preoccupations*, 37. In another lecture of 1978, "Yeats as an
Example," Heaney does argue for Yeats as a possible model for his own
practice, and his ongoing resistance to (and eventual association with)
Yeats provides quite a different model of poetic influence: see ibid., 100.

151 Ibid., 67.

152 Ibid., 61, 62.

153 See Swann, "The Poet as Critic," 361.

154 Heaney, *Preoccupations*, 62.

155 Ibid.

156 Ibid., 63, 65.

157 Heaney, *Death of a Naturalist*, 14.

158 Ibid., 4.

159 Wordsworth, *The Prelude*, 1850: I, 55–8. I follow Heaney's lead here in
quoting the 1850 version of *The Prelude*; the 1805 version features
slightly different punctuation.

160 Ibid., 1850: I, 51–4. The 1805 passage is slightly different: "To the open
fields I told / A prophesy; poetic numbers came / Spontaneously, and
clothed in priestly robe / My spirit, thus singled out, as it might seem, /
For holy services. Great hopes were mine!": ibid., 1805: I, 59–63.

161 Heaney, *Preoccupations*, 63, 65.

162 Ibid., 66–7.

163 Ibid., 68; Wordsworth and Wordsworth, *Home at Grasmere*, 224, italics in
original.

164 Heaney, *Preoccupations*, 68.

165 Heaney, *Field Work*, 35.

Notes to pages 102–4

166 Corcoran argues that after the Joycean denouement of *Station Island* (1984) Heaney "discovers a way of flying free of all exemplars and instructors": Corcoran, *Poets of Modern Ireland*, 106.

167 Stephen James discusses Heaney's "Commanding Voices" (especially Robert Lowell), with particular focus on his fluvial imagery: James, "Dividing Lines: Robert Frost and Seamus Heaney".

168 Heaney, *Finders Keepers*, 65, emphasis added.

169 Marggraf Turley, "Johnny's in the Basement," 187. See Robinson, "Seamus Heaney's Seeing Things," 48; Alcobia-Murphy, *Sympathetic Ink*, 151.

170 Heaney, "Envies and Identifications," 5.

171 Heaney, *Finders Keepers*, 28.

172 O'Driscoll, *Stepping Stones*, 396–7.

173 Heaney, Introduction, *W.B. Yeats: Poems*, xx, xxiv.

174 Heaney, *Preoccupations*, 79.

175 Heaney, *Field Work*, 44; Corcoran, *Poets of Modern Ireland*, 95.

176 Heaney, *Preoccupations*, 220; Heaney, *The Government of the Tongue*, 7, 69; O'Driscoll, *Stepping Stones*, 195.

177 O'Driscoll, *Stepping Stones*, 191; Heaney, *The Government of the Tongue*, 116; Heaney, *Preoccupations*, 156. Patricia Horton argues that in "The Makings of a Music" "Heaney uses Wordsworth to limit the influence of Yeats and so establish his own authority within the Irish poetic canon": Horton, "A Truly Uninvited Shade," 17.

178 Heaney, *Preoccupations*, 156.

179 Stafford, *Starting Lines*, 294, 302.

180 Heaney, *Preoccupations*, 97. The emphasis on the "humanizing" qualities of Wordsworth's verse perhaps suggests a debt to Geoffrey Hartman's introduction to a 1970 collection of Wordsworth's verse, which describes the processes of "naturalization" and "humanization" in the first two books of *The Prelude*: Hartman, "Nature and the Humanization of the Self in Wordsworth," 131–2.

181 Bate, *Romantic Ecology*; Bate, "Department of One." For an argument about how allusion can become a "source of energy and gratitude," see Ricks, *Allusion to the Poets*, 12.

182 Bate, *The Burden of the Past and the English Poet*, 102. Longley, "Musarum Sacerdos," 62.

183 Heaney, *The Government of the Tongue*, 30. See also Ricks, *Allusion to the Poets*, 189, where he suggests, discussing Tennyson, that "We have powers of speech as a community, here in the present, only because we form a community with the past."

272   Notes to pages 104–10

184 Corcoran, *Poets of Modern Ireland*, 135.
185 Muldoon too is also often described as treating precursors as peers: see Kirkland, "Ways of Saying/Ways of Reading," 76.
186 Heaney, "Place, Pastness, Poems," 38.
187 Ibid., 32.
188 Bloom, *Anatomy of Influence*, 9. Bloom makes similar claims in *The Anxiety of Influence* (1973) and *The Anatomy of Influence* (2011). See Newlyn, Foreword, viii. Heaney himself, glossing Wallace Stevens, describes poets facing a "labyrinth" of "given experience": Heaney, *The Redress of Poetry*, 2.
189 Heaney, "Place, Pastness, Poems," 37. Heaney, *North*, 7.
190 Heaney, "Place, Pastness, Poems," 47.
191 McConnell, *Northern Irish Poetry and Theology*, 54.
192 Stafford, *Local Attachments*, 11.
193 Ramazani, "Seamus Heaney's Globe," 45.
194 See Alcobia-Murphy, *Sympathetic Ink*, 4; Corcoran, *Poets of Modern Ireland*, 134; Buxton, *Robert Frost and Northern Irish Poetry*, 15.
195 Longley, *The Living Stream*, 51.
196 Muldoon, *To Ireland, I*, 24–5. Edna Longley notes that "Whereas Hardy is obsessed, to use Samuel Hynes's phrase, with 'the irreversible pastness of the past,' Irish writers are more likely to be obsessed with its irreversible presentness": Longley, *The Living Stream*, 150.
197 O'Driscoll, *Stepping Stones*, 187.
198 Heaney, "The Prelude," 1.
199 Ibid., 2.
200 Heaney, *The Redress of Poetry*, 22. O'Driscoll, *Stepping Stones*, 433.
201 *Tempest* 3:2: 128–9: Shakespeare, *The Norton Shakespeare*, 3247.
202 Longley, *The Living Stream*, 60. Heaney dedicates "Wraith" in *Human Chain* to Carson: Heaney, *Human Chain*, 66–8.

CHAPTER THREE

1 Heaney, "Yank," 14. The poem had been presented to the Belfast Group, and a draft of it is kept in the Michael Longley papers at Emory University (Box 60, FF 7).
2 Wordsworth and Coleridge, *Lyrical Ballads*, 185.
3 Ibid., 182.
4 Ibid.
5 Ibid., 193–4.
6 Heaney, "Yank," 14.

Notes to pages 110–16

7 Heaney first heard MacLean read his poetry in Dublin in the 1970s: see Heaney, "The Trance and the Translation."

8 Heaney, "Yank," 15.

9 Ibid., 14.

10 Ibid., 14–15.

11 I am grateful to Patrick Crotty for the suggestion that *The Backward Look* was also the title of an influential survey of Irish literature by Frank O' Connor, published in 1967. The idea that Irish experience "involves an often contradictory, even paradoxical combination of the 'backward look' and breakneck modernization" has come to be a mainstay of Irish studies: see Goodby, *Irish Studies*, vii.

12 Heaney, "Last Look," 7.

13 Heaney, "Bachelor Deceased," 5. Heaney talks about Pat McGuckian in O'Driscoll, *Stepping Stones*, 402.

14 Heaney, *Wintering Out*, 11.

15 Heaney, *Human Chain*, 73.

16 Ibid., 19–20.

17 See Heaney's essay "Joy or Night: Last Things in the Poetry of W.B. Yeats and Philip Larkin": "When language does more than enough, as it does in all achieved poetry, it opts for the condition of overlife, and rebels at limit"; Heaney, *The Redress of Poetry*, 158.

18 Heaney, *Wintering Out*, 12.

19 Heaney, *North*, 33–4.

20 Mackay, "Memory, the Bog, Seamus Heaney."

21 Wordsworth, *The Prose Works of William Wordsworth*, 1974, 2:85.

22 Heaney, "Obituary": this was submitted to the Belfast Group between 1963 and 1966 and is held in the National Library of Ireland archives.

23 Eliot, *The Complete Poems and Plays*, 195.

24 Heaney, "Letter to Michael Longley," 4 January 1978.

25 Heaney, *Preoccupations*, 132.

26 Ibid., 131.

27 Ibid., 131, 133. Gail McConnell argues that Heaney's view of landscape – and poetic form – in this lecture is "half-pagan, half-Christian": McConnell, *Northern Irish Poetry and Theology*, 60.

28 Heaney, *Preoccupations*, 132.

29 Ibid., 135.

30 Ibid., 141.

31 Ibid., 147.

32 Lysaght, "Robert Lloyd Praeger," 891.

33 Heaney, *Preoccupations*, 145.

274 Notes to pages 116–19

34 The phrase "one dear perpetual place" comes from Yeats's 1921 "Prayer for My Daughter": Yeats, *W.B. Yeats*, 213. Herbert Lindenberger had related Yeats's poem to Book IX of *The Prelude*, suggesting that they share the "same zeal for rootedness," as well as to Eliot and Burke: Lindenberger, *On Wordsworth's Prelude*, 250.

35 Heaney, *Preoccupations*, 145.

36 Praeger, *The Way That I Went*, 102.

37 Ibid.

38 Heaney, *Preoccupations*, 145.

39 In Heaney's 1975 essay on Kavanagh, "From Monaghan to the Grand Canal," (later published in *Preoccupations*) Wordsworth appears as a foil for Kavanagh, in terms of the growth of the poetic mind as subject matter, and the consciousness, as in "Tintern Abbey," that the "real value of the moment" does not lie in "its present feelings" but "in its potential flowering, its blooming, in the imagination": ibid., 117.

40 Praeger, *The Way That I Went*, 1.

41 Lysaght, "Contrasting Natures," 447.

42 Heaney, *Preoccupations*, 148–9.

43 Mac Mathúna, "*Dinnseanchas*," 299–300.

44 Praeger, *The Way That I Went*, 101. For a discussion of the continuing importance of this genre, see Mac Giolla Léith, "*Dinnseanchas* and Modern Gaelic Poetry."

45 Wordsworth and Coleridge, *Lyrical Ballads*, 272–3.

46 Ibid., 285.

47 Bate, *Romantic Ecology*, 104.

48 See Burris, *The Poetry of Resistance*, 79. Simon Armitage's rewriting of "Michael" makes explicit how the poem can be read as an agon between a (liberal) father and (potentially murderous) son, with the suggestion that your first "crime" will determine your life's course: Armitage, *Seeing Stars*, 10–11.

49 In the 1799 *Prelude* "Nature" and the "spirits" in Nature are interchangeable. By the 1805 *Prelude* the "spirits" have become "Nature" and the spiritual concealed in the natural.

50 Wordsworth, *The Prelude*, 1805: I, 572–4.

51 Wordsworth came under criticism from the Unitarian Miss Patty Smith for confusing Nature with God. See Moorman, *William Wordsworth: The Later Years*, 227.

52 Quoted in Hill, "Wordsworth, Comenius and the Art of Education," 303.

53 Wordsworth and Coleridge, *Lyrical Ballads*, 271.

54 Heaney, *Preoccupations*, 145.

55 See McConnell, *Northern Irish Poetry and Theology*, 160.

Notes to pages 119–24

56 Heaney, *Preoccupations*, 133, 132.
57 Ibid., 147.
58 Longley, *The Living Stream*, 96. Heaney had earlier (albeit with a slightly ambiguous tone) lauded Hewitt in a 1969 review of his *Collected Poems* for providing "all subsequent Northern writers with a hinterland of reference": Heaney, "The Poetry of John Hewitt," 73.
59 Heaney, *Preoccupations*, 147.
60 Ibid., 149; Corkery, *Synge and Anglo-Irish Literature*, 14. For eighteenth- and nineteenth-century foundational imaginings of the bog, see Trumpener, *Bardic Nationalism*, 37–66.
61 Trumpener, *Bardic Nationalism*, 23; Heaney, *North*, 64.
62 Deane, *The French Revolution and Enlightenment in England*, 149.
63 Ibid., 151.
64 Wordsworth and Coleridge, *Lyrical Ballads*, 268. See Harrison, *Wordsworth's Vagrant Muse*, 75–6.
65 Heaney, *Wintering Out*, 17.
66 Lysaght, "Contrasting Natures," 444.
67 For Heaney's own discussions of this poem, see Heaney, *Among Schoolchildren*, 10; Heaney, *Finders Keepers*, 350.
68 Braidwood, *The Ulster Dialect Lexicon*, 27. As well as containing the example of the boortrees, Braidwood's lecture also provided the transliterations of Irish names for the snipe that Heaney uses in "The Backward Look" in *Wintering Out*.
69 Murphy, *Seamus Heaney*, 23; Corcoran, *The Poetry of Seamus Heaney*, 47. As Eugene O' Brien has pointed out, Irish does not appear in the poem except in a ghostly form: "Broagh" is an anglicized transliteration of "bruach" rather than a Gaelic term itself: O'Brien, *Seamus Heaney and the Place of Writing*, 60.
70 Heaney, *Preoccupations*, 20.
71 See Bate, *Romantic Ecology*, 103, where he argues that "A naming poem stands between a naturalized 'dwelling poem' and an alienated 'prospect poem.'"
72 Heaney, *Field Work*, 35.
73 Beckett, *Waiting for Godot*, I, 46.
74 Heaney, "Field Work Manuscripts," 15.
75 O'Driscoll, *Stepping Stones*, 198.
76 Ibid.
77 Ibid., 197.
78 O'Brien, "Seamus Heaney and William Wordsworth," 187, 189.
79 Heaney, *Field Work*, 33.

276 Notes to pages 124–7

80 Heaney, "Two Poems," 64.
81 O'Driscoll, *Stepping Stones*, 194; Heaney, "Interview with Frank Kinahan," 404–14.
82 Heaney, "Interview with James Randall," 21. Bernard O'Donoghue reminds us that this use of the first-person pronoun is still a "rhetorical trope" rather than transparent access to reality: O'Donoghue, *Seamus Heaney and the Language of Poetry*, 74.
83 Heaney, "Interview with Frank Kinahan," 412. Heaney characteristically demurs, suggesting "I distrust this attitude too, of course."
84 Heaney, *North*, 59.
85 Corcoran, *The Poetry of Seamus Heaney*, 101.
86 Heaney, *North*, 44; Heaney, *Field Work*, 34.
87 Heaney, *Field Work*, 33.
88 Browning, *The Poems*, 1:71; Chatterton, *The Complete Works of Thomas Chatterton*, 1:592; MacDiarmid, *Complete Poems*, 1:335. See Kinsella, "Poet to Poet," 114; O'Grady, "Heaney Redivivus: The Fine Art of Renovation," 77.
89 Heaney, *Stations*, 21.
90 Heaney, *North*, 67.
91 Heaney, *Preoccupations*, 56–7.
92 Heaney, *Field Work*, 39. Bate, *The Song of the Earth*, 250–1.
93 See Corcoran, *The Poetry of Seamus Heaney*, 101–6; McLoughlin, "An Ear to the Line," 213. Both Andrew Waterman and Elmer Kennedy-Andrews find that the book is perhaps *too* open to Lowell's influence: Waterman, "The Best Way Out Is Always Through," 23; Kennedy-Andrews, *Northern Irish Poetry*, 96.
94 Heaney, *Field Work*, 33.
95 Miłosz, *Selected and Last Poems, 1931–2004*, 93. Heaney quotes this in a 2002 interview with Harry Thomas: Thomas, *Talking with Poets*, 65–6; he also used a quotation from the poem (which had been written in Berkeley in 1968) as the title for a short essay on Miłosz: Heaney, "The Door Stands Open."
96 Heaney, *Field Work*, 44.
97 Bloom, *The Anxiety of Influence*, 30, italics in original.
98 Ibid., 147. There are perhaps echoes here of Robert Frost's staring into a well in "For Once, Then, Something," a poem modulated quite differently in Heaney's "Personal Helicon" in *Death of a Naturalist* (1966) and Muldoon's "The More a Man Has the More a Man Wants" in *Quoof* (1983). See also Buxton, *Robert Frost and Northern Irish Poetry*, 26–32; James, "Dividing Lines," 63–77.

Notes to pages 127–30

99 Bloom, *The Anxiety of Influence*, 16.
100 Bate, "Department of One," a review of *The Anatomy of Influence*, outlines many of Bloom's faults; Bielik-Robson, *The Saving Lie*, offers a measured exposition and defence of his theories.
101 Corcoran, *Poets of Modern Ireland*, 130–1. Corcoran traces Bloomian echoes in Muldoon's poetry and Muldoon's early comments about Bloom's theories: ibid., 124–33. As Fran Brearton comments, responding to Corcoran, *The Anxiety of Influence* is "an enormously seductive text with which to read Paul Muldoon. But its very seductiveness sends warning signals": Brearton, "For Father Read Mother," 58–9.
102 Muldoon, *The End of the Poem*, 46; Muldoon, "Letter to Seamus Heaney."
103 Corcoran, *The Poetry of Seamus Heaney*, 103; Foster, *Seamus Heaney*, 97; Andrews, *The Poetry of Seamus Heaney*, 118.
104 Heaney, *Preoccupations*, 145, 65; McLoughlin, "An Ear to the Line," 204; Foster, *Seamus Heaney*, 80.
105 Heaney, *Field Work*, 36.
106 McLoughlin, "An Ear to the Line," 201.
107 Ibid., 202.
108 Heaney, *Field Work*, 41.
109 Ibid., 33. See Corcoran, *The Poetry of Seamus Heaney*, 103: "Boris Pasternak's 'Hamlet,' the first of the *Doctor Zhivago* poems, ends with a Russian proverb which Robert Lowell translates, in *Imitations*, 'To live a life is not to cross a field.'"
110 Heaney, *Field Work*, 35.
111 Heaney, "Interview with Frank Kinahan," 412.
112 Heaney, *Field Work*, 35.
113 Bloom, *The Anxiety of Influence*, 64.
114 Heaney, *Field Work*, 34, 36.
115 Ibid., 37.
116 Gillis, "The Modern Irish Sonnet," 73. Similarly, Corcoran suggests that Heaney discovers in Glanmore "a new point of confirmation and resolution, a firmer ground" while Andrew Murphy argues that "Heaney celebrates his family's stint of living in County Wicklow with a kind of ease and freedom that 'Exposure' signally lacks": Corcoran, *The Poetry of Seamus Heaney*, 101; Murphy, *Seamus Heaney*, 74.
117 Bloom, *The Anxiety of Influence*, 36, 39. See Brearton, "For Father Read Mother," 54, 58 for a discussion of the importance of the Covering Cherub, and its opposite, the Sphinx, to Paul Muldoon's poetry.
118 Bloom, *The Anxiety of Influence*, 39.

278 Notes to pages 130–4

119 Heaney, *Field Work*, 40, 41.
120 Ibid., 41.
121 Ibid.
122 McLoughlin, "An Ear to the Line," 212. See also Gifford, *Ulysses Annotated*, 22.
123 Heaney, *Field Work*, 42.
124 Ibid., 35.
125 Ibid., 40. Corcoran, *The Poetry of Seamus Heaney*, 105. See also Collins, *Seamus Heaney*, 129.
126 O'Donoghue, "Heaney's Classics and the Bucolic," 119; Longley, *Poetry & Posterity*, 106.
127 Heaney, *Field Work*, 41.
128 Corcoran, *The Poetry of Seamus Heaney*, 106.
129 Guinn Batten suggests that Heaney "developed a politics and poetics of embodiment inseparable from his politics and poetics of displacement": Batten, "Heaney's Wordsworth and the Poetics of Displacement," 180.
130 Bielik-Robson, *The Saving Lie*, 37.
131 Muldoon, *Why Brownlee Left*, 22. The argument in this section draws on points made in Mackay, "The End of 'Home.'"
132 Lindop, "News & Notes," 3. In a letter to Ron Schuhard in 1983, Heaney had described a recent visit to Grasmere as "salutary and enhancing"; writing from Grasmere when delivering the lecture he describes it as "a time of terrific buoyancy and genial spirits – Wordsworth's vocabulary is in the air up here": Heaney, "Letter to Ron Schuhard." The original publication of the lecture features a brief introduction by Heaney about the occasion: Heaney, *Place and Displacement*, 1.
133 Batten, "Heaney's Wordsworth and the Poetics of Displacement," 184.
134 The importance of Heaney's American bilocation cannot be overstated, but neither can the extent to which it was not an inevitable part of his immediate poetic and cultural environment: for a poet so conscious of his place in different traditions, it can be seen – on poetic historiographical grounds – as an adoption of and negotiation with other poetic traditions to complicate those he had weighed against each other in "Singing School."
135 Heaney, "Current Unstated Assumptions about Poetry," 645.
136 For further discussion of Heaney's use of Eastern European poetry, see Quinn, "Heaney and Eastern Europe."
137 Heaney, "Current Unstated Assumptions about Poetry," 651.
138 Ibid.
139 Heaney, *Preoccupations*, 153.

Notes to pages 134–8

140 Begley, *Rambles in Ireland*, 167. Heaney has used the Jungian concept of the collective unconscious and Jung's understanding of the process of individuation in his criticism, but it would still be a stretch to describe him as "Jungian," notwithstanding that when asked to give his own version of Eliot's "famous self-description: classicist in literature, royalist in politics, Anglo-Catholic in religion," he famously replied "Probably Jungian in religion, torpid in politics and … Passionate" in literature: Heaney, "Interview with Frank Kinahan," 409.

141 Heaney, *North*, 67.

142 Heaney, *The Government of the Tongue*, xvi–xix, 97.

143 Ibid., 54, 108. For these images, see "The Interesting Case of Nero, Chekhov's Cognac and a Knocker," "Osip and Nadezhda Mandelstam," "Atlas of Civilization," and the title lecture of *The Government of the Tongue* (1986).

144 Heaney, *Finders Keepers*, 112.

145 Ibid., 114.

146 Heaney, *North*, 67.

147 Jerome McGann had argued in 1983 (in response to Geoffrey Hartman) that the need to "return" to a sense of unity was a central concern of Wordsworth's: McGann, *The Romantic Ideology*, 40; Hartman, *Beyond Formalism*, 302–3.

148 Jung, *The Essential Jung*, 19.

149 Ibid., 227. Heaney, *Finders Keepers*, 112.

150 Heaney, *Finders Keepers*, 117–18. As Henry Hart and Rachel Buxton argue, this position is almost Kantian in its appeal to a sublime beyond the quotidian: Buxton, *Robert Frost and Northern Irish Poetry*, 80; Hart, "What Is Heaney Seeing in Seeing Things?," 37.

151 Heaney, *Finders Keepers*, 118.

152 Ibid., 114–15.

153 Ibid., 115. M.H. Abrams in *The Mirror and the Lamp* (1953) had similarly used Wordsworth and his peers as a parallel for poets between the world wars (and their anxieties about the value of poetry): Abrams, *The Mirror and the Lamp*, 326. See also Ross, "In Search of Enabling Light," 112.

154 Heaney, *Finders Keepers*, 115.

155 Haughton, "Power and Hiding Places," 64. See also Larrissy, "Seamus Heaney and Romanticism," 105–6.

156 Haughton, "Power and Hiding Places," 75. See also Hartman, "Nature and the Humanization of the Self in Wordsworth," 127.

157 Newlyn, Foreword, ix. See also McGann, *The Romantic Ideology*, 100.

280 Notes to pages 138–43

158 O'Neill, *The All-Sustaining Air*, 140, quoting Heaney, *The Redress of Poetry*, 260. O'Neill suggests that "For Stan Smith, such healing follows a path from Wordsworthian predicament to Keatsian negative capability ... But to pursue Heaney's debt to Romanticism in terms of switched allegiances would be to oversimplify. Wordsworth certainly does not drop away"; he is discussing Smith, "Seamus Heaney."

159 Abrams, *Natural Supernaturalism*, 145.

160 Heaney, *The Haw Lantern*, 7.

161 Bhabha, *The Location of Culture*, 111.

162 Cooke, "Harriet Cooke Talked to the Poet Seamus Heaney," 8.

163 Heaney, *Preoccupations*, 37.

164 O'Driscoll, *Stepping Stones*, 113.

165 Heaney, *Station Island*, 32.

166 Corcoran, "The Melt of the Real Thing," 8.

167 Heaney, *Station Island*, 32–3.

168 Heaney, *Stations*, 16.

169 Heaney, *Station Island*, 58.

170 Heaney, *Stations*, 19.

171 Wordsworth, *The Prelude*, 1805: II, 367–71.

172 Ibid., 1850: II, 76–7. Heaney would also quote from these lines from *The Prelude* much later, in the 2000 Lafcadio Hearn lecture published in the *Guardian* in 2007: Heaney, "The Pathos of Things," 20–1.

173 Heaney, "In Glenelly Valley." This poem was submitted for consideration to the Belfast Group, between 1963 and 1966.

174 Heaney, *Station Island*, 32.

175 Ibid., 32. Ruth "stood in tears amid the alien corn" of Boaz, to borrow the famous phrase from Keats' "Ode to a Nightingale"; see the book of Ruth 2–3.

176 Heaney, *Station Island*, 32.

177 Wordsworth, *The Prelude*, 1805: I, 1–2.

178 Heaney, *Station Island*, 32.

179 Ibid.

180 Ibid., 51.

181 Wordsworth and Coleridge, *Lyrical Ballads*, 178.

182 Heaney, *Station Island*, 52.

183 The logic of this loss is similar to Rousseau's when he identifies deforestation as one of the first movements towards a "civilized" and un-natural existence: Rousseau, *The Social Contract and Discourses*, 352; Bate, *The Song of the Earth*, 43.

184 Heaney, *Station Island*, 52.

Notes to pages 143–52

185 Heaney, *Sweeney Astray*, 37.
186 Horton, "Romantic Intersections," 33.
187 It would also be a location, much later, for the poem "In a Loaning": Heaney, *District and Circle*, 74.
188 Heaney, *Station Island*, 51–2.
189 Ibid., 51.
190 Ibid.
191 Ibid.
192 Ibid.
193 Heaney, *North*, 67.
194 Mandelstam, *Selected Poems*, 122.
195 Heaney, *Station Island*, 52.
196 See the note by Dante's translator, Michael Palma, to Canto XIII: 58–9 in Alighieri, *Inferno*, 146.
197 Heaney, *Station Island*, 52.
198 Ibid.
199 Ibid., 51.
200 Ibid., 51–2.
201 Ibid., 93–4.
202 Ibid., 55.
203 Heaney, Foreword, *A Portrait of the Artist as a Young Girl*, ix.
204 Ibid., ix. This idea of being "licked into poetic shape" had also been expressed in "Feeling into Words" and Thomas, *Talking with Poets*, 53.
205 Heaney, Foreword, *A Portrait of the Artist as a Young Girl*, x.
206 Ibid., ix–x.
207 Ibid., x.

CHAPTER FOUR

1 Heaney, "Verses for a Fordham Commencement," 22.
2 Ibid., 23.
3 Wordsworth, *The Prelude*, 1850: IV, 356; I, 392–5.
4 Heaney, "Verses for a Fordham Commencement," 23.
5 Ibid.
6 Wordsworth and Coleridge, *Lyrical Ballads*, 293.
7 Heaney uses this quotation in programs in 1973 and 1978, once to darken Kavanagh's hopeful "light of the imagination," and once to discuss a novel by Michael McLaverty: Heaney, "Explorations: Bitter Honey"; Heaney, "Explorations 2: Call My Brother Back."

282 Notes to pages 152–5

8 For a discussion of Heaney's broadcasting career in this period, see Russell, *Seamus Heaney's Regions*, 66–100.

9 "Education and Community," 6. Another of Heaney's *Education Times* essays, published 20 December 1973, was collected in *Preoccupations* as part 2 of "Mossbawn": see Heaney, "Seamus Heaney Recalls."

10 Heaney, "Poetic Sweetness and Light in the Classroom," 14. Heaney may have been heartened by the inclusion of his own "Blackberry-Picking" in *Poeimata*, with the Heaneyesque/Muldoonian exercise: "Write in verse (or prose) about your own experience picking mushrooms (or if you like blackberries)": Egan and Rice, *Poiemata*, 20. Egan, alongside Michael Hartnett, also published Heaney's "Servant Boy" in their anthology *Choice*: Egan and Hartnett, *Choice*, 38–9.

11 Heaney, "Poetic Sweetness and Light in the Classroom," 14.

12 Ibid.

13 Heaney, "Cool and Complex Weaving of Myth and Language," 12.

14 Ibid.

15 Heaney, "Adroitest of Makers," 17.

16 Ibid.

17 Ibid.

18 Haffenden, *Viewpoints*, 59.

19 Leavis, *How to Teach Reading*, 40; Day, *Re-reading Leavis*, xii.

20 Haffenden, *Viewpoints*, 60. The retrospect is less rosy, however: looking back in "My Education" (1997) he described "the frustration of not having a closer and more nurturing relationship with individuals. It was conveyor-belt teaching, really, dealing with crowds of people": Quinn, *My Education*, 175.

21 Quoted in McSweeney, "The Poet's Picture of Education," 139. The interview was carried out on 8 May 1981. While Heaney contributed the foreword to their anthology *The School Bag* (1997), Ted Hughes wrote an "Afterword: Memorising Poems," which makes the case, drawing on centuries of memory techniques, for the importance of learning by rote: Heaney and Hughes, *The School Bag*, 563–9. See also Stafford, *Starting Lines*, 294.

22 McSweeney, "The Poet's Picture of Education," 141.

23 Ibid., 140.

24 Part of this lecture was published in the journal *Fortnight* in September 1983, where it is noted, "John Malone, who died on February 14, 1982, was Director of the School Support Service. A lifelong supporter of comprehensive education, he was formerly a lecturer in education at QUB,

Notes to pages 155–7

a Director of the Schools Curriculum Project, and headmaster of Orangefield Secondary School": Heaney, *Among Schoolchildren*, 18.

25 This tripartite structure is in part derived from Eliot's essay *The Three Voices of Poetry*, and also C.K. Stead's discussion of this in his *New Poetics*: see Eliot, *Three Voices of Poetry* and Dennison, *Seamus Heaney and the Adequacy of Poetry*, 113. Herbert Lindenberger, in his 1963 study *On Wordsworth's Prelude*, had applied Eliot's essay to Wordsworth's work.

26 Heaney, *Among Schoolchildren*, 6–7.

27 Ibid., 5, 7. He quotes from *The Teachers Handbook of the Primary School Curriculum*. There are possible parallels here with the work of Anthony D. Smith, who argues that when nationalist movements aim for "social regeneration through education," "Education here stands for more than mere enlightenment. It is a process of self-development, of drawing out of oneself hidden and suppressed potentialities, until full self-realisation has been attained. Such education is closely linked to the elevation of culture as the source of politics": Smith, "Neo-Classicist and Romantic Elements in the Emergence of Nationalist Conceptions," 83; see also Wright, *Representing the National Landscape in Irish Romanticism*, 75–6.

28 Lloyd, *Anomalous States*, 19.

29 Heaney, *Among Schoolchildren*, 17.

30 Ibid., 15, 16.

31 Heaney, *Finders Keepers*, 115.

32 Heaney, "The Prelude," 3.

33 Heaney, *Among Schoolchildren*, 16.

34 Ibid., 5.

35 Ibid., 16.

36 Dennison, *Seamus Heaney and the Adequacy of Poetry*, 108. See also Foster, "Crediting Marvels"; and McConnell, *Northern Irish Poetry and Theology*, 84. As Ed Larrissy notes, "it would be a grave mistake simplistically to identify Heaney's Wordsworth with the transcendentalist seer of popular imagining" not least because "he pays scant attention to the transcendentalist framework Wordsworth attempted to foist on *The Prelude* from the early 1800s": Larrissy, "Seamus Heaney and Romanticism," 105.

37 "What Heaney, in his stoic joy, fails to consider is the possibility of a poetry of belief which – because of God's assumption in the incarnation of our creaturely forsakenness and fallenness, and the Holy Spirit's refining, cruciform work – has no need to effect some final and notional transcendence, indeed which, because this is so, can descend the *via negativa*": Dennison, *Seamus Heaney and the Adequacy of Poetry*, 169–70.

284 Notes to pages 158–61

38 Ibid., 185.

39 O'Brien, "The Anxiety of Influence," 122–3; Blanchot, *The Space of Literature*, 200.

40 Heaney, "Further Language," 16. See the next chapter for discussion of this lecture.

41 Heaney, *Among Schoolchildren*, 16.

42 Heaney, *Station Island*, 66. This section was first published in summer 1983: Heaney, "Station Island." There is perhaps an odd echo here of God talking to Elijah with a "still small voice" (1 Kings 19).

43 Heaney, *Among Schoolchildren*, 5: "What I am involved in here is more autobiography than argument, carried on in the faith that the educational process is a matter of sympathetic recognition."

44 Ibid., 9.

45 Ibid.

46 Ibid., 10, 12.

47 Shane Alcobia-Murphy identifies three other instances in which Heaney discusses this scene: "John Bull's Other Island," "The Interesting Case of John Alphonsus Mulrennan," and "A Tale of Two Islands." See Alcobia-Murphy, *Sympathetic Ink*, 223n47.

48 Heaney, *Among Schoolchildren*, 12.

49 Ibid.

50 Ibid., 16. This quotes Derek Mahon, "The Sea in Winter," first published in a special edition of the same name in 1979. The "mysterious" aspect of teaching is something Heaney will elucidate further in "Poet as Professor," where he argues for the important role that practising poets can have in the teaching of poetry: Heaney, *Finders Keepers*, 71.

51 Heaney, *Among Schoolchildren*, 17.

52 MacKenzie, *Escape from the Classroom*, 88.

53 Heaney, *The Government of the Tongue*, 149.

54 Ibid., 148.

55 Ibid., 153.

56 Wordsworth and Coleridge, *Lyrical Ballads*, 134.

57 Heaney, *The Government of the Tongue*, 154.

58 Ibid., 159. The structure of "The Indefatigable Hoof-Taps" is very similar to Heaney's discussion of Derek Walcott's career in "The Murmur of Malvern," where it is measured (approvingly) against Yeats's: ibid., 23.

59 Ibid., 163.

60 Lloyd, "Pap for the Dispossessed," 325, 328.

61 Heaney, *The Government of the Tongue*, 169.

62 Ibid., 169, 168.

Notes to pages 162–8

63 Ibid., 168, 148.
64 Ibid., 170. As Haughton notes, in this lecture Heaney "Discreetly smuggl[es] in T.S. Eliot's wartime notion of poetry as a raid on the inarticulate, Matthew Arnold's notion of poetry as 'criticism of life,' and Auden's meditations on Shakespeare's Ariel and Prospero": Haughton, "Power and Hiding Places," 64–5.
65 Heaney, *The Government of the Tongue*, 163.
66 O'Neill, *The All-Sustaining Air*, 138.
67 Wordsworth and Coleridge, *Lyrical Ballads*, 178.
68 Brearton, "For Father Read Mother, " 80–1.
69 Haughton, "Power and Hiding Places," 67–8.
70 Heaney, *The Government of the Tongue*, 18–19.
71 Heaney, *The Redress of Poetry*, 158–9. See Wheatley, "Professing Poetry," 132.
72 Heaney, "The Peace of the World Is Always with You."
73 Heaney, "Voices behind a Door," 32.
74 By coincidence, Heaney's old mentor Philip Hobsbaum published a selection of Wordsworth's poetry and prose with Routledge the following year. In a letter to Heaney, Hobsbaum, "over the moon," applauds him on his treatment of the "Two-Book Prelude" and inclusion of "Redundance" and fragments from the Alfoxden Notebook: Hobsbaum, "Letter to Seamus Heaney"; Wordsworth, *Selected Poetry and Prose*.
75 Heaney, Introduction, *Essential Wordsworth*, viii.
76 Ibid., vii.
77 Ibid.
78 Haughton, "Power and Hiding Places," 65.
79 Heaney, Introduction, *Essential Wordsworth*, vii, ix, x.
80 Ibid., xi.
81 Ibid.
82 Ibid., xi–xii.
83 Heaney, *The Redress of Poetry*, 120.
84 Heaney, Introduction, *Essential Wordsworth*, xii.
85 Heaney, *The Haw Lantern*, 14.
86 Heaney, *Station Island*, 100, 98.
87 Heaney, *The Haw Lantern*, 7.
88 Ibid., 32. Italics added.
89 Heaney, *Station Island*, 68.
90 Heaney, *The Haw Lantern*, 32.
91 Wordsworth and Coleridge, *Lyrical Ballads*, 178.
92 Heaney, *The Government of the Tongue*, 3–4.

286 Notes to pages 168–74

93 Wordsworth, *The Prose Works of William Wordsworth*, 2:58.
94 Ibid., 2:57–8; Heaney, *Station Island*, 83; Heaney, *Field Work*, 17–18.
95 Heaney, *The Haw Lantern*, 31.
96 Auden, *Collected Poems*, 247.
97 Yeats, *The Major Works*, 85–7. Czesław Miłosz's 1965 "Bobo's Metamorphosis," which deals with trees that exist in the imagination alone, may also inform the "Clearances." It is, however, ambivalent about the process of idealizing objects: the narrator "blushes" and turns away from the suggestion that "Only the object which does not exist / Is perfect and pure": Miłosz, *Collected Poems 1931–1987*, 164.
98 Heaney, *The Haw Lantern*, 32.
99 Tobin, *Passage to the Center*, 273.
100 Heaney, *The Haw Lantern*, 7.
101 Ibid., 6.
102 Hall, "Cultural Identity and Diaspora," 110–12.
103 Heaney, *The Haw Lantern*, 13.
104 Ibid., 18.
105 Heaney, *Station Island*, 56.
106 Heaney, *The Haw Lantern*, 1.
107 Ibid., 1–2.
108 Ibid., 3.
109 Matthews, "Translations," 120.
110 Heaney, *The Haw Lantern*, 19.
111 Lee, "Writing in Colonial Space," 400.
112 Heaney, *The Haw Lantern*, 18.
113 Ibid., 17.
114 Kerrigan, "'Knowing the Dead …' for Pete Laver 1947–83," 15.
115 Vendler, *Seamus Heaney*, 75.
116 Heaney, *The Haw Lantern*, 17.
117 It is also Hugh MacDiarmid territory. "On a Raised Beach," his great exploration of how we can describe the physical world, starting from the haptic quality of stones, sees the poet striving towards "the silence of supreme creative power, / The direct and undisturbed way of working / Which alone leads to greatness": MacDiarmid, *Complete Poems*, I: 428–9.
118 Wordsworth, *The Ruined Cottage and The Pedlar*, 73.
119 Lee, "Writing in Colonial Space," 400.
120 Heaney, *The Haw Lantern*, 48.
121 Ibid.
122 Ibid.
123 Ibid., 48–9.

Notes to pages 174–8

124 Ibid., 48.
125 Ibid., 49.
126 Ibid., 6.
127 Ibid., 49.
128 O'Driscoll, *Stepping Stones*, 32.
129 Wordsworth and Coleridge, *Lyrical Ballads*, 199.
130 Cole, "The Art of Poetry, No.75." Paul Muldoon has a poem, "Our Lady of Ardboe" (originally published in the 1977 collection *Mules*), based on the apparitions: Muldoon, *Poems, 1968–1998*, 50–1. There may also be another divine apparition lurking behind the poem, based on the most famous "visionary" gable in Ireland. In Knock in County Mayo in 1879, a group of people witnessed a vision of Mary, Joseph, John the Evangelist, and John the Baptist on the gable of the parish church, for over two hours on the evening of Thursday, 21 August (there were subsequent, less well documented, visions as well). The church confirmed the validity of this holy manifestation, and the face of the gable wall was quickly chipped away by pilgrims wanting relics, souvenirs, and cures. The church has subsequently become a major pilgrimage site, even if, as has plausibly been suggested, the manifestations were most likely the result of a magic lantern show put on by the Knock parish priest Archdeacon Bartholomew Cavanagh: the divine nature (or otherwise) of the visions is not necessarily tied into their power. See Berman, "Knock: Some New Evidence"; Carpenter, "Mimesis, Memory, and the Magic Lantern." For a discussion of how the magic lantern controversy at Knock appears in Joyce's story "Grace," see Brown, "Joyce's Magic Lantern." For a more orthodox, dogmatic approach, see Duggan, "Lessons from Our Lady of Knock."
131 Heaney, *The Haw Lantern*, 49.
132 Bate, *Romantic Ecology*, 34; Heaney, *The Haw Lantern*, 49.
133 Heaney, *The Haw Lantern*, 50.
134 Deane, "Powers of Earth and Visions of Air," 275–6.
135 Wordsworth, *Poems in Two Volumes*, 428.
136 Ibid., 275.
137 Wordsworth, *William Wordsworth: The Borders of Vision*, 19. Emphasis in original.
138 Thomas Docherty makes a similar argument about the spectre of Heaney's father in *Seeing Things*: "It is as if Heaney's father's very disappearance is what guarantees his very existence": Docherty, *Alterities*, 34. See also Andrews, "The Spirit's Progress," 228.
139 Vendler, *Seamus Heaney*, 136.
140 Hart, "What Is Heaney Seeing in *Seeing Things*?," 160.

288 Notes to pages 178–83

141 See Weiskel, *The Romantic Sublime*, 4.

142 For Richard Rankin Russell, "The volume's title likely draws on the determination of one of his favourite poets, Wordsworth, to 'see into the life of things'": Russell, *Seamus Heaney*, 142.

143 Heaney, *Seeing Things*, 17.

144 Andrews, *The Poetry of Seamus Heaney*, 145. John Wilson Foster similarly describes "Heaney's third poetry, a poetry of light, air, glimmer, manoeuvre": Foster, *The Achievement of Seamus Heaney*, 51.

145 Deane, "Powers of Earth and Visions of Air," 151. See O'Brien, *Searches for Answers*, 47–8, for a discussion of Heaney's "I" and "eye."

146 Heaney, *Seeing Things*, 50. See Parker, *Seamus Heaney*, 217.

147 Heaney, *Seeing Things*, 55.

148 Vendler, *Seamus Heaney*, 140; Heaney, *Seeing Things*, 55.

149 Heaney, *Seeing Things*, 55.

150 Ibid.

151 Heaney, *The Government of the Tongue*, 57; Herbert, *Barbarian in the Garden*, 48.

152 Burnside and Fazzini, "John Burnside in Conversation with Marco Fazzini," 95; Fazzini, "Kenneth White and John Burnside," 120.

153 Foster, *The Achievement of Seamus Heaney*, 51; Docherty, *Alterities*, 22; Vendler, *Seamus Heaney*, 138; Auge, *A Chastened Communion*, 138.

154 Hughes to Heaney, 8 October 1989, in Hughes, *Letters of Ted Hughes*, 564.

155 Andrews, "The Spirit's Progress," 231.

156 Heaney, *The Cure at Troy*, 74.

157 Heaney, *The Spirit Level*, 12; O'Driscoll, *Stepping Stones*, 475, quoting Wordsworth, *The Prelude*, 1805: X, 727.

158 Brown, "The Witnessing Eye and the Speaking Tongue," 190. As Eugene O'Brien suggests, this point-of-view *in extremis* can be seen to permit a view from within culture (Spinoza's view *sub specie durationis*) as well as the view of eternity (*sub specie aeternitatis*). O'Brien, "The Place of Writing," 55–9. See Spinoza, *Ethics*, 85.

159 Heaney, *District and Circle*, 3–4.

160 Vendler, *Seamus Heaney*, 138.

161 Heaney, *Seeing Things*, 61, 60.

162 Ferguson, *Wordsworth: Language as Counter-Spirit*, xiv.

163 Heaney, *Seeing Things*, 16.

164 See Docherty, *Alterities*, 33–4.

165 Heaney, *Seeing Things*, 18.

166 Salvesen, *The Landscape of Memory*, 35–6.

167 Heaney, *Seeing Things*, 18.

Notes to pages 183–7

168 Muir, *Collected Poems*, 61; MacLean, *Caoir Gheal Leumraich*, 230–5.

169 Heaney, *Seeing Things*, 18.

170 Heaney, *The Spirit Level*, 62.

171 Heaney, *Seeing Things*, 22.

172 Ibid.

173 Heaney, *District and Circle*, 15.

174 Heaney, *Seeing Things*, 104, italics in original. Heaney and Ted Hughes include Vaughan's "They Are All Gone into the World of Light" in Heaney and Hughes, *The School Bag*, 519.

175 Heaney, *Seeing Things*, 104.

176 Ibid.

177 Ibid., 17.

178 Corcoran, *The Poetry of Seamus Heaney*, 173–4.

179 O'Brien, *Searches for Answers*, 23, 68. "Field of force" is a translation of Theodor Adorno's "Kraftfeldt."

180 Heaney, *Seeing Things*, 16, 31, 32, 47.

181 Ibid., 28–9.

182 Heaney, *The Government of the Tongue*, 108.

183 Heaney, *The Cure at Troy*, 77; Heaney, *Finders Keepers*, 47. See O'Brien, *Searches for Answers*, 52.

184 Heaney, *The Government of the Tongue*, 94. Heaney is discussing Robert Frost's "The Figure a Poem Makes," in which he claims that "No one can really hold that the ecstasy should be static and stand still in one place": Frost, *The Collected Prose of Robert Frost*, 132.

185 Heaney, *The Government of the Tongue*, 108.

186 Ibid., 121.

187 Murphy, *The Annals of Clonmacnoise*, 118. The appearance of these ships may in some way be connected to the snow of "wonderfull Greatness that there was in no man's memory such seen" that fell this year and killed most of the cattle.

188 Heaney, *Seeing Things*, 62.

189 Ibid.

190 Heaney, "Further Language," 12–13.

191 Frost, *The Poetry of Robert Frost*, 121–3. Heaney uses the image of the overflowing cup in "Burns' Art Speech" and "Muldoon's *The Annals of Chile*": Heaney, *Finders Keepers*, 356, 395. It is similar to another image Heaney adopts from Frost's work, that of the poem as an ice cube "riding on its own melting" in "The Figure a Poem Makes"; Heaney reworks this in "The Rescue" where the poet "came to / Like water in a dream of thaw": Heaney, *Seeing Things*, 45.

290 Notes to pages 187–90

192 Heaney, *Seeing Things*, 42.
193 Ibid., 80.
194 Yeats, *Collected Poems*, 225.
195 Daniel Albright in Yeats, *The Poems*, 643n12. See also Beer, *Wordsworth in Time*, 60. The idea of an epiphany that is characterized by rising (rather than gushing) waters is suggested in the later poem "In Iowa," which ends with "the slush and rush and hiss / Not of parted but as of rising waters"; the slightly intrusive "as" introduces the epiphanic distance into the image: Heaney, *District and Circle*, 52.
196 Heaney, *Seeing Things*, 13.
197 Ibid.
198 Coleridge, *Shakespearean Criticism*, II, 103. See Heaney's lecture "The Frontiers of Writing" where he says of his Oxford Lectures that he "wanted to affirm that within our individual selves we can reconcile two orders of knowledge which we might call the practical and the poetic; to affirm also that each form of knowledge redresses the other and that the frontier between them is there for the crossing": Heaney, *The Redress of Poetry*, 203.
199 Lévinas also considers death, the Other, and works of art to be futural, or "promissory," as Heaney suggests: see Lévinas, *The Levinas Reader*, 41, 44, 139 and O'Brien, *Searches for Answers*, 37.
200 Another poem in *Electric Light*, "Ten Glosses," does, however, playfully warn against Auden's "pause for po-ethics": Heaney, *Electric Light*, 13, 55. That such "nonsensical" openness and recognition is still required is suggested by Colin Graham's recent exploration of the usefulness of Lévinas's thinking for the future of Northern Irish culture. For Graham, what might be required is an understanding of peace that is based on "the 'desire and goodness' *for* the other"; however, writing in 2017 Graham can still only hope that such an enjoyable future might only "be a matter of time, of a 'fecundity of time,' in Lévinas's terms"; it is perhaps a matter of openness forever deferred. See Graham, "The Future in Northern Irish Culture," 395, 403. Graham quotes Lévinas, *Totality and Infinity*, 306.
201 Heaney, *Seeing Things*, 31.
202 Ibid., 19.
203 Ibid., 59, 66.
204 Ibid., 107.
205 Ibid.
206 Ibid.
207 Ibid., 108.
208 Eliot, *Four Quartets*, 3.

Notes to pages 190–6

209 Heidegger, *The Concept of Time*, 14.
210 Heaney, *The Redress of Poetry*, 15, 16. The metaphor of the field of vision persists and morphs through Heaney's work: by "Out of the Bag," say, he is exploring a "precinct of vision": Heaney, *Electric Light*, 8.
211 Heaney, *Seeing Things*, 55.
212 Heaney, *The Redress of Poetry*, xiii, xviii.
213 Ibid., xviii.
214 McGann, *The Romantic Ideology*, 134.
215 I am grateful to Henry Hart for the suggestion that it is a *feeling* rather than *idea* of transcendence that is important to Heaney.
216 Eliot, *Four Quartets*, 40. Heaney used this passage to conclude a keynote address to the Annual Conference of the Ireland Funds in 1988 (Heaney, "Correspondences.") In this address Heaney stresses the both/and (instead of either/or) doubleness of Irish existence.
217 Docherty, *Alterities*, 19.
218 Corcoran, *The Poetry of Seamus Heaney*, 192. See also Murphy, *Seamus Heaney*, 93.
219 Although the IRA cessation (begun in August 1994) ended in February 1996, it resumed in July 1997 in the peace talks that would lead up to the Belfast Agreement of 1998, the terms of which still, for the moment, hold.
220 Heaney, *The Spirit Level*, 4.
221 Ibid.
222 Ibid., 69. Murphy, *Seamus Heaney*, 103.
223 Heaney, *The Redress of Poetry*, 187.
224 Heaney, *The Spirit Level*, 6.
225 It is possible, at a stretch, to see the rye crop waving beside the ruins as refiguring another nationalist refrain, Robert Dwyer Joyce's 1861 song about the 1798 rebellion, "The Wind that Shakes the Barley": Joyce, *Ballads, Romances, and Songs*, 252–4.
226 Heaney, "The Regional Forecast," 19. This lecture was originally delivered at an academic conference in Aberdeen in 1986, but not published until 1989.
227 Heaney and Miller, *Seamus Heaney in Conversation with Karl Miller*, 28.
228 Heaney, *The Spirit Level*, 4.
229 Ibid., 6.
230 Ibid., 37.
231 Ibid.
232 Wordsworth, *The Prelude*, 1805: II, 377–81; Heaney, "Introduction to Essential Wordsworth," vii.
233 Heaney, *The Redress of Poetry*, 2.

292   Notes to pages 196–202

234 Ibid., 9.
235 Heaney, *The Spirit Level*, 47.
236 Ibid. In "Lupins" in *Electric Light*, being there "for good" metamorphoses into the flowers that are "there / for sure. Sure and unbending"; the lupins, like the "Mint" in *The Spirit Level*, are a symbol of persistence; they "stood for something. Just by standing": Heaney, *Electric Light*, 5.
237 Murphy, *Seamus Heaney*, 98.
238 Weil, *Gravity and Grace*, 2–3, 151. Heaney, *The Redress of Poetry*, 3.
239 Heaney, *The Spirit Level*, 17.
240 Ibid.
241 Ibid., 30.
242 Ibid., 17. See Yeats, *Oxford Book of Modern Verse, 1892–1935*, xxxiv.
243 Heaney, *The Spirit Level*, 18.
244 Ibid.
245 Ibid., 19.
246 Ibid., 40. This image will later be reshaped in "The Real Names": "Airiness from the start, / Me on top of the byre, seeing things": Heaney, *Electric Light*, 46.

CHAPTER FIVE

1 O'Driscoll, *Stepping Stones*, 95.
2 Ibid., 94.
3 Vendler, *Seamus Heaney*, 158.
4 Wordsworth, *Poems in Two Volumes*, 276–7.
5 Heaney, *The Spirit Level*, 6.
6 Heaney, *Electric Light*, 70.
7 Ibid., 70–1.
8 Heaney, *Spelling It Out*, 13.
9 Heaney, *Electric Light*, 4.
10 Heaney, *Spelling It Out*, 13.
11 Heaney and Miller, *Seamus Heaney in Conversation with Karl Miller*, 36. This was not the first time Heaney had pushed against his secular schooling in this way. As Neil Corcoran notes, in leaving Queen's University Belfast to go to Carysfort Teacher Training College and supplying an article called "The Poet as a Christian" in 1978 to an Irish Catholic theological journal, Heaney was "visibly and publicly assuming, in a time of crisis, positions against which Joyce had uttered, through his autobiographical self-representation Stephen Dedalus, his *non serviam* sixty years earlier": Corcoran, *Poets of Modern Ireland*, 116.

Notes to pages 203–8 293

12 Heaney, *Finders Keepers*, 70. This was originally delivered as the Inaugural Darcy O'Brien Memorial Lecture at the University of Tulsa.

13 Heaney, "Heaney on the Haw Lantern," 12.

14 Brandes, "Seamus Heaney: An Interview," 11; Heaney, "Review of 'A Fugitive from Utopia,'" 2.

15 Wordsworth and Coleridge, *Lyrical Ballads*, 301.

16 Heaney, *Finders Keepers*, 69.

17 Heaney, *Crediting Poetry*, 19.

18 Heaney, *Finders Keepers*, 68.

19 Ibid., 69.

20 Heaney, *The Redress of Poetry*, 24.

21 Ibid., 185. Heaney is here responding to Samuel Johnson's suggestion in *Rasselas* that "Human life is everywhere a state in which much is to be endured, and little to be enjoyed": Johnson, *Selected Writings*, 217. A celebration of endurance and persistence had been a feature of his prose for much longer, however: see Heaney, *Preoccupations*, 159.

22 Heaney, *Crediting Poetry*, 15–16, 27.

23 Heaney, *The Redress of Poetry*, 143.

24 Freud, *The Freud Reader*, 625.

25 Heaney, *The Redress of Poetry*, 158.

26 Letter to John Taylor, 27 February 1818: Keats, *The Letters of John Keats*, 238.

27 Heaney, *The Redress of Poetry*, 83.

28 Ibid., 36–7.

29 Heaney, introduction, *Essential Wordsworth*, viii.

30 Thomas, *Talking with Poets*, 53–4.

31 Ibid., 53, 52.

32 Ibid., 54, emphasis in original. Such "extraness" also finds explicit expression in Heaney's poetry in his description of "the gypsies" in the prose poem "The Tall Dames": "Every time they landed in the district, there was an extra-ness in the air, as if a gate had been left open in the usual life, as if something might get in or get out": Heaney, *District and Circle*, 38–9.

33 Thomas, *Talking with Poets*, 53.

34 Ibid., 54–5.

35 Heaney, "Words of Advice for Graduates on the Threshold of the Millennium," A11.

36 Merleau-Ponty, *The Merleau-Ponty Aesthetics Reader*, 66. Merleau-Ponty is discussing the paintings of Cézanne.

37 Heaney, *Seeing Things*, 29.

38 Heaney, *Electric Light*, 51.

39 Longley, *Poetry & Posterity*, 104.

40 Heaney, "Fisher," 11. It could be seen, in modified form, in the echoing rhymes of "Personal Helicon" and the suggestion in "The Plantation" that "You had to come back / To learn how to lose yourself": Heaney, *Death of a Naturalist*, 46; Heaney, *Door into the Dark*, 38–9.

41 Heaney, *Crediting Poetry*, 11.

42 Quinn, *My Education*, 175–6; Longley, *Poetry & Posterity*, 104.

43 Heaney, *The Haw Lantern*, 3.

44 Boym, *The Future of Nostalgia*, 16.

45 Heaney, "Fretwork," 24. This article is published in various places, with minor changes: see also, for example, Heaney, "The Drag of the Golden Chain."

46 Schiller, "On Naïve and Sentimental Poetry," 191; Heaney, "Further Language," 10. The lecture was first delivered at Queen's University Belfast in 1995.

47 Heaney, *North*, 46.

48 Heaney, "Further Language," 10; Buckley, *Cutting Green Hay*, 28.

49 Brown, *In the Chair*, 76.

50 To some extent, Heaney pre-empts Bruno Latour's thinking: for Latour, "We do have a future and a past, but the future takes the form of a circle expanding in all directions, and the past is not surpassed but revisited, repeated, surrounded, protected, recombined, reinterpreted and reshuffled"; as such, our experiences are "polytemporal": Latour, *We Have Never Been Modern*, 75.

51 Heaney, *Electric Light*, 57.

52 Brown, *In the Chair*, 79.

53 Ibid., 83.

54 Ibid., 77.

55 Heaney, "Bags of Enlightenment," B6. In their discussion on the composition of *The School Bag* it is clear that Heaney and Hughes shared the opinion that Wordsworth was "truly great": letter of 20 January 1990 in Hughes, *Letters of Ted Hughes*, 574.

56 This was originally delivered at the Prince of Wales's Summer School, Norwich in July 2003 and subsequently published in the *Guardian*.

57 Heaney and Hughes, *The Rattle Bag*, 19; Heaney, "Bags of Enlightenment," B4.

58 Heaney, "Bags of Enlightenment," B4.

59 Ibid., B5.

60 Ibid., B4.

61 Ibid.

62 Freud, *The Freud Reader*, 625.

63 Heaney, Foreword, *Childhood and Its Discontents*, xv.

64 Ibid., xiv.

65 Ibid.

66 Ibid., xiv–xv.

67 Ibid., xv.

68 This was first delivered as the Jayne Lecture at the American Philosophical Society on 23 April 2004.

69 Heaney, "Title Deeds," 413; Devlin, "In Spite of Sea and Centuries," 85. See also O'Brien, *Seamus Heaney as Aesthetic Thinker*, 269–75.

70 Heaney, "Title Deeds," 419.

71 Heaney, *Electric Light*, 80–1. Heaney used this phrase, "There-you-are-where-are-you?," as the basis for a video tour of Bellaghy, on show at the Bellaghy Bawn Museum before the advent of the Seamus Heaney HomePlace. By "The Aerodrome" in *District and Circle*, Heaney was once more willing to turn this unsettling self-positioning into a "location" or "stance": "If self is a location, so is love: / Bearings taken, markings, cardinal points, / Options, obstinacies, dug heels and distance, / Here and there and now and then, a stance": Heaney, *District and Circle*, 12.

72 Murray Pittock cites an unpublished intervention by Ian Duncan at the "Scottish Romanticism in World Literature" conference, at the University of California at Berkeley, 9 September 2006 for the phrase "chronotopic sedimentation": see Pittock, *Scottish and Irish Romanticism*, 213.

73 Heaney, *Electric Light*, 3.

74 See Heaney, "At Toomebridge."

75 Heaney, *Beowulf*, ix.

76 Heaney and Miller, *Seamus Heaney in Conversation with Karl Miller*, 42.

77 See Trumpener, *Bardic Nationalism*, 11, on the cultural nationalist dimension of the 1798 rising, and also Beiner, "The Enigma of 'Roddy McCorley Goes to Die.'"

78 Heaney, *The Redress of Poetry*, 83.

79 Heaney, *Human Chain*, 28–32.

80 Heaney, "Further Language," 12.

81 Heaney, *Door into the Dark*, 35. "Slime" was particularly important for Heaney in *Death of a Naturalist* and *Door into the Dark* as an alien, horrific, and imagination-expanding substance. It was also, suggestively, rhymed with "rhyme" in "Personal Helicon": Heaney, *Death of a Naturalist*, 46.

82 Heaney, *Electric Light*, 27.

296 Notes to pages 220–5

83 Ibid., 26. Wordsworth and Coleridge, *Lyrical Ballads*, 178.
84 Heaney, *Electric Light*, 26.
85 Ibid.
86 Leopardi, *Selected Prose and Poetry*, 268–9.
87 Heaney, *Electric Light*, 6, 8.
88 Ibid., 21.
89 Ibid., 22.
90 Ibid., 38.
91 Ní Ríordáin, "Puddling at the Source," 174, 176.
92 Heaney, *Beowulf*, xxx.
93 Ibid., Mandelstam's description of Acmeism as "nostalgia for world culture" appears repeatedly in Heaney's criticism of the 1990s. See, for example, "John Clare's Prog": Heaney, *The Redress of Poetry*, 82.
94 Heaney, *Beowulf*, xxv.
95 Murphy, *Seamus Heaney*, 120; Heaney, *District and Circle*, 56.
96 Schiller, "On Naïve and Sentimental Poetry," 191; Heaney, "Further Language," 10.
97 Heaney, *Among Schoolchildren*, 12; Heaney, "Further Language," 10.
98 Examples of a four-nations or archipelagic approach to literary studies include Stafford, *Starting Lines*; Ryan, *Ireland and Scotland*; Norquay and Smyth, *Across the Margins*; McIlvanney and Ryan, *Ireland and Scotland*; Kerrigan, *Archipelagic English*; Mackay, Longley, and Brearton, *Modern Irish and Scottish Poetry*; Brannigan, *Archipelagic Modernism*. The interdisciplinary series *Belfast Studies in Language, Culture and Politics*, published by Cló Ollscoil na Banríona, and the *Journal for Irish and Scottish Studies* (published by the Research Institute for Irish and Scottish Studies at Aberdeen University) also offer important contributions to the field, as does Draper, *The Literature of Region and Nation*, in which Heaney's "The Regional Forecast" appears.
99 Heaney, "An Open Letter," 24.
100 Heaney, "The Regional Forecast," 22–3.
101 See Crotty, "Seamus Heaney and Scotland."
102 Heaney, "The Regional Forecast," 23.
103 Heaney, "The Pathos of Things," 20–1. This article, published in the *Guardian* in 2007, is an abridgement of Heaney's 2000 Lafcadio Hearn lecture; it was also included in De Angelis and Woods, *Our Shared Japan*. A similar juxtaposition of Old Irish poetry and the eclogic tradition appears in "Glanmore Eclogue": Heaney, *Electric Light*, 35–7.
104 Heaney, *The Redress of Poetry*, 200.
105 Dennison, *Seamus Heaney and the Adequacy of Poetry*, 173.173.

Notes to pages 225–32

106 Heaney, *The Spirit Level*, 28; Heaney, *Electric Light*, 54. Heaney had also earlier asked himself this in "Place, Pastness, Poems."
107 Heaney, *North*, 7.
108 Heaney, *The Spirit Level*, 28.
109 Heaney, *Crediting Poetry*, 23.
110 Heaney, *Finders Keepers*, 378–9; Kearney, *The British Isles*, 5–8.
111 Heaney, *Finders Keepers*, 366.
112 Ibid., 366, 379.
113 Longley, "Ulster Protestants and the Question of 'Culture,'" 119–20.
114 Kearney, *The British Isles*, 7–8.
115 Norquay and Smyth, *Across the Margins*, 7.
116 Randolph, *Close to the Next Moment*, 202.
117 This was later published as an article in the *Guardian*: Heaney, "The Heart of a Vanished World."
118 Heaney, introduction, *The People of the Sea*, xv, xiii.
119 Heaney, *Finders Keepers*, 252.
120 Heaney, introduction, *The People of the Sea*, xiv.
121 Ibid., xi.
122 O'Driscoll, *Stepping Stones*, 251.
123 Heaney, "The Trance and the Translation," 4. This was first delivered at the Edinburgh Book Festival in 2002, as the inaugural Sorley MacLean Lecture.
124 Ibid., 6.
125 This was published in the *Hudson Review* in 2008 and based on a lecture delivered at the Morgan Library and Museum two years earlier.
126 Heaney, "Apt Admonishment," 19.
127 Ibid.
128 Ibid., 21.
129 Ibid., parentheses in original.
130 Ibid., 23.
131 Ibid., 26.
132 Ibid., 27.
133 Ibid., 27–8.
134 Heaney, *Seeing Things*, 22. The ability of poetry to redeem lives that are attenuated is also questioned in "The Real Names" with the bathetic exclamation "But not Bobby Sings": Heaney, *Electric Light*, 50.
135 Wordsworth, *Poems in Two Volumes*, 128. Heaney, *Seeing Things*, 22.
136 Heaney, "Apt Admonishment," 28; Heaney, *Electric Light*, 13.
137 Heaney, "Apt Admonishment," 32–3.
138 Ibid., 33.

298   Notes to pages 233–7

139 Wordsworth and Coleridge, *Lyrical Ballads*, 158.
140 Stafford, *Local Attachments*, 38. Stafford is responding to Appleton, *The Experience of Landscape*.
141 John Whale and Stephen Copley claim that "Appearing after the event, and in the wake of its literary objects, the Romantic is always already retrospective": Whale and Copley, *Beyond Romanticism*, 6. One of the tensions, however, within the Romantic is how to turn the retrospective into the prospective.
142 Wordsworth, *Poems in Two Volumes*, 1983, 275.
143 O'Driscoll, *Stepping Stones*, 304.
144 Bate, *Romantic Ecology*, 4.
145 Bornstein, *Transformations of Romanticism*, 45.
146 Shelley, *The Complete Works of Shelley*, 1:206.
147 Bornstein, *Transformations of Romanticism*, 45.
148 See Walford Davies, "Blake and Dylan Thomas," 34; Thomas, *Collected Letters*, 26.
149 Yeats, *Autobiographies*, 235.
150 Bornstein, *Transformations of Romanticism*, 46; Yeats, *Mythologies*, 342. Yeats had a torn relationship to England ("I owe my soul to Shakespeare, to Spenser and to Blake, perhaps to William Morris, and to the English language in which I think, speak and write … everything I love has come to me through English; my hatred tortures me with love, my love with hate"), yet still railed against "Wordsworth, that typical Englishman": Ramazani, *The Hybrid Muse*, 38–9; Yeats, *Later Essays*, 211.
151 Macrae, "Seamus Heaney's New Voice," 60; Corcoran, "Heaney and Yeats," 169. See also Cavanagh, *Professing Poetry*, 92.
152 Haughton, "Power and Hiding Places," 66.
153 Muldoon, *Madoc*. Southey too was fond of "prospects" and commented on his proposed Pantisocratic community in America that "No prospect in life gives me half the pleasure this visionary one affords": Southey, *The Life and Correspondence of Robert Southey*, I, 193–4; Roe, "Bringing It All Back Home," 173.
154 Heaney, introduction, *Essential Wordsworth*, xi.
155 Heaney, *The Redress of Poetry*, 120.
156 O'Driscoll, *Stepping Stones*, 391.
157 Ibid., 374, 346, 466.
158 Randolph, *Close to the Next Moment*, 203, 209.
159 O'Driscoll, *Stepping Stones*, 32.
160 Wordsworth, *Poems in Two Volumes*, 147.

Notes to pages 237–43

161 Heaney, "Holding Patterns: Arts, Letters and the Academy," 14; Wordsworth and Coleridge, *Lyrical Ballads*, 302.
162 O'Driscoll, *Stepping Stones*, 58.
163 Ibid., 404.
164 Ibid., 451–2.
165 Ibid., 366.
166 Ibid., 214.
167 Wordsworth, *Journals of Dorothy Wordsworth*, 36.
168 Heaney, *District and Circle*, 70.
169 Wordsworth, *Journals of Dorothy Wordsworth*, 36.
170 Heaney, *District and Circle*, 70. The 2005 publication of the poem in *Irish Pages* had a typographical mistake – "footballs" for "footfalls" – which spurred Edna Longley to write a punning response: Heaney, "Home Fires"; Longley, "The Lake Poets and the Beautiful Game."
171 Heaney, *District and Circle*, 70.
172 Morrissey, *Parallax*, 11.
173 Heaney, *District and Circle*, 22.
174 Heaney, *Preoccupations*, 46, quoting Wordsworth, *The Prelude*, 1850: I, 433–4; 1805, I 460–1.
175 Heaney, *District and Circle*, 22; Heaney, "Wordsworth at Grasmere."
176 Heaney, *District and Circle*, 22.
177 McAlpine, *The Poet's Mistake*, 157.
178 Heaney, *Electric Light*, 56.
179 Laird, "*Human Chain* by Seamus Heaney."
180 Heaney, *Human Chain*, 3.
181 Ibid., 13.
182 Ibid., 53, 58, 59.
183 Ibid., 18.
184 Ibid., 17.
185 Heaney, "Cutaways," 25.
186 Heaney, *Human Chain*, 16.
187 Heaney, *District and Circle*, 57.
188 Ibid., 5.
189 Wills, "Late Openings," 117, 120.
190 Heaney, *Human Chain*, 24. As Nick Laird notes, "Derek Hill was an English painter who lived at St Colomb's Rectory near Churchill in Donegal and whose visit from Greta Garbo was recently the subject of Frank McGuinness's play *Greta Garbo Came to Donegal*": Laird, "Human Chain by Seamus Heaney."

191 Heaney, *Human Chain*, 63; Heaney, "The Boule Miche of the North," 19.
192 Haughton usefully reads this collection alongside Helen Vendler's 2010 book *Last Looks, Last Books*: Haughton, "Seamus Heaney: First and Last Things."
193 Heaney, *Human Chain*, 83; Heaney, "Seamus Heaney Recalls," 7.
194 Heaney, *Human Chain*, 84.
195 Heaney, *Spelling It Out*, 13.
196 Wheatley, "Professing Poetry," 132–3. Wheatley is discussing Tim Kendall's and, especially, Peter McDonald's responses to Heaney's criticism.
197 Abrams, *Natural Supernaturalism*, 431; see Wheatley, "Professing Poetry," 132.
198 O'Driscoll, *Stepping Stones*, 475.
199 Heaney, *Human Chain*, 85.
200 Heaney, *Wintering Out*, 6; Heaney, *Human Chain*, 85.
201 Heaney, *New Selected Poems*, 218.
202 Ibid.

Works Cited

Abrams, M.H. *The Correspondent Breeze: Essays on English Romanticism.* Edited by Jack Stillinger. New York: Norton, 1984.
– *The Mirror and the Lamp: Romantic Theory and the Critical Tradition.* London:
Oxford University Press, 1979.
– *Natural Supernaturalism: Tradition and Revolution in Romantic Literature.* London: Oxford University Press, 1971.
Alcobia-Murphy, Shane. *Sympathetic Ink: Intertextual Relations in Northern Irish Poetry.* Liverpool: Liverpool University Press, 2006.
Alighieri, Dante. *Inferno: A New Verse Translation, Backgrounds and Contexts, Criticism.* Translated by Michael Palma. New York: W.W. Norton, 2008.
Allen, Michael, ed. *Seamus Heaney: Contemporary Critical Essays.* Basingstoke, Hampshire: Macmillan, 1997.
Allen, Nicholas. "Seamus Heaney and Water." *Irish Review* 49/50 (Winter/ Spring 2014/2015): 173–82.
Allison, Jonathan. "'Friendship's Garland' and the Manuscripts of Seamus Heaney's 'Fosterage.'" In Irish Writing since 1950, special issue, *The Yearbook of English Studies* 35, (2005): 58–71.
– "Seamus Heaney and the Romantic Image." *Sewanee Review* 106, no. 2 (Spring 1998): 184–201.
Andrews, Elmer. *The Poetry of Seamus Heaney: All the Realms of Whisper.* Basingstoke: Macmillan, 1988.
– "The Spirit's Progress." In *Seamus Heaney: A Collection of Critical Essays,* edited by Elmer Andrews, 208–32. Basingstoke: Macmillan, 1993.
– ed. *Seamus Heaney: A Collection of Critical Essays.* Basingstoke: Macmillan, 1993.

Appleton, Jay. *The Experience of Landscape*. London; New York: Wiley, 1975.

Armitage, Simon. *Seeing Stars*. London: Faber & Faber, 2010.

Arnold, Matthew. *Essays on English Literature*. London: University of London Press, 1965.

Auden, W.H. *Collected Poems*. Edited by Edward Mendelson. London: Faber, 2004.

Auge, Andrew J. *A Chastened Communion: Modern Irish Poetry and Catholicism*. 1st ed. Irish Studies. Syracuse: Syracuse University Press, 2013.

Bacon, Francis. *The Advancement of Learning and New Atlantis*. Edited by Arthur Johnston. Repr. Oxford: Clarendon Press, 1980.

Bate, Jonathan. "Department of One." *Prospect Magazine*, June 2011. http://www.prospectmagazine.co.uk/arts-and-books/jonathan-bate-harold-bloom-review-anatomy-of-influence.

– *Romantic Ecology: Wordsworth and the Environmental Tradition*. London; New York: Routledge, 1991.

– *Shakespeare and the English Romantic Imagination*. Oxford: Clarendon Press, 1992.

– *The Song of the Earth*. London: Picador, 2000.

Bate, Walter Jackson. *The Burden of the Past and the English Poet*. New York: Norton, 1972.

– *John Keats*. Cambridge: Belknap Press of Harvard University Press, 1963.

Batten, Guinn. "Heaney's Wordsworth and the Poetics of Displacement." In O'Donoghue, *The Cambridge Companion to Seamus Heaney*, 178–91.

Beckett, Samuel. *Waiting for Godot: A Tragicomedy in Two Acts*. London: Faber & Faber, 2006.

Beer, John B. "Coleridge and Wordsworth: Influence and Confluence." In *New Approaches to Coleridge: Biographical and Critical Essays*, edited by Donald Sultana, 191–211. Critical Studies Series. London: Vision Press, 1981.

– *Wordsworth in Time*. London; Boston: Faber & Faber, 1979.

Begley, Monie. *Rambles in Ireland and a County-by-County Guide for Discriminating Travelers*. Old Greenwich, CT: Devin-Adair Co., 1977.

Beiner, Guy. "The Enigma of 'Roddy McCorley Goes to Die': Forgetting and Remembering a Local Rebel Hero in Ulster." In *Rhythms of Revolt: European Traditions and Memories of Social Conflict in Oral Culture*, edited by Eva Guillorel, David M. Hopkin, and William Pooley, 327–57. Abingdon; New York: Routledge, 2018.

Works Cited

Bell, Andrew. *An Experiment in Education, Made at the Male Asylum of Madras*. London and Edinburgh: Cadell and Davies; and W. Creech, 1797.

Berman, David. "Knock: Some New Evidence." *The British and Irish Skeptic* 1, no. 1 (January–February 1987), 9.

Bhabha, Homi K. *The Location of Culture*. Routledge Classics. London; New York: Routledge, 2004.

Bielik-Robson, Agata. *The Saving Lie: Harold Bloom and Deconstruction*. Evanston: Northwestern University Press, 2011.

Bizot, Richard. "Mastering the Colonizer's Tongue: Yeats, Joyce and Their Successors in Their Irish Schoolroom." *Studies in the Literary Imagination* 30, no. 2 (Fall 1997): 63–6.

Blanchot, Maurice. *The Space of Literature*. Translated by Ann Smock. Lincoln; London: University of Nebraska Press, 2010.

Bloom, Harold. *The Anatomy of Influence: Literature as a Way of Life*. New Haven: Yale University Press, 2011.

– *The Anxiety of Influence: A Theory of Poetry*. 2nd ed. New York: Oxford University Press, 1997.

– *A Map of Misreading*. 2nd ed. New York: Oxford University Press, 2003.

Bornstein, George. *Transformations of Romanticism in Yeats, Eliot, and Stevens*. Chicago: University of Chicago Press, 1976.

Boym, Svetlana. *The Future of Nostalgia*. New York: Basic Books, 2001.

Boyson, Rowan. *Wordsworth and the Enlightenment Idea of Pleasure*. Cambridge; New York: Cambridge University Press, 2012.

Braidwood, John. *The Ulster Dialect Lexicon: An Inaugural Lecture Delivered before the Queen's University of Belfast on 23 April 1969*. Belfast: Queen's University of Belfast, 1975.

Brandes, Rand. "Seamus Heaney: An Interview." *Salmagundi* 80 (Fall 1988): 4–21.

– "Seamus Heaney's Working Titles: From 'Advancements of Learning' to 'Midnight Anvil.'" In O'Donoghue, *The Cambridge Companion to Seamus Heaney*, 19–36.

– and Michael J. Durkan. *Seamus Heaney: A Bibliography 1959–2003*. London: Faber & Faber, 2008.

Brannigan, John. *Archipelagic Modernism: Literature in the Irish and British Isles, 1890–1970*. Edinburgh: Edinburgh University Press, 2015.

Brearton, Fran. "For Father Read Mother: Muldoon's Antecedents." In *Paul Muldoon: Critical Essays*, edited by Tim Kendall and Peter McDonald, 45–61. Liverpool: Liverpool University Press, 2004.

304   Works Cited

– *The Great War in Irish Poetry: W.B. Yeats to Michael Longley*. Oxford; New York: Oxford University Press, 2000.
– "Heaney and the Feminine." In O'Donoghue, *The Cambridge Companion to Seamus Heaney*, 73–91.
– Michael Allen, and Eamonn Hughes, eds. *Last before America: Irish and American Writing*. Belfast: Blackstaff, 2001.
Brown, John. *In the Chair: Interviews with Poets from the North of Ireland*. Cliffs of Moher, County Clare, Ireland: Salmon, 2002.
Brown, Terence. "Joyce's Magic Lantern." *James Joyce Quarterly* 28, no. 4 (1991): 791–9.
– "The Witnessing Eye and the Speaking Tongue." In Andrews, *Seamus Heaney: Collection of Critical Essays*, 182–92.
Browning, Robert. *The Poems*. Edited by John Pettigrew and Thomas J. Collins. Vol. 1. 2 vols. Harmondsworth: Penguin, 1981.
Brownlee, Marina S. "The Untranscendent Vision." In The Philology of the Couple, Supplement No. 1, *French Forum* 14, (December 1989): 475–85.
Buckley, Vincent. *Cutting Green Hay: Friendships, Movements and Cultural Conflicts in Australia's Great Decades*. Melbourne: Allen Lane / Penguin, 1983.
Burnside, John, and Marco Fazzini. "John Burnside in Conversation with Marco Fazzini." *Il Tolomeo* 1, no. 8 (2008), 95–8.
Burris, Sidney. *The Poetry of Resistance: Seamus Heaney and the Pastoral Tradition*. Athens: Ohio University Press, 1990.
Butler, James A. "Poetry 1798–1807: Lyrical Ballads and Poems, in Two Volumes." In *The Cambridge Companion to Wordsworth*, edited by Stephen Charles Gill, 38–54. Cambridge; New York: Cambridge University Press, 2003.
Butler, Marilyn. "Repossessing the Past." In *Rethinking Historicism: Critical Readings in Romantic History*, edited by Marjorie Levinson, 64–84. Oxford: Blackwell, 1989.
Buxton, Rachel. *Robert Frost and Northern Irish Poetry*. Oxford; New York: Clarendon Press; Oxford University Press, 2004.
Carpenter, Paul. "Mimesis, Memory, and the Magic Lantern: What Did the Knock Witnesses See?" *New Hibernia Review / Iris Éireannach Nua* 15, no. 2 (Summer 2011): 102–20.
Carson, Ciarán. *The Star Factory*. London: Granta Books, 1998.
Cavanagh, Michael. *Professing Poetry: Seamus Heaney's Poetics*. Washington: Catholic University of America Press, 2010.
Chatterton, Thomas. *The Complete Works of Thomas Chatterton: A*

Bicentenary Edition. Edited by Donald S. Taylor. Vol. 1. 2 vols. Oxford: Clarendon Press, 2014.

Clutterbuck, Catriona. "'Pilot and Stray in One': Sustaining Nothingness in the Travel Poems of Early Heaney." *Irish Review* 49/50 (2014/2015): 106–21.

Cole, Henri. "The Art of Poetry, No.75." *Paris Review* 144 (Fall 1997): 88–138.

Coleridge, Samuel Taylor. *Samuel Taylor Coleridge: The Major Works*. Edited by H.J. Jackson. Oxford World's Classics. Oxford; New York: Oxford University Press, 2008.

– *Shakespearean Criticism*. Edited by Thomas Middleton Raysor. 2 vols. Everyman's Library. London: Dent, 1960.

Collins, Floyd. *Seamus Heaney: The Crisis of Identity*. Newark: London: University of Delaware Press; Associated University Presses, 2003.

Cook, Eleanor. *Against Coercion: Games Poets Play*. Stanford: Stanford University Press, 1998.

Cooke, Harriet. "Harriet Cooke Talked to the Poet Seamus Heaney." *Irish Times*, 28 December 1973, 8.

Corcoran, Neil. "Heaney and Yeats." In O'Donoghue, *The Cambridge Companion to Seamus Heaney*, 165–77.

– "The Melt of the Real Thing." *Irish Review* 49/50 (Winter/Spring 2014/2015): 5–18.

– *The Poetry of Seamus Heaney: A Critical Study*. London: Faber & Faber, 1998.

– *Poets of Modern Ireland: Text, Context, Intertext*. Cardiff: University of Wales Press, 1999.

– *Seamus Heaney*. Faber Student Guides. London; Boston: Faber & Faber, 1986.

Corkery, Daniel. *Synge and Anglo-Irish Literature: A Study*. Cork: Cork University Press, 1931.

Coughlan, Patricia. "'Bog Queens': The Representation of Women in the Poetry of John Montague and Seamus Heaney." In Allen, *Seamus Heaney: Contemporary Critical Essays*, 185–205.

Craft, Maurice. "Education for Diversity." In *Education and Cultural Pluralism*, 5–26. Milton: Taylor and Francis, 2017.

Crotty, Patrick. "The Context of Heaney's Reception." In O'Donoghue, *The Cambridge Companion to Seamus Heaney*, 37–55.

– "Seamus Heaney and Scotland." In *Seamus Heaney in Context*, edited by Geraldine Higgins. Cambridge University Press, forthcoming.

Crowder, Ashby Bland. "Seamus Heaney's Revisions for 'Death of a Naturalist.'" *New Hibernia Review / Iris Éireannach Nua* 19, no. 2 (Summer/Samhreadh 2015): 94–112.

Cuda, Anthony J. "The Use of Memory: Seamus Heaney, T.S. Eliot, and the Unpublished Epigraph to 'North.'" *Journal of Modern Literature* 28, no. 4 (2005): 152–75.

Davis, Dick. "Door into the Dark." In *The Art of Seamus Heaney*, edited by Tony Curtis, 27–36. Brigend, Mid Glamorgan: Seren, 2001.

Day, Gary. *Re-reading Leavis: Culture and Literary Criticism*. New York: St. Martin's Press, 1996.

Deane, Seamus. "The Famous Seamus." *New Yorker*, 20 March 2000, 54.

– *The French Revolution and Enlightenment in England, 1789–1832*. Cambridge: Harvard University Press, 1988.

– "Powers of Earth and Visions of Air." *Times Literary Supplement*, 16 March 1990, 275–6.

– *Strange Country: Modernity and Nationhood in Irish Writing since 1790*. Clarendon Lectures in English Literature 1995. Oxford: Clarendon Press, 1998.

De Angelis, Irene, and Joseph Woods, eds. *Our Shared Japan: An Anthology of Contemporary Irish Poetry*. Dublin: Dedalus Press, 2007.

De Man, Paul. *The Rhetoric of Romanticism*. New York: Columbia University Press, 1984.

Dennison, John. *Seamus Heaney and the Adequacy of Poetry*. Oxford: Oxford University Press, 2015.

Dentith, Simon. "Heaney and Walcott: Two Poems." *Critical Survey* 11, no. 3 (1999): 92–9.

Desmond, John F. *Gravity and Grace: Seamus Heaney and the Force of Light*. Studies in Christianity and Literature 2. Waco: Baylor University Press, 2009.

Devlin, Brendan. "In Spite of Sea and Centuries: An Irish Gael Looks at the Poetry of Sorley Maclean." In *Sorley Maclean: Critical Essays*, edited by Raymond J. Ross and Joy Hendry, 81–90. Edinburgh: Scottish Academic Press, 1986.

Docherty, Thomas. *Alterities: Criticism, History, Representation*. Oxford; New York: Clarendon Press, 1996.

Draper, Ronald P., ed. *The Literature of Region and Nation*. Houndsmills, Basingstoke, Hampshire: Palgrave Macmillan, 1989.

Duggan, Paul E. "Lessons from Our Lady of Knock." *The Priest*, August 1999, 17–20.

Editorial. "Education and Community." *Education Times*, 26 April 1973, 6.

Works Cited

Egan, Desmond, and Michael Hartnett, eds. *Choice: An Anthology of Irish Poetry Selected by the Poets Themselves with a Comment on Their Choice*. Dublin: The Goldsmith Press, 1973.

– and Gerard Rice, eds. *Poiemata: Readings in Poetry and Prose for Young People*. Dublin: Fallon, 1972.

Eilenberg, Susan. *Strange Power of Speech: Wordsworth, Coleridge, and Literary Possession*. New York: Oxford University Press, 1992.

Eliot, T.S. *The Complete Poems and Plays*. London: Faber & Faber, 2004.

– *Four Quartets*. London: Faber & Faber, 2001.

– "Professional, Or." *The Egoist* 5, no. 4 (April 1918): 61.

– *Selected Prose of T.S. Eliot*. London: Faber & Faber, 1975.

– *The Three Voices of Poetry*. London: Cambridge University Press (for the National Book League), 1953.

– *The Use of Poetry and the Use of Criticism*. London and Cambridge, MA: Faber, 1933.

Ellis, David. *Wordsworth, Freud, and the Spots of Time: Interpretation in The Prelude*. Cambridge; New York: Cambridge University Press, 1985.

Fazzini, Marco. "Kenneth White and John Burnside." In *The Edinburgh Companion to Contemporary Scottish Poetry*, edited by Matt McGuire and Colin Nicholson, 111–25. Edinburgh: Edinburgh University Press, 2009.

Ferguson, Frances. *Wordsworth: Language as Counter-Spirit*. New Haven: Yale University Press, 1977.

Ferguson, Samuel. *The Poems of Samuel Ferguson*. Edited by Alfred Perceval Graves. Dublin: Talbot Press, 1916.

Flynn, Leontia. "Radically Necessary: Heaney's Defence of Poetry." *Irish Review* 49/50, (Winter/Spring 2014): 208–18.

Foster, John Wilson. *The Achievement of Seamus Heaney*. Dublin: The Lilliput Press, 1995.

– "Crediting Marvels: Heaney after 50." In O'Donoghue, *The Cambridge Companion to Seamus Heaney*, 206–23.

– "The Poetry of Seamus Heaney [Wintering Out]." In Garratt, *Critical Essays on Seamus Heaney*, 25–38.

Foster, Thomas C. *Seamus Heaney*. Dublin: O'Brien, 1989.

Freud, Sigmund. *The Freud Reader*. Edited by Peter Gay. London: Vintage, 1995.

Frost, Robert. *The Collected Prose of Robert Frost*. Edited by Mark Richardson. Cambridge: Belknap Press of Harvard University Press, 2009.

– *The Poetry of Robert Frost: The Collected Poems*. Edited by Edward Connery Lathem. New York: Henry Holt, 1979.

Works Cited

Frye, Northrop. "The Drunken Boat: The Revolutionary Element in Romanticism." In *Romanticism Reconsidered: Selected Papers from the English Institute*, edited by Northrop Frye, 1–25. New York: Columbia University Press, 1963.

– *A Study of English Romanticism*. New York: Random House, 1968.

Garratt, Robert F., ed. *Critical Essays on Seamus Heaney*. New York; London: G.K. Hall; Prentice Hall International, 1995.

Gifford, Don. *Ulysses Annotated: Notes for James Joyce's* Ulysses. 2nd ed., revised and enlarged, 20th anniversary ed. Berkeley: University of California Press, 2008.

Gilbert, Sandra M., and Susan Gubar. *The Madwoman in the Attic: The Woman Writer and the Nineteenth-Century Literary Imagination*. 2nd ed. New Haven: Yale University Press, 2000.

Gillis, Alan A. "The Modern Irish Sonnet." In *The Oxford Handbook of Modern Irish Poetry*, edited by Fran Brearton and Alan A. Gillis, 567–87. Oxford: Oxford University Press, 2012.

Goodby, John, ed. *Irish Studies: The Essential Glossary*. London; New York: Arnold; Distributed in the United States of America by Oxford University Press, 2003.

Gottfried, Leon. *Matthew Arnold and the Romantics*. London: Routledge & Kegan Paul, 1963.

Graham, Colin. "Foreword: 'Crumpled Metal' and 'A Gift of a Melon': The Future in Northern Irish Culture." In Northern Irish Writing, Supplement, *Irish University Review* 49 (2017): 395–404.

Gwynn, E.J. "Fosterage." In *Encyclopaedia of Religion and Ethics*, 6:104–9. Edinburgh: T&T Clark, 1913.

Haffenden, John, ed. *Viewpoints: Poets in Conversation with John Haffenden*. London; Boston: Faber & Faber, 1981.

Hall, Stuart. "Cultural Identity and Diaspora." In *Contemporary Postcolonial Theory: A Reader*, edited by Padmini Mongia, 110–21. London; New York: Bloomsbury Academic, 1996.

Hamilton, Paul. "From Sublimity to Indeterminacy: New World Order or Aftermath of Romantic Ideology." In *Romanticism and Postmodernism*, edited by Edward Larrissy, 13–28. Cambridge; New York: Cambridge University Press, 1999.

Hardiman, J., ed. "A Statute Enacted in Kilkenny, A.D. 1367," Vol. 2. Dublin: Irish Archaeological Society, 1843.

Harrison, Gary Lee. *Wordsworth's Vagrant Muse: Poetry, Poverty, and Power*. Detroit: Wayne State University Press, 1994.

Works Cited

Hart, Henry. *Seamus Heaney, Poet of Contrary Progressions*. Irish Studies. Syracuse: Syracuse University Press, 1992.
– "What Is Heaney Seeing in *Seeing Things?*" *Colby Quarterly* 30, no. 1 (1994): 32–42.
Hartman, Geoffrey H. *Beyond Formalism: Literary Essays 1958–1970*. New Haven: Yale University Press, 1975.
– "Nature and the Humanization of the Self in Wordsworth." In *English Romantic Poets: Modern Essays in Criticism*, edited by M.H. Abrams, 2nd ed., 123–32. Oxford: Oxford University Press, 1975.
– "On Traumatic Knowledge and Literary Studies." *New Literary History* 26, no. 3 (1995): 537–63.
– *Wordsworth's Poetry, 1787–1814*. New Haven: Yale University Press, 1964.
The Harvard Crimson. "Getting Along Seamus-ly." 10 October 2002. https://www.thecrimson.com/article/2002/10/10/getting-along-seamus-ly-ralph-waldo-emerson/?print=1.
Haughton, Hugh. "The Irish Poet as Critic." In *The Oxford Handbook of Modern Irish Poetry*, edited by Fran Brearton and Alan A. Gillis, 513–33. Oxford: Oxford University Press, 2012.
– "'Power and Hiding Places': Wordsworth and Seamus Heaney." In *The Monstrous Debt: Modalities of Romantic Influence in Twentieth-Century Literature*, edited by Damian Walford Davies and Richard Marggraf Turley, 61–100. Detroit: Wayne State University Press, 2006.
– "Seamus Heaney: First and Last Things." *Irish Review* 49/50 (Winter/Spring 2014/ 2015): 194–207.
Heaney, Seamus. "Adroitest of Makers." *Education Times*, 6 February 1975, 17.
– "An Advancement of Learning." *Irish Times*, 9 March 1963, 8.
– *Among Schoolchildren: A John Malone Memorial Lecture*. Belfast: Queen's University, 1983
– "'Apt Admonishment': Wordsworth as an Example." *Hudson Review* 61, no. 1 (Spring 2008): 19–33.
– "At Toomebridge." *Thumbscrew* 11 (Autumn 1998): 3.
– "Autobiographical Borings." *Irish Times*, 8 July 1975, supplement: 1.
– "Bachelor Deceased." *Honest Ulsterman* 2 (June 1968): 5.
– "Bags of Enlightenment." *Guardian*, 25 October 2003, sec. B.
– *Beowulf: A Translation*. London: Faber & Faber, 1999.
– "The Boule Miche of the North." *Fortnight* 207 (September 1984): 18–21.

- "Confessions and Histories." *Outposts*, 1965, 21–4.
- "Cool and Complex Weaving of Myth and Language." *Education Times*, 16 May 1975, 12.
- "Correspondences: Emigrants & Inner Exiles." In *Migrations: The Irish at Home & Abroad*, edited by Richard Kearney, 21–31. Dublin: Wolfhound Press, 1990.
- *Crediting Poetry: The Nobel Lecture*. 1st ed. New York: Farrar, Straus & Giroux, 1996.
- *The Cure at Troy: Sophocles' Philoctetes*. London: Faber & Faber, 2017.
- "Current Unstated Assumptions about Poetry." *Critical Inquiry* 7, no. 4 (1981): 645–51.
- "Cutaways." *Irish Pages* 4, no. 1 (2007): 24–5.
- *Death of a Naturalist*. London: Faber & Faber, 1966.
- *District and Circle*. London: Faber & Faber, 2006.
- *Door into the Dark*. London: Faber & Faber, 1969.
- "The Door Stands Open." In Miłosz, *Selected and Last Poems, 1931–2004*, xiii–xvi. London: Penguin, 2014.
- "The Drag of the Golden Chain." *Times Literary Supplement*, 12 November 1999, 14–16.
- "Earning a Rhyme." *Poetry Ireland Review* 25 (1989): 95–100.
- Editor's Note. *Soundings '72: An Annual Anthology of New Irish Poetry*, 5–6. Belfast: Blackstaff Press, 1972.
- Editor's Note. *Soundings 2: An Annual Anthology of New Irish Poetry*, 5–6. Belfast: Blackstaff Press, 1974.
- "Educating the Epsilons." *Hibernia* (September 1964): 10–11.
- *Electric Light*. London: Faber & Faber, 2001.
- "Envies and Identifications: Dante and the Modern Poet." *Irish University Review*, 1985, 5–19.
- "Evangelists." *New Statesman*, 9 July 1965, 54–5.
- "An Evening at Killard," *The Irish Press*, 29 November 1969, 19.
- "Explorations 2: Call My Brother Back," 12 January 1978. MSS 960, Box 99, FF 12. Seamus Heaney papers, Stuart A. Rose Manuscript, Archives, and Rare Book Library, Emory University.
- "Explorations: Bitter Honey," c 1973. MSS 960, Box 99, FF 5. Seamus Heaney papers, Stuart A. Rose Manuscript, Archives, and Rare Book Library, Emory University.
- *Field Work*. London; Boston: Faber & Faber, 1979.
- "Field Work Manuscripts." Manuscript and typescript drafts of poems taken from a folder marked "Field Work." National Library of Ireland.

Works Cited

Department of Manuscripts., n.d. MS 49,493/51. Seamus Heaney Literary Papers, 1963–2010.

– *Finders Keepers: Selected Prose 1971–2001*. London: Faber & Faber, 2002.
– "Fisher." *Irish Times*, 8 February 1964, 11.
– "Five Derry Glosses." In *32 Counties: Photographs of Ireland*, by Donovan Wylie, 69–71. London: Secker & Warburg, 1989.
– "For Joy and for Fun." In *The High Towers: The Early Years of* BBC *Schools Broadcasting in Northern Ireland*, edited by Douglas Carson, 12. BBC Northern Ireland, 2011.
– Foreword. In *Childhood and Its Discontents: The First Seamus Heaney Lectures*, edited by Joseph Dunne and James Kelly, xiii–xvi. Dublin: Liffey Press, 2003.
– Foreword. In *A Portrait of the Artist as a Young Girl*, edited by John Quinn, ix–x. London; Dublin: Mandarin; RTÉ, 1986.
– "Fretwork: On Translating Beowulf." *In Other Words: The Journal for Literary Translators* no. 13/14 (Autumn/Winter 1999/2000): 23–33.
– "From 'Private Excursions.'" *Dublin Review* Spring (2001): 40–5.
– *Front Row*, BBC Radio 4. Interview by Mark Lawson. 6 March 2005.
– "Further Language." *Studies in the Literary Imagination* 30, no. 2 (Fall 1997): 7–16.
– "Heaney on the Haw Lantern." *The Listener*, 23 July 1987, 12.
– "Holding Patterns: Arts, Letters and the Academy." In Seamus Heaney, *Articulations: Poetry, Philosophy and the Shaping of Culture*, 11–24. Dublin: Royal Irish Academy, 2008.
– "The Gentle Flame." Draft poems. National Library of Ireland. Department of Manuscripts., n.d. MS 49,493/57. Seamus Heaney Literary Papers, 1963–2010.
– *The Government of the Tongue: The 1986 T.S. Eliot Memorial Lectures and Other Critical Writings*. London; New York: Faber & Faber, 1988.
– *The Haw Lantern*. London: Faber & Faber, 1987.
– "The Heart of a Vanished World." *Guardian*, 24 February 2001, Saturday Review 1–2.
– "Home Fires." *Irish Pages* 3, no. 1 (2005): 29.
– *Human Chain*. London: Faber & Faber, 2010.
– "In Glenelly Valley." Draft poem. National Library of Ireland. Department of Manuscripts, n.d. MS 49,493/1. Seamus Heaney Literary Papers, 1963–2010.
– "The Interesting Case of John Alphonsus Mulrennan." *Planet*, 1978, 34–40.

Works Cited

– "Interview with Frank Kinahan." *Critical Inquiry* 8, no. 3 (Spring 1982): 405–14.
– "Interview with Mike Murphy." In *Reading the Future: Irish Writers in Conversation with Mike Murphy,* edited by Mike Murphy and Clíodhna Ní Anluain, 81–97. Dublin: Lilliput Press, 2000.
– "Interview with James Randall." *Ploughshares* 5, no. 3 (1979): 7–22.
– Introduction. In *Collected Short Stories,* by Michael McLaverty, xi–xiii. Belfast: Blackstaff Press, 2002.
– Introduction. In *The Essential Wordsworth*, vii–xii. London: Faber & Faber, 1988.
– Introduction. In *The People of the Sea*, by David Thomson, ix–xvii. Edinburgh: Canongate, 2011.
– Introduction. In *A Way of Life, Like Any Other*, by Darcy O'Brien, v–x. New York: New York Review Books, 2001.
– Introduction. In *W.B. Yeats: Poems*, xi–xxv. London: Faber & Faber, 2004.
– "January Review: The Arts in Ireland," 23 January 1973. MSS 960, Box 199, FF 1. Seamus Heaney papers, Stuart A. Rose Manuscript, Archives, and Rare Book Library, Emory University.
– "John Bull's Other Island." *Listener*, 29 September 1977, 397–9.
– "Kicking Against the Code." *New Statesman*, 12 November 1965, 748.
– "Last Look." *Outposts* Spring (1968): 7.
– "Lecture on Composition." Holograph outline for lecture with early teaching materials, c 1966. MSS 960, Box 100, FF 3. Seamus Heaney papers, Stuart A. Rose Manuscript, Archives, and Rare Book Library, Emory University.
– "Letter to Seamus Deane," 3 December 1977. MSS 1210, Box 20, FF 2. Seamus Deane Collection, Stuart A. Rose Manuscript, Archives, Rare Book Library, Emory University.
– "Letter to Michael Longley," March 1975. MSS 744, Box 15a, FF 6. Michael Longley Collection, Stuart A. Rose Manuscript, Archives, Rare Book Library, Emory University.
– "Letter to Michael Longley," 4 January 1978. MSS 744, Box 15a, FF 2. Michael Longley Collection, Stuart A. Rose Manuscript, Archives, Rare Book Library, Emory University.
– "Letter to Ron Schuhard," 24 April 1983. MSS 1005, Box 1, FF 2. Ron Schuhard papers, Stuart A. Rose Manuscript, Archives, and Rare Book Library, Emory University.
– "Michael McLaverty: Part of His Own Posterity." *Fortnight* 306 (1992): 31.
– *New Selected Poems: 1988–2013.* London: Faber & Faber, 2014.

Works Cited

– *North*. London: Faber & Faber, 1975.

– "Obituary." Draft poem. National Library of Ireland. Department of Manuscripts., n.d. MS 49,493/1. Seamus Heaney Literary Papers, 1963–2010.

– "An Open Letter." In *Ireland's Field Day*, edited by Seamus Deane, 21–30. Belfast: Field Day Theatre Company, 1983.

– "Out of London: Ulster's Troubles." *New Statesman*, 1 July 1966, 23–4.

– "The Pathos of Things." *Guardian*, 24 November 2007, sec. Review.

– "The Peace of the World Is Always with You." *Sunday Times*, 17 January 1999, Culture 10–11.

– *Place and Displacement: Recent Poetry of Northern Ireland*. Pete Laver Memorial Lecture Delivered at Grasmere, 2 August 1984. Grasmere: Trustees of Dove Cottage, 1984.

– "Place, Pastness, Poems: A Triptych." The Literary Imagination and the Sense of the Past, special issue, *Salmagundi* 68/69 (1985/1986): 30–47.

– "The Play Way." *Outposts* 62 (Autumn 1964): 14.

– "The Podium: 'Are You Doing Any Poetry with Them?'" *American Scholar* 70, no. 4 (Autumn 2001): 40–5.

– "Poetic Sweetness and Light in the Classroom." *Education Times*, 26 April 1973, 14.

– "The Poetry of John Hewitt." *Threshold* (Summer 1969): 73–7.

– "The Power of T.S. Eliot." *Boston Review* (October 1989): 7–9, 22.

– "The Prelude," n.d. MSS 653, Box 1, FF 9. Seamus Heaney papers, Stuart A. Rose Manuscript, Archives, and Rare Book Library, Emory University.

– *Preoccupations: Selected Prose, 1968–1978*. London; Boston: Faber & Faber, 1980.

– *The Redress of Poetry: Oxford Lectures*. London; Boston: Faber & Faber, 1995.

– "The Regional Forecast." In Draper, *The Literature of Region and Nation*, 10–23.

– "Review of *A Fugitive from Utopia: The Poetry of Zbigniew Herbert* by Stanislaw Baranczak." *Erato (The Harvard Book Review)* 7–8 (Winter 1988): 2–3.

– "Seamus Heaney Recalls … When Li'l Abner Breezed in from Castledawson." *Education Times*, 20 December 1973, 7.

– "The Seductive Muse: A Superfluous and Unsolicited Editorial." *Gorgon* Hilary term (1961): 4–6.

– *Seeing Things*. London; Boston: Faber & Faber, 1991.

– "The Singing Classes." *Education Today* (Spring 1993): 17.

Works Cited

– "Something to Write Home About." *Princeton University Library Chronicle* 59, no. 3 (1998): xx.

– *Spelling It Out: In Honour of Brian Friel on His 80th Birthday.* Loughcrew, Ireland: The Gallery Press, 2009.

– *The Spirit Level.* London: Faber & Faber, 1996.

– "Station Island." *The Hudson Review* 36, no. 2 (summer 1983): 257–64.

– *Station Island.* London; Boston: Faber & Faber, 1984.

– *Stations.* Belfast: Ulsterman Publications, 1975.

– "Stations Drafts." Manuscript drafts of *Stations*. National Library of Ireland. Department of Manuscripts., n.d. MS 49,493–31 I.v. "Stations." Seamus Heaney Literary Papers, 1963–2010.

– *Sweeney Astray.* London: Faber & Faber, 1983.

– "A Tale of Two Islands: Reflections on the Irish Literary Revival." In *Irish Studies*, edited by P.J. Drury, 1–20. Cambridge: Cambridge University Press, 1980.

– "There's Rosemary." *Gorgon*, Hilary term (1961): 29–32.

– "Title Deeds: Translating a Classic." *Proceedings of the American Philosophical Society* 148, no. 4 (December 2004): 411–26.

– *Today Programme*, BBC Radio 4. Interview by John Humphrys. 6 February 2005.

– "The Trance and the Translation." *Guardian*, 30 November 2002, Review 4, 6.

– *A Tribute to Michael McLaverty.* Belfast: Linen Hall Library, 2005.

– "Two Poems." *Prospice* 5 (1976): 64–5.

– "Two Voices." *London Review of Books*, 20 March 1980, 8.

– "'Untitled': Script for *Explorations*, BBC Northern Ireland Schools Department." Emory University, 1 May 1968. Michael Longley Collection, Stuart A. Rose Manuscript, Archives, Rare Book Library, Emory University.

– "Verses for a Fordham Commencement by Seamus Heaney, Fordham University May 23, 1982." *Irish Literary Supplement*, Autumn (1982): 22–3.

– "Violence and Repose." *Hibernia*, 19 January 1973, 13.

– "'Voices behind a Door': Robert Frost." *Poetry Review* 83, no. 4 (Winter 1993): 31–2.

– "Winter Seeds." Annotated typescript drafts of poems for inclusion in "Winter Seeds." National Library of Ireland. Department of Manuscripts., n.d. MS 49,493/21. Seamus Heaney Literary Papers, 1963–2010.

– *Wintering Out.* London: Faber & Faber, 1972.

Works Cited

– "Woodcut." *Workshop* 11 (1971): 4.
– "Words of Advice for Graduates on the Threshold of the Millennium." Edited by Jodi Wilgroen. *New York Times*, 29 May 2000, A11.
– "Wordsworth at Grasmere." Carbon typescript with editorial notes written by Seamus Heaney, c 1974. MSS 960, Box 100, FF 28. Seamus Heaney papers, Stuart A. Rose Manuscript, Archives, and Rare Book Library, Emory University.
– "Writer and Teacher." *Irish Times*, 20 February 1965, 8.
– "Yank." *Everyman* 2 (1969): 14–15.
– "Yeats's Nobility." *Fortnight* 271 (March 1989): ii–iii.
– and Robert Hass. *Sounding Lines: The Art of Translating Poetry*. Berkeley: Doreen B. Townsend Center for the Humanities, 2000.
– and Ted Hughes, eds. *The Rattle Bag*. London; Boston: Faber & Faber, 1982.
– eds. *The School Bag*. London: Faber & Faber, 1997.
– and Karl Miller. *Seamus Heaney in Conversation with Karl Miller*. London: Between the Lines, 2000.
Heidegger, Martin. *The Concept of Time*. Translated by William McNeill. Oxford, UK; Cambridge, MA: Wiley-Blackwell, 1992.
Herbert, Zbigniew. *Barbarian in the Garden*. Translated by Michael March and Jaroslaw Anders. Manchester: Carcanet, 1985.
Hickey, Alison. *Impure Conceits: Rhetoric and Ideology in Wordsworth's "Excursion."* Stanford: Stanford University Press, 1997.
Hill, Alan G. "Wordsworth, Comenius and the Art of Education." *Review of English Studies* 26, no. 103 (August 1975): 301–12.
Hillan, Sophia. "Michael McLaverty, Seamus Heaney and the Writerly Bond." *Irish Times*, 20 October 2017, https://www.irishtimes.com/culture/books/michael-mclaverty-seamus-heaney-and-the-writerly-bond-1.3263062.
– "Wintered into Wisdom: Michael McLaverty, Seamus Heaney, and the Northern Word-Hoard." *New Hibernia Review / Iris Éireannach Nua* 9, no. 3 (Fómhar/Autumn 2005): 86–106.
Hobsbaum, Philip. "Letter to Seamus Heaney," 8 July 1988. MSS 960, Box 40, FF 11. Seamus Heaney papers, Stuart A. Rose Manuscript, Archives, and Rare Book Library, Emory University.
Holbrook, David. *English for the Rejected: Training Literacy in the Lower Streams of the Secondary School*. Cambridge: Cambridge University Press, 1964.
Holt, John. *How Children Fail*. Harmondsworth, Middlesex: Penguin, 1964.

Horton, Patricia. "Romantic Intersections: Romanticism and Contemporary Northern Irish Poetry." PhD thesis, Queen's University Belfast, 1996.

– "'Time That Was Extra, Unforeseen and Free' – Representations of Childhood in the Poetry of Seamus Heaney.'" In *Returning to Ourselves: Second Volume of Papers from the John Hewitt International Summer School*, edited by Eve Patten, 287–96. Belfast: Lagan Press, 1995.

– "'A Truly Uninvited Shade': Romantic Legacies in the Work of Seamus Heaney and Paul Muldoon." In Brearton, Allen, and Hughes, *Last before America: Irish and American Writing*, 16–28.

Hughes, Eamonn. "Representation in Modern Irish Poetry." In Allen, *Seamus Heaney: Contemporary Critical Essays*, 78–94.

Hughes, Ted. *Letters of Ted Hughes*. Edited by Christopher Reid. London: Faber & Faber, 2007.

Hulme, Thomas E. *Selected Writings*. Edited by Patrick McGuinness. Manchester: Fyfield, 2003.

Jackson, Brian, ed. *English Versus Examinations*. London: Chatto and Windus, 1965.

Jacobus, Mary. "The Art of Managing Books: Romantic Prose and the Writing of the Past." In *Romanticism and Language*, edited by Arden Reed, 215–46. Ithaca: Cornell University Press, 1984.

James, Stephen. "Dividing Lines: Robert Frost and Seamus Heaney." *Symbiosis* 3, no. 1 (1999): 63–77.

Janus, Adrienne. "Mnemosyne and the Mislaid Pen: The Poetics of Memory in Heaney, Longley and McGuckian." In Brearton, Hughes, and Allen, *Last before America: Irish and American Writing*, 54–68.

Johnson, Samuel. *Selected Writings*. Edited by Reginald Thorne Davies. London: Faber & Faber, 1965.

Johnston, Dillon. "Irish Influence and Confluence in Heaney's Poetry." In O'Donoghue, *The Cambridge Companion to Seamus Heaney*, 150–64.

– "Irish Poetry after Joyce (Heaney and Kavanagh)." In Garratt, *Critical Essays on Seamus Heaney*, 196–206.

Joyce, James. *A Portrait of the Artist as a Young Man*. Edited by Seamus Deane. London: Penguin, 2000.

– *Stephen Hero: Part of the First Draft of "A Portrait of the Artist as a Young Man."* London: Jonathan Cape, 1944.

– *Ulysses*. London: The Bodley Head, 1960.

Joyce, Robert Dwyer. *Ballads, Romances, and Songs*. Dublin and London: James Duffy, 1861.

Jung, Carl Gustav. *The Essential Jung*. Edited by Anthony Storr. London: Fontana, 1998.

Kavanagh, Patrick. *Collected Prose*. London: MacGibbon and Kee, 1967.

Kearney, Hugh F. *The British Isles: A History of Four Nations*. Cambridge; New York: Cambridge University Press, 1989.

Kearney, Richard. *Navigations: Collected Irish Essays, 1976–2006*. Syracuse: Syracuse University Press, 2006.

Keats, John. *Keats's Poetry and Prose: Authoritative Texts Criticism*. Edited by Jeffrey N. Cox. New York: Norton, 2009.

– *The Letters of John Keats: 1814–1821*. Edited by Hyder Edward Rollins. Cambridge: Harvard University Press, 1958.

Kelly, Fergus. *A Guide to Early Irish Law*. Early Irish Law Series, v. 3. Dublin: Dublin Institute for Advanced Studies, 1988.

Kendall, Tim. *Paul Muldoon*. Bridgend: Seren, 1996.

Kennedy-Andrews, Elmer. *Northern Irish Poetry: The American Connection*. Houndsmills, Basingstoke, Hampshire; New York: Palgrave Macmillan, 2014.

Kermode, Frank. *The Sense of an Ending: Studies in the Theory of Fiction: With a New Epilogue*. Oxford; New York: Oxford University Press, 2000.

Kerrigan, John. *Archipelagic English: Literature, History, and Politics, 1603–1707*. Oxford; New York: Oxford University Press, 2008.

– "'Knowing the Dead …' for Pete Laver 1947–83." *January*, 1987, 11–42.

Kinsella, Michael. "Poet to Poet: Seamus Heaney's Wordsworth." PhD thesis, University of York, 2003.

Kirkland, Richard. "Towards a Disciplinary History of Irish Studies." Genetics and the Irish People, special issue. *Irish Review* 48 (Summer 2014): 65–80.

– "Ways of Saying/Ways of Reading: Materiality, Literary Criticism and the Poetry of Paul Muldoon." In Brearton, Hughes, and Allen, *Last before America: Irish and American Writing*, 69–79.

Laird, Nick. "*Human Chain* by Seamus Heaney: Review." *Telegraph*, 2 September 2010, Review 21.

Larrissy, Edward, "Seamus Heaney and Romanticism." In *Romantic Presences in the Twentieth Century*, edited by Mark Sandy, 105–16. Aldershot, England; Burlington, VT: Ashgate, 2012.

– ed. *Romanticism and Postmodernism*. Cambridge; New York: Cambridge University Press, 1999.

Works Cited

Latour, Bruno. *We Have Never Been Modern*. Translated by Catherine Porter. Cambridge: Harvard University Press, 1993.

Lau, Beth. *Keats's Paradise Lost*. Gainesville: University Press of Florida, 1998.

Lavan, Rosie. "Explorations: Seamus Heaney and Education." *Irish Review*, no. 49–50 (2015): 54–70.

– "Heaney and the Audience." *Essays in Criticism* 66, no. 1 (2016): 54–71.

Leavis, F.R. *How to Teach Reading: A Primer for Ezra Pound*. Cambridge: Minority Press, 1932.

Lee, Dennis. "Writing in Colonial Space." In *The Post-Colonial Studies Reader*, edited by Bill Ashcroft, Gareth Griffiths, and Helen Tiffin, 2nd ed., 397–401. London; New York: Routledge, 2006.

Leopardi, Giacomo. *Selected Prose and Poetry*. Edited by Iris Origo and John Heath-Stubbs. London: Oxford University Press, 1966.

Lerner, Lawrence. *Domestic Interior and Other Poems*. London: Hutchison, 1959.

Lévinas, Emmanuel. *The Levinas Reader*. Edited by Seán Hand. Blackwell Readers. Oxford, UK; Cambridge, MA: Blackwell, 1989.

– *Totality and Infinity: An Essay on Exteriority*. Translated by Alphonso Lingis. Pittsburgh: Duquesne University Press, 1969.

Lindenberger, Herbert Samuel. *On Wordsworth's Prelude*. Princeton: Princeton University Press, 2015.

Lindop, Grevel. "News & Notes: Obituary of Pete Laver." *PN Review* 35, no. 10 (January–February 1984): 3.

Liu, Alan. *Wordsworth: The Sense of History*. Stanford: Stanford University Press, 1989.

Lloyd, David. *Anomalous States: Irish Writing and the Post-Colonial Moment*. Dublin: Lilliput Press, 1993.

– "'Pap for the Dispossessed': Seamus Heaney and the Poetics of Identity." On Humanism and the University II: The Institutions of Humanism. *Boundary* 2 13, no. 2/3 (Winter–Spring 1985): 319–42.

– "The Two Voices of Seamus Heaney's *North*." *Ariel* 10, no. 4 (October 1979): 5–13.

Longley, Edna. "Heaney – Poet as Critic." *Fortnight* (December–January 1980/1981): 15–16.

– "The Lake Poets and the Beautiful Game." In *From the Small Back Room: A Festschrift for Ciaran Carson*, edited by W.R. Irvine, 128–9. Belfast: Netherlea Press, 2008.

– *The Living Stream: Literature & Revisionism in Ireland*. Newcastle upon Tyne: Bloodaxe Books, 1994.

Works Cited

– *Poetry & Posterity*. Highgreen, Tarset, Northumberland: Bloodaxe Books, 2000.

– "Ulster Protestants and the Question of 'Culture.'" In Brearton, Hughes, and Allen, *Last before America: Irish and American Writing*, 99–120.

Longley, Michael. "Musarum Sacerdos: An Interview." *Poetry Review* 96, no. 4 (Winter 2006–7): 61–4.

Lysaght, Seán. "Contrasting Natures: The Issue of Names." In *Nature in Ireland*, edited by John Wilson Foster, 440–60. Dublin: Lilliput Press, 1997.

– "Robert Lloyd Praeger." In *The Encyclopaedia of Ireland*, edited by Brian Lalor, 891. Dublin: Gill & Macmillan, 2003.

McAlpine, Erica. *The Poet's Mistake*. Princeton and Oxford: Princeton University Press, 2020.

McConnell, Gail. *Northern Irish Poetry and Theology*. Houndsmills, Basingstoke, Hampshire; New York: Palgrave Macmillan, 2014.

MacDiarmid, Hugh. *Complete Poems*. Edited by Michael Grieve and W.R. Aitken. Vol. 1. 2 vols. Manchester: Carcanet Press, 1993.

McDiarmid, Lucy. "Heaney and the Politics of the Classroom." In Garratt, *Critical Essays on Seamus Heaney*, 110–20.

McDonald, Peter. "Faiths and Fidelities: Heaney and Longley in Mid-career." In Brearton, Hughes, and Allen, *Last before America: Irish and American Writing*, 3–15.

– *Mistaken Identities: Poetry and Northern Ireland*. Oxford; New York: Clarendon Press, 1997.

– "The Poet and 'The Finished Man': Heaney's Oxford Lectures." *Irish Review* 19 (1996): 98–108.

– "Seamus Heaney as Critic." In *Poetry in Contemporary Irish Literature*, edited by Michael Kenneally, 174–89. Gerrards Cross, Buckinghamshire: Colin Smythe, 1995.

McGann, Jerome J. *The Romantic Ideology: A Critical Investigation*. Chicago: University of Chicago Press, 2004.

Mac Giolla Léith, Caoimhín. "*Dinnseanchas* and Modern Gaelic Poetry." In *The Poet's Place: Ulster Society and Literature: Essays in Honour of John Hewitt*, edited by John Wilson Foster and Gerald Dawe, 157–68. Belfast: Institute of Irish Studies, 1991.

McIlvanney, Liam, and Ray Ryan, eds. *Ireland and Scotland: Culture and Society, 1700–2000*. Dublin; Portland, OR: Four Courts Press, 2005.

Mackay, Peter. "The End of 'Home': Heaney, Muldoon and the Return of the Dead." In *British Literature in Transition, 1960–1980: Flower-Power*, edited by Kate McLoughlin, 289–302. Cambridge: Cambridge University Press, 2019.

320 Works Cited

– "Memory, the Bog, Seamus Heaney." *Ecloga* 7, (Spring 2009): 80–97.

– Edna Longley, and Fran Brearton, eds. *Modern Irish and Scottish Poetry.* Cambridge: Cambridge University Press, 2011.

MacKenzie, R.F. *Escape from the Classroom.* London: Collins, 1965.

MacLean, Sorley. *Caoir Gheal Leumraich / White Leaping Flame: Collected Poems in Gaelic with English Translations.* Edited by Christopher Whyte and Emma Dymock. Edinburgh: Polygon, 2011.

McLoughlin, Deborah. "'An Ear to the Line': Modes of Receptivity in Seamus Heaney's Glanmore Sonnets." *Papers on Language and Literature* 25, no. 2 (Spring 1989): 201–15.

Mac Mathúna, Liam. "*Dinnseanchas.*" In *The Encyclopaedia of Ireland,* edited by Brian Lalor, 299–30. Dublin: Gill & Macmillan, 2003.

Macrae, Alasdair. "Seamus Heaney's New Voice in *Station Island.*" In *Irish Writers and Society at Large: Conference of IASAIL-JAPAN at Waseda University, Tokyo, in September 1984,* edited by Masaru Sekine, 122–38. Gerrards Cross, Buckinghamshire: Colin Smythe, 1985.

McSweeney, Siobhan. "The Poet's Picture of Education." *The Crane Bag* 7, no. 2 (1983): 134–42.

Mahon, Derek. *The Sea in Winter.* Dublin: Gallery Press; Old Deerfield, MA: Deerfield Press, 1979.

Makdisi, Saree. *Romantic Imperialism: Universal Empire and the Culture of Modernity.* Cambridge: Cambridge University Press, 1998.

Mandelstam, Osip. "Conversation about Dante." In *The Poet's Dante,* translated by Jane Gary Harris and Constance Link, 40–93. New York: Farrar, Straus and Giroux, 2002.

– *Osip Mandelstam: Selected Poems.* Translated by Clarence Brown and W.S. Merwin. Harmondsworth, Middlesex: Penguin, 1977.

Marggraf Turley, Richard. "'Johnny's in the Basement': Keats, Bob Dylan and the End of Influence." In Walford Davies and Marggraf Turely, *The Monstrous* Debt, 181–204.

Matthews, Steven. "Translations: Difference and Identity in Recent Poetry from Ireland and the West Indies." In *Irish and Postcolonial Writing: History, Theory, Practice,* edited by Glenn Hooper and Colin Graham, 109–26. Houndsmills, Basingstoke, Hampshire; New York: Palgrave Macmillan, 2002.

– *Yeats as Precursor: Readings in Irish, British, and American Poetry.* New York: St. Martin's Press, 2000.

Merleau-Ponty, Maurice. *The Merleau-Ponty Aesthetics Reader: Philosophy and Painting.* Edited by Galen A. Johnson. Translated by Michael B. Smith. Evanston: Northwestern University Press, 1993.

Works Cited

Miłosz, Czesław. *Collected Poems 1931–1987*. London: Viking, 1988.

– *Selected and Last Poems, 1931–2004*. London: Penguin, 2014.

Moorman, Mary. *William Wordsworth, a Biography: The Later Years 1803–1850*. Oxford: Oxford University Press, 1965.

Morrissey, Sinéad. "Against All Rhyme and Reason." *Fortnight*, April 2003, 16–17.

– "'And Fostered Me and Sent Me Out': Muldoon Reading Heaney." *Irish Review* 49/50 (2014/2015): 137–40.

– *Parallax*. Manchester: Carcanet, 2013.

Muir, Edwin. *Collected Poems*. London: Faber & Faber, 2003.

Muldoon, Paul. *The End of the Poem*. London; New York: Faber & Faber; Farrar, Straus and Giroux, 2006.

– "Letter to Seamus Heaney," 21 November 1999. MSS 960, Box 42, FF 10. Seamus Heaney papers, Stuart A. Rose Manuscript, Archives, and Rare Book Library, Emory University.

– *Madoc: A Mystery*. London; New York: Faber & Faber; Farrar, Straus and Giroux, 1990.

– *New Weather*. London: Faber & Faber, 1973.

– *Poems, 1968–1998*. London: Faber & Faber, 2001.

– *Quoof*. London: Faber & Faber, 1983.

– *To Ireland, I: An Abccedary of Irish Literature*. London: Faber & Faber, 2000.

– *Why Brownlee Left*. London; Boston: Faber & Faber, 1980.

Murphy, Andrew. *Seamus Heaney*. 3rd ed. Writers and Their Work. Tavistock, Devon : [London]: Northcote; British Council, 2010.

Murphy, Denis, ed. *The Annals of Clonmacnoise: Being Annals of Ireland from the Earliest Period to A.D. 1408*. Translated by Conell Mageoghagan. Felinfach: Llanerch, 1993.

Newlyn, Lucy. *Dorothy and William Wordsworth: "All in Each Other."* Oxford: Oxford University Press, 2013.

– Foreword. In Walford Davies and Marggraf Turley, *The Monstrous Debt: Modalities of Romantic Influence in Twentieth-Century Literature*, viii–xiii.

Nichols, Ashton. *The Poetics of Epiphany: Nineteenth-Century Origins of the Modern Literary Moment*. Tuscaloosa: University of Alabama Press, 1987.

Ní Chonaill, Bronagh. "Fosterage: Child-Rearing in Medieval Ireland." *History Ireland* 5, no. 1 (1997): 28–31.

Ní Ríordáin, Clíona. "'Puddling at the Source': Seamus Heaney and the Classical Text." *Études anglaises* 56, no. 2 (2003): 173–83.

322 Works Cited

Norquay, Glenda, and Gerry Smyth, eds. *Across the Margins: Cultural Identity and Change in the Atlantic Archipelago*. Manchester; New York: Manchester University Press, 2002.

O'Brien, Darcy. "Seamus Heaney and William Wordsworth: A Correspondent Breeze." In Garratt, *Critical Essays on Seamus Heaney*, 187–95.

O'Brien, Eugene. "The Anxiety of Influence: Heaney and Yeats and the Place of Writing." *Nordic Irish Studies* 4 (2005): 119–36.

– "The Place of Writing: Place, Poetry and Politics in the Writing of Seamus Heaney." *Hermathena* (Winter 1996): 52–67.

– *Seamus Heaney: Creating Irelands of the Mind*. Dublin: Liffey Press, 2002.

– *Seamus Heaney: Searches for Answers*. London; Sterling, VA: Pluto Press, 2003.

– *Seamus Heaney and the Place of Writing*. Gainesville: University Press of Florida, 2002.

– *Seamus Heaney as Aesthetic Thinker: A Study of the Prose*. Syracuse: Syracuse University Press, 2016.

O'Brien, Karen. "Imperial Georgic, 1660–1789." In *The Country and the City Revisited: England and the Politics of Culture, 1550–1850*, edited by Gerald M. MacLean, Donna Landry, and Joseph P. Ward, 160–79. Cambridge; New York: Cambridge University Press, 1999.

Ó Cadha, Stiofán. "Pattern." In *Encyclopedia of Ireland*, 861. Dublin: Gill and Macmillan, 2003.

O'Donoghue, Bernard. "Heaney's Classics and the Bucolic." In O'Donoghue, *The Cambridge Companion to Seamus Heaney*, 106–21.

– Introduction. In O'Donoghue, *The Cambridge Companion to Seamus Heaney*, 1–18.

– *Seamus Heaney and the Language of Poetry*. Germantown: Prentice Hall, 1994.

– , ed. *The Cambridge Companion to Seamus Heaney*. Cambridge; New York: Cambridge University Press, 2009.

O'Driscoll, Dennis. *Stepping Stones: Interviews with Seamus Heaney*. London: Faber & Faber, 2008.

O'Grady, Thomas. "Heaney Redivivus: The Fine Art of Renovation." *Poetry Ireland Review* 60 (Spring 1999): 76–9.

O'Neill, Michael. *The All-Sustaining Air: Romantic Legacies and Renewals in British, American, and Irish Poetry since 1900*. Oxford; New York: Oxford University Press, 2007.

Oratory of St Philip Neri, London. *The Catholic Hymn Book*. Edited by Patrick Russill. Leominster, Herefordshire: Gracewing, 1998.

Works Cited   323

Parker, Michael. *Seamus Heaney: The Making of the Poet*. Houndsmills: Macmillan, 1997.

Parkes, Peter. "Celtic Fosterage: Adoptive Kinship and Clientage in Northwest Europe." *Comparative Studies in Society and History* 48, no. 2 (2006): 359–95.

– "Fosterage, Kinship and Legend: When Milk Was Thicker than Blood?" *Comparative Studies in Society and History* 46, no. 3 (2004): 587–615.

Pittock, Murray. *Scottish and Irish Romanticism*. Oxford; New York: Oxford University Press, 2008.

Pointon, Barry. *Wordsworth and Education*. Lewes: The Hornbook Press, 1998.

Potkay, Adam. *Wordsworth's Ethics*. Baltimore: Johns Hopkins University Press, 2015.

Praeger, Robert Lloyd. *The Way That I Went: An Irishman in Ireland*. Dublin: Allen Figgis, 1937.

Quinn, John, ed. *My Education*. Dublin: Town House, 1997.

Quinn, Justin. "Heaney and Eastern Europe." In O'Donoghue, *The Cambridge Companion to Seamus Heaney*, 92–105.

Ramazani, Jahan. *The Hybrid Muse: Postcolonial Poetry in English*. Chicago: University of Chicago Press, 2001.

– *Poetry of Mourning: The Modern Elegy from Hardy to Heaney*. 2nd ed. Chicago: University of Chicago Press, 1994.

– "Seamus Heaney's Globe." *Irish Review* 49/50 (Winter/Spring 2014): 38–53.

Randolph, Jody Allen. *Close to the Next Moment: Interviews from a Changing Ireland*. Manchester: Carcanet, 2010.

Reiman, Donald Henry. *The Romantics Reviewed: Contemporary Reviews of British Romantic Writers*. New York: Garland, 1976.

Rickard, John. "Stephen Dedalus among Schoolchildren: The Schoolroom and the Riddle of Authority in *Ulysses*." *Studies in the Literary Imagination* 30, no. 2 (1997): 17–37.

Ricks, Christopher. *Allusion to the Poets*. Oxford: Oxford University Press, 2002.

– *The Force of Poetry*. Oxford; New York: Clarendon Press, 1984.

– "Review of *Death of a Naturalist*." In Allen, *Seamus Heaney: Contemporary Critical Essays*, 21–4.

Robinson, Alan. "Seamus Heaney's *Seeing Things*: Familiar Compound Ghosts." In *Anglisentag 1992 Stuggart*, edited by Hans Ulrich Seeber and Walter Göbel, 46–56. Tubingen: Max Niemeyer Verlay, 1992.

Roe, Nicholas. "Bringing It All Back Home: Pantisocracy, Madoc, and the

Poet's Myth." In Brearton, Hughes, and Allen, *Last before America: Irish and American Writing*, 172–85.

– "'Wordsworth at the Flax-Dam': An Early Poem by Seamus Heaney." In *Critical Approaches to Anglo-Irish Literature*, edited by Angela Wilcox and Michael Allen, 166–71. Gerrards Cross, Buckinghamshire: Colin Smythe, 1989.

Ross, Daniel. "In Search of Enabling Light: Heaney, Wordsworth, and the Poetry of Trauma." *Nordic Irish Studies* 5 (2016): 109–21.

Rousseau, Jean-Jacques. *Émile, ou, De l'éducation*. Edited by André Charrak. Paris: Flammarion, 2009.

– *The Social Contract and Discourses*. Edited by J.H. Brumfitt and John C Hall. Translated by G.D.H. Cole. New York: Dutton, 1979.

Russell, D.A., and Michael Winterbottom, eds. *Ancient Literary Criticism: The Principal Texts in New Translations*. Oxford: Clarendon Press, 1972.

Russell, Richard Rankin. *Seamus Heaney: An Introduction*. Edinburgh: Edinburgh University Press, 2016.

– *Seamus Heaney's Regions*. Notre Dame: University of Notre Dame Press, 2014.

Ryan, Ray. *Ireland and Scotland: Literature and Culture, State and Nation, 1966–2000*. Oxford English Monographs. Oxford; New York: Clarendon Press; Oxford University Press, 2002.

Salvesen, Christopher. *The Landscape of Memory: A Study of Wordsworth's Poetry*. London: Edward Arnold, 1965.

Schiller, Friedrich. "On Naïve and Sentimental Poetry." In *German Aesthetic and Literary Criticism: Winckelmann, Lessing, Hamann, Herder, Schiller, Goethe*, edited by H.B. Nisbet, translated by Julius A. Elias. Cambridge; New York: Cambridge University Press, 1985.

Shakespeare, William. *The Norton Shakespeare: Based on the Oxford Edition*. Edited by Stephen Greenblatt, Walter Cohen, Suzanne Gossett, Jean E. Howard, Katharine Eisaman Maus, and Gordon McMullan. 2nd ed. New York: Norton, 2008.

Shelley, Percy Bysshe. *The Complete Works of Shelley*. Edited by Roger Ingpen and Walter E. Peck. Vol. 1. 10 vols. New York: Gordian Press, 1965.

– *The Poems of Shelley: Volume 3, 1819–1820*. Edited by Jack Donovan, Geoffrey Matthews, Cian Duffy, Michael Rossington, and Kelvin Everest. Harlow: Longman, 2011.

Smith, Anthony D. "Neo-Classicist and Romantic Elements in the Emergence of Nationalist Conceptions." In *Nationalist Movements*, edited by Anthony D. Smith, 74–87. London: Macmillan, 1976.

Works Cited

Smith, Stan. "Seamus Heaney: The Distance Between." In *The Chosen Ground: Essays on the Contemporary Poetry of Northern Ireland*, edited by Neil Corcoran, 35–64. Bridgend, Mid Glamorgan: Seren Books, 1992.

Southey, Robert. *The Life and Correspondence of Robert Southey*. Edited by Charles Cuthbert Southey. Vol. 1. 6 vols. London: Longman, Brown, Green and Longmans, 1849.

Spinoza, Benedict de. *Ethics*. Edited by Tom Griffith. Translated by W.H. White and A.K. Stirling. Hertfordshire: Wordsworth Editions Limited, 2001.

Stafford, Fiona J. *Local Attachments: The Province of Poetry*. Oxford; New York: Oxford University Press, 2010.

– *Starting Lines in Scottish, Irish, and English Poetry: From Burns to Heaney*. Oxford: Oxford University Press, 2000.

Stanford Encyclopedia of Philosophy. "David Hartley." Stanford University Press, 2008. http://plato.stanford.edu/.

Stead, C.K. *The New Poetic: Yeats to Eliot*. London: Continuum, 2005.

Stephen, J.K. *Lapsus Calami*. Cambridge: Macmillan and Bowes, 1891.

Stevens, Wallace. *The Collected Poems of Wallace Stevens*. Edited by John N. Serio and Chris Beyers. London: Vintage, 2015.

– *The Necessary Angel: Essays on Reality and the Imagination*. New York: Vintage Books, 1951.

Stevenson, Anne. "Stations: Seamus Heaney and the Sacred Sense of the Sensitive Self." In *The Art of Seamus Heaney*, edited by Tony Curtis, 4th ed., 45–52. Brigend, Mid Glamorgan: Seren, 2001.

Swann, Joseph. "The Poet as Critic: Seamus Heaney's Reading of Wordsworth, Hopkins and Yeats." In *Literary Interrelations: Ireland, England, and the World*, edited by Wolfgang Zach and Heinz Kosok, 2:361–70. Tübingen: G. Narr Verlag, 1987.

Taylor, L.C., ed. *Experiments in Education at Sevenoaks*. London: Prentice Hall Europe, 1965.

Thomas, Dylan. *The Collected Letters*. Edited by Paul Ferris. London: Dent, 2000.

Thomas, Harry, ed. *Talking with Poets: Interviews with Robert Pinsky, Seamus Heaney, Philip Levine, Michael Hofmann, and David Ferry*. New York: Handsel Books, 2002.

Thompson, Thomas William. *Wordsworth's Hawkshead*. Edited by Robert Woof. London, New York: Oxford University Press, 1970.

Tobin, Daniel. *Passage to the Center: Imagination and the Sacred in the Poetry of Seamus Heaney*. Lexington: University Press of Kentucky, 1999.

Trumpener, Katie. *Bardic Nationalism: The Romantic Novel and the British Empire*. Princeton: Princeton University Press, 1997.

Vendler, Helen Hennessy. "Anglo-Celtic Attitudes." *New York Review of Books*, 6 November 1997, 57–60.

– *Last Looks, Last Books: Stevens, Plath, Lowell, Bishop, Merrill*. Princeton University Press, 2010.

– *Seamus Heaney*. London: HarperCollins, 1998.

Walford Davies, Damian. "Blake and Dylan Thomas: 'Altarwise by Owl-Light.'" In Walford Davies and Marggraf Turely, *The Monstrous Debt: Modalities of Romantic Influence in Twentieth-Century Literature*, 11–40.

– and Richard Marggraf Turley, eds. *The Monstrous Debt: Modalities of Romantic Influence in Twentieth-Century Literature*. Detroit: Wayne State University Press, 2006.

Waterman, Andrew. "The Best Way Out Is Always Through." In Andrews, *Seamus Heaney: Collection of Critical Essays*, 11–38.

Weil, Simone. *Gravity and Grace*. London; New York: Ark Paperbacks, 1987.

Weiskel, Thomas. *The Romantic Sublime: Studies in the Structure and Psychology of Transcendence*. Baltimore: Johns Hopkins University Press, 1986.

Whale, John C., and Stephen Copley, eds. *Beyond Romanticism: New Approaches to Texts and Contexts, 1780–1832*. London; New York: Routledge, 1992.

Wheatley, David. "Professing Poetry: Heaney as Critic." In O'Donoghue, *The Cambridge Companion to Seamus Heaney*, 122–35.

Wills, Clair. "Late Openings." *The Poetry Ireland Review* 102 (December 2010): 117–24.

– *Reading Paul Muldoon*. Newcastle upon Tyne: Bloodaxe, 1998.

Wilson, David. "William Wordsworth Lived Here: Seamus Heaney at Dove Cottage." BBC 2, 28 November 1974.

Wimsatt, William K. *The Verbal Icon: Studies in the Meaning of Poetry*. Edited by Monroe C. Beardsley. Lexington: University Press of Kentucky, 1989.

Wolfson, Susan J. "Wordsworth's Craft." In *The Cambridge Companion to Wordsworth*, edited by Stephen Charles Gill, 108–24. Cambridge; New York: Cambridge University Press, 2003.

Wordsworth, Dorothy. *Journals of Dorothy Wordsworth: The Alfoxden Journal, 1798, the Grasmere Journals, 1800–1803*. Edited by Mary

Works Cited

327

Trevelyan Moorman. 2nd ed. Oxford Letters & Memoirs. Oxford; New York: Oxford University Press, 1991.

– and William Wordsworth. *Home at Grasmere: Extracts from the Journal of Dorothy Wordsworth (Written between 1800 and 1803) and from the Poems of William Wordsworth*. Edited by Colette Clark. London: Penguin Books, 1986.

Wordsworth, Jonathan. *William Wordsworth: The Borders of Vision*. Oxford: New York: Clarendon Press; Oxford University Press, 1982.

Wordsworth, William. *Early Poems and Fragments, 1785–1797*. Edited by Carol Landon and Jared R. Curtis. The Cornell Wordsworth. Ithaca: Cornell University Press, 1997.

– *The Excursion*. Edited by Sally Bushell, James Butler, Michael C. Jaye, and David Garcia. The Cornell Wordsworth. Ithaca: Cornell University Press, 2007.

– *Lyrical Ballads, and Other Poems, 1797–1800*. Edited by James Butler and Karen Green. The Cornell Wordsworth. Ithaca: Cornell University Press, 1992.

– *Poems in Two Volumes, and Other Poems, 1800–1807*. Edited by Jared R. Curtis. The Cornell Wordsworth. Ithaca: Cornell University Press, 1983.

– *The Prelude 1799, 1805, 1850*. Edited by Jonathan Wordsworth, M.H. Abrams, and Stephen Gill. London; New York: Norton, 1979.

– *The Prose Works of William Wordsworth*. Edited by W.J.B. Owen and Jane Worthington Smyser. Vol. 3. 3 vols. Oxford: Oxford University Press, 1974.

– *The Prose Works of William Wordsworth*. Edited by W.J.B. Owen and Jane Worthington Smyser. Vol. 2. 3 vols. Oxford: Oxford University Press, 1974.

– *The Ruined Cottage and The Pedlar*. Edited by James Butler. The Cornell Wordsworth. Ithaca: Cornell University Press, 1979.

– *Selected Poetry and Prose*. Edited by Philip Hobsbaum. Routledge English Texts. London; New York: Routledge, 1989.

– and Samuel Taylor Coleridge. *Wordsworth and Coleridge: Lyrical Ballads*. Edited by R.L. Brett and Alun R. Jones. London; New York: Routledge, 2005.

– and Dorothy Wordsworth. *The Letters of William and Dorothy Wordsworth*. Edited by Ernest De Selincourt, Chester L. Shaver, Mary G. Moorman, and Alan G. Hill. 8 vols. Oxford: Clarendon Press, 1969.

Wright, Julia M. *Representing the National Landscape in Irish Romanticism*. 1st ed. Syracuse: Syracuse University Press, 2014.

Yeats, William Butler. *Autobiographies*. London: Macmillan, 1955.

– *Collected Poems*. London; Basingstoke: Picador, 1995.

– *Later Essays*. Edited by William H. O'Donnell. New York: Charles Scribner's Sons, 1994.

– *The Major Works; Including Poems, Plays, and Critical Prose*. Edited by Edward Larrissy. Oxford: Oxford University Press, 2008.

– *Mythologies*. New York: Simon & Schuster, 1998.

– *The Poems*. Edited by Daniel Albright. London: Campbell, 1992.

– *W.B. Yeats: Poems*. Edited by Seamus Heaney. London: Faber & Faber, 2004.

– ed. *Oxford Book of Modern Verse, 1892–1935*. Oxford: Oxford University Press, 1978.

Index

Abrams, M.H., 11, 138, 244, 279n153. *See also* Greater Romantic Lyric

Achilles, 182

afterlife, 168, 181, 189–91, 245

Agenbyt of Inwyt, 131

Alcobia-Murphy, Shane, 77, 91, 250n62, 284n47

amplification, 29, 54–5, 160, 206–11, 243; and education, 33, 208

Annals of Clonmacnoise, 186

Armitage, Simon, 274n48

Arnold, Matthew, 52, 244; "Sweetness and Light," 43–4, 150, 152; touchstones, 68–9, 72, 81

auctoritas / authority, 68, 76–84, 102, 128

Auden, W.H., 103, 153–4, 168, 239, 290n200

auditory imagination, 69, 71, 160, 263n21

Auschwitz, 25–6, 233

authenticity, 77, 81, 89, 172, 176

Bacon, Francis, 47–8, 258n93

Bate, Jonathan, 18, 93, 104, 234; on dwelling in language, 126, 275n71; on W's work, 118, 176

Batten, Guinn, 15, 83–4, 133, 248n22, 278n129

Beer, John, 5, 290n195

Beethoven, Ludwig van, 43, 45, 64

befitting emblems of adversity, 67, 78, 83, 125

Bell, Andrew, 35

Bellaghy, 116, 222, 295n71

Bhabha, Homi, 139–40

bifocal approaches to poetry, 21–3, 115, 180. *See also* vision

Bloom, Harold, 20, 40, 105, 107; anxiety of influence, 67, 126–7, 129–30

boat-stealing, 39–40, 86, 150

Bornstein, George, 21 41, 234

Braidwood, John, 122

Brandes, Rand, 47

Brearton, Fran, 163, 259n102, 277n101

Britannic approach to poetry. *See* four-nations approach

330 Index

Brown, Terence, 181
Browning, Robert, 125, 127
Buckley, Vincent, 209–10, 223
Buile Suibhne, 139, 143, 221
Burns, Robert, 16, 20, 150, 223, 224
Burnside, John, 181

Carson, Ciaran, 107–8, 258n87
Cavanagh, Michael, 79, 252n87, 255n50
Celtic Twilight, 115, 228, 267n100
childhood and influence on adulthood 6, 148, 195, 212–13
Christianity, 54, 119, 180; Christian humanist wager, 25–7
Clare, John, 223
Clutterbuck, Catriona, 50
Coleridge, Samuel Taylor, 32, 63, 95, 187, 188; friendship with W, 107, 121, 165; "Frost at Midnight," 86
community, 30, 82–3, 202, 214, 242–3; and education, 152; with past, 104, 106, 271n183
Cook, Eleanor, 66
Corcoran, Neil, 97, 104, 122, 124, 140; on "Glanmore Sonnets," 128, 131, 132, 277n116; on H and Yeats 13, 234; on influence, 70, 103, 127, 247n9
Corkery, Daniel, 22, 87, 120
corresponding breeze, 64, 92, 129
Coughlan, Patrick, 84
craft and technique, 32, 54, 81, 96
Crotty, Patrick, 19, 260n128, 273n11

Dante, 102, 103, 126, 145–6, 168, 231

Deane, Seamus, 107, 120, 155, 171; *Gradual Wars*, 56–7; on "Mud Vision," 176; on *Seeing Things*, 179
defence of poetry, 24–5, 27, 72, 150–2, 252n86. *See also* liberal humanism
de Man, Paul, 20
Dennison, John, 25, 57, 157, 225, 252n92, 283n37
de Quincey, Thomas, 128
Devlin, Brendan, 214
dinnseanchas, 116–17, 121–2, 171
Diogenes, 139, 169, 181
displacement, 16, 23, 61, 132–9, 210
divination, 76–7, 83
Docherty, Thomas, 192, 287n138
Dove Cottage, 23, 73–6
dúchas, 214, 218, 227
Duncan, Ian, 215
dwelling, 76, 116, 118, 139, 145; in language, 126, 128; in two places at once, 10, 23

education, 30, 49, 150, 152, 257n84; national systems of, 35–7; and poetry, 41–4; shaky local voice of, 158–9
Eilenberg, Susan, 94
Eliot, T.S., 76, 77, 181; "Burnt Norton," 190; "Little Gidding," 71, 82, 114, 192, 258n90; "Tradition and the Individual Talent," 69–72; *The Waste Land*, 43. *See also* auditory imagination
emotion recollected in tranquillity, 7, 19, 45, 230
epiphany, 39, 46, 48, 51–5; in *Electric Light*, 291–2; rejection

of, 7, 112, 174; in "The Thorn,"
83; and violence, 55–6. *See also*
haecceity; Joyce
excess, 187, 202, 205–7, 245

faith, 43, 60, 195, 226–7; 232; bad
faith, 18, 113; language of, 202
falling, 43–4, 51–3, 216–17,
260n118
Farber, Frederick W., 262n156
fear, 55, 63, 92, 117, 213; beauty
and, 58, 84, 86; ministries of, 86,
124; in natural world, 40, 49–50,
131, 143, 155
Ferguson, Frances, 182
Ferguson, Samuel, 267n100
Flanagan, Tom, 267n96
fortification, 5, 30, 169, 182, 211,
213
Foster, Thomas, 128
fosterage, 15, 27, 60, 85, 91; as
biographical fact, 87–8; in
Brehon law, 88–9; and festering,
92–3; as poetic influence, 66–109
four-nations approach to poetry,
15, 223–7
freedom. *See* liberation
Friel, Brian, 201–2
friendship, 70, 91, 107–8, 199, 202
Freud, Sigmund, 31, 45, 84, 231;
pleasure principle, 205, 212
Frost, Robert, 105, 164, 187, 210,
259n100, 276n98

Gaelic Ireland, 69, 89, 112, 139,
143 ,167
Garner, Alan, 153
gendering of language and landscape, 96–8, 115
Gillis, Alan, 55, 130

Glanmore, 123–4
Graham, Colin, 290n200
Grasmere, 73–6, 123
Greater Romantic Lyric, 40–1, 50,
220
Greene, Graham, 86

haecceity, 43, 51–2, 54, 260n116
half-creation, 39, 77, 96, 113,
269n136
Hall, Stuart, 169
Hamilton, Paul, 260n118
Hardy, Thomas, 109, 182
Hart, Henry, 47, 51–2, 105, 178,
291n215
Hartley, David, 39, 94, 255n47
Hartman, Geoffrey 9, 18, 51–2,
138, 271n180
Harvey, W.J., 68, 99
Haughton, Hugh, 18, 62, 72, on
displacement, 138; on H's use of
W's work 14, 15, 85, 114n68,
269n137; on "Indefatigable
Hoof-taps," 163; on late W, 234;
on "Makings of a Music," 96;
on *William Wordsworth Lived
Here*, 73
haunting, 58, 68, 124–32, 221,
232
Heaney, Marie, 62, 102, 123, 130
Heaney, Seamus, biography: career
as reviewer, 31–3, 56–7, 152–5;
fosterage of his father, 88; opening of Jerwood Centre, 23–4;
proposed thesis on Wordsworth,
30–1; relationship with
Catholicism / Christianity, 25–6,
105, 119; school education, 4–5,
14, 60, 88; teaching career,
29–30, 46–7, 154, 204

332 Index

Heaney's interviews and media: "The Art of Poetry," 267n92; *Close to the Next Moment*, 227, 236; *Explorations*, 44, 152; *Front Row*, BBC Radio 4, 24; Interview with Harriet Cooke, 54, 140; Interview with John Haffenden, 154; Interview with Karl Miller, 202, 217; Interview with Monie Begley, 134; *In the Chair*, 12, 210; "My Education," 34, 47, 208–9, 282n20; *Reading the Future*, 83; *Stepping Stones*, 4, 103, 107; ampler prospects, 29–30; Christian humanist wager, 25–6; late style, 235–6; persistence 3, 8, 11, 235–37; visionary moments, 174, 233, 236; *Talking with Poets*, 98, 206; *Today*, BBC Radio 4, 24; *William Wordsworth Lived Here*, 13, 58, 73–6, 92, 240

Heaney's poetry, plays, and translations: "Act of Union," 124; "An Advancement of Learning," 48, 49, 51; "The Aerodrome," 295n71; "An Afterwards," 103, 126; "Alphabets," 88, 170–2, 174, 184, 209; "The Ash Plant," 189; "At Toomebridge," 215–19; "Autobiographical Borings," 60; "Bachelor Deceased," 111; "The Badgers," 130; "The Baler," 243; "Ballynahinch Lake," 220; "The Barn," 48, 49; *Beowulf*, 139, 209–10, 222; "Blackberry-Picking," 48; "The Bookcase," 208; "Broagh," 121, 159; *Burial at Thebes*, 214; "The Butts," 241;

"Casting and Gathering," 188–9; "Cauled," 61; "Chanson d'Aventure," 242; "Churning Day," 43; "Clearances," 167–9; "Cloistered," 60; "The Clothes Shrine," 220; *The Cure at Troy*, 181, 221; "Cutaways," 242; *Death of a Naturalist*, 14–15, 43, 47, 51–7, 119, 170–1, 213; "Death of a Naturalist," 48–9, 92; "Digging," 100; "The Disappearing Island," 176, 177–8; "The Discharged Soldier," 62; *District and Circle*, 26; "The Diviner," 82; *Door into the Dark*, 57, 295n81; "Earning a Rhyme," 102; "Eelworks," 219; "Electric Light," 215; "England's Difficulty," 61, 140; "Exposure," 125, 135; "Field of Vision," 183–4, 232; *Field Work*, 103, 124, 139–40, 179; "Fil súil nglais," 112; "Finding a Voice," 60; "Fisher," 208; "Flanders," 63; "Follower," 99; "Fosterage," 51, 88; "Fosterling," 88; "The Fragment," 210; "From the Frontier of Writing," 169; "From the Land of the Unspoken," 170, 172; "From the Republic of Conscience," 170; "Funeral Rites," 105; "Gifts of Rain," 33; "Glanmore Revisited," 189; "Glanmore Sonnets," 23–5, 86, 97, 102, 123–33, 208; "The Gravel Walks," 197–8; "Had I not Been Awake," 241; "The Harvest Bow," 30; *The Haw Lantern*, 88, 112, 139, 166–72; "The Haw Lantern," 167, 169;

174; *Human Chain*, 14, 112, 241; "Human Chain," 244; "Incertus," 78; "In Iowa," 290n195; "In Glenelly Valley," 141; "Inquisition," 62; "In the Attic," 244; "In Time," 245; "July," 62, 64–5; "Kernes," 61; "The King of the Ditchbacks," 141, 170, 216; "Kinship," 92, 113; "Kite for Aibhín, A," 245; "The Known World," 221; "Land," 111, 112; "Last Look," 111, 112; "Late in the Day," 200–1; "Lightenings," 179–80, 182, 186, 189; "The Loaning," 142–7, 167, 169, 170; "Loughanure," 243; "The Lough Neagh Sequence," 216, 219; "Lupins," 292n236; "Making Strange," 140, 141–2, 144, 188; *The Midnight Verdict*, 222; "The Ministry of Fear," 86; "Mint," 194–5, 200, 201; "Miracle," 242; "Montana," 189, 232; "The Mud Vision," 173–6, 178, 179, 194; "Mycenae Lookout," 195, 197; *North*, 51, 53, 58, 84, 98, 124, 134; "Obituary," 113; "On His Work in the English Tongue," 251n74; *Opened Ground*, 97; "An Open Letter," 23; "Oral English," 65; "Out of Shot," 184; "Out of the Bag," 220, 291n210; "Out of this World," 26; "The Peninsula," 121; "Perch," 202; "Personal Helicon," 14, 294n40; "The Plantation," 294n40; "The Play Way," 42–4, 45–6, 64, 156; "The Poet's Chair," 97, 196; "Postscript," 238; "Preludes in

Glanmore," 123; *The Rattle Bag*, 211; "The Real Names," 292n246, 297n134; "Reaping in Heat," 248n16; "Requiem for the Croppies," 218; "A Retrospect," 187; "Route 110," 242; "The Sabbath-Breakers," 62; "The Sandpit," 6, 28, 147; *The School Bag*, 211; "Scrabble," 185, 189; "A Scuttle for Dorothy Wordsworth," 238–40; *Seeing Things*, 112, 179–92, 196; "Seeing Things," 179, 182–3, 185; "Settings," 184, 187; "The Settle Bed," 185, 208; "A Shiver," 243; "Sibyl," 92; "The Singer's House," 130; "The Singing Classes," 43; "Singing School," 58, 84–6, 88, 278n134; "Sinking the Shaft," 62; "The Smell," 92; *The Spirit Level*, 65, 192–8, 217; "Squarings," 181, 184–5, 189–90; *Station Island*, 53, 112, 130, 133, 139–41, 167; "Station Island," 146–7, 167, 168; *Stations*, 17, 57–65, 140–1; "The Stone Verdict," 172–3; "Storm on the Island," 50; "A Stove Lid for W.H. Auden," 239–40; "The Strand," 183; "The Strand at Lough Beg," 140, 168; "Summer 1969," 120; "Summer Home," 92; *Sweeney Astray*, 143–4, 167, 221; "Sweeney Redivivus," 141; "The Tall Dames," 293n32; "Ten Glosses," 241, 290n200; "Terminus," 90, 92; "To a Dutch Potter in Ireland," 193, 194; "Tollund," 193; "The Tollund Man in Springtime," 222, 242;

334 Index

"The Toome Road," 130;
"Triptych," 130; "The Turnip
Snedder," 182; "Ugolino," 103,
130; "Undine," 216; "Verses for
a Fordham Commencement,"
150–2, 157, 162; "The
Wanderer," 141; "Waterfalls,"
53; "Weighing In," 196–7;
Wintering Out, 33, 53, 57, 112,
117, 134; "Woodcut," 64, 95;
"Wordsworth's Skates," 238,
240–1; "Writer and Teacher," 46;
"Yank," 109–11, 112, 118, 132,
139
Heaney's prose: "1972," 98;
"Adroitest of Makers," 153–4;
Among Schoolchildren, 23,
155–60, 162, 194; "Apt
Admonishment," 13, 230–1;
"The Atlas of Civilisation," 180;
"Bags of Enlightenment," 211;
"The Boule Miche of the North,"
47, 243; "Burns' Art Speech,"
289n191; *Childhood and Its
Discontents*, 212–13; "Cool and
Complex Weaving of Myth and
Language," 153; "Counting to a
Hundred," 204–5; *Crediting
Poetry*, 106, 205, 208, 230,
264n46; "Current Unstated
Assumptions about Poetry," 134;
"The Door Stands Open,"
276n95; "Dylan the Durable,"
205; Editorial for *Gorgon*, 45;
"Educating the Epsilons," 44;
"Edwin Muir," 10; "Envies and
Identifications," 102; *Essential
Wordsworth*, 14, 164–6, 195,
235; "Evangelists," 31, 81;
"Extending the Alphabet,"

204–6; "Feeling into Words," 13,
17, 22–3, 25, 231; epiphany, 39,
54, 92; liberation, 132; poetic
authority, 76–81; "The Fire i' the
Flint," 98, 155; *Finders Keepers*,
24, 47, 165; Foreword to *A
Portrait of the Artist as a Young
Woman*, 147–8; "Fretwork,"
209; "From Monaghan to the
Grand Canal," 274n39;
"Frontiers of Writing," 193–4;
"The Fully Exposed Poem," 19;
"Further Language," 187,
208–10, 219, 222; *The Gentle
Flame*, 30; *The Government of
the Tongue*, 134; "The
Government of the Tongue,"
185–6; "The Heart of a Vanished
World," 55; "Holding Patterns,"
237; "Indefatigable Hoof-Taps,"
160–6, 209; Introduction to
People of the Sea, 227–8; "John
Clare's Prog," 296n93; "Joy or
Night," 273n17; "Kicking
against the Code," 31–2;
"Learning from Eliot," 69, 103;
"The Main of Light," 164; "The
Makings of a Music," 13, 14–15,
96–102, 162; "Mossbawn," 216;
"Muldoon's *The Annals of
Chile*," 289n191; "The Murmur
of Malvern," 161, 284n58;
"Omphalos," 8–9, 122; "On
Composition," 81; "On Poetry
and Professing," 203–4; "Out of
London: Ulster's Troubles," 92;
"The Pathos of Things," 12, 224,
280n172; "The Peace of the
World Is Always with You," 164;
Place and Displacement, 13, 14,

114, 133–8, 166; "The Placeless Heaven," 168; "Place, Pastness, Poems," 105–6; 297n106; "The Poet as a Christian," 292n11; "Poetic Sweetness and Light in the Classroom," 152–3; *Preoccupations*, 8, 24, 133; *The Redress of Poetry*, 22, 190, 255n50; "The Redress of Poetry," 195; "The Regional Forecast," 194; "The Sense of Place," 69, 93–6, 114–23; "Something to Write Home About," 90, 92; "Sounding Auden," 78, 186; *Soundings*, 3, 81; *Spelling It Out*, 201–2; "Speranza in Reading," 205; "There's Rosemary," 7, 167; "Title Deeds," 214–15; "Traditions and an Individual Talent," 70–2; "Two Voices," 54; Unpublished lecture on *The Prelude*, 66; "Voices behind a Door," 164; "Words of Advice for Graduates," 207

Heidegger, Martin, 76, 93, 126, 139, 190

Herbert, Zbigniew, 134, 136, 180

Hermes, 172

Hewitt, John, 114–15, 119–20, 223

Hill, Geoffrey, 57–8

Hobsbaum, Philip, 285n74

Horton, Patricia, 14–15, 18, 97, 144, 271n177

Hughes, Eamonn, 85

Hughes, Ted, 107, 134, 190, 235; fishing, 188, 197, 199; influence, 13, 20, 103, 107; on "Squarings," 181

idleness, 36, 38, 42

inscape / instress, 4, 68, 260n116

inwardness, 19, 44, 103, 155–6, 210–11; Wordsworthian introspection, 60, 201

Irish Republican Army, 91, 125, 193–4

Jackson Bate, Walter, 81, 94

Jacobus, Mary, 95

Jarrell, Randall, 154

Jesus, 135–6, 162, 186

Johnson, Samuel, 203–4, 207, 293n21

Joyce, James, epiphany, 52, 71–2, 88, 179, 231–2; *Portrait of the Artist as a Young Man*, 21, 78, 150; *Ulysses*, 9, 131, 146

Jung, C.G., 55, 134, 279n140; theory of individuation, 133, 136–7, 154, 157, 166

Kant, Immanuel, 178–9, 279n150

Kavanagh, Patrick, 223; on kettles of potatoes, 21; sense of place, 93, 115, 116

Keats, John, 75, 104, 280n175; and influence, 68, 78, 81, 84; "Ode on a Grecian Urn," 87

Kendall, Tim, 268n111, 300n196

Kennedy-Andrews, Elmer, 48, 50–1, 128, 179

Kinsella, Michael, 15, 249n52, 264n28, 264n31

Laird, Nick, 299n190

landscape, and divine presence, 118–19; and education, 37, 39–41, 58, 87–8; humanizing force of, 93–5, 122, 174; as

336 Index

memory, 109–11, 113, 124, 134; mental landscapes, 9, 73, 147, 196; and national identity, 8, 21–2, 114–17, 119–20

Landweer, Sonja, 193

language, as counter-spirit, 113; of faith, 100, 202; and gender, 96–8; and sectarianism, 60–1; as time-charged medium, 105, 122

Larkin, Philip, 164

Larrissy, Ed, 15, 283n36

last looks, 111–12, 244

late style, 27, 200–3

Latour, Bruno, 294n50

Lavan, Rosie, 269n131

Leavis, F.R., 20, 154, 244

Lee, Dennis, 172

Leopardi, Giacomo, 220

Lerner, Lawrence, 53

Lévinas, Emmanuel, 188, 290n200

liberal humanism, 155, 164, 192, 202–3, 236; and historical continuity, 11, 64–5

liberation, 42, 114, 192–4, 258n90; and entrapment, 46–7; and transcendence, 158–9

Liu, Alan, 18

Lloyd, David, 18–19, 22, 156, 87, 161

Long, Richard, 175

Longinus, 93

Longley, Edna, 18, 23, 208, 260n118, 268n123; on intertextuality, 106, 107; on pastness, 272n196; on representations of Ireland, 19, 119

Longley, Michael, 19, 104, 114

Lowell, Robert, 53, 102, 107, 120, 130,

Lysaght, Seán, 117, 121

McConnell, Gail, 26, 54, 105, 119, 273n27

MacDiarmid, Hugh, 70–2, 125, 166, 223–4, 286n117

McDonald, Peter, 260n126, 269n133

McGann, Jerome, 18, 138, 191, 279n147

MacKenzie, R. F., 31, 32–3, 159

McLaverty, Michael, 46, 51, 88, 146–7, 204

MacLean, Sorley, 110, 183, 229–30

McLoughlin, Deborah, 128, 131

MacNeice, Louis, 13, 22, 29, 225–6

Macrae, Alasdair, 234

McSweeney, Siobhan, 154–5

Mahon, Derek, 22, 107, 159, 224, 284n50

Mandelstam, Nadezhda, 104, 134–5

Mandelstam, Osip, 134–5, 145, 162, 222; citations as cicadas, 67, 107

Marggraf Turley, Richard, 102

marvels, crediting of, 26, 88, 192

Matthews, Stephen, 171

memory, 7, 24, 113, 154, 183. *See also* Eliot: "Little Gidding"

Merriman, Brian, 139, 222

Middleton, Colin, 243

Miłosz, Czesław, 25–6, 235, 286n97; as father figure, 85, 100, 102; as touchstone, 69, 126, 134

Milton, John, 45, 68

Montague, John, 114–16, 261n140

Morrissey, Sinéad, 240, 250n62

Muir, Edwin, 10, 183, 228

Muldoon, Paul, 17, 91, 106, 127, 235; "Dancers at the Moy," 65; "Our Lady of Ardboe,"

287n130; *Why Brownlee Left*, 112, 133
Murphy, Andrew, 122, 196, 222, 277n116

naming of places, 161. *See also* dinnseanchas
nature, as humanizing influence, 93–4, 116, 118–19; as teacher, 38–9. *See also* landscape
neighbourliness, 105, 225–6
Newlyn, Lucy, 138, 268n123
Ní Ríordáin, Clíona, 221

O'Brien, Darcy, 12, 15, 124, 249n39
O'Brien, Eugene, 158, 250n57, 275n69, 288n158
O'Connor, Frank, 273n11
O'Donoghue, Bernard, 276n82
omphalos, 9, 89
O'Neill, Hugh, 90–1
O'Neill, Michael, 14, 21–3, 138
openness, 52, 124–5
Orpheus, 205, 222, 230
Ovid, 139, 222
Owen, Wilfred, 142

pantheism, 38
Parker, Michael, 85
Parkes, Peter, 89
Pasternak, Boris, 129
pastness, 68, 69, 104–6
Plath, Sylvia, 160–4
ploughing, 96–7, 99, 125, 129, 140, 263n9
poetic influence, as beneficent, 68, 103–4; as cannibalistic, 103; metaphors for, 65–7; and music, 5, 99, 108; river imagery, 5, 28

Poiemata, 152–4
postcolonial approaches, 17, 20–1, 172, 222; H's resistance to, 209, 226, 251n74
post-secularism, 15, 18, 202. *See also* secularism
Potkay, Adam, 252n89
Praeger, Robert Lloyd, 93, 115–17, 120
prospects in/of the mind, 122–3, 141, 196, 207, 233, 237; and allusion, 96; and friendship, 107; Heaney's use of, 9, 10, 223, 228
Protestantism, 34, 260n125, relationship to land, 60, 115, 119

quidditas. *See* haecceity

Ramazani, Jahan, 44, 106
redemption, 174
redress, 5, 190–1, 196
restoration, 28, 75–6, 79, 83, 205; of self, 10
return, 41, 96; of the dead, 126–8; of the native, 109–11; to source, 113, 130, 195
revelation, 49, 51, 54, 77, 79
revisioning, 17, 124, 126, 163, 223
Ricks, Christopher, 48, 271n183
Romanticism, 16–18, 20–2, 53, 176; H's discussion of, 19–20
Rousseau, Jean-Jacques, 33, 37, 39
Russell, Richard Rankin, 248n16, 282n8

Salvesen, Christopher, 183
Schiller, Friedrich, 38, 110, 114, 138–9, 141
sectarianism, 34, 60–1, 64, 121, 156

338 Index

secularism, 27, 101, 173–6, 181, 192, 292n11. *See also* post-secularism

self-discovery and self-realization, 33–4, 44, 52, 151–2

sexual knowledge, 49, 97–8, 101, 216; as humanizing, 94, 104, 131–2

Shakespeare, William, 45, 158, 209, 233, 298n150

Shelley, Percy Bysshe, 41, 52, 63–4, 142, 234

Sidney, Philip, 126, 128, 205–7

silence, 43, 56–7, 172–3, 261n135; and creativity, 97, 286; and listening, 112, 143, 163, 168

Simpson, David, 138

Simpson, Louis, 140

Smith, Anthony D., 283n27

Socrates, 135–6, 162, 196

solitude 141, 162, 191, 201, 143; and inspiration, 9, 48–9, 150–1; as strange loneliness, 131

soundings, 3–4, 30, 115

Southey, Robert, 298n153

spirit, 83–4, 179–80, 189–90, 202; of the past, 75, 77, 81; in *The Prelude*, 80, 274n49; secularization of, 59–60, 163, 202; universal spirit, 39–40, 168, 172–6

spots of time, 24, 52, 90, 199–200; as generative structure, 3–4, 9, 19, 261n144; in "Glanmore Sonnets," 128; in *Stations*, 57–60, 62

Stafford, Fiona, 16, 21, 48, 104, 106, 233

Stephen, J.K., 261n128

Stevens, Wallace, 51, 127, 235, 265n52

Storr, Anthony, 136

subterranean currents, 6, 28, 30, 102, 147–8, 253n100

Sweeney, 112, 139

sweetness and light, 43, 150

technique. *See* craft and technique

Thatcher, Margaret, 91, 193–4

Thomas, Dylan, 102, 205, 234

Thomson, David, 200–1

Tobin, Daniel, 52

touchstones, 68–71, 81, 134

transcendence, 19, 26, 192; necessity of idea of, 156–8, 176, 178

Treasure Island, 63, 244

Trumpener, Kate, 89, 120

trust, 124, 129, 159, 176, 188, 237; anxiety of, 67

truthfulness, opposing conditions of, 137–8, 156, 158, 159, 191–2

Vaughan, Henry, 184

Vendler, Helen, 172, 178, 180–2, 200, 261n130

violence, 25, 65, 78, 91, 265n52, in Heaney's poetry, 49–50, 60, 64, 92, 130; and repose, 55–7

Virgin Mary at Ardboe, the, 175

vision, 25, 30, 42, 49; in *Among Schoolchildren*, 156–7; borders of, 183, 190; double-vision, 21, 115, 180, 183; ebbing of, 41, 51, 165, 173–8, 183; fields of, 181, 190, 291n210; and obstinacy, 25, 27, 233–6; trust in, 179–81, 186–7. *See also* bifocal approaches

Index

Waiting for Godot, 123
Weil, Simone, 196
Weiskel, Thomas, 178
Wheatley, David, 244, 248n21
Wilde, William, 200
Wills, Clair, 243
wise passiveness, 38–9, 56, 99–100, 128, 135
Wolfson, Susan, 40
Wordsworth, Dorothy, 37, 74, 107, 131, 165; journal entries, 101, 231, 239
Wordsworth, Jonathan, 177, 190
Wordsworth, William: educational theories, 34–42; and fear, 50; fosterage in Hawkshead, 87; friendship with Andrew Bell, 35–7
Wordsworth's prose: "Essays on Epitaphs," 113, 168; Fenwick Notes, 176–7; Preface to *Lyrical Ballads,* 5, 24, 45; on pleasure, 203–4, 212; on truth, 161, 191; "Reply to Mathetes," 94; "Speech at the Laying of the Foundation Stone," 34
Wordsworth's poetry: "The Brothers," 109–11, 113, 118, 147; "Composed upon Westminster Bridge," 237; "Daffodils," 201; "Elegiac Stanzas," 166; *The Excursion,* 36; "Expostulation and Reply," 38; "Extempore Effusion upon the Death of James Hogg," 235–6; "Fidelity," 4–5, 14; "Lines on the Bicentenary of Hawkshead School," 34; "Lines Written a Few Miles above *Tintern Abbey,*" 38, 39, 205–6,

233, 245, 274n39; "Lines Written at a Small Distance from My House," 38; "Lines Written in Early Spring," 37; "Loud Is the Vale," 14, 210; *Lyrical Ballads,* 37, 218 (*See also* Wordsworth: Preface); "Michael," 5, 14, 93–5, 174; and rootedness, 117–19; "Nutting," 39–40; "Ode: Intimations of Immortality," 14, 25, 27, 165–6, 190; epiphany, 40–1, 52, 174; late style, 200, 205, 233; the prison house, 152; translation, 177–8; *Poems in Two Volumes,* 41; "Poems on the Naming of Places," 121; "Point Rash-Judgement," 121, 184; *The Prelude,* 14, 25, 37, 62–3, 161–2; blessedness and cheer, 97, 100, 124; childhood, 195, 213, 240; education, 39–40, 118; fosterage, 58–9, 84, 87–8; the French Revolution, 10–11, 136, 137; hiding places, 75, 76, 79–80; imagination 5, 92, 150; literary community, 11, 68, 83; and *Paradise Lost,* 68, 99 (*See also* boat-stealing; corresponding breeze; Nature; prospects in/of the mind; restoration; solitude; spirit; spots of time); "Resolution and Independence," 5, 14, 25, 184, 232; "The Ruined Cottage," 14, 100, 173, 210; "Simon Lee," 151; "A Slumber Did My Spirit Seal," 14, 64, 175; "The Solitary Reaper," 14, 28, 46, 228–9; "Stepping Westward," 177;

340 Index

"Surpris'd by Joy," 257n80; "The Tables Turned," 38; "There Was a Boy," 39–40, 143, 160–4, 168, 190, 220; "The Thorn," 14, 82–3, 92; "Thought of a Briton on the Subjugation of Switzerland," 261n128; *Two-Part Prelude*, 14; "We are Seven," 104
Wright, Julia, 22

Yeats, W.B., 13, 21, 75, 97–9, 103, 164; "Among Schoolchildren," 157–8, 160; *Autobiographies*, 84–5; "Easter 1916," 169; as example, 230, 235, 270n150; "Meditations in Time of Civil War," 78, 187; *Oxford Book of Modern Verse*, 197; and Wordsworth, 24, 85, 98, 234